IMAGINING

THE

SACRAMENTO–
SAN JOAQUIN

RIVER DELTA

IMAGINING

THE

SACRAMENTO–

SAN JOAQUIN

RIVER DELTA

AN ANTHOLOGY OF VOICES ACROSS CENTURIES

Robert R. Benedetti, PhD

AMERICA
THROUGH TIME®
ADDING COLOR TO AMERICAN HISTORY

*For the Delta Protection Commission and two Executive Directors,
Margit Aramburu and Eric Vink, who provided guidance
throughout the evolution of this project.*

America Through Time is an imprint of Fonthill Media LLC
www.through-time.com
office@through-time.com

Published by Arcadia Publishing by arrangement with Fonthill Media LLC
For all general information, please contact Arcadia Publishing:
Telephone: 843-853-2070
Fax: 843-853-0044
E-mail: sales@arcadiapublishing.com
For customer service and orders:
Toll-Free 1-888-313-2665

www.arcadiapublishing.com

First published 2022

ISBN 978-1-63499-395-1

Typeset in 10pt on 13pt Sabon
Printed and bound in England

Preface

There is a place in the heart of California called the Sacramento–San Joaquin River Delta.

We mainly know it today as the hub of California's fresh water circulatory system, where waters from the state's two largest rivers—the Sacramento and San Joaquin—come together and get divided, some destined for human use in far-flung parts of the state and some flowing through the Carquinez Strait to San Pablo and San Francisco Bays, then ultimately the Pacific Ocean. It is the largest delta on the west coast of the Americas.

Prior to the arrival of Spanish settlers in the eighteenth century, the Sacramento–San Joaquin River Delta was inhabited—for millennia—by Native Americans from a number of tribes. These First People existed within the natural conditions of the Sacramento–San Joaquin River Delta in an era before dams and upstream reservoirs, with the Mediterranean climate delivering torrential flows during winter storms and spring snowmelt, as well as trickles during drought. Native peoples generally settled to the east of the marshland of what we know as the present-day Sacramento–San Joaquin River Delta. Their settlements are thought to have the highest population density in North America prior to the arrival of Europeans, exceeded only by Central Mexico.

In the post-European contact era, Sacramento–San Joaquin River Delta waterways first became important as the route to Sacramento and Stockton and the goldfields beyond. In the following decades, the region transformed from what was regarded then as mosquito-infested swampland (landscapes we view today with greater charity and appreciation) to the productive agricultural region it is known as today. That transformation—one of the great engineering marvels of the late nineteenth and early twentieth centuries—

was defined by pluck and perspiration, presided over by succeeding waves of migrants from throughout Europe and labored over by waves of migrant workers from Asia. The dredge spoils sweated over by the laborers (including many Chinese immigrants) literally accrued to building the levees and the wealth of the European-settler landowners. Filipino, Japanese, Sikh, Mexican, and other laborers built the wealth further, including to this day.

The era of reclamation brings us to a more modern era—of bold visions (and even greater engineering prowess) that has created a waterworks in the Sacramento–San Joaquin River Delta without peer, and with that hydraulic marvel, an era of pitched battle over water culminating in the multi-decade battles over how much flow and where the water should go. All of these features led Congress to proclaim the Sacramento–San Joaquin River Delta as a National Heritage Area in 2019 legislation, recognizing its significance as a place where natural, cultural, historic, and recreation resources combine to form a cohesive, nationally important landscape. See Fig. 51.

Dr. Benedetti has done a great service in compiling this collection of writings about the delta. Historically organized, the writings travel centuries to the present and even imagine the future. What unifies it all? Probably a sense of the place—a place where land formed from water, and where human imagination and nature dueled and reached a sort of truce, or maybe just a hint of a truce. Through the words that follow, I hope you see the region for what it was and what it remains. It is a place that captivates and confounds— the Sacramento–San Joaquin River Delta.

Erik Vink
Executive Director
Delta Protection Commission
State of California
Fall, 2021

Acknowledgments

This book is built upon the foundation of the Delta Narratives project funded by the Delta Protection Commission, state of California. The project allowed scholars and museum professionals to explore a variety of historical themes and resulted in a series of public forums and four research essays. The participants included Margit Aramburu, former executive director of the Delta Protection Commission; William Swagerty and Reuben Smith from the department of history, University of the Pacific; David Stuart, former director of the San Joaquin County Historical Museum; Tod Ruhstaller, former CEO of the Haggin Museum; Gregg Camfield, department of English and office of the provost, University of California, Merced; Marcia Eymann, Center for Sacramento History and city historian; Michael Wurtz, head of special collections, University of the Pacific's Holt Atherton Library; Philip Garone, department of history, CSU Stanislaus; Jennifer Helzer, department of anthropology and geography, CSU Stanislaus; Dylan McDonald, former archivist, Center for Sacramento History; Leigh Johnsen, former archivist, San Joaquin County Historical Museum; Blake Roberts, Delta Protection Commission; and Margo Lentz-Meyer, public history program, CSU Sacramento. The editor benefited greatly from our conversations and the insightful research that resulted from the Delta Narratives project.

The second foundation of this anthology was an exploratory board of editors that was formed to assess the options that might be considered in presenting such a collection. The decision to publish this book was taken by the editor, Robert Benedetti, alone, but benefited greatly from the advice of the exploratory board. Members included: Paula Sheil, San Joaquin Delta Community College, the Write Place, and Tuleburg Press; Barbara Barrigan-Parrilla, executive director, Restore the Delta; Erik Vick, executive director,

Delta Protection Commission; and Tama Brisbane, poet laureate, Stockton, California. This book would not exist save for the wisdom and guidance provided by this group, which was generous with their suggestions and warnings.

The exploratory board was supported by an intern at the Delta Protection Commission, Carrie Alexander. The Delta Protection Commission acted as the home base for the collection of materials for the anthology, and the assistance of their staff is much appreciated.

Prior to assembling the anthology, the editor offered classes on the Sacramento–San Joaquin River Delta as part of the Renaissance Society program at CSU Sacramento. The senior citizens who enrolled included past and current residents of the Sacramento-San Joaquin River Delta. They offered readings and identified themes that later became the building blocks of this book. It was an honor for the editor to receive their wisdom, and they have strengthened the project considerably. In addition, the editor has presented lectures based on this material at the Rio Vista Museum, the Sacramento River Historical Society, and the Osher Life Long Learning Institute, the University of the Pacific. The feedback from these audiences also helped to fashion the final product.

The editor is also indebted to several residents of the Sacramento–San Joaquin River Delta who shared insights and identified sources. Thomas Herzog is the president of the Sacramento River Historical Society (SRHS) and owns Strange Cargo, a book store and gift shop in Locke. He has delved deeply into the archives held by SRHS and knows much of the history of the region by heart. Philip Pezzaglia has written on the history of Rio Vista and has served at the Rio Vista Museum. He has been generous with his wide knowledge of the area. Carol Jensen, in addition to serving as a volunteer editor of this volume, has shared her insights and materials about Contra Costa County generally and Byron Hot Springs specifically. Her help has strengthened this selection in countless ways.

During the early development of this collection, the editor was a research associate at the Center for California Studies, CSU Sacramento. The center organized a symposium focused on the Delta Narratives Project and provided an academic affiliation for the editor of the anthology. The former executive director of the center, Steve Boilard, and the current executive director, Leonor Ehling, were generous with their resources and incorporated the project into the ongoing business of the center.

As readers will notice, many of the pictures included are from two photographers: Dorothea Lange and Carol Highsmith. The work of both are collected and preserved by the Library of Congress. Their artistry has allowed the telling of Delta stories with force and immediacy.

In addition, this volume could not have been completed without the editorial help of Margit Aramburu and Carol Jensen. The mistakes are the editor's, but there would have been many more without their help.

Finally, my wife, Susan, has had to live with this anthology for months on end. I appreciate her patience. Without her counsel and support, this volume would not be.

Contents

Introduction

This book is an introduction to the Sacramento–San Joaquin River Delta as a cultural area. Recent legislation focused on Sacramento–San Joaquin River Delta preservation draws attention to the region's "sense of place." This phrase foregrounds the interaction between human inhabitants and the natural endowment of the Sacramento–San Joaquin River Delta. What is collected here is a sampling of the journals, poems, fiction, and non-fiction commentaries that record such encounters at different points in the evolution of the Sacramento–San Joaquin River Delta's history. In assembling this collection, every attempt was made to identify material that reflected the lived lives of Sacramento–San Joaquin River Delta inhabitants. In many cases, the authors were themselves living in the Sacramento–San Joaquin River Delta when they wrote their reflections or had long acquaintance with the area before writing.

The opinions of some of these authors may be offensive to readers. Frequently, authors express ideas that betray prejudicial assumptions. The opinions of these authors are not the opinions of the editor or publisher of this volume. The inclusion of such materials is meant to demonstrate the mindset of individuals who experienced the Sacramento–San Joaquin River Delta at a particular time. Not to include materials that today we may find offensive would falsify the historic record. Where available, perspectives from a wide range of inhabitants at a particular period are included to help balance perceptions regarding the social life and cultural norms of the era. The editor confesses that the selection does not include the voices of many living in the Delta during each historical segment. This collection is an attempt to organize available resources with the hope that other researchers will deepen the understanding of the historical record as other materials become available. In other words, this collection is offered as a rough road map for future exploration.

What ties the many items collected here together is the context. Every author is in a dialogue with the Sacramento-San Joaquin River Delta. The Sacramento–San Joaquin River Delta changes over time and therefore so does the context to which authors react. Also shifting is the lens that the inhabitants and hence the authors bring to their view of the area. As a result, this collection is a history of an evolving space and an evolving set of attitudes.

The definition of the Sacramento–San Joaquin River Delta has been a contested topic. Most attention has been paid to the water and land use patterns of the area. However, the cultural boundaries are larger. Roughly speaking, the cultural Sacramento–San Joaquin River Delta runs from the Suisun Marsh and Benicia on the west to Sacramento on the Northeast and Stockton on the southeast along both sides of two major rivers, the Sacramento and the San Joaquin. The map with the plates was prepared by the Delta Narratives project sponsored by the Delta Protection Commission (scholarlycommons.pacific.edu/cop-facreports/7/). It is similar to the Delta Heritage Area map and useful here because it tracks most of the locations mentioned in readings that compose this volume. See Fig. 1.

Much has been written by those who study American literature of the particular engagement of American authors with nature. Possibly the most enduring is Frederick Jackson Turner's discussion of the "Frontier" (nationalhumanitiescenter.org/pds/gilded/empire/text1/turner.pdf). Using Turner's lens, the Sacramento–San Joaquin River Delta is a constantly modified, but never fully stabilized, place. It nurtures small communities and customs, but promises little more than subsistence. It is a place to pursue one's goals and style of life in isolation. This may be the view of the Sacramento–San Joaquin River Delta, which attracts visitors from the world cities of San Francisco or San Jose who ventures along Highway 160 and have the sense that they are traveling back in time to what much of America was when the nation was ever expanding westward.

A second lens is provided by Leo Marx in his *The Machine in the Garden* (New York: Oxford University Press, 2000). Here the vision is of a tension between a garden that requires a respect for organic and natural processes and technology that may improve the productivity of land but has destructive side effects. Clearly, while native peoples had technologies, they are seen as respectful of natural processes, viewing their role as nature's collaborator. On the other hand, settlers from other worlds have relied on technologies that have literally remade the Sacramento–San Joaquin River Delta, including the dredge machines, the tractor, the levees, steamboats, cars, trains, and bridges. This lens directs attention to the continuing attempts of inhabitants to tame nature and the unanticipated consequences of those efforts. Some of these consequences are paid by the land itself, others by social groups who are oppressed by the implementation of new means of production (for example, the canneries).

A third lens is suggested by Carey McWilliams who saw in Californian agriculture the evolution of "factories" in the fields (Carey McWilliams, *Factories in the Fields: The Story of Migrant Labor in California* (Berkeley: UC Press, 2000)). With this lens, the focus is on the labor required to make the Sacramento–San Joaquin River Delta productive. The degradation of nature is seen as a byproduct of the oppression of a class of workers. The story of the Sacramento–San Joaquin River Delta tracks the burdens placed on native peoples first by the mission system and then by the rancheros. Then the Sacramento–San Joaquin River Delta participated in the evolution of the Gold Rush and later land rush from providing opportunities to the many to the domination of large investors. As the nineteenth century closed, the Sacramento–San Joaquin River Delta developed forms of agricultural land holding, which invited tenant farmers and migrant labor. World market pressure and the profit focus of owners resulted in the degradation of the labor as expressed most graphically by the poet Edwin Markham in this collection. These tendencies are then made more intense by racial and ethnic discrimination.

The diverse voices in this collection can provide support for the insights provided by each of these three lenses. The Sacramento–San Joaquin River Delta remains a frontier, a garden in tension with technology, and a factory in the field. In addition, this collection also highlights the aesthetic dimension of the Sacramento–San Joaquin River Delta. Despite its challenges both socially and environmentally, the Sacramento–San Joaquin River Delta is a place of rare beauty. To be sure, it does not have the dramatic effect of the Sierras, but as William Everson the poet has written in this collection, "The valley after the storms can be beautiful beyond the telling." Two aspects of the Sacramento–San Joaquin River Delta—the Sacramento River and Mt. Diablo—endure as subjects across time. Highway 160 has been rightly designated as a scenic highway by the state of California, and the writing collected here is itself a testament to the provocative nature of the Sacramento–San Joaquin River Delta and its history.

Finally, the Sacramento–San Joaquin River Delta has endured as a place where visitors can experience the evolution of California history. Unlike much of the rest of the state, those who travel Highway 160 and the legacy towns along the way can glimpse the life led by native peoples, appreciate the awe of Spanish explorers, understand the promise seen by the rancheros, follow the path of so many to the gold fields, witness the agricultural bounty of the region, see farm equipment in action, participate in a range of ethnic celebrations, witness the places that stood against prohibition, experience migrant camps and segregated schools, enjoy marinas and leisure time on the river, fish, witness the migrations along the Western Flyway, and come to understand the multiple attempts to re-route California's mighty rivers and save endangered species. Come and see.

N.B.: Several of the authors included here used dashes where current usage would either omit them or use commas. The current practice has been followed except where dashes continue to be used today or where to change their usage would undermine the authors' meanings. The latter is particularly the case with poems where the punctuation has been transcribed intact.

Also, some authors have adopted spelling that is now outdated or is simply wrong. The usage of the authors has been replicated in such cases without the repeated use of [*sic.*].

Even where authors do not put foreign words in italics, that practice has been adopted here for clarity.

Much of the material and many of the pictures reproduced here are in the public domain. Where this is not the case, permissions to republish have been obtained. In these cases, the selections are so marked.

Robert Benedetti
Sacramento, 2021

Introductory Poem

[Editor's note: This poem by Leo Briones serves a prologue for this anthology. It raises many of the themes expressed by other contributors and provides a summary of the evolution of a dialogue between the natural endowment of the Sacramento–San Joaquin River Delta and its varied inhabitants. Mr. Briones was born and raised in Texas, published his first book of poems in 2006, and currently owns a communications firm in Los Angeles. (*poemhunter.com/poem/the-blues-in-the-delta-breeze/, by permission*). See Fig. 2.]

The Blues in the Delta Breeze

(Delta) water, mostly runoff from mountain snowpack, flows through a web of channels to mammoth pumps in the southern delta, sending billions of gallons of water to 25 million Californians.

The Sacramento Bee, 2009

I.

On a clear day
in site of the Golden Gate,
twenty-five miles off the coast
of the Fabled City, separated
by the deep murky blue
and rolling foamy swells,
a small out-cropping of craggily isles—
Drake's Islands of St. James—
the mysterious Farallones.

There
every October
off its rocky shores
and in its myrtle green lagoons,
Great White sharks gather
to feast on Stellar sea lions and Northern fur seals—
an annual ritual of crimson and want.

It is said that when these Great Whites feed
they are roused to such a frenzy
that their bodies bounce like quicksilver from the sea
in the precise motion of a volcanic convulsion—
as rows of triangular razor teeth clutch their prey
the blood brewed ocean turns cinnabar red.

The Great White's mighty thrust
lifts them from the sea;
their eyes roll into their sockets
and become two tiny pure white beads.
There is an ole' fisherman's legend that swears,
that on the rare day that the sun shines
through the Pacific gloom
and reflects off those colorless eyes,
that one can catch the very glare
of Lucifer as St. Michael cast him into the fiery pit.

Twenty miles behind the shore in the Fabled City—
high rises lift open palms to the Pacific Rim,
vomit and syringes swarm the Tenderloin,
proud descendants of the Romans and Celts

hide behind the picket fences of the Sunset,
leather boys strut the Castro humming freedom,
tourists cross the Golden Gate in search of the western-most dream.

II.

But it has not always been like this
10,000 years ago, before the earth last melted,
the Farallones formed the cold coastline of the Pacific
and the Fabled City was but a depression of sand and grass.
Nearly yearlong gusts swept
sand from the sea to the valleys—
as miles and miles of frigid dunes formed far, far inland.

Then slowly
the sun warmed to an epoch
of eternal Spring on California's north coast.
As the ice melted, the Farallones drifted into a rocky mystery,
the Fabled City became the thumb of the Pacific
and furious salt water chiseled the San Francisco Bay.

Inland
the Sacramento and San Joaquin rivers
roared and merged to form the great Sacramento Delta.
Meandering waterways of slough and marsh,
of sandhill cranes, waterfowl, and raptor.
For thousands of years,
in this resplendent kingdom
of the natural world—bear and elk, deer and beaver,
fox and possum wandered the Tully fog and peat mashes
in search of Salmon and the tender spouts of Spring.

III.

Then one-day
people came,
first Miwok and Yokut
then, it is said, ancient Chinese wanderers.
Man and land lived like a melody,
unbroken timbre of life—

until the settlers arrived; manifest and heartened
leather Forty-Niner and denim farmer.

Slowly they drained the peat marshes
to form islands named after themselves—
Sherman and Brannon, Bethel and Woodward—
then erected levees to make rigid waterways.

Soon in an easterly dash for refugee
the grizzly bear and mule deer
fled to the Sierra Nevada.
The land was plowed and tilled and sowed
to became bread mother of the earth;
rice and alfalfa, walnut and pear.

All along in this Golden State
of innovators and speculators,
of growers and growth merchants—
cities grew and suburbs sprawled.

To fulfill this thirst for prosperity
delta streams were clutched, enchased, transformed–
modern wonders of the world–
great dams named Oroville and Shasta,
quenched massive steel pumps sucking water
to the yearning fields of the mighty San Joaquin Valley
and south to the Shadow Motherland of fortune and modernity—
bear and deer retreated further and further
to the Canaan of the valleys and Jerusalem of the Sierra's snowy peaks.

IV.

Along the narrow winding roads
that circle and twist the delta like a tangle of wire
some the world greatest engineers travel in big silver tour buses.
With a black microphone in hand
they speak to the obscurity of turbidity and salinization,
explain to jittery farmers and impatient developers
that the piper is calling his golden children home
and the tiny, endangered Delta Smelt, no bigger
than the palm of your hand is the paragon of this tale.

In a junction
between north and south the tourist bus stops.
The travelers walk into an open field
where Bovine cattle graze and a slow delta breeze
preserves the morning chill.

This small herd of humanity
moves toward a wood and barb wire fence.
A woman complains that she should
have worn pants, as she is cold in her pinned stripped skirt.
Another man looking awkward in a fleece pullover,
denim jeans, and cowboy boots leans on the fence.
He asks, "The land looks odd. Sort of like rolling …"

The engineer like a smug professor
interrupts the man in mid-sentence,
"… like sandy dunes. Yes, that exactly what they are.
you see 10,000 years ago at the end of the last Ice Age
when the Farallon Islands were actually the shoreline
of the Pacific and San Francisco was a valley …
sand blew across the delta and formed…."
He goes on and on.

But soon the travelers are not listening.
Another cold Delta breeze gusts through them
and brings a still silence and then a cold voice on the air,
as if to say Great White or sandy dune,
I was here before you walked two-legged and erect.
I will be here long after you cease.

V.

There is a great white dome that hovers
over the southern entry of California's Capitol.
On the walls of the staircases are portraits
of California Governors: Pioneers and 49ers,
screen actors, recalled and reformist, statesmen,
forward thinkers and forgers of movements.
Peter Hardeman Burnett, Pat and Jerry Brown,
Ronald Reagan, Gray Davis and Arnold Schwarzenegger,
Hiram Johnson and Earl Warren.

What has been chiseled in their homage
and what shall said of future generations of the powerful?
Shall they ride like a primeval reminder on the coastal tides
and Sierra watersheds that ebb and flow
on the great fanning Sacramento Delta:
Aquarius bearing water to quench an unbearable thirst—
both buried and laid bare.

A Native American Paradise

[Editor's note: Native peoples inhabited the Sacramento–San Joaquin River Delta region between 10,000 and 12,000 years before Europeans arrived. The small villages, often called "triblets," that they established were later categorized by the language groups into which their spoken language most naturally fell: Miwok, Yokut, and Ohlone. They lived along the rivers within the Sacramento San Joaquin River Delta: the Sacramento, San Joaquin, American, Calaveras, Cosumnes, Tuolumne, and Mokelumne. They shared customs and aspects of their religions which included close relationships with animals and the natural environment. See Fig. 3.

Anthropologists have collected some of their folk tales. A sample is presented here concluding with a modern reflection by a representative of these tribes. The villages were destroyed first by disease and the recruitment of labor by the Spanish/Mexican missions and later by attacks from those associated with rancheros and gold mines. In the early twentieth century, survivors were assembled and moved to reservations—for example, the Shingle Springs Rancheria. David Stuart has published a useful summary with a timeline of the native settlements in the Sacramento San Joaquin River Delta in the *Soundings Magazine* ("Paradise Lost: An Indigenous History Timeline for the Sacramento–San Joaquin Delta," June 25, 2021). He also helped in the identification of these folk tales. The final selection by Joyce Rummerfield has been selected to be placed on a commemorative plaque at the Blue Mountain Coalition for Youth and Families near West Point, CA and at the Calaveras County Governmental Center, San Andreas, CA. It reflects the sorrow and anger that native peoples carry forward.]

The Creation

[Editor's note: Reprinted in Kroeber, A. L., "The Patwin and Their Neighbors," *Publications in Archaeology and Ethnography, Vol. 29, No. 4* (Berkeley, CA: University of California, 1935), pp. 304–305.]

There was a great flood which drowned [everything]. The birds flew to the sky. There Falcon drew a feather from the right arm of each, and killed them all, except four pairs. With him were … Coyote, who was … his mother's brother; and … Turtle. Coyote suggested that Turtle dive. They tied a long line to his ankle and in the evening, he dived. At last the line ran to the end: they reached an arm into the water to let him go as far as he could. Then they began to draw him up. It was morning when he came to the surface. They made a fire for him and asked if he had reached bottom. He said he had not; but [Falcon] with a little stick scraped the dirt from under his nails and patted it flat in his palm. Telling Coyote and Turtle to go to sleep, he put the little disk of earth through the sky-hole onto the water. The water went down: in the morning, the world was dry. Then, on successive days, [Falcon] sent out each of the pairs of four birds he had not killed. They were to fly south along the river to the ocean, then west, north, east, south, all around the world and back upstream. On the first day went … [Red-tailed] Hawk; on the second, … a wading bird with curved bill, who reported water encircling the world; on the third [White-tailed Kite]—[Falcon] had told him to eat grass if he found it; on the fourth, Dove, who was to eat pinole seeds.

After eight days Coyote was lonely and wanted to make man. [Falcon] said, "You do it. You are old and wise." So, Coyote made a brush fence. Into it he put a pair of elder sticks wrapped together with grass. At night [Falcon] awoke. "Mother's brother, wake up," he said, "they [humans] are talking!" All night he listened. In the morning talk was going on all around them.

After four days, Coyote wanted to know how people would live. [Falcon] said: "You know how to make it." That night Coyote made all the animals and plants (a long enumeration follows). After four days, [Falcon] wanted to know how people would eat. That night Coyote made the ways of preparing food (another enumeration). After four days more, [Falcon] asked how they would cook with fire. Coyote took a drill, had [Falcon] hold the hearth, and drilled fire. From the feathers which [Falcon] had plucked out of the birds which came to the sky, Coyote made towns; and when he had gone about the world making them, he showed human beings how to grind, soak, and parch their food.

The Theft of Fire

[Editor's note: Told by William Fuller; reprinted in Gifford, E.W., "Miwok Myths," *Publications in Archaeology and Ethnography*, Vol. 12, No. 6, (Berkeley, CA: University of California, 1917), pp. 332–333.]

Lizard saw the smoke. He said: "Smoking below, smoking below, smoking below, smoking below...." Flute-player (Mouse) was sent ... to secure the fire. Flute-player departed, taking with him two flutes. He finally arrived at the assembly house from which the smoke was issuing. He found it crowded, but he was welcomed and the people persuaded him to play. He played and he played. Then they put a feather mat over the smoke hole at the top of the house and shut the feathers in the door. They closed the door with the feather dress. They told the doorkeeper to close the door tight.

Flute-[player] played continuously. The people fell asleep and snored. Flute-player remained awake and played. Finally, he concluded that all were fast asleep. He arose and took two coals from the fire, placing them in his flute. Then he put two coals in the second flute. He proceeded to the door, cut loose the feathers, passed [through], and started homeward.

The people awoke to find him gone and with him the fire. Hail and Rain were sent in pursuit, for they were the two swiftest travelers among [those] people. Hail went, but Flute-[player] heard Hail and Rain coming, so he threw one of his flutes under a buckeye tree. Rain asked him what he had done with the fire. "You stole our fire," Rain said. Flute-player denied it. Then Rain returned home. The placing of the flute, with the coals in it, under the buckeye tree resulted in the fire always being in the buckeye.

Flute-[player] took his fire from under the buckeye and again proceeded homeward. He arrived at home safely and brought the fire into the assembly house. He told the people that Rain had taken one flute with coals in it. He said, "Rain took one flute from me. I have only one left." The chief told Flute-player to build a fire, and the latter produced the coals from his remaining flute. A large fire was made. It was then that people lost their language. Those close to the fire talked correctly. The people at the north side of the assembly house talked brokenly. Those at the south side talked altogether different; so did those at the west side and at the east side.

Falcon and the Music Tree

[Editor's note: Merriam, C. Hart, *The Dawn of the World: Myths and Weird Tales Told by the Mewan Indians of California* (Cleveland, OH: The Arthur K. Clark Company, 1910), pp. 67–73.]

In the beginning, there was ... the California Condor. His home was on ... Mount Diablo, whence he could look out over the world—westerly over San Francisco Bay and the great ocean; easterly over the tules and the broad flat Joaquin Valley. Every morning [Condor] went off to hunt, and every evening he came back to roost on a large rock on the east side of the mountain. One morning he noticed that something was the matter with the rock, but did not know what the trouble was, or what to do for it. So he went off to consult the doctors.

The doctors were brothers, two dark snipe-like little birds who lived on a small creek near the foot of the mountain. He told them his rock was sick and asked them to go with him and led them to it. When they saw the rock they said, "The rock is your wife; she is going to give you a child;" and added, "we must make a big fire." Then all three set to work packing wood; they worked hard and brought a large quantity and made a big fire. Then they took hold of the rock, tore it loose, rolled it into the fire, and piled more wood around it.

When the rock became hot, it burst open with a great noise, and from the inside out darted ... Falcon. As he came out he ... flew over all the country—north, south, east, and west—to see what it was like.

At that time, there were no people. And there were no [elderberry trees] except a single one far away to the east in the place where the Sun gets up. There, in a den of rattlesnakes on a round topped hill grew the [elderberry tree].

Its branches, as they swayed in the wind, made a sweet musical sound. The tree sang; it sang all the time, day and night, and the song was good to hear. [Falcon] looked and listened and wished he could have the tree. Nearby he saw two ... Star-people, and as he looked he perceived that they were ... the great and beautiful women-chiefs of the Star-people. One was the Morning Star, the other Pleiades.... They were watching and working close by the [elderberry tree].

[Falcon] liked the music and asked the Star-women about it. They told him that the tree whistled songs that kept them awake all day and all night so they could work all the time and never grow sleepy. They had the rattlesnakes to keep the birds from carrying off the elderberries.

Then [Falcon] returned to his home on ... Mount Diablo and told [Condor] his father what he had seen. He said he had seen the beautiful Star-women and had heard the soft whistling song of the elderberry tree that keeps one from feeling sleepy. He asked his father how they could get the music tree and have it at their home on [Mount Diablo].

[Condor] answered, "My son, I do not know; I am not very wise; you will have to ask your grandfather; he knows everything."

"Where is my grandfather?" asked [Falcon].

"He is by the ocean," Condor replied.

"I never saw him," said [Falcon].

His father asked, "Didn't you see something like a stump bobbing in the water and making a noise as it went up and down?"

"Yes," said [Falcon], "I saw that."

"Well," replied Condor, "that is your grandfather."

"How can I get him?" asked [Falcon].

"You can't get all of him, but perhaps you can break off a little piece and in that way, get him."

So [Falcon] flew off to the ocean, found the stump bobbing in the water, and tore off a little piece and brought it home. When he awoke next morning, the little piece had changed into Coyote, who was already living in a little house of his own on top of the mountain. Coyote told Falcon that he was his grandfather. [Falcon] told Condor his father and added, "Now I've got my grandfather."

Condor replied, "Ask him what you want to know; he knows everything."

So [Falcon] asked [Coyote], " How are we going to get the elderberry music?"

"Ho-ho" answered [Coyote], "that is very difficult; you might have bad luck and might be killed."

But [Falcon] continued, "I want it."

Then the wise [Coyote] said: "All right, go and buy it, but mind what I tell you or you will be killed. You will find the Star-women pleasant and pretty. They will want you to stay and play with them. If you do so, you will die. Go and do as I tell you."

So [Falcon] went. He flew fast and far, far away to the east, to the place where the Sun gets up. There he found ... the Starwomen and ... the elderberry tree. The Starwomen were people of importance; both were chiefs. [Falcon] had taken with him long strings of ... shell money, which as he flew streamed out behind. This he gave them for the elderberry music.

The Star-women liked the [shell money] and accepted it and led [Falcon] to the elderberry tree and told him to break off a little piece and take it home and he would have all. But when he reached the tree the rattlesnakes stood up all around and hissed at him to frighten him, for he was a stranger. The Star-women told him not to be afraid, they would drive the snakes away. So they scolded the snakes and sent them down into their holes. Then [Falcon] took his [digging stick] and pried off a piece of the tree.

The Star-women began to play with him and wanted him to stay with them, but remembering what [Coyote] his grandfather had told him, he paid no attention to them but took the piece of elderberry tree and carried it swiftly home to [Mount Diablo]. When he arrived, he said to [Coyote], "Grandfather, I've brought the music-tree; what shall we do with it so we can have the music?"

Coyote laughed as he replied, "Do you really think you have it?"

"Yes," answered [Falcon], "here it is."

Then [Coyote] said, "We must put it in the ground over all the country to furnish music for the [Indian people] we are going to make, for pretty soon we shall begin to make the people."

... Then they went out and traveled over all the country and planted the elderberry tree so that by and by it would furnish music and food and medicine for the Indian people they were going to make. Coyote told Falcon that the berries would make food, the roots and blossoms medicine, and the hollow branches music.

Joyce Rummerfield, "Keepers of the Land"

[Editor's note: "Keepers of the Land," Joyce Rummerfield (Northern Sierra Miwok) as reported in the *Stockton Record*, January 21, 2011. (*By permission*). See Fig. 4.]

This is a truth about the tragic destruction of a way of life—
It happened for only one reason. Our people abandoned so many
Indian villages in Calaveras County alone!
The Miwok lived a quiet, simple life, so close to nature they changed with the seasons.
One time the men were many miles away from the village hunting for wild game. They felt a sense of sadness,
uneasiness. Something was out of the ordinary.
Something was different. Something was strange.
The women and children were down by the river pounding acorns
and singing some of their songs. The deer and grey squirrel running
past them in panic were the first to signal something was wrong.
Suddenly there were strangers standing in the water pointing at shiny yellow
stuff and yelling words The People didn't understand.
There was no need for the yellow stuff when all they needed was
provided when Creator made this land. The attack on the village came
violent and quick—women running and trying to protect their children;
seeing some bashed with rocks, some killed with a noisy stick ...
The old Hyapo (Chief) wounded and bleeding, heart-broken too see such
an ugly sight looked skyward and prayed toward the Heavens.
He cried—Creator, why is this happening?
Creator, this just isn't right!
Creator, look what they've done to my family.
Creator, I'll stand here and fight!
Of course they were out-numbered by many.

No mercy towards women, children or the very old.
Nothing or no one would stand in their way—these strangers
were after gold! Perhaps, if not so consumed with greed,
The People might have shown them where to find it or given a
helping hand, for Miwok people are caretakers of Mother Earth and Keepers
of the Land.
This is a dedication to Indian People of so long ago .
To the ones that died, the ones sold as slaves, to the ones stolen away and
forced to attend boarding schools and cut their hair, never to speak their own
language.
This is a dedication to the People who had no choice but to learn a whole new
way of survival.
If not for you, we wouldn't exist today.
A-Ho
In loving memory of Our People and my uncle Dave Jeff (Northern Sierra
Miwok) Keeper of the Language

2

Journaling with Spanish Explorations

[Editor's note: By 1776, the Spanish had begun to explore the territory north of Monterey and east of San Francisco. Typically, the explorations were directed by military officers, but the notes were taken by Catholic clergy. As is seen in the passages below from the journals of Padre Pedro Font with the Anza expedition (1776) and of Narciso Duran with the Argüello expedition, the state of the terrain and of the condition of native settlements are of most interest to these explorers. It was recognized from the beginning that travel in and around the Sacramento–San Joaquin River Delta was going to be difficult. For a comparison with other journaling of expeditions in California at about the same time, see Rose Marie Beebe and Robert Senkewicz (eds.), *Lands of Promise and Despair: Chronicles of Early California: 1535–1846* (Norman: University of Oklahoma Press, 2015).]

Padre Pedro Font from the De Anza Exploration

[Editor's note: "The Journal of Pedro Font" as translated and edited in Alan K. Brown, *With Anza to California, 1775-76* (Norman, OK: Arthur H. Clark, 2011). Footnotes and material added in subsequent drafts of Font's Journal are omitted. (*By permission*). See Fig. 5.]

[April] 3, Wednesday. I said Mass. The weather was very clear and without chill at daybreak; we would even have had a hot day save for the northwest wind's blowing soft and cool. We were not bothered by mosquitoes during today's travel, and we noted that all of the country we rode through today was very dry either because there has been no rain this year or because it only rains in summer in these parts, and for that reason the grass was almost dry. We set out from the *Arroyo de Santa Angela de Fulgino* at a quarter past seven in the morning and upon an east-northeasterly course crossed the plain upon which we had stopped, which is much grown over with white oaks and through the midst of which goes a stream, much overgrown with cottonwoods and other trees, but which we found wholly dry. There is good soil there. We traveled through it for some three leagues, which is the size that it has both in length and in width between the edge of the stream and the foot of mountains that have two high peaks, and with a good deal of trees visible on them. As we started out, a number of Indians from the thieves' village met us as we went and presented us with *cacomites* and a small dried fruit strung on cords, a bit larger than a hazelnut, grey-colored and having a hard, little pit inside. The soldiers said it was what they call *tascal*, but larger than the kind that grows in Sonora, and it is fairly sweet. Yet not even that made me approve of those Indians, as thievish and ill-willed as they had shown themselves yesterday.

We then came into hills and hollow leading out upon a large plain at the edge of the river, and having traveled through the hollow for about a league northeastward we came to the top of the hill, I myself saw the river split, not into three branches but into many, making several islets of which I counted many as seven, some of them of some size and others small, all of them consisting of flats and appearing long and narrow. A portion of water visible in the farthest distance seemingly was coming as a branch from the north, turning or ascending eastward, while closer by, the other portion of water, or larger branch, extended east-northeastward until it became hidden behind hills grown over with trees, and we saw that the tree growth continued onward across the plains. Upon the other side, nothing was to be seen but low bare hills, such those we saw yesterday, following the margin of the river.

Up until here we had traveled for about four leagues, at a distance from the river of around a league or a bit more. We came down, then, from the hill and directed our way on a course east by north, going toward the range that was hiding the river's course from us, and upon which and beyond it about southeastward we saw a good deal of trees extending onward. As soon as we had come down to the plain, of which there must be about two leagues between the foot of the hills and the water, we saw on the plain not very far from the water and at a distance of about one short league a big herd of the great deer that I think are called *buras* in New Mexico, which are some seven *cuartas* in height and have antlers about two *varas* wide with a number of branches. Although an attempt was made to get one, it failed because of their great speed in running, particularly at the present time when they happened to be without their big horns, which they undoubtedly shed seasonally judging by the great amount of antlers that we saw cast off thereabouts. Along the way we had already seen many of their tracks and likewise had found a number of their very large horns. I was moved to measure one and found it six *cuartas* long, with five branches each about *tercia* in size. We stopped here for about two hours. The soldiers, as soon as we had seen them, wanted to go and chase them to see if they could get one. Our captain gave them leave and they changed their horses and followed after the great deer until they were tired; but the deer were faster and they were unable to catch any. These animals are nearly gray colored, and as large as a two-year-old calf. They got as far as the stream from which we had set out and when they came back, reported they had found over twenty Indians returning from fishing, each man laden with four or five salmon; and near the spot we had set out from they had met Indians coming from the mountains to hunt in the plain who were carrying a stag head. One Indian had been painted the color of the great deer. These Indians went along with them for a little while but as soon as they began getting near the thieves' village in the Llano de Santa Angela they refused to go farther with them, indicating by signs that those people were their enemies. These great deer are very plentiful in this entire area; it has entirely the appearance of there being some extremely large estancia of livestock thereabouts, because of the tracks that we encountered this day and the next and which are like those of cattle.

After the chase, we continued on all across the plain, leaving to our right hand at the foot of the hills the brackish stream that was the final end of the expedition made by Señor Fages when he came surveying this river. And upon traveling some four leagues on an east by north course we came to a rather large village (whose Indians, who are like the others in their hue and in every way, received us peaceably and even fearfully) that was located in the plain at the foot of the small ranges that we were coming in search of, and so close up to the water that there could not have been twelve paces' distance between water and the huts.

We stopped for a bit here at this village, in which the huts were not grass-built and wretched like the ones we had seen during this journey, but rather large, round and well built like the ones on the channel, made out of good, large tule rush mats with a framework of poles inside to maintain their roundness, and a door; and with the usual sweathouse for everyone. Our commander sought to treat them to a present of beads to remove the fear they had shown the moment they saw us, to the degree that the Indian women went and closed themselves inside their huts and the men stayed outside talking loudly (none of which we could understand)—not, however, with any weapons. One of them went in great a haste to set a long pole on top of the sweathouse, with a plume of feathers at its end and a long piece of rabbit skin in two strips, with the hair on it, hanging from the pole like pennant, which we supposed to be the sign of peace under which we were being received. At the same time, however, the little children and some women put out into the water, boarding their tule balsas. They have a great many of them, and very well made of tule rush with raised sides and a bow and stern terminating in a high point, and furnished all along the side with poles bent as though to provide a railing or backrest. The Indians paddled away with great ease and speed using small paddles. The Indian men responded to our gift by giving us feathers, small sticks, and other trinkets in token of their esteem, to the point of insisting that we take them. These Indians are just as ugly and dark as all of the ones we have seen up to here—not bearded, however.

Here we no longer suspected but became convinced that what was being called a river is no river but a very large lake of fresh water, with no flow, that reaches throughout these boundless plains in a number of branches and bends. Our animals went down on foot to drink from it and we ourselves tasted it and found it very fresh and good.

We were intending to keep on along the river or shore of the water in the same direction from here in order to go up to the top of the small wooded range—which is not very high—to get a view of the land and the course of the water. However, we had scarcely left the village when a swamp or small water arm with a tule rush marsh lay directly in our way, forcing us to change course. Therefore, heading east-southeastward and leaving to our left the little ranges we had been in search of, we traveled over the ridge of a little low hill and came at once onto a rather large plain—although the soil was dry, it had a good many white oaks which were the trees we had seen about southeastward from the hill. And having traveled thus for a bit over one league we came to a very bare hill that was not very high.

In order to get good view of the land we went up to the top of this hill, which overlooks the entire plain, and from there, we saw a tangle of water, tule marshes, bit of woods near the mountains on the south, and an enormous stretch of flat land, never in my life I have seen so nor do I expect to see this again great an expanse of horizon.

Looking eastward, we saw a large and very long, snowy mountain range upon the other side of the plain and some thirty leagues away, white from its summit to its skirts, running crosswise from south-southeast to north-northwest. I judged what I could demarcate of its bearing that upon the south this range might possibly have some connection with the snowy range that comes off from the main California range above the *Puerto de San Carlos*, or to put it better, that it is the same main range extending about northwestward as far as Mission San Gabriel and beyond.

Turning westward, we could see along the course of the river the hills that we had been leaving behind us as we traveled, and in among which the gathered waters shot in or entered; and that on the other side of the water, the ranges open out a great deal, as though running northward, as far as the final end of them that can be made out, which is very far in the distance.

Looking southward, we could see very far off long high mountain range running about from southeast to northwestward, and this is the range that

I talk about under March 8 and that we left upon our right hand during the whole way we came, all the way from the vicinity of Mission San Luis until the mouth of the river where it ends, the whole of it being formed by a chain of mountains and hills that are bare upon the outside but have a great deal of trees in their center and on whose skirts lie the valleys of Santa Delfina (through which the Monterey River runs), of San Bernardino, and still others, including the *Llano de los Robles* going toward the mouth of San Francisco harbor. A Monterey soldier declared and affirmed that he recognized a peak that was visible to the southeastward at the limit of what could be seen of this range, and said that it was not very far from a spot they call Buenavista which was scouted by the soldiers when they went to the tule rush swamps which lie toward Mission San Luis in search of some deserters, and that if we were to head that way we would come out in the vicinity of Mission San Luis or Mission San Antonio.

Looking back northward, we saw that between the snowy range and the low hills northwest on the other side of the river, there is a great emptiness of horizon with no end to be seen to it, the sky joining with the earth so that the eye loses its objective and there is no telling whether what follows beyond is water or land. We saw a boundless plain, that seemed to run in the same direction as the snowy range on its far side did, but opening out on the other side about to westward, so widely that it took in almost half the circle of the horizon. This is the great plain whose edge we stand upon, in which can be seen nothing except water in branches, tule rush marshes, and flat land without mountains or hills standing out anywhere in all this wide portion of the world's extent.

In view of this our commander decided to go down and camp at the water's edge, having in mind to keep on ahead for a few days' march and cross the plain and approach the snowy range in order to prolong the exploring (which during the previous expedition was carried out only so far as the vicinity of this spot) as far in that direction as might be before exhausting the provisions we had with us-or, rather, for whatever distance they would reach while still enabling us to return. Therefore, coming down from the hill, we traveled about a league over the plain on a northeastward course through level, fairly dense wood of small live oaks and some white oaks, but before reaching the water, already close to it, we came upon a small tule marsh and bog that barred our way; so we changed course and, by traveling about a quarter-league westward, reached the water's edge at a spot having an abandoned village, where there was a good deal of grass and enough firewood, and here we camped at a little after a half past four o'clock in the afternoon, having traveled about ten leagues in all.

Here finally we came to the realization that the river is no river-unless it becomes one farther up—but instead a great lake of fresh, very good water that, because it has very little drainage into the sea, keeps fresh the water that reaches inland. As soon as we had halted we went to view the water and to taste it, and we found it very crystalline, fresh, sweet, and good; and our animals went down to water at it without any trouble. We noted that it has a shore like the beach of a small sea, with little waves, and plants and some trees growing all the way down into the water. And we saw that, caused by the wind, it had a soft motion striking upon the edge or shore with gentle waves; we could perceive no current in it, however. In order to test whether it did have any, our commander seized a middling-sized stick that ended in a knob and threw it as strongly as he could out onto the water. Yet we soon saw that instead of drifting downstream, it was brought back to the shore by the little waves in the water, so that we recognized that it has no flow, or if it does have any it must be a very little one and out in the middle of the water, the width of which is almost the same as at the mouth. However, we at once noticed a more unusual fact, which was that it has a flow and ebb like the sea, and that the tide was going out. There were no deposits of flooding on the shore or trash, except for a bit of dried tule rushes, from which we deduced it is not a river. If it had been, it would have deposits of timber and signs of its having flooded—of the snowy range. Naturally it would do, being as it is within view.

Our captain set a marker on the shore at the point that was being reached by the little waves on the water. An hour and a quarter went by and we returned to view the water and noted that it had uncovered a distance of over four *varas* away from the marker that had been set up and that the water had dropped about two *tercias*—judging by the uncovered trunks of some trees there on the shore, ones which we had seen submerged earlier. We concluded from this that the water has its own ebb and flow like the sea and that the tide was going out at that time. From all of this it results that the river is no longer a river, so that henceforth we shall call it a lake until God pleases for us to discover otherwise. For this reason, our lieutenant, along with a servant, was charged with taking care to observe when the tide should be at its lowest during the course of the night and with measuring whatever amount of the beach or shore it uncovered, and with later observing how far up it came at high tide. As I shall tell, this was performed during this night and the morning of the following day.

[April] 4, Holy Thursday. The weather was quite clear at daybreak although with a very strong northwest wind that had begun about midnight and continued all day until sunset, troubling us a great deal. After dinner before midnight our lieutenant went to see whether the water of the lake had gotten lower, and he found it had drawn back so far that we determined from the measurement he made that it had uncovered sixteen and one-half *varas'* width of shore. My servant Silva, who was charged with going after midnight to see how much it had risen, went before dawn and saw that the water had risen so far that it lifted it the dry tule rushes that had washed onto the bank. At sunrise, our commander and I went and saw that the tide was already beginning to ebb and that, what with the northwest wind blowing so hard today, the water was a bit more disturbed, with the little waves out on it turning white the way they do at sea, under the gales (as they are called), and with rather big waves along the shore. Using a level (I had a level along with me for whatever occasion might arise), I took the difference in the water's height, and determined thereby that the water had gone down a bit over three *varas* where it left the shore bare from its height at high tide, measured down at low tide. I shall note that the water was pooled up here and must have had very nearly the same width as at the mouth, and the shore was not steep in the way it is elsewhere but very low-sloping, and along we saw some little shells, almost flat, and as shiny as though made of mother-of-pearl, but thin and in fragments. I took the difference in the water's height in the following way: I measured two *varas'* worth of the shore down from the highest point on it reached by the water at high tide, and by leveling this portion I read off, by the level, one and one-fourth *cuarta* at the farther end of the distance, so that by estimating this amount against the sixteen *varas* of sloping shoreline uncovered at low tide, determined by the triangle that the water had dropped some three *varas,* which is a pretty large drop. From all the above, and from these tests—and most of all because of the tide, which we experienced as being all the greater because it was the day of the full moon—we concluded, and became finally assured, that the river was no river but lake, and I was confirmed in the conjecture that I had had earlier, that that lake was formed from the great tule swamps that exist in this vicinity and that it discharges through here into the sea, but not enough so as to count, since it has no current other than the ebb and flow of the tide. And if after all—granting that it is fresh water someone claims that it can be called a river just because it has some motion with the ebb and flow, then by the same reasoning we can call the sea a river.

Our commander still insisted on the decision that he had reached yesterday to go around the lake until he saw the end of it and proceed to the snowy range so as to follow along it, if the tule marshes would allow us to do so. We set out, then, from the spot (where we felt only a little chilliness because of the wind) at a quarter past seven and traveled for a short way on an eastward course, intending to keep on along the water, either beside its edge or else in view of it. Immediately, however, the tule rush marsh and bogs that hindered us shore yesterday lay in our way, making us alter our course from reaching its and commencing to separate us from the water so that we had no further sight of it. We took up an east-southeastward course and in that way traveled some three leagues, keeping to our right the wood of small live oaks which at about two leagues continued on as one of quite big tall white oaks at the foot of the southern mountain range. We followed it along to a distance of a bit over six or seven leagues, with the tule marsh on the left taking us farther and farther away from the water. Since we wanted to see if the tule marshes would allow us a way across, we turned east-northeastward with some veering to northeast and traveled in this way about a further league, but at once the tule marshes hindered us from following in that direction and although we tried to keep eastward, we commenced winding about, to the east-southeast, sometimes southeast, and also to the south, without being able to gain any distance toward the snowy range but rather getting farther out of the way.

We saw the many well-trodden trails that are made by the great deer—whose hoof or track perfectly resembles that of cattle—as they go down to the water across that plain, and we followed some of them; always in vain, however, for we would come up immediately against a mire or an impassible ditch of water that made us turn back. Finally, we came across a little path with human tracks on it that we thought led toward a small village that we saw in the distance on a small elevation within the tule marsh. Although we tried to follow it, we immediately found ourselves faced with a bog our animals were unable to get through and that even on foot could only be crossed with difficulty. Accordingly, two soldiers crossed through the first bad spot on foot and, with some trouble, their animals, and as we were so desirous of following this trail, our commander said that on foot or not, we would follow it until unable to go farther. He ordered a soldier to go out in front and inspect whether there would be any other bad spot ahead. When he had gone only a short way, we saw him and the mule he was riding not only stop but fall. By this we recognized the difficulty, and the fact that penetrating the tule swamp was impossible.

We went on in this way, eastward to southward, east-southeastward and southeastward, until over four leagues, making our way with some toil across the tule marshes, which were dry for a good stretch, and treading over loose, rotten soil full of dry scum, and with such a biting dust raised by the wind from the ashes of burned tule rushes that it blackened us and burned harshly in our eyes, making us cry and hardly able to see, so that we had a very unpleasant day and departed from here with very red, inflamed eyes.

We headed to the south and I said to our commander that if he thought it well, we would do better to return toward Monterey, in view of the fact that the tule marshes where we were are the same ones that run on until close to Mission San Luis and were taking us farther away from the range with every step, for it was already clear that a what had been called a river had turned out to be a lake. But our commander, although already of the same opinion, had not yet entirely abandoned his determination to see whether we might approach the snowy range, and he chose to pursue the task a little farther just in find higher ground farther down that would give us case we might an easier way across. And so, going on a short way we began heading eastward, and traveled for about three leagues, following a somewhat trodden trail for a good while.

It was already about two o'clock in the afternoon. Corporal Robles, who went out in front as a guide, halted as if he were thinking about where to go and which direction to lead us in Our commander asked him, "What do you think? Is there any hope we can reach the mountain range today or tomorrow?" The corporal answered, "I don't know, Sir. What I can say is that once I came out past the point of that range there (the one that we saw looking southward from the hill yesterday, and that runs southeast to northwest) and I spent a day and a half trying to get around a tule swamp and saw that it still ran onward, and did so on the other side as well, but I did not get to the end of it nor did I see I anything more, since I turned back from there."

Thereupon I said, "Sir, it is futile to involve ourselves in establishing a fact already known. We are sure that the river we were looking for is a lake. The most we can learn is whether some rivers run into it from the snowy range, something that for our current purpose is not very important to learn and is likely enough to be true. It is also the fact that verifying this will require more days than what we suppose it will and that we can only accomplish this by rounding the whole tule marsh, which must occupy a district of about thirty leagues on this plain. Meanwhile, the day is drawing to an end and if we go onward any farther our animals will spend a bad night. Unless we head to the mountains in time to look for a stopping place, we will spend the night here on these plains with no water, no firewood, and no grass: no grass and no firewood because there is none to be had, and no water because the bogs and extensive mires in the tule swamps keep us from reaching it. So, since there is nothing more to be seen here, it is better for us to return to Monterey."

Our commander, seeing all the difficulty that would be involved in approaching the snowy range as he had planned, then decided on our returning to Monterey. The soldiers, however, said that in order to do so it would be necessary to return to the place we had set out from. From there we would go the way we had come by, since they knew of no route hereabouts and no Spaniards had ever traveled in this area. This seemed hard to our commander and to me. I said that judging from the way that we had come, Monterey was to the south of us. If we could bring ourselves to cross the range in front of us, I dared to affirm that we would I come out at the San Bernardino valley along this course or at worst, at the Santa Delfina valley.

Therefore, changing our course, we headed toward the range on a south-southwestward course. After going one league we came to very bare hill ranges which we called the *Lomas de las Tuzas* because we saw a number of gophers in them and they were undermined with gopher holes. We went into them through a hollow made by hills from which we saw that there was a white oak grove upon the plain, about at the end of the tule marsh we had just left, and continuing very far onward. We traveled through the hills, going up and down over them, for a bit over two leagues on a south-southwestward course though veering to one side or the other because of the way the hills turned. And, having climbed to their top, we saw a spacious valley to our right that is formed between the hills we were crossing through and those others that we had kept upon our right while on the way to the mouth of the lake. It is the valley through which Captain Fages came out on his return after leaving the *Arroyo de Santa Angela de Fulgino*, and they called it Santa Coleta. Opposite us, far off, we made out the range of pines that runs toward the San Francisco harbor and ends at *Punta de Almejas*. Then, having surveyed the country and seen we were on a right course, we went down from the top of the hills, kept on through them for about two leagues upon the same south-southwest ward course, and proceeded straight toward hills that had trees upon them in hope of finding water there, which we did, although only little. We reached them a bit after five o'clock in the afternoon and the pack train arrived at six o'clock. We had traveled some fifteen leagues in all, at a good pace, and we halted upon a small height next to a hollow in which a little water was found.

In the tule marshes we saw a great many dead snails and turtles, and a number of great deer in the woods, but we did not see a single Indian along the whole route today, and encountered only human footprints pressed into the dried mud. I thought it so poor a land as not to be easy for people to dwell in. I, at least, was left without any wish to travel back and see this piece of country again, for besides the burning in the eyes that I have brought away from there and my mouth inflammation that had already mended but which broke out again today, I have not seen an uglier country than this. For, although when seen from afar it strikes the eye as being something fine, so level and with a distant view stretching to so wide a horizon, in reality, however, it is an arid country, nitrous, all water and mires, not containing anything to please me or strike me as useful, except for the great deer that seemingly have their lair hereabouts.

Fray Narciso Duran from the Expedition on the Sacramento and San Joaquin Rivers

[Editor's note: From *Expedition on the Sacramento and San Joaquin Rivesr in 1817: Diary of Fray Narciso Duran,* edited by Charles Edward Chapman (Berkeley: University of California: 1911). See Fig. 6.]

Viva Jesús.
    Diary of the exploring expedition made, in the month of May, 1817, by the commandant of the royal presidio of our father San Francisco, Lieutenant

Don Luis Argüello, with his launch San Rafael or La Fina, and by the fathers, Fray Ramón Abella, minister of the mission of our father San Francisco, and Fray Narciso Duran, of that of San José, with the launch named San José or La Pescadora, on the only two rivers, called the Sacramento and San Joaquin, which flow into the port of our father San Francisco.

May 13. We started from the beach of the presidio at ten o'clock this morning, with a fresh wind which lasted until we crossed the entrance of the port, and at noon we came, rowing, to the large island called Isla de Los Angeles, where we had lunch. At five o'clock in the afternoon we set out from the island, and, having doubled the Punta de San Pablo, which is the point of the mainland on the San José side, we stopped at eight o'clock at night, having travelled in the whole day six leagues toward the northeast.

May 14. We started at six o'clock in the morning, and with a light wind came at midday to the end of the strait of the *Chupcanes*. The village of this name is Christian, [belonging] partly to San José and partly to San Francisco; it is fourteen leagues northeast of the latter, and seventeen leagues north-northwest of the former. After lunch, we set out with a fresh wind, which in the middle of the afternoon became a storm, heading for the *Ompines* toward the east. This is where the only two rivers that flow into the port through the said strait unite.

One comes from the north and northeast and is called the Sacramentó, and the other from the east and southeast and is called the San Joaquin, and the two, united at their mouth, appear to be the river which the maps put down under a single name, *Rió de San Francisco*. I call them the only two rivers, because it seems that the many streams or branches which are formed by numerous little wooded islands and tule patches, as well as some other rivers farther up, all discharge their waters into these two rivers; so that, although the western slopes of the Sierra Nevada may form some rivers, as they say, yet all lose their identity and mingle with the two principal rivers already mentioned.

Then, as night had fallen and advanced a little, the commandant's launch stopped on the San José side of the mainland at the mouth of the San Joaquin, and we, the two fathers, with the other launch, followed the course agreed upon, entering the Sacramento and ascending until we could find land on the opposite side which is in the country of the *Ompines*; for, although we passed near the other launch and saw a fire, it was already impossible to go back because of the storm. We landed on a small island of tule which at high tide was covered with water, and we had to take refuge upon some places full of brambles to protect ourselves from the water until it receded. We passed a very uncomfortable night, although in good spirits; and the commandant could not have passed a better night, because, while we had water without fire, he had wind without shelter. We travelled in the whole day twelve leagues toward the northeast and east.

May 15. The storm has continued all night. At five o'clock in the morning
the commandant again joined us, arriving with his mainmast broken, but
without loss of life, thanks to the Lord, and it seems rather miraculous that it
did not break someone's head or kill someone at the time of its fall. Presently
we set out to seek a suitable place to say mass, as it was Ascension Day.
Having gone five or six leagues up the Sacramento River with the same storm,
we alighted on dry land, where the mass was sung. But, as the place was very
unsheltered and cold, we started in the middle of the afternoon, after lunch,
and at night fall reached the end of the *Lomas de los Ompines*, these hills
sheltering us from the storm. This place is called *Los Ciervos*. About a league
before arriving, the launch San José struck upon a submerged log, which
frightened us, but upon examination afterwards, it appeared that no harm
was done, thank God. We travelled in the whole day eight leagues toward the
east and northeast.

May 16. The storm from the northwest has continued all night, stopping
at dawn; there was a heavy fog, and it almost rained. We started with a light
wind at eight o'clock in the morning going toward the northeast. After going
a league, we came to a stream to starboard leading to the east, and they say
that this is the turn which the principal river makes. In case that is so, we here
left the said river, which surrounds the island called *Isla de los Quenemsias*,
and followed a branch with a course to the north and northwest, intending to
explore the village called *Rancherias de los Chucumnes*. After going another
league, we came upon another stream or branch to port, and instantly it
seemed that it was going to lead to the said village.

Nevertheless, we left this, and followed the same stream as before. This
morning we saw some rafts with people and some houses without, because
they rushed away at the noise of the launches. After going six leagues we came
to another stream to starboard, toward the northeast. Either this stream or the
former is the main stream of the Sacramento. We left it and went on, following
the same stream as before. All along this river it is like a park, because of
the verdure and luxuriance of its groves of trees. Still, it is difficult to land,
because everything is inundated, due to the rise in the rivers from the melting
of the snow. We stopped at six o'clock, having rowed eight leagues toward the
northeast, north, and somewhat to the northwest.

May 17. There has been a strong wind all night. We set out at six o'clock in
the morning. After going a league, we came to the stream that we left yesterday
on our left. In a very short time we came to the village of the *Chucumnes*, but
there were no people there. We counted thirty-five houses, some being from
forty to fifty paces in circumference, which indicates a considerable people.
We called to the natives, but no one appeared. This village is at a place where
the river subdivides into some three branches: one goes to the south, which
is the one that I say we passed yesterday on our left; another, to the west,

and we do not know where it empties, although it is presumed that it makes some turn to the southwest and goes to join the stream to the south; and the other branch goes to the north. Well, we had lunch and started at two o'clock in the afternoon, and took the said branch to the north. The same groves as yesterday continue, and both banks are under water. At six o'clock we stopped in front of a stream which they say leads to the village called *Ranchería de los Ilamnes*. In the whole day, we went but four leagues, because the river carries a considerable current. Our course during this whole day has been northwest, north, and northeast.

May 18. After having said mass, as it was Sunday, we set out toward the northeast following the same river. We went a league (which cost us much labor to go, on account of the great strength of the current), and came upon the main stream of the Sacramento which runs from north to south. This is the same that we left on our right, or to starboard, on the 18th although I cannot figure out which of the two said streams it is, whether the first or the second. Well, continued up the river, which is very wide and of great depth; after going half a league we stopped to eat. We had hardly finished, when our party suddenly got excited, saying that natives were coming to molest us; but no one appeared. We set out at two o'clock in the afternoon, going up the river. At a distance of a league there is a stream on the right which makes a turn and leads to the same river two leagues farther up. At about five o'clock, looking to the northeast through a gap in the grove of the river bank, we discerned the famous Sierra Nevada. The white part of this Sierra seemed to all to be snow, although, as they say, it also has a species of white rock which looks like snow. We went a little farther up the river, and stopped at sunset, having travelled during the day some five leagues toward the northeast, north, and northwest.

May 19. We started at seven o'clock in the morning, continuing up the river, and, after going a league, came upon a village on the eastern bank called *Chuppumne*, whose people fled at the noise of the launches, leaving but two old women, each over sixty years of age. After instructing them in the Christian faith, I baptized them, because we thought that they would die before Divine Providence might arrange another fitting time when they could be baptized at some mission. We left this village at ten o'clock, and stopped to eat at midday. We again set out at two o'clock in the afternoon, and in the distance, saw two villages with people, and another by the water abandoned some time since. The river is much swollen and is flooded on both sides, so that one can scarcely alight upon land. We stopped at sunset, having travelled during the day ten leagues toward the north and northwest.

May 20. We started up the river at six o'clock in the morning, intending to look for an open place, in order to put up a cross, and there to stop in our ascent, and to go back down the river. We had gone three leagues, when upon the launches touching the western bank, some rafts were descried in a nearby tule patch. Some neophytes went to inspect them and found a village of natives, who came toward them armed and with a fierce shout, as is their custom. Presently the commandant went with the soldiers and the other neophytes to talk to them, and they became pacified and made an apology, saying that they had armed themselves in the belief that we were a hostile people. They gave us *toróus*, which is a kind of pounded soaproot, and they went away in peace, telling us that their village was a little farther up the river, and that they would await us there to give us some fish. We had lunch and set out, going one league farther up the river; but we neither came upon nor saw either village or native, except a poor old man, asleep upon a log, and he had known nothing of the launches. We gave him some pinole and sent him away. Seeing that no one was near we carved a cross on an oak-tree, and this having been blessed and adored by the people, marked the end of our ascent. One may come to this place by land in the dry season, to judge by appearances, because, although one sees tule patches in the vicinity, it seems that in October everything must be dry, for there is no water except the floods from the river. This being so, the course of the river from here on could be followed better by land than by water, and the vast lands to the end of the Sierra Nevada be examined, which lands, it is likely, maybe settled by innumerable natives. Once the pass in the Sierra is discovered, which the said end seems to offer, we would be able to ascertain the truth of what the Indians have told us for some years past, that on the other side of the Sierra Nevada there are people like our soldiers. We have never been able to clear up the matter and know whether they are Spanish from New Mexico, or English from the Columbia, or Russians from La Bodega.

At about ten leagues to the northwest of this place we saw the very high hill called by soldiers that went near its slope *Jesús María*. It is entirely covered with snow. They say that a great river of the same name runs near it, and that it enters the Sacramento River, and they conjecture that it may be some branch of the Columbia. This I have heard from some soldier; let the truth be what it may. To-day we went four leagues up the river toward the north and northwest. At four o'clock in the afternoon we began to go down the river, and at sunset stopped on the western bank in front of the place where we were on the 18th, having travelled fourteen leagues in three or four hours because of the great force of the current course toward the south and southeast.

May 21. We started at seven o'clock in the morning, and, in a little while, came to the stream on the right, by which on the 18th we entered the principal river. Leaving that stream and continuing along this river for a league, we came upon a village of forty houses called *Ranchería de Ochejamnes;* but there were no people there. In a little while we came upon the point of the island called *Isla de los Quenemisas*. Here, on our right, we left the principal stream of the Sacramento, which runs to the southwest, and took a stream to the left which runs to the southeast, at the entrance of which, in the year [1813], the natives killed the late Julio, *alcalde* of San José. The launches are proceeding with difficulty because of the many logs that there are. After going six leagues we came upon the village of the *Guaypéms,* with some people in it; and there seven souls amongst the old, the sick, and the infants, were baptized. Here we had lunch, and having set out at three o'clock in the afternoon, stopped at the place called *Las Cruces*, intending to start to-morrow to find the San Joaquin River, and to ascend it to the village called *Ranchería de los Passasimas.* In the whole day we travelled fifteen leagues, steering to the south and southeast.

May 22. We started at seven o'clock in the morning, and in a little while, upon reaching the end of this stream or branch, which we entered yesterday, we found another on our left which comes from the northeast. We passed it and followed a very broad canyon to the south and southeast, leading to the San Joaquin River. Here the launches separated. That of the commandant headed to the west and northwest to explore two or three islands where some fugitives from San José are living together in hiding. We, with the other launch took a course to the south and southeast, ascending the San Joaquin River, being desirous of exploring the villages of the tule regions. After going four leagues we stopped at a miry little resting-place, because of the extreme heat which enervated the rowers. We started at six o'clock in the afternoon intending to travel all night.

May 23. We have travelled all night, except for a brief stop in the launch itself, and at eight o'clock drew near the village of the *Passasimas.* During the night, we passed on our right the village of the *Notótemnes* who have already become Christians at San José; they used to live almost in the center of the tule region. On our left, we passed the *Tauquimnes* and *Yatchicomnes;* the said *Passasimas* live on that side, with the *Muquélemnes* a little to the northeast of them. Some Passasimas came out to receive us in a peaceful manner, which is not surprising, because they have been at the mission many times, and some of them have been baptized. After lunch, we went on foot to visit some houses of the same people, and there I baptized four heathen who were from sixty to seventy years of age. Having proclaimed God to them, and the necessity of thinking about becoming Christians, we returned to the launch, accompanied by the self-same natives. Here they again told us the stories of there being civilized people on the other side of the Sierra Nevada (from which we should be ten leagues distant), without being able to verify the statements, as has been said on May 20th. At four o'clock in the afternoon we embarked to return by the same course by which we came. We had travelled but a short distance when we found waiting for us one hundred and thirteen natives, part *Yatchicomnes* and part Muquélemnes, half of them painted and armed, with an aspect of war. We overtook them, and, after we had spoken to them, they put aside their arms and asked for peace. Most of these natives live on the mainland, and one may visit them on horseback, if, perchance, it should be necessary to do so. They reach to the slope of the Sierra Nevada, and inform us that that which appears white is rock and not snow, although it most certainly seems that the Sierra contains snow as well as white rock which looks like snow. At six o'clock we took leave of them, giving them wheat, etc., and they promised us that they would come on a trip to the mission. The distance travelled yesterday and last night is about eleven or twelve leagues, toward the south and southeast. We started to travel all night toward the north and northwest.

May 24. At daybreak, we were about at the same parallel as we were when we set out on May 22, and at eight o'clock we arrived at the place called *Los Méganos* in front of *Los Julpunes*, where we had breakfast. At midday, we set out to join the commandant at the strait of the *Chupcane*s, which were reached at six o'clock in the afternoon, finding the said gentleman there; he had arrived in the morning. We travelled this afternoon as far as the mouth of the San Joaquin. It is necessary to pass this at high tide, because there is a sand-bar, and the launches are blocked by it. There is this difference between the Sacramento and San Joaquin; the latter carries less volume of water, although in some places it is wider, and in all that part which we have travelled there is nothing but tule, without a tree under which the navigator may find shade, nor a stick of firewood with which to warm himself; whereas the Sacramento, when it is not flooded, has dry land on both banks covered with May poplar groves, as has been said, and it seems to carry a greater abundance of water. Last night and to-day we travelled twenty leagues toward the north, northwest, and west.

May 25. The day of Pentecost dawned and a mass was sung; after this, in order that the presidio might not be without a mass for the two days following, we set out at nine o'clock with a head wind and a considerable head sea which lasted through the whole strait; the strait is about two leagues long, and a little more or less than half that in width. As we came out of this the sea became calm, and at three o'clock in the afternoon we arrived at a place called the *Punta de Olegario* near the *Isla de los Angeles* where we stopped, having travelled some ten leagues toward the southwest.

May 26. At two o'clock in the morning, before the tide stopped going out, we passed the entrance of the port, arriving almost at dawn at the beach of the presidio. After having said mass there, we returned to the mission of our father San Francisco, with all felicity, thanks to the Lord, to whom be the glory forever and ever. Amen. Fray Narciso Duran.

3

The Rancheros

[Editor's note: The Spanish focus on the Sacramento–San Joaquin River Delta was dominated by security concerns and the recruitment of labor for Mission agriculture and conversion. By 1830, the Spanish project in California was exhausted and Spanish institutions were taken over by Mexican authorities. Their focus was on economic gain. They consolidated missions and sold land through a "land grant" system. Major land grants in the Sacramento–San Joaquin River Delta were purchased by Dr. John Marsh and John Sutter among others. John Bidwell talks of coming to California and visiting Marsh and then Sutter; for more of Bidwell's story and reflections, see Michael J. Gillis and Michael Magliari (eds.), *John Bidwell California: The Life and Writings of a Pioneer: 1841–1900* (Spokane, Washington: Arthur H. Clark, 2004). John Sutter describes how he sought to organize his grant of land into a profitable agricultural manor. Theodore Cordua describes the challenges of those who followed Sutter and criticizes Sutter's labor practices. Clearly, the promise of the land was great but equal were the challenges. Dan Hanel fictionalizes these some of these struggles in *In the Shadow of Diablo: Mystery of the Great Stone House* (Creative Space Independent Publishing, 2012). See Fig. 7.]

John Bidwell, from Echoes of the Past

[Editor's note: John Bidwell's Arrival in California, from John Bidwell, *Echoes of the Past about California*, Library of Congress: loc.gov/item/29000935/.]

Dr. Marsh's ranch, the first settlement reached by us in California, was located in the eastern foothills of the Coast Range Mountains, near the northwestern extremity of the great San Joaquin Valley and about six miles east of Monte Diablo, which may be called about the geographical center of Contra Costa County. There were no other settlements in the valley; it was, apparently, still just as new as when Columbus discovered America, and roaming over it were countless thousands of wild horses, of elk, and of antelopes. It had been one of the driest years ever known in California. The country was brown and parched, and wheat, beans, and everything had failed. Cattle were almost starving for grass, and the people, except perhaps a few of the best families, were without bread, and were eating chiefly meat, and that often of very poor quality.

Benjamin E. L. Bonneville was a native of France, born about the year 1795, who came to America and graduating from West Point in 1815 spent his life as an officer in the U.S. Army. He became a captain of infantry in 1825 and from 1831 to 1836 was engaged in various explorations in the Rocky Mountains and California. His journal, amplified and edited by Washington Irving, was published by the latter in 1837 with the title, *Adventures of Captain Bonneville, U.S.A., in the Rocky Mountains and the Far West.* On Sept. 9, 1861, Bonneville (now a colonel) was retired from active service for disability, and from 1862 to 1865 he commanded Benton Barracks, at St. Louis. He died June 12, 1878, being at the time the oldest officer on the retired list of the U.S. army.

Dr. Marsh had come into California four or five years before by way of New Mexico. He was in some respects a remarkable man. In command of the English language I have scarcely ever seen his equal. He had never studied medicine, I believe, but was a great reader; sometimes he would lie in bed all day reading, and he had a memory that stereotyped all he read, and in those days in California such a man could easily assume the role of doctor and practice medicine. In fact, with the exception of Dr. Marsh there was then no physician of any kind anywhere in California. We were overjoyed to find an American, and yet when we became acquainted with him we found him one of the most selfish of mortals. The night of our arrival he killed two pigs for us. Men reduced to living on poor meat and almost starving have an intense longing for anything fat. We felt very grateful, for we had by no means recovered from starving on poor mule meat, and when he set his Indian cook to making tortillas (little cakes) for us, giving one to each—there were thirty-two in our party—we felt even more grateful, and especially when we learned that he had had to use some of his seed wheat, for he had no other.

Hearing that there was no such thing as money in the country, and that butcher-knives, guns, ammunition, and everything of that kind were better than money, we expressed our gratitude the first night to the doctor by presents, one giving a can of powder, another a bar of lead or a butcher-knife, and another a cheap but serviceable set of surgical instruments.

The next morning, I rose early, among the first, in order to learn from our host something about California—what we could do, and where we could go—and, strange as it may seem he would scarcely answer a question. He seemed to be in an ill humor, and among other things he said: "The company has already been over a hundred dollars' expense to me, and God knows whether I will ever get a *reál* of it or not." I was at a loss to account for this, and went out and told some of the party, and found that others had been snubbed in a similar manner. We held a consultation and resolved to leave as soon as convenient. Half our party concluded to go back to the San Joaquin River, where there was much game, and spend the winter hunting, chiefly for otter, the skins being worth three dollars apiece. The rest—about fourteen—succeeded in gaining information from Dr. Marsh by which they started to find the town of San José, about forty miles to the south, then known by the name of Pueblo de San José; now the city of San José. More or less of our effects had to be left at Marsh's, and I decided to remain and look out for them, and meantime to make short excursions about the country on my own account.

The *reál* was a small Spanish silver coin.

After the others had left I started off, traveling south, and came to what is now called Livermore Valley, then known as Livermore's ranch, belonging to Robert Livermore, a native of England. He had left a vessel when a mere boy, and had married and lived like the native Californians, and, like them, was very expert with the lasso. Livermore's was the frontier ranch, and more exposed than any other to the ravages of the Horse-thief Indians of the Sierra Nevadas, before mentioned. That valley was full of wild cattle, thousands of them, and they were more dangerous to one on foot, as I was, than grizzly bears. By dodging into the gulches and behind trees I made my way to a Mexican ranch at the extreme west end of the valley, where I stayed all night. This was one of the noted ranches, and belonged to a Californian called Don José Maria Amador, more recently to a man named Dougherty. The rancheros marked and branded their stock differently so as to distinguish them. But it was not possible to keep them separate. One would often steal cattle from the other. Livermore in this way lost cattle by his neighbor Amador. In fact, it was almost a daily occurrence, a race to see which could get and kill the most of the other's cattle. Cattle in those days were often killed for the hides alone. One day a man saw Amador kill a fine steer belonging to Livermore. When he reached Livermore's, ten or fifteen miles away, and told him what Amador had done, he found Livermore skinning a steer of Amador's!

Next day, seeing nothing to encourage me, I started to return to Marsh's ranch. On the way, as I came to where two roads, or rather paths, converged, I fell in with one of the fourteen men, M.C. Nye, who had started for San José. He seemed very much agitated, and reported that at the mission of San

José, some fifteen miles this side of the town of San José, all the men had been arrested and put in prison by General Vallejo, Mexican commander-in-chief of the military under Governor Alvarado, he alone having been sent back to tell Marsh and to have him come forth-with to explain why this armed force had invaded the country. We reached Marsh's after dark. The next day the Doctor started down to the mission of San José, nearly thirty miles distant, with a list of the company, which I gave him. He was gone about three days. Meanwhile we sent word to the men on the San Joaquin River to let them know what had taken place, and they at once returned to the ranch to await results.

When Marsh came back, he said ominously: "Now, men, I want you all to come into the house and I will tell you your fate." We all went in, and he announced, "You men that have five dollars can have passports and remain in the country and go where you please." The fact was, he had simply obtained passports for the asking; they had cost him nothing. The men, who had been arrested at the mission, had been liberated as soon as their passports were issued to them, and they had at once proceeded on their way to San José. But five dollars! I don't suppose anyone had five dollars; nine-tenths of them probably had not a cent of money. The names were called and each man settled, giving the amount in something, and if unable to make it up in money or effects he would give his note for the rest. All the names were called except my own. There was no passport for me. Marsh had certainly not forgotten me, for I had furnished him with the list of our names myself. Possibly his idea was—as others surmised and afterwards told me—that lacking a passport, I would stay at his ranch and make a useful hand to work.

The next morning before day found me starting for the mission of San José to get a passport for myself. Mike Nye, the man who had brought the news of the arrest, went with me. A friend had lent me a poor old horse, fit only to carry my blankets. I arrived in a heavy rain-storm, and was marched into the calaboose and kept there three days with nothing to eat, and the fleas were so numerous as to cover and darken anything of a light color. There were four or five Indians in the prison. They were ironed, and they kept tolling a bell, as a punishment, I suppose, for they were said to have stolen horses; possibly they belonged to the Horse-thief tribes east of the San Joaquin Valley. Sentries were stationed at the door. Through a grated window I made a motion to an Indian boy outside and he brought me a handful of beans and a handful of *manteca*, which is used by Mexicans instead of lard. It seemed as if they were going to starve me to death. After having been there three days, I saw through the door a man whom, from his light hair, I took to be an American although he was clad in the wild picturesque garb of a native Californian, including serape and the huge spurs used by the vaquero. I had the sentry at the door hail him. He proved to be an American, a resident of the pueblo of San José, named Thomas Bowen, and he kindly went to Vallejo, who was right across the way in the big mission building, and procured for me the passport. I think I have that passport now, signed by Vallejo and written in Spanish by Victor Pruden. Everyone at the mission pronounced Marsh's action an outrage; such a thing was never known before.

We had already heard that a man by the name of Sutter was starting a colony, a hundred miles away to the north in the Sacramento Valley. No other civilized settlement had been attempted anywhere east of the Coast Range; before Sutter came the Indians had reigned supreme. As the best thing to be done I now determined to go to Sutter's, afterwards called Sutter's Fort, or New Helvetia.

Johann August Sutter, from his Diary

[Editor's note: *The Diary of John Augustus Sutter*, Library of Congress, loc. gov/item/34013250/ and on the website of the Museum of the City of San Francisco, sfmuseum.net/hist2/sutdiary1.html (Sutter's spelling, capitalization and abbreviations have been kept). See Fig. 8.]

April, 1838

I left the State of Missouri (where I has resided for a many years) on the 1th April, 1838, and travelled with the party of Men under Capt Tripps, of the Amer. fur company, to their Rendezvous in the Rocky Mountains (Wind River Valley); from there I travelled with 6 brave Men to Oregon, as I considered myself not strong enough to cross the Sierra Nevada and go direct to California.

Under a good Many Dangers and other troubles I have passed the Different forts or trading posts of the Hudsons Bay Company, and arrived at the Mission at the Dalls on Columbia River. From this place, I crossed right strait through thick & thin and arrived to the great astonishment of the inhabitants. I arrived in 7 days in the Valley of the Willamette, while others with good guides arrived only in 17 days previous my Crossing. At fort Vancouver I has been very hospitably received and invited to pass the Winter with the Gentlemen of the Company, but as a Vessel of the Compy was ready to sail for the Sandwich Islands, I took a passage in her, in hopes to get Soon a Passage from there to California, but 5 long Months I had to wait to find an Opportunity to leave, but not direct to California, except far out of my Way to the Russian American Colonies on the North West Coast, to Sitka the Residence of the Gov'r', I remained one Month there and delivered the Cargo of the Brig Clementine, as I had Charge of the Vessel, and then sailed down the Coast in heavy Gales, and entered in Distress in the Port of San Francisco, on the 2nd of July 1839. An Officer and 15 Soldiers came on board and ordered me out, saying that

Monterey is the Port of entry, & at last I could obtain 48 hours to get provisions (as we were starving) and some repairings done on the Brig.

In Monterey, I arranged my affairs with the Custom House, and presented myself to Govr. Alvarado, and told him my intention to Settle here in this Country, and that I have brought with me 5 White Men and 8 *Kanacas* (two of them married). 3 of the Whitemen were Mechanics, he was very glad to hear that, and particularly when I told him, that I intend to Settle in the interior on the banks of the river Sacramento, because the Indians then at this time would not allow white Men and particularly of the Spanish Origin to come near them, and was very hostile, and stole the horses from the inhabitants, near San Jose. I got a General passport for my small Colony and permission to select a Territory where ever I would find it convenient, and to come in one year's time again in Monterey to get my Citizenship and the title of the Land, which I have done so, and not only this, I received a high civil Office ("*Representante del Govierno en las fronteras del Norte, y Encargado de la Justicia*").

When I left Yerba Buena (now San Francisco) after having leaved the Brig and dispatched her back to the S. J. I bought several small Boats (Launches) and Chartered the Schooner "Isabella" for my Exploring Journey to the inland Rivers and particularly to find the Mouth of the River Sacramento, as I could find Nobody who could give me information, only that they Knew that some very large Rivers are in the interior. William Heath Davis commanded the *Isabella* and *Nicholas* which Sutter had chartered from Nathan Spear.

It took me eight days before I could find the entrance of the Sacramento, as it is very deceiving and very easy to pass by, how it happened to several Officers of the Navy afterwards which refused to take a pilot. About 10 miles below Sacramento City I fell in with the first Indians which was all armed & painted & looked very hostile; they were about 200 Men, as some of them understood a little Spanish I could make a Kind of treaty with them, and the two which understood Spanish came with me, and made me a little better acquainted with the Country. All other Indians on the up River hided themselves in the Bushes, and on the Mouth of Feather River they runned all away so soon they discovered us. I was examining the Country a little further up with a Boat, while the larger Crafts let go their Ankers. On my return, all the white Men came to me and asked me how much longer I intended to travel with them in such a Wilderness. I saw plain that it was a Mutiny. I answered them that I would give them an answer the next Morning and left them and went in the Cabin.

The following Morning I gave Orders to return, and entered in the American River, landed at the former Tannery on the 12th Augt. 1839. Gave Orders to get everything on Shore, pitch the tents and mount the 3 Cannons, called the white Men, and told them that all those which are not contented could leave on board the Isabella next Morning and that I would settle with them immediately and remain alone with the *Canacas*, of 6 Men 3 remained, and 3 of them I gave passage to Yerba buena.

The Indians was first troublesome, and came frequently, and would it not have been for the Cannons they would have Killed us for sake of my property, which they liked very much, and this intention they had very often, how they have confessed to me afterwards, when on good terms.

I had a large Bull Dog which saved my life 3 times, when they came slyly near the house in the Night: he got hold of and marked them most severely. In a short time removed my Camps on the very spot where now the Ruins of Sutters fort stands, made acquaintance with a few Indians which came to work for a short time making Adobes, and the *Canacas* was building 3 grass houses, like it is customary on the Sandwich Islands. Before I came up here, I purchased Cattle & Horses on the Rancho of Senor Martinez, and had great difficulties & trouble to get them up, and had to wait for them long time, and received them at least on the 22d October 1839. Not less than 8 Men wanted to be in the party, as they were afraid of the Indians and had good reasons to be so.

Before I got the cattle we were hunting Deer & Elk etc. and so afterwards to safe the Cattle as I had then only about 500 head, 50 horses & a *manada* of 25 mares. One Year, that is in the fall 1840, I bought 1000 head of Cattle of Don Antonio Sunol and as many horses more of Don Joaquin Gomez and others. In the fall 1839, I have built an Adobe house, covered with Tule and two other small buildings in the middle of the fort; they were afterwards destroyed by fire. At the same time, we cut a Road through the Woods where the City of Sacramento stand, then we made the New Embarcadero, where the old Zinkhouse stands now. After this it was time to make a Garden, and to sow some Wheat &c. We broke up the soil with poor Californian ploughs, I had a few Californians employed as Baqueros, and 2 of them making Cal. Carts & stocking the ploughs etc.

In the Spring 1840, the Indians began to be troublesome all around me, Killing and Wounding Cattle, stealing horses, and threatening to attack us en Mass I was obliged to make Campaigns against them and punish them severely, a little later about 2 a 300 was approaching and got United on Cosumne River, but I was not waiting for them. Left a small Garrison at home, Canons & other Arms loaded, and left with 6 brave men & 2 *Baquero's* in the night, and took them by surprise at Day light. The fighting was a little hard, but after having lost about 30 men, they was willing to make a treaty with me, and after this lecon they behaved very well, and became my best friends and Soldiers, with which I have been assisted to conquer the whole Sacramento and a part of the San Joaquin Valley.

They became likewise tolerable good laborers and the boys had to learn mechanical trades; teamster's, Vaquero's, etc. At the time, the Communication with the Bay was very long and dangerous, particularly in open Boats; it is a great Wonder that we got not swamped a many times, all time with an Indian Crew and a Canace at the helm. Once it took me (in December 1839.) 16 days to go down to *erbabuena* and to return. I went down again on the 22nd to Yerba buena and on account of the inclemency of the Weather and the strong current in the River I need a whole month (17 days coming up) and nearly all the provisions spoiled.

March the 18th. I dispatched a party of White men and Indians in search for pine timber and went not further up on the Amer. River as about 25 miles, found and cut some but not of a good quality and rafted it down the River. On the end of the month of March there was another conspiracy of some Indians, but was soon quelled when I succeeded to disarm them.

August 17th. The men who crossed with me the Rocky Mountains with two others had a chance to come from Oregon on board an Amer. Vessel which landed them at Bodega, at the time occupied by the Russians. When they told the Russian Governor that they wanted to join me, he received them very kindly and hospitable, furnished them with fine horses, new Saddles etc. at a very low rate and gave them direction whereabout they would have to travel, without being seen by some Spaniards, which would have them brought to Sonoma in the prison and after a many difficulties they found me at last. I was of Course very glad having these brave men again with me, and employed them, and so I became strong at once.

August 23rd. Capt. Ringold of Comadore Wilkes' Exploring Squadron arrived on the Embarcadero, piloted by one of the Launches Indian crew; without this they would not have found so easy the entrance of the Sacramento. They had 6 Whaleboats & 1 Launch, 7 Officers and about 50 men in all. I was very glad indeed to see them, sent immediately saddled horses for the Officers, and my Clerk with an invitation to come and see me. At their arrival I fired a salut, and furnished them what they needed. They was right surprised to find me up here in this Wilderness, it made a very good impression upon the Indians to see so many whites are coming to see me, they surveyed the River as far as the Butes. Ringgold of Commodore Wilkes' expedition.

September 4th. Arrived the Russian Govr. Mr. Alexander Rottcheff on board the Schooner Sacramento, and offered me their whole Establishment at Bodega & Ross for sale, and invited me to come right of with him, as there is a Russian Vessel at Bodega, and some Officers with plein power, to transact this business with me, and particularly they would give me the preference, as they became all acquainted with me, during a month's stay at Sitka. I left and went with him down to the Bay in Company with Capt. Ringold's Expedition. What for a fleet we thought then, is on the River. Arriving at Bodega, we came very soon to terms, from there we went to fort Ross where they showed me everything and returned to Bodega again, and before the Vessel sailed we dined on board the Helena, and closed the bargain for $30,000, which has been paid. And other property, was a separate account which has been first paid. The clerk was John Bidwell.

September 28th. I dispatched a number of men and my Clerk by Land to Bodega, to receive the Cattle, Horses, Mules & Sheep, to bring them up to Sutter's fort, called then New Helvetia, by crossing the Sacramento they lost me from about 2000 head about a 100, which drowned in the River, but of most of them we could safe the hides, our Cal. Banknotes at the time.

I did send a Clerk with some men in charge of these Establishments and left the necessary horses and Cattle there. The Schooner Sacramento keept up the communication between the Coast and here, and brought me as freight the Lumber, to finish the House in the fort. I was just building and errecting the fort at the time in Aug. & Sept. for protection of the Indians and of the Californians which became bery jealous seeing these fortifications and 12 Canons and a field piece mounted, and two other brass pieces unmounted at the time.

1844 Fremont's first appearance in California.

October 18th. A party of Comodore Wilkes' Exploring Squadron, arrived from Oregon by land, consisting of the Scientific Corps, a few Naval Officers, Marine Soldiers and Mountaineers as Guides under Command of Lieut. Emmons. I received them so well as I could, and then the Scientific Corps left by Land for San Jose and the Naval Officers & Marines I dispatched them on board of one of my Vessels.

Capt. Fremont arrived at the fort with Kit Carson, told me that he was an officer of the U. S. and left a party behind in Distress and on foot, the few surviving Mules was packed only with the most necessary. I received him politely and his Company likewise as an old acquaintance. The next Morning, I furnished them with fresh horses, & a Vaquero with a pack Mule loaded with Necessary Supplies for his Men. Capt. Fremont found in my Establishment everything what he needed, that he could travel without Delay. He could have not found it so by a Spaniard, perhaps by a great Many and with losing a great deal of time. I sold him about 60 Mules & about 25 horses, and fat young Steers or Beef Cattle, all the Mules & horses got Shoed. On the 23d March, all was ready and on the 24th he left with his party for the U. States. As an Officer of the Govt. it was my duty to report to the Govt., that Capt. Fremont arrived. Genl. Micheltorena dispatched Lieut. Col. Telles (afterwards Gov. of Sinaloa) with Capt., Lieut. and 25 Dragoons, to inquire what Captain Fremont's business was here; but he was en route as they arrive only on the 27th. From this time on Exploring, Hunting & Trapping parties has been started, at the same time Agricultural & Mechanical business was progressing from Year to year, and more Notice has been taken of my establishment. It became even a fame, and some early Distinguished Travellers like Doctor Sandells, Wasnesensky & others, Captains of Trading Vessels & Super Cargos,

& even Californians (after the Indians was subdued) came and paid me a visit, and was astonished to see what for Work of all kinds has been done. Small Emigrant parties arrived, and brought me some very valuable Men, with one of those was Major Bidwell (he was about 4 Years in my employ). Major Reading & Major Hensley with 11 other brave Men arrived alone, both of those Gentlemen has been 2 Years in my employ, with these parties excellent Mechanics arrived which was all employed by me, likewise good farmers. We made immediately Amer. ploughs in my Shops and all kind of work done. Every year the Russians was bound to furnish me with good iron & Steel & files, Articles which could not be got here, likewise Indian Beeds and the most important of all was 100 lb of fine Rifle & 100 lb of Canon powder, and several 100 lb of Lead (every year). With these I was carefull like with Gold.

The Bartle son party which included John Bidwell arrived in November, 1841 Reading and Hensley came in 1843. From the Hudsons Bay Company I received likewise great supplies, and particularly Powder, lead, and Shot, Beaver Trapps and Clothing (on Credit, to be paid for in Beaver and Otter Skins). They would not have done this to everyone; but as I has been highly recommended to these gentlemen from England and personally acquainted, they have done so. Once I received a visit of Mr. Douglas, who was the Commander in Chief of the establishments on the Pacific & the mountains, after Dr. McLaughlin resigned. With such a supply of Powder, Amunition & Arms, I made a bold appearance. The fort was built in about 4 years of time, as it was very difficult to get the necessary lumber we was sawing by hand Oak timber. Under Gen'l Micheltorena our Govr. I received the rank and Title Capt. of the Mexican Army. He found it his Policy to be friend with me, as he was all time threatened with a Revolution of the Californians notwithstanding having about 1000 troupes (Mexicans). Having the rank as Capt. and Military Comander of the Northern frontieres, I began to drill the Indians, with the assistance of two good Non-Commissioned Officers from my Country, which I promoted to Capt & first Lieut't & got their Comissions and from the time I had a self-made Garrison, but the Soldiers to earn for their Uniforms & food etc. had to work when they was not on Duty. During this time, my Stock was increasing; had about then 8000 head of Cattle and 2000 horses and breeding Mares and about 4000 Sheep. Of the Wool we made our own blankets, as we established under great Difficulties a factory. blankets, like nearly all other articles was very scarce and sold to very high prices at the time.

Emigration continued in small parties, just strong enough to protect themselves travelling through a Country of hostile Indians, all of them was always hospitably received under my roof and all those who could or would not be employed, could stay with me so long as they liked, and when leaving, I gave them Passports which was everywhere respected. Was some trouble below, all came immediately to me for protection. Of the different unfortunate

Emigrations which suffered so much in the Snow, it is unnecessary to speak of, as it was published in the papers throughout the States.

In the fall 1844, I went to Monterey with Major Bidwell and a few armed men (Cavallada & Servants); how it was customary to travel at these times, to pay a Visit to Gen'l Micheltorrena. I has been received with the greatest Civil and Military honors. One day he gave a great Diner, after Diner all the Troupes were parading, and in the evening a balloon was sent to the higher regions, etc., etc. At the time, it looked very gloomy; the people of the Country was arming and preparing to make a Revolution, and I got some sure and certain information, of the British Consul and other Gentlemen of my acquaintance which I visited on my way to Monterey. They did not know that the General and myself were friends, and told and discovered me the whole plan, that in a short time the people of the Country will be ready to blockade the General and his troupes in Monterey, and then take him prisoner and send him and his Soldiers back to Mexico, and make a Gov'r of their own people etc. I was well aware what we could expect should they succeed to do this; they would drive us foreigners all very soon out of the Country, how they have done it once, in the winter 1839. Capt. Vioget has already been engaged by Castro & Alvarado to be ready with his vessel to take the Gen'l and his Soldiers to Mexico.

I had a confidential Conversation with Genl. Micheltorena who received me with great honors and Distinction in Monterey. After having him informed of all what is going on in the Country, he took his measures in a Counsel of war in which I has been present. I received my Orders to raise such a large auxiliary force as I possibly could, and to be ready at his Order, at the same time I received some Cartridges and some small Arms which I had shipped on board the Alert, and took a Passage myself for San Francisco (or then Yerba Buena). If I had travelled by land, Castro would have taken me a Prisoner in San Juan, where he was laying in Ambush for me. In Yerba Buena I remained only a few hours as my Schooner was ready to receive me on board, having waited for me at Yerba Buena. I visited the Officers of the Custom house and Castro's Officer, which immediately after I left received an order to arrest me, but I was under fair way to Sacramento.

Theodore Cordua from "The Pioneer of the New Mecklenburg"

[Editor's note: Erwin G. Gudde, editor and translator, "The Memoirs of Theodor Cordua: The Pioneer of New Mecklenburg in the Sacramento Valley," *Quarterly of the California Historical Society*, volume 12, Number 4 (Berkeley: UC Press, 1933); See online: corduan.com/images/Ted_Cordua_Memoirs.pdf#:~:text=memoirs%20of%20Theodor%20Cordua%2C%20

the%20first%20settler%20in,translate%20and%20publish%20the%20
manuscript.%20The%20following%20account, pp 6ff. Ellipses indicate
where passages have been omitted to compress the excerpt. See Fig. 9.]

The beginning of November we returned to the Bay of San Francisco and
anchored at the small town of Yerba Buena which at that time could be called
neither village nor city. Here I met my German compatriot, Mr. Flugge from
Hanover, who was in the service of Sutter, and who induced me to return to
Nova Helvetia with him. The idea of settling in Sutter's neighborhood in the
Sacramento Valley I had almost given up in the meantime. I had heard many
complaints about Sutter, especially that he had contracted many debts and
did not think of repaying them; for this reason, I naturally somewhat lost my
confidence in him. Mr. Carl Flugge, whose uncle I had known since 1815, in
Grossen Helle, Mecklenburg, as a very worthy and respectable man, had been
in California for some time and was better acquainted with the conditions
than I was. Therefore, I followed his advice although he was a friend of Sutter
and had been his pal from the time they had met in St. Louis. He advised me
not to give up my plan and I returned to Sutter's Fort with him. Sutter, who
owned a grant of thirty leagues (about thirty German square miles or one
hundred and fifty thousand acres) in the Sacramento Valley, wished to have
settlers in his neighborhood. He also wanted to buy the goods which I had
brought from the Sandwich Islands and which he needed very badly just then.
His many promises finally led to a deal.

To Mr. Sutter I sold goods valued at about $8,000, for which I was to receive
in exchange heifers at $4 a head, wild cows at $6, domesticated cows and
oxen at $15, wild mares at $3, domesticated mares at $15, and well-broken
horses at $20. Mr. Flugge guaranteed everything and became my partner for a
few months. Sutter, in accordance with his promises, also gave me all the land
north of the Yuba to which he held claim. This permission to live on a part
of his holdings and to use it at my pleasure for nine years was given to me by
contract. If I would move away at the end of nine years, Sutter would pay me
for the newly constructed buildings, but if I were to use the land another nine
years, the buildings, too, would become Sutter's property.

In addition to the five leagues I received from Sutter, I applied to the
Mexican Government a little later for a grant of seven more leagues, situated
at the boundary of Sutter's grant. The size of this additional property was
probably ten leagues, but I have never received a written document for it. I was
loath to take the trip to Monterey or to the distant Pueblo de Los Angeles, the
residence of the last two Mexican Governors, Micheltorena and Pico. Neither
was I willing to bribe the government officials at those places. Nevertheless,
everybody considered me as the owner of the Honcut Ranch. This name I had
given my ten-league grant, because the Honcut River formed the northern

boundary of my entire holdings of about fifteen square miles. On the east, my possessions were bounded by the foothills of the Sierra Nevada, on the south by the Yuba and on the west by the Feather River.

According to the Mexican laws I could consider the six to seven thousand Indians inhabiting the land as my subjects. They were not allowed to work for any other settler, but received wages and board from me whenever I needed them.

My ranch was in every respect one of the finest farms in California suitable for soil cultivation as well as for cattle raising. The whole estate was a valley with hardly any trees. There were only a few beautiful oaks. The banks of the river were lined with oaks, alders, willows, and sycamores; here and there were arbors of wild grapes. By the rivers spread the finest meadows and the most beautiful grazing land, lowlands of five hundred to two thousand acres. On the whole plain of the Sacramento River not a single shrub is found, only here and there near the river are a few oaks. But it is covered with fine grasses, and in the month of March many flowers blossom. At this time, it resembles a carpet of all colors. The soil of this plain is a yellow loam, toward the mountains it becomes reddish-brown and is less fertile. In the lowlands by the rivers are alluvial lands, light soil mixed with much humus and hence very fertile. The luxurious growth of grass makes this sufficiently evident.

Thus, I established myself in the late fall of 1842, as a farmer or ranchero on the Yuba River, within the fork formed by the Yuba and Feather rivers, 39° 20' north latitude, not far from the place where the Yuba empties into the Feather River. I called my whole settlement Neu-Mecklenburg, hoping that I would be able to share it with many of my own countrymen. In the beginning, I had to struggle with unspeakable difficulties. The virgin soil had to be broken with the plowshare, and it was extremely difficult to instruct the laborers on account of the language. The first good ox-hide served as a mattress, and the saddle as a pillow, the stumps of trees as a table and chairs. Mr. Flugge left me after a few months. He had invested nothing in the business, yet he was not satisfied with fifty per cent, of the profits which, to be sure, would amount to very little during the first few years. He wanted to make his fortune as soon as possible and went to the southern part of Upper California. Everything I saw and heard was "Greek" to me, although I had been born and reared in the country and was not entirely unacquainted with cattle raising and agriculture. But the cattle were treated here in a manner which not only would have surprised the Mecklenburg farmer, but would have intimidated him. Until 1844, I was the only settler of the Upper Sacramento Valley, in a distant part of the unknown California, almost without neighbors and surrounded by thousands of wild Indians. I lived two hundred miles away from Yerba Buena, and all the necessities had to be carried up the Sacramento, Feather and Yuba rivers by boat or canoe. Captain Sutter was my only neighbor, yet he lived fifty miles as the crow flies, or seventy-five miles along the stream, from me. Under such circumstances, and especially since I saw everything around me in a wild state, my courage changed sometimes to despondency and all my dreams in anticipation of a pleasant life in this beautiful wilderness seemed to fade. But with persistent industry and courageous efforts I finally reached my goal, and—since a human being is a victim of habit—I became satisfied with everything that had been foreign to me at first.

Until the end of the year 1844, we lived a tranquil life. Everything followed a general routine. Diseases and illnesses among the animals and men were known but little. In December of this year, however, a dark cloud arose on the horizon. The country resounded with revolution and civil war. In Europe this sounds terrible. but in the large and small Spanish republics such a thing was taken with great calmness because everyone knew that the unsettled situation would not last long. From Mexico several hundreds of freed convicts had been sent to California as soldiers. These offended the good Californian citizens because they did not shrink from robbery and murder. The officers, to be sure, were a noticeable exception, especially their general, Governor Micheltorena, who was a good man and a friend to everyone—only a little too lenient in dealing with these vagabonds. Now, the citizens, who wanted to keep Micheltorena but send the soldiers home, took up arms. Captain Sutter, who wished to receive forgiveness for a former offense against Mexico, sided with the Governor. Through a number of intrigues, he succeeded in gathering about two hundred Europeans and Americans as well as two hundred and fifty Indians. Some of those who did not wish to volunteer were forced to join. I was one of these. The foreigners were mostly settlers from the Sacramento Valley and Upper California. Sutter proposed to elect a leader, firmly expecting that he himself would be chosen. The choice, however, fell upon the brave Captain Gant, an old doughty American, who formerly had been in the service of the United States. For his adjutant Captain Rufuss, a German was selected. Sutter and I remained unnecessary associates. In the Salinas Valley, near Monterey, we united with the troops of Micheltorena. Our whole army consisted of about eight hundred men, a copper field piece, and two old rusty cannon. Our batteries were placed upon an old ox-cart. All good Californian citizens as well as the foreigners below Monterey opposed us with an army of about the same strength.

The year 1847 ended with the greatest expectations and it seemed that the following year would crown my success. Around my dwelling, whose doors were never locked, the former wilderness had changed into gardens and large fields of various kinds of grain. The antelope and deer had been replaced by large herds of cattle and horses which grazed unhampered and unguarded. Even the wild Indians appeared to be not unimpressionable by culture and civilization. With my Indians, I always lived in peaceful and harmonious relations. What they lost by my cattle as to acorns, grass seeds, etc., I replaced with wheat, corn, melons, etc., which I planted and shared with them.

Almost in all directions I now had neighbors, so that the social relations were considerably improved. In addition, I enjoyed the greatest freedom which any human being could enjoy and was frequently in a position to give the deciding vote in a judgment over life and death. Then gold was found in my district and my great hopes came to naught.

Without paying much attention to the discovery of gold I embarked at the end of April with twenty-five Indians for San Francisco in order to fetch the twelve hired Americans and with them to prepare the contracted hay in the Napa Valley at the Bay of San Francisco. But all of them had gone off already to the rich gold mines. At the time when I had left Neu-Mecklenburg there had been no panning for gold as yet, neither at the Yuba River nor at the Feather River. All had streamed to the mill at the American Fork. The twelve Americans had gone there too. With much effort and great difficulties, I succeeded in getting other laborers, but only at higher wages. Most of these workers stayed but a short time, and finally I could not get any help even for fifty dollars a day. Only my Indians remained loyal to me. One hundred and forty tons of hay were pressed and baled ready for delivery; over one hundred tons still lay unpressed on the ground. My hay contract was thus filled on my part as well as it was possible under the circumstances, although under the conditions at that time no contract was respected. The soldiers left their posts with arms, horses, and saddles; the sailors left their ships; officers, mates, captains, citizens, lawyers, officials, alcaldes—all hurried to the gold regions in the Sacramento Valley. Yet, the agent of the United States, Quartermaster Folsom, did not treat me very honorably. He was not ashamed to deduct one thousand dollars for fifty tons of hay which had not been pressed. Thus I did not get any profit from my contract although I had filled it as loyally as it was possible! Had I been less honorable and plain-dealing what could I not have done with my twenty-five Indians during this time in the mines! I would have considered Folsom's procedure not unreasonable if his government would have had any disadvantage in this deal. Later he could find no ships to freight the hay and had to let the whole shipment lie with the exception of a few tons, until the fall and winter rain spoiled everything.

At the end of June, I returned to my ranch. My majordomo received me, but he was intoxicated to such an extent that he could not stand on his legs. At the time when gold was discovered, I had in my employ a German, Adolf Brüheim from Hamburg, for a butcher and cook, an American for majordomo, an American for blacksmith, three Englishmen and a Scotchman as carpenters, and an Englishman for captain of my boat and my canoes. With the exception of a few Indians and the intoxicated majordomo all of my people had left me.

When the news of the discovery of gold in California reached Europe many of my countrymen, even my brother, wanted to come to California. Now, however, I could not advise them to do so any longer. Everything was too late! On the first of January, 1849, I transferred my Neu-Mecklenburg to the new owner, and left it with tears in my eyes the end of February. I went with three hundred pounds (4,800 ounces = 120,000 *talers*) of the finest gold which had been gathered at the Yuba and Feather Rivers down-stream to San Francisco. My intention was to embark for Europe, but there was no opportunity to do so. Steam shipping was not yet in existence. To make matters worse, all Europe was in a state of revolution, according to the letters of my brother, and many of my affairs had not been settled. Thus, I remained for the time being in San Francisco ...

The Indian easily learns how to work and knows how to help himself when in need or distress. Everything he starts he wishes to complete as soon as possible. His work is therefore very often unsatisfactory. If he has started something of which he cannot see the end he becomes easily discouraged. He can carry immense burdens for miles and he is a good marksman with the bow and arrow. The river Indians are excellent divers and swimmers. In general, the Indian is rather cowardly. He never trusts a man again who once has broken a promise to him. When he is offended he always tries to take revenge. If an Indian is killed by a white man the relatives of the Indian will kill the first white man who crosses their path. With the beginning of civilization and the introduction of the Christian religion in California the misfortune of the Californian Indian started. In consequence of the founding of the great missions the happily living children of nature were forced to leave their home, to live closely together in the barrack-like buildings of the missions and to work for foreigners. Populations of whole villages, even in the Sacramento Valley, were forced into these institutions. Old and incapable people were baptized immediately and then killed with a dagger. The Indians who were capable of working, as well as the children, were driven into the missions. When Sutter established himself in 1839 in the Sacramento Valley, new misfortune came upon these peaceful natives of the country. Their services were demanded immediately. Those who did not want to work were considered as enemies. With other tribes, the field was taken against the hostile Indian. Declaration of war was not made. The villages were attacked usually before daybreak when everybody was still asleep. Neither old nor young was spared by the enemy, and often the Sacramento River was colored red by the blood of the innocent Indians, for these villages usually were situated at the banks of the rivers. During a campaign one section of the attackers fell upon the village by way of land. All the Indians of the attacked village naturally fled to find protection on the other bank of the river. But there they were awaited by the other half of the enemy and thus the unhappy people were shot and killed with rifles from both sides of the river. Seldom an Indian escaped such an attack, and those who were not murdered were captured. All children from six to fifteen years of age were usually taken by the greedy white people. The village was burned down and the few Indians who had escaped with their lives were left to their fate. Sutter usually claimed the children as a payment for the cost of the war. They became regular commercial objects because the inhabitants of the coast preferred the Indians of the Sacramento Valley as servants, and paid good prices for them. In this way, a regular trade of human beings developed. Gradually there came to our settlements rude hunters who had crossed over the Rocky Mountains. They were mostly vagabonds without feeling and character who had fled from the United States on account of some crime. These were the real enemies of the Indians. They have committed many atrocious deeds without being called to justice. Sutter had been appointed as *Alcalde* and Commander of the North by the Mexican Government. As such he should have been the protector of all people, but he often failed because of selfish interest. As fast as the immigration from the United States into California increased, just so rapidly the number of Indians in the country decreased. Where the Anglo-Saxon appears the red-skin has to yield, says the American. He does not realize that the disappearance of The Indian is usually the consequence of the many diseases and vices which the white man brings along. By these the innocent and inexperienced natives are ruined, although it cannot be denied that at the western boundary of the United States, in the Rocky Mountains, many tribes can still be found, being forced west by the young American nation. The Californian Indians could neither be driven out nor could they emigrate, because the neighboring Indians refused to admit them into their territories.

From my first appearance in California until my departure from this beautiful country I lived in peace with all the neighboring tribes in the valley as well as in the mountains. I could travel among them entirely alone and without fear of being annoyed whenever I wanted. Days and nights, I have stayed with them without thinking of any danger. I have never participated in any of Sutter's campaigns against them, but have rather regretted these attacks. Only once, in the fall of 1846, was I forced to take up arms against a tribe which lived in the mountains about forty miles away from me. These were the Indians of the Luckno villages. They were hostile to the Indians who surrounded me and had stolen three horses and ten heads of cattle from me. As soon as my intention was known among the surrounding tribes all declared their willingness to participate in the campaign. With seven chiefs, about two hundred Indians, and two Europeans, Mr. Stevens, an old Holsteiner, and Mr. O'Fallan, an Irishman, I took the field against the Luckno villages in warlike fashion. We reached their places on the afternoon of the second day. At our approach, there arose in the valley where the villages were situated such a ghastly war-cry of the enemy that it echoed in the mountains. In a few moments, I was deserted by everybody and heard only the howl in the distance. To my great pleasure I soon found the two Europeans. Shortly after twilight my Indians brought in four prisoners, among them the first chief of the enemy. Stevens, in his rage, drew a long knife out of the scabbard and wanted to decapitate the chief. I asked him, however, to wait with the punishment until the next morning. He was satisfied therefore to tie the prisoners' hands behind their backs. We found skulls and skeletons of the stolen animals in the villages, which proved sufficiently that they were guilty and the confessions of the captured Indians confirmed everything. A tent was pitched for myself and my two companions and in front of it a large fire was lighted. The Indians camped in the open around small fires. The four prisoners sat at the fire near our tent and were strictly guarded. Pondering about the fate of the poor Indians I lay on my straw bed without being able to sleep. Suddenly a shot fell nearby. The whole camp was aroused at once. The prisoners who had sat close together with their hands on their backs had untied themselves unnoticed. The chief had run away with a handsome young Indian. Stevens, who was on guard, had sent a bullet after them in vain. He was beside himself with anger while I was secretly pleased. I lay down again hoping that that two other Indians would follow the example of their companions. To my regret, I found them the next morning at the same place where I had left them. Both had confessed to having participated in the theft and the other Indians had confirmed this. Thus, there was nothing left except to give a judgment. Stevens, O'Fallan and all of the Indians were for capital punishment. As their chief, I was forced to agree with them for leniency was out of the question. Both delinquents were tied and placed on a large rock. Stevens, an old soldier who had fought at Waterloo under Napoleon, executed the sentence. We placed the bodies on the rock, put the bones of the cattle in their hands and left the camp and place of the execution. O'Fallan had taken two beautiful young Indian girls of six and seven years as prisoners of war. I bought both of them for a tame cow. After two months, I gave the children back to their mother, the wife of the chief, and forwarded a few presents along with them. In this manner, the Indians of Luckno became my friends.

Since the cattle were not guarded in the open and since many Indians lived around us, we could not deal with cattle thieves otherwise than by punishing them with execution. If we had allowed the Indians to become accustomed to beef or horse meat, even capital punishment would not have kept them in check. Therefore, it was better to sacrifice a victim at the beginning than to be obliged to destroy whole tribes later on. In the San Joaquin Valley and the surrounding mountains lived many Indians who formerly belonged to the missions. These ate mainly horse meat and millions [!] of horses had been killed by them and thousands of tame horses are still stolen every year from the herds near the settlements on the coast.

On May, 1852, after a stay of ten years I left California. Many people had I befriended, hundreds had I entertained at my table, my house always had been open and a free hotel for all travelers. Yet I did not leave a single friend behind. When my glance had fallen upon Yerba Buena for the first time there had been but six houses and ten huts, and the many bare sand hills had offered a sad sight. Now the barren hills had disappeared together with the old name of Yerba Buena. The parting glance fell upon the large and beautiful City of San Francisco, the queen of commerce of the whole western coast of America. A city of the size of Bremen, built from material and by people of all nations of the world. At points where ten years ago ships anchored there were large warehouses. This tremendous metamorphosis had taken place in hardly four years! He who knows me will realize that I am little inclined to sentimentality. Yet in this moment I had a feeling as if my chest was to burst open and I had to hide in a quiet corner in order to collect myself.

4

Highway to Gold

[Editor's note: With the rush for gold, the Sacramento and San Joaquin rivers as well as the towns along became the focus of immigrants in search of their fortunes. The river towns were primitive and the target of satire like the one included here by George Derby using the pen name "Squibob." Bret Harte offers a short story that illustrates the incompatible value systems of the Spanish and the new immigrants coming to California to search for gold. Samuel Clements (Mark Twain), reporting for the San Francisco *Call*, describes a disaster that befell one of the riverboats as it was heading to Sacramento and the Northern mines, and the bravery of its captain.]

George Derby, alias Squibob, Benicia in 1850

[Editor's note: George Horatio Derby, *Phoenixiana: Or Sketches and Burlesque* (New York: D. Appleton, 1903), pp. 95–105. Derby was a West Point graduate in California to make maps for military use. See Fig. 10.]

LEAVING the metropolis last evening by the gradually-increasing-in-popularity steamer, "West Point," I "skeeted" up Pablo Bay with the intention of spending a few days at the world-renowned seaport of Benicia. Our Captain (a very pleasant and gentlemanly little fellow by the way) was named Swift, our passengers were emphatically a fast set, the wind blew like well-watered rose bushes, and the tide was strong in our favor. All these circumstances tended to impress me with the idea that we were to make a wonderfully quick passage, but alas, "the race is not always to the Swift," the "Senator" passed us ten miles from the wharf, and it was nine o'clock, and very dark at that, when we were roped in by the side of the "ancient and fishlike" smelling hulk that forms the broad wharf of Benicia.

As I shouldered my carpet-bag, and stepped upon the wharf among the dense crowd of four individuals that were there assembled, and gazing upon the mighty city whose glimmering lights, feebly discernible through the Benician darkness, extended over an area of five acres, an overpowering sense of the grandeur and majesty of the great rival of San Francisco affected me. I felt my own extreme insignificance, and was fain to lean upon a pile of watermelons for support. "Boy!" said I, addressing an intelligent specimen of humanity who formed an integral portion of the above-mentioned crowd, "Boy! can you direct me to the best hotel in this city?"—"Ain't but one," responded the youth, "Winn keeps it; right up the hill thar." Decidedly, thought I, I will go in to Winn, and reshouldering my carpet-bag, I blundered down the ladder, upon a plank foot-path leading over an extensive morass in the direction indicated, not noticing, in my abstraction, that I had inadvertently retained within my grasp the melon upon which my hand had rested. "*Saw yer!*" resounded from the wharf as I retired—"*Saw yer!*" repeated several individuals upon the foot-path.

For an instant, my heart beat with violence at the idea of being seen accidentally appropriating so contemptible an affair as a watermelon; but hearing a man with a small white hat and large white mustache shout "Hello!" and immediately rush with frantic violence up the ladder, I comprehended that Sawyer was his proper name, and by no means alluded to me or my proceedings; so, slipping the melon in my carpet-bag, I tranquilly resumed my journey. A short walk brought me to the portal of the best and only hotel in the city, a large two-story building dignified by the title of the "Solano Hotel," where I was graciously received by mine host, who welcomed me to Benicia in the most *winning* manner. After slightly refreshing my inner man with a feeble stimulant, and undergoing an introduction to the oldest inhabitant, I calmly seated myself in the barroom, and contemplated with intense interest the progress of a game of billiards between two enterprising citizens; but finding, after a lapse of two hours, that there was no earthly probability of its ever being concluded, I seized a candle-stick and retired to my room. Here I discussed my melon with intense relish, and then seeking my couch, essayed to sleep. But, oh! the fleas! skipping, hopping, crawling, biting! "Won't someone establish an agency for the sale of D. L. Charles & Co.'s Fleabane, in Benicia?" I agonizingly shouted, and echo answered through the reverberating halls of the "Solano Hotel," "Yes, they won't!" What a night! But everything must have an end (circles and California gold excepted), and day at last broke over Benicia. Magnificent place!

I gazed upon it from the attic window of the "Solano Hotel," with feelings too deep for utterance. The sun was rising in its majesty, gilding the red wood shingles of the U.S. Storehouses in the distance; seven deserted hulks were riding majestically at anchor in the bay; clothes-lines, with their burdens, were flapping in the morning breeze; a man with a wheelbarrow was coming down the street! Everything, in short, spoke of the life, activity, business, and bustle of a great city. But in the midst of the excitement of this scene, an odoriferous smell of beefsteak came, like a holy calm, across my olfactories, and hastily drawing in my *cabeza*, I descended to breakfast.

This operation concluded, I took a stroll in company with the oldest inhabitant, from whom I obtained much valuable information (which I hasten to present), and who cheerfully volunteered to accompany me as a guide to the lions of the city. There are no less than forty-two wooden houses, many of them two stories in height, in this great place—and nearly twelve hundred inhabitants, men, women and children! There are six grocery, provision, dry goods, auction, commission, and where-you-can-get-almost-any-little-thing-you-want stores, one hotel, one school-house—which is also a *brevet* church—three billiard-tables, a post-office—from which I actually saw a man get a letter—and a tenpin-alley, where I am told a man once rolled a whole game, paid $1.50 for it, and walked off chuckling. Then there is a "monte bank"—a Common Council, and a Mayor, who, my guide informed me, was called "*Carne*," from a singular habit he has of eating roast beef for dinner. But there isn't a tree in all Benicia. "There was one," said the guide, "last year—only four miles from here, but they chopped it down for firewood for the 'post.' Alas! Why didn't the woodman spare that tree?"

The dwelling of one individual pleased me indescribably—he had painted it a vivid green! Imaginative being. He had evidently tried to fancy it a tree, and in the enjoyment of this sweet illusion, had reclined beneath its grateful shade, secured from the rays of the burning sun, and in the full enjoyment of rural felicity even among the crowded streets of this great metropolis. How pretty is the map of Benicia! We went to see that, too. It's all laid off in squares and streets, for ever so far, and you can see the pegs stuck in the ground at every corner, only they are not exactly in a line, sometimes; and there is Aspinwall's wharf, where they are building a steamer of iron, that looks like a large pan, and Semple Slip, all divided on the map by lines and dots, into little lots of incredible value; but just now they are all under water, so no one can tell what they are actually worth. Oh! decidedly Benicia is a great place. "And how much, my dear sir," I modestly inquired of the gentlemanly recorder who displayed the map; "how much may this lot be worth?" and I pointed with my finger at lot No. 97, block 16,496—situated, as per map, in the very center of the swamp. "That, sir," replied he with much suavity, "ah! it would be held at about three thousand dollars, I suppose."—I shuddered—and retired. The history of Benicia is singular. The origin of its name as related by the oldest inhabitant is remarkable. I put it right down in my note-book as he spoke, and believe it religiously, every word. "Many years ago," said that aged man, "this property was owned by two gentlemen, one of whom, from the extreme candor and ingenuousness of his character, we will call Simple; the other being distinguished for waggery, and a disposition for practical joking, I shall call—as in fact he was familiarly termed in those days—Larkin. While walking over these grounds in company, on one occasion, and being naturally struck by its natural advantages, said Simple to Larkin, 'Why not make a city here, my boy? have it surveyed into squares, bring up ships, build houses, make it a port of entry, establish depots, sell lots, and knock the center out of Yerba Buena straight?' (Yerba Buena is now San Francisco, reader.) 'Ah!' quoth Larkin with a pleasant grin diffusing itself over his agreeable countenance, 'that would be nice, hey?'" Need we say that the plan was adopted—carried out—proved successful—and Larkin's memorable remark: "*be nice, hey,*" being adopted as the name of the growing city, gradually became altered and vulgarized into its present form, Benicia!

A curious history, this, which would have delighted Horne Took beyond measure. Having visited the Masonic Hall, which is really a large and beautiful building, reflecting credit alike on the Architect and the fraternity, being by far the best and most convenient hall in the country, I returned to the Solano Hotel, where I was accosted by a gentleman in a blue coat with many buttons, and a sanguinary streak down the leg of his trousers, whom I almost immediately recognized as my old friend, Captain George P. Jambs, of the U.S. Artillery, a thorough-going *adobe*, as the Spaniard has it, and a member in high and regular standing of the Dumfudgin Club.

He lives in a delightful little cottage, about a quarter of a mile from the center of the city, being on duty at the Post—which is some mile, mile and a half or two miles from that metropolis—and pressed me so earnestly to partake of his hospitality during my short sojourn, that I was at last fain to pack up my property, including the remains of the abstracted melon, and in spite of the blandishments of my kind host of the Solano, accompany him to his domicile, which he very appropriately names "Mischief Hall." So here I am installed for a few days, at the expiration of which I shall make a rambling excursion to Sonoma, Napa and the like, and from whence perhaps you may hear from me. As I sit here looking from my airy chamber upon the crowds of two or three persons thronging the streets of the great city; as I gaze upon that man carrying home a pound and a half of fresh beef for his dinner; as I listen to the bell of the Mary (a Napa steam packet of four cat power) ringing for departure, while her captain in a hoarse voice of authority requests the passengers to "step over the other side, as the larboard paddle-box is under water;" as I view all these unmistakable signs of the growth and prosperity of Benicia, I cannot but wonder at the infatuation of the people of your village, who will persist in their absurd belief that San Francisco will become a *place*, and do not hesitate to advance the imbecile idea that it may become a successful rival of this city. Nonsense!—Oh Lord! at this instant there passed by my window the—prettiest—little—I can't write any more this week; if this takes, I'll try it again.

Yours forever,
SQUIBOB.

Bret Harte, "The Legend of Monte del Diablo"

[Editor's note: Bret Harte, "The Legend of Monte del Diablo" first published in *The Atlantic* in 1863. For online edition see: gutenberg.org/files/2599/2599-h/2599-h.htm#link2H_4_0002. See Fig. 11.]

The cautious reader will detect a lack of authenticity in the following pages. I am not a cautious reader myself, yet I confess with some concern to the absence of much documentary evidence in support of the singular incident I am about to relate. Disjointed memoranda, the proceedings of *ayuntamientos* and early departmental juntas, with other records of a primitive and superstitious people, have been my inadequate authorities. It is but just to state, however, that though this particular story lacks corroboration, in ransacking the Spanish archives of Upper California I have met with many more surprising and incredible stories, attested and supported to a degree that would have placed this legend beyond a cavil or doubt. I have, also, never lost faith in the legend myself, and in so doing have profited much from the examples of divers grant-claimants, who have often jostled me in their more practical researches, and who have my sincere sympathy at the skepticism of a modern hard-headed and practical world.

For many years after Father Junipero Serra first rang his bell in the wilderness of Upper California, the spirit which animated that adventurous priest did not wane. The conversion of the heathen went on rapidly in the establishment of missions throughout the land. So sedulously did the good Fathers set about their work, that around their isolated chapels there presently arose adobe huts, whose mud-plastered and savage tenants partook regularly of the provisions, and occasionally of the Sacrament, of their pious hosts. Nay, so great was their progress, that one zealous Padre is reported to have administered the Lord's Supper one Sabbath morning to "over three hundred heathen savages." It was not to be wondered that the Enemy of Souls, being greatly incensed thereat, and alarmed at his decreasing popularity, should have grievously tempted and embarrassed these holy Fathers, as we shall presently see.

Yet they were happy, peaceful days for California. The vagrant keels of prying Commerce had not as yet ruffled the lordly gravity of her bays. No torn and ragged gulch betrayed the suspicion of golden treasure. The wild oats drooped idly in the morning heat or wrestled with the afternoon breezes. Deer and antelope dotted the plain. The watercourses brawled in their familiar channels, nor dreamed of ever shifting their regular tide. The wonders of the Yosemite and Calaveras were as yet unrecorded. The holy Fathers noted little of the landscape beyond the barbaric prodigality with which the quick soil repaid the sowing. A new conversion, the advent of a saint's day, or the baptism of an Indian baby, was at once the chronicle and marvel of their day.

At this blissful epoch, there lived at the Mission of San Pablo Father José Antonio Haro, a worthy brother of the Society of Jesus. He was of tall and cadaverous aspect. A somewhat romantic history had given a poetic interest to his lugubrious visage. While a youth, pursuing his studies at famous Salamanca, he had become enamored of the charms of Doña Carmen de Torrencevara, as that lady passed to her matutinal devotions. Untoward circumstances, hastened, perhaps, by a wealthier suitor, brought this amour to a disastrous issue, and Father José entered a monastery, taking upon himself the vows of celibacy. It was here that his natural fervor and poetic enthusiasm conceived expression as a missionary. A longing to convert the uncivilized heathen succeeded his frivolous earthly passion, and a desire to explore and develop unknown fastnesses continually possessed him. In his flashing eye and sombre exterior was detected a singular commingling of the discreet Las Casas and the impetuous Balboa.

Fixed by this pious zeal, Father José went forward in the van of Christian pioneers. On reaching Mexico he obtained authority to establish the Mission of San Pablo. Like the good Junipero, accompanied only by an acolyte and muleteer, he unsaddled his mules in a dusky *cañon*, and rang his bell in the wilderness. The savages—a peaceful, inoffensive, and inferior race—presently flocked around him. The nearest military post was far away, which contributed much to the security of these pious pilgrims, who found their open trustfulness and amiability better fitted to repress hostility than the presence of an armed, suspicious, and brawling soldiery. So the good Father José said matins and prime, mass and vespers, in the heart of sin and heathenism, taking no heed to himself, but looking only to the welfare of the Holy Church. Conversions soon followed, and on the 7th of July, 1760, the first Indian baby was baptized,— an event which, as Father José piously records, "exceeds the richness of gold or precious jewels or the chancing upon the Ophir of Solomon." I quote this incident as best suited to show the ingenious blending of poetry and piety which distinguished Father José's record.

The Mission of San Pablo progressed and prospered, until the pious founder thereof, like the infidel Alexander, might have wept that there were no more heathen worlds to conquer. But his ardent and enthusiastic spirit could not long brook an idleness that seemed begotten of sin; and one pleasant August morning in the year of grace 1770 Father José issued from the outer court of the mission building, equipped to explore the field for new missionary labors.

Nothing could exceed the quiet gravity and unpretentiousness of the little cavalcade. First rode a stout muleteer, leading a pack-mule laden with the provisions of the party, together with a few cheap crucifixes and hawks' bells. After him came the devout Padre José, bearing his breviary and cross, with a black serape thrown around his shoulders; while on either side trotted a dusky convert, anxious to show a proper sense of his regeneration by acting as guide into the wilds of his heathen brethren. Their new condition was agreeably shown by the absence of the usual mud plaster, which in their unconverted state they assumed to keep away vermin and cold. The morning was bright and propitious. Before their departure, mass had been said in the chapel, and the protection of St. Ignatius invoked against all contingent evils, but especially against bears, which, like the fiery dragons of old, seemed to cherish unconquerable hostility to the Holy Church.

As they wound through the *cañon*, charming birds disported upon boughs and sprays, and sober quails piped from the alders; the willowy watercourses gave a musical utterance, and the long grass whispered on the hillside. On entering the deeper defiles, above them towered dark green masses of pine, and occasionally the *madroño* shook its bright scarlet berries.

As they toiled up many a steep ascent, Father José sometimes picked up fragments of scoria, which spoke to his imagination of direful volcanoes and impending earthquakes. To the less scientific mind of the muleteer Ignacio they had even a more terrifying significance; and he once or twice snuffed the air suspiciously, and declared that it smelt of Sulphur. So, the first day of their journey wore away, and at night they encamped without having met a single heathen face.

It was on this night that the Enemy of Souls appeared to Ignacio in an appalling form. He had retired to a secluded part of the camp and had sunk upon his knees in prayerful meditation, when he looked up and perceived the Arch-Fiend in the likeness of a monstrous bear. The Evil One was seated on his hind legs immediately before him, with his fore paws joined together just below his black muzzle. Wisely conceiving this remarkable attitude to be in mockery and derision of his devotions, the worthy muleteer was transported with fury. Seizing an arquebus, he instantly closed his eyes and fired. When he had recovered from the effects of the terrific discharge, the apparition had disappeared. Father José, awakened by the report, reached the spot only in time to chide the muleteer for wasting powder and ball in a contest with one whom a single *ave* would have been sufficient to utterly discomfit. What further reliance he placed on Ignacio's story is not known; but, in commemoration of a worthy Californian custom, the place was called "*La Cañada de la Tentacion del Pio Muletero*," or "The Glen of the Temptation of the Pious Muleteer," a name which it retains to this day.

The next morning the party, issuing from a narrow gorge, came upon a long valley, sear and burnt with the shadeless heat. Its lower extremity was lost in a fading line of low hills, which, gathering might and volume toward the upper end of the valley, upheaved a stupendous bulwark against the breezy north. The peak of this awful spur was just touched by a fleecy cloud that shifted to and fro like a bannerette. Father José gazed at it with mingled awe and admiration. By a singular coincidence, the muleteer Ignacio uttered the simple ejaculation "Diablo!"

As they penetrated the valley, they soon began to miss the agreeable life and companionable echoes of the *cañon* they had quitted. Huge fissures in the parched soil seemed to gape as with thirsty mouths. A few squirrels darted from the earth and disappeared as mysteriously before the jingly mules. A gray wolf trotted leisurely along just ahead. But whichever way Father José turned, the mountain always asserted itself and arrested his wandering eye. Out of the dry and arid valley it seemed to spring into cooler and bracing life. Deep cavernous shadows dwelt along its base; rocky fastnesses appeared midway of its elevation; and on either side huge black hills diverged like massy roots from a central trunk. His lively fancy pictured these hills peopled with a majestic and intelligent race of savages; and looking into futurity, he already saw a monstrous cross crowning the dome-like summit. Far different were the sensations of the muleteer, who saw in those awful solitudes only fiery dragons, colossal bears, and breakneck trails. The converts, Concepcion and Incarnacion, trotting modestly beside the Padre, recognized, perhaps, some manifestation of their former weird mythology.

At nightfall, they reached the base of the mountain. Here, Father José unpacked his mules, said vespers, and, formally ringing his bell, called upon the Gentiles within hearing to come and accept the holy faith. The echoes of the black frowning hills around him caught up the pious invitation and repeated it at intervals; but no Gentiles appeared that night. Nor were the devotions of the muleteer again disturbed, although he afterward asserted that, when the Father's exhortation was ended, a mocking peal of laughter came from the mountain. Nothing daunted by these intimations of the near hostility of the Evil One, Father José declared his intention to ascend the mountain at early dawn, and before the sun rose the next morning he was leading the way.

The ascent was in many places difficult and dangerous. Huge fragments of rock often lay across the trail, and after a few hours' climbing they were forced to leave their mules in a little gully and continue the ascent afoot. Unaccustomed to such exertion, Father José often stopped to wipe the perspiration from his thin cheeks. As the day wore on a strange silence oppressed them. Except the occasional pattering of a squirrel, or a rustling in the chamisal bushes, there were no signs of life. The half-human print of a bear's foot sometimes appeared before them, at which Ignacio always crossed himself piously. The eye was sometimes cheated by a dripping from the rocks, which on closer inspection proved to be a resinous oily liquid with an abominable sulphurous smell. When they were within a short distance of the summit, the discreet Ignacio, selecting a sheltered nook for the camp, slipped aside and busied himself in preparations for the evening, leaving the holy Father to continue the ascent alone. Never was there a more thoughtless act of prudence, never a more imprudent piece of caution. Without noticing the desertion, buried in pious reflection, Father José pushed mechanically on, and, reaching the summit, cast himself down and gazed upon the prospect.

Below him lay a succession of valleys opening into each other like gentle lakes, until they were lost to the southward. Westerly the distant range hid the bosky *cañada* which sheltered the Mission of San Pablo. In the farther distance the Pacific Ocean stretched away, bearing a cloud of fog upon its bosom, which crept through the entrance of the bay, and rolled thickly between him and the northeastward; the same fog hid the base of the mountain and the view beyond. Still from time to time the fleecy veil parted, and timidly disclosed charming glimpses of mighty rivers, mountain defiles, and rolling plains, sear with ripened oats and bathed in the glow of the setting sun. As father José gazed, he was penetrated with a pious longing. Already his imagination, filled with enthusiastic conceptions, beheld all that vast expanse gathered under the mild sway of the holy faith and peopled with zealous converts. Each little knoll in fancy became crowned with a chapel; from each dark *cañon* gleamed the white walls of a mission building. Growing bolder in his enthusiasm and looking farther into futurity, he beheld a new Spain rising on these savage shores. He already saw the spires of stately cathedrals, the domes of palaces, vineyards, gardens, and groves. Convents, half hid among the hills, peeping from plantations of branching limes, and long processions of chanting nuns wound through the defiles. So completely was the good Father's conception of the future confounded with the past, that even in their choral strain the well-remembered accents of Carmen struck his ear. He was busied in these fanciful imaginings, when suddenly over that extended prospect the faint distant tolling of a bell rang sadly out and died. It was the Angelus. Father José listened with superstitious exaltation.

The Mission of San Pablo was far away, and the sound must have been some miraculous omen. But never before, to his enthusiastic sense, did the sweet seriousness of this angelic symbol come with such strange significance. With the last faint peal, his glowing fancy seemed to cool; the fog closed in below him, and the good Father remembered he had not had his supper. He had risen and was wrapping his serape around him, when he perceived for the first time that he was not alone.

Nearly opposite, and where should have been the faithless Ignacio, a grave and decorous figure was seated. His appearance was that of an elderly hidalgo, dressed in mourning, with mustaches of iron-gray carefully waxed and twisted round a pair of lantern-jaws. The monstrous hat and prodigious feather, the enormous ruff and exaggerated trunk-hose, contrasted with a frame shriveled and wizened, all belonged to a century previous. Yet Father José was not astonished. His adventurous life and poetic imagination, continually on the look-out for the marvelous, gave him a certain advantage over the practical and material-minded. He instantly detected the diabolical quality of his visitant, and was prepared. With equal coolness and courtesy, he met the cavalier's obeisance.

"I ask your pardon, Sir Priest," said the stranger, "for disturbing your meditations. Pleasant   they must have been, and right fanciful, I imagine, when occasioned by so fair a prospect.

"Worldly, perhaps, Sir Devil,—for such I take you to be," said the holy Father, as the stranger bowed his black plumes to the ground; "worldly, perhaps; for it hath pleased Heaven to retain even in our regenerated state much that pertaineth to the flesh, yet still, I trust, not without some speculation for the welfare of the Holy Church. In dwelling upon yon fair expanse, mine eyes have been graciously opened with prophetic inspiration, and the promise of the heathen as an inheritance hath marvelously recurred to me. For there can be none lack such diligence in the true faith but may see that even the conversion of these pitiful salvages hath a meaning. As the blessed St. Ignatius discreetly observes," continued Father José, clearing his throat and slightly elevating his voice, "'the heathen is given to the warriors of Christ, even as the pearls of rare discovery which gladden the hearts of shipmen.' Nay, I might say"—

But here the stranger, who had been wrinkling his brows and twisting his mustaches with well-bred patience, took advantage of an oratorical pause. "It grieves me, Sir Priest, to interrupt the current of your eloquence as discourteously as I have already broken your meditations; but the day already waneth to night. I have a matter of serious import to make with you, could I entreat your cautious consideration a few moments."

Father José hesitated. The temptation was great, and the prospect of acquiring some knowledge of the Great Enemy's plans not the least trifling object. And, if the truth must be told, there was a certain decorum about the stranger that interested the Padre. Though well aware of the Protean shapes the Arch-Fiend could assume, and though free from the weaknesses of the flesh, Father José was not above the temptations of the spirit. Had the Devil appeared, as in the case of the pious St. Anthony, in the likeness of a comely damsel, the good Father, with his certain experience of the deceitful sex, would have whisked her away in the saying of a paternoster. But there was, added to the security of age, a grave sadness about the stranger,—a thoughtful consciousness, as of being at a great moral disadvantage, which at once decided him on a magnanimous course of conduct.

The stranger then proceeded to inform him that he had been diligently observing the holy Father's triumphs in the valley. That, far from being greatly exercised thereat, he had been only grieved to see so enthusiastic and chivalrous an antagonist wasting his zeal in a hopeless work. For, he observed, the issue of the great battle of Good and Evil had been otherwise settled, as he would presently show him. "It wants but a few moments of night," he continued, "and over this interval of twilight, as you know, I have been given complete control. Look to the west."

As the Padre turned, the stranger took his enormous hat from his head and waved it three times before him. At each sweep of the prodigious feather the fog grew thinner, until it melted impalpably away, and the former landscape returned, yet warm with the glowing sun. As Father José gazed a strain of martial music arose from the valley, and issuing from a deep *cañon* the good Father beheld a long cavalcade of gallant cavaliers, habited like his companion. As they swept down the plain, they were joined by like processions, that slowly defiled from every ravine and *cañon* of the mysterious mountain. From time to time the peal of a trumpet swelled fitfully upon the breeze; the cross of Santiago glittered, and the royal banners of Castile and Aragon waved over the moving column. So, they moved on solemnly toward the sea, where, in the distance, Father José saw stately caravels, bearing the same familiar banner, awaiting them. The good Padre gazed with conflicting emotions, and the serious voice of the stranger broke the silence.

"Thou hast beheld, Sir Priest, the fading footprints of adventurous Castile. Thou hast seen the declining glory of old Spain, declining as yonder brilliant sun. The sceptre she hath wrested from the heathen is fast dropping from her decrepit and fleshless grasp. The children she hath fostered shall know her no longer. The soil she hath acquired shall be lost to her as irrevocably as she herself hath thrust the Moor from her own Granada."

The stranger paused, and his voice seemed broken by emotion; at the same time, Father José, whose sympathizing heart yearned toward the departing banners, cried in poignant accents:

"Farewell, ye gallant cavaliers and Christian soldiers! Farewell, thou, Nuñes de Balboa! thou, Alonzo de Ojeda! and thou, most venerable Las Casas! farewell, and may Heaven prosper still the seed ye left behind!"

Then turning to the stranger, Father José beheld him gravely draw his pocket-handkerchief from the basket-hilt of his rapier and apply it decorously to his eyes.

"Pardon this weakness, Sir Priest," said the cavalier apologetically; "but these worthy gentlemen were ancient friends of mine, and have done me many a delicate service, much more, perchance, than these poor sables may signify," he added, with a grim gesture toward the mourning suit he wore.

Father José was too much preoccupied in reflection to notice the equivocal nature of this tribute, and, after a few moments' silence, said, as if continuing his thought:

"But the seed they have planted shall thrive and prosper on this fruitful soil."

As if answering the interrogatory, the stranger turned to the opposite direction, and, again waving his hat, said, in the same serious tone, "Look to the east!"

The Father turned, and, as the fog broke away before the waving plume, he saw that the sun was rising. Issuing with its bright beams through the passes of the snowy mountains beyond appeared a strange and motley crew. Instead of the dark and romantic visages of his last phantom train, the Father beheld with strange concern the blue eyes and flaxen hair of a Saxon race. In place of martial airs and musical utterance, there rose upon the ear a strange din of harsh gutturals and singular sibilation. Instead of the decorous tread and stately mien of the cavaliers of the former vision, they came pushing, bustling, panting, and swaggering. And as they passed, the good Father noticed that giant trees were prostrated as with the breath of a tornado, and the bowels of the earth were torn and rent as with a convulsion. And Father José looked in vain for holy cross or Christian symbol; there was but one that seemed an ensign, and he crossed himself with holy horror as he perceived it bore the effigy of a bear.

"Who are these swaggering Ishmaelites?" he asked, with something of asperity in his tone.

The stranger was gravely silent.

"What do they here, with neither cross nor holy symbol?" he again demanded.

"Have you the courage to see, Sir Priest?" responded the stranger quietly.

Father José felt his crucifix, as a lonely traveler might his rapier, and assented.

"Step under the shadow of my plume," said the stranger.

Father José stepped beside him and they instantly sank through the earth.

When he opened his eyes, which had remained closed in prayerful meditation during his rapid descent, he found himself in a vast vault, bespangled overhead with luminous points like the starred firmament. It was also lighted by a yellow glow that seemed to proceed from a mighty sea or lake that occupied the centre of the chamber. Around this subterranean sea dusky figures flitted, bearing ladles filled with the yellow fluid, which they had replenished from its depths. From this lake, a mysterious flood penetrated like mighty rivers the cavernous distance. As they walked by the banks of this glittering Styx, Father José perceived how the liquid stream at certain places became solid. The ground was strewn with glittering flakes. One of these the Padre picked up and curiously examined. It was virgin gold.

An expression of discomfiture overcast the good Father's face at this discovery; but there was trace neither of malice nor satisfaction in the stranger's air, which was still of serious and fateful contemplation. When Father José recovered his equanimity, he said bitterly:

"This, then, Sir Devil, is your work! This is your deceitful lure for the weak souls of sinful nations! So, would you replace the Christian grace of Holy Spain!"

"This is what must be," returned the stranger gloomily. "But listen, Sir Priest. It lies with you to avert the issue for a time. Leave me here in peace. Go back to Castile, and take with you your bells, your images, and your missions. Continue here, and you only precipitate results. Stay! promise me you will do this, and you shall not lack that which will render your old age an ornament and a blessing;" and the stranger motioned significantly to the lake.

It was here, the legend discreetly relates, that the Devil showed—as he always shows sooner or later—his cloven hoof. The worthy Padre, sorely perplexed by this threefold vision, and, if the truth must be told, a little nettled at this wresting away of the glory of holy Spanish discovery, had shown some hesitation. But the unlucky bribe of the Enemy of Souls touched his Castilian spirit. Starting back in deep disgust, he brandished his crucifix in the face of the unmasked Fiend, and in a voice that made the dusky vault resound cried:

"*Avaunt* thee, Sathanas! Diabolus, I defy thee! What! wouldst thou bribe me, me, a brother of the Sacred Society of the Holy Jesus, Licentiate of Cordova and Inquisitor of Guadalaxara? Thinkest thou to buy me with thy sordid treasure? *Avaunt*!"

What might have been the issue of this rupture, and how complete might have been the triumph of the holy Father over the Arch-Fiend, who was recoiling aghast at these sacred titles and the flourishing symbol, we can never know, for at that moment the crucifix slipped through his fingers.

Scarcely had it touched the ground before Devil and holy Father simultaneously cast themselves toward it. In the struggle they clinched, and the pious José, who was as much the superior of his antagonist in bodily as in spiritual strength, was about to treat the Great Adversary to a back somersault, when he suddenly felt the long nails of the stranger piercing his flesh. A new fear seized his heart, a numbing chillness crept through his body, and he struggled to free himself, but in vain. A strange roaring was in his ears; the lake and cavern danced before his eyes and vanished, and with a loud cry he sank senseless to the ground.

When he recovered his consciousness, he was aware of a gentle swaying motion of his body. He opened his eyes, and saw it was high noon, and that he was being carried in a litter through the valley. He felt stiff, and looking down, perceived that his arm was tightly bandaged to his side.

He closed his eyes, and, after a few words of thankful prayer, thought how miraculously he had been preserved, and made a vow of candlesticks to the blessed Saint José. He then called in a faint voice, and presently the penitent Ignacio stood beside him.

The joy the poor fellow felt at his patron's returning consciousness for some time choked his utterance. He could only ejaculate, "A miracle! Blessed Saint José, he lives!" and kiss the Padre's bandaged hand. Father José, more intent on his last night's experience, waited for his emotion to subside, and asked where he had been found.

"On the mountain, your Reverence, but a few *varas* from where he attacked you."

"How? you saw him then?" asked the Padre in unfeigned astonishment.

"Saw him, your Reverence! Mother of God! I should think I did! And your Reverence shall see him too, if he ever comes again within range of Ignacio's arquebus."

"What mean you, Ignacio?" said the Padre, sitting bolt-upright in his litter.

"Why, the bear, your Reverence, the bear, holy Father, who attacked your worshipful person while you were meditating on the top of yonder mountain."

"Ah!" said the holy Father, lying down again. "Chut, child! I would be at peace."

When he reached the mission, he was tenderly cared for, and in a few weeks, was enabled to resume those duties from which, as will be seen, not even the machinations of the Evil One could divert him. The news of his physical disaster spread over the country, and a letter to the Bishop of Guadalaxara contained a confidential and detailed account of the good Father's spiritual temptation. But in some way the story leaked out; and long after José was gathered to his fathers, his mysterious encounter formed the theme of thrilling and whispered narrative.

… The mountain was generally shunned. It is true that Señor Joaquin Pedrillo afterward located a grant near the base of the mountain; but as Señora Pedrillo was known to be a termagant half-breed, the *señor* was not supposed to be over-fastidious.

Such is the legend of Monte del Diablo. As I said before, it may seem to lack essential corroboration. The discrepancy between the Father's narrative and the actual climax has given rise to some skepticism on the part of ingenious quibblers. All such I would simply refer to that part of the report of Señor Julio Serro, Sub-Prefect of San Pablo, before whom attest of the above was made. Touching this matter, the worthy Prefect observes, "That although the body of Father José doth show evidence of grievous conflict in the flesh, yet that is no proof that the Enemy of Souls, who could assume the figure of a decorous elderly caballero, could not at the same time transform himself into a bear for his own vile purposes."

Bayard Taylor from *Eldorado: Adventures in the Path of Empire*

[Editor's note: Bayard Taylor, *Eldorado: Adventures in the Path of Empire* (New York: G.P. Putnam, 1850), Chapter 21. Library of Congress, loc.gov/ item/rc01000822/. Taylor portrays the Sacramento River and environs just as the gold rush begins; there is chaos and natural beauty in and around the Sacramento–San Joaquin River Delta in those years. See Fig. 12.]

Sacramento River and City

The change of temperature following the heavy shower which fell the day after my arrival at San Francisco, seemed to announce the near approach of the rainy season. I made all haste, therefore, to start on my tour through the northern placers, fearing lest it might be made impossible by a longer delay. The schooner James L. Day was advertised to leave for Sacramento City about the time we had finished distributing the mail, and as no preparation is required for a journey in California, I took my sarape and went down to Clark's Point, which is to San Francisco what Whitehall is to New York. The fare was $14, which included our embarkation—a matter of some little consequence, when $5 was frequently paid to be rowed out to a vessel. There were about seventy passengers on board, the greater part of whom had just arrived in the steamer *Panama*. The schooner was a trim, beautiful craft, that had weathered the gales of Cape Horn. A strong wind was blowing from the south, with a rain coming up, as we hove anchor and fired a parting gun. We passed the islands of Yerba Buena and Alcatraz, looked out through the Golden Gate on the Pacific, and dashed into the strait connecting the Bay of San Francisco with Pablo Bay, before a ten-knot breeze. This strait, six miles in length and about three in breadth, presents a constant variety of scene, from the irregularity of its mountain-shores. In the middle of it stands an island of red volcanic rock, near which are two smaller ones, white with guano, called The Brothers. At the entrance of Pablo Bay are two others, The Sisters, similar in size and form.

Pablo Bay is nearly circular, and about twelve miles in diameter. The creeks of Napa, Petaluma and San Rafael empty into it on the northern side, opposite Mare Island, so called from a wild mare who was formerly seen at the head of a band of elk, galloping over its broad meadows. We had but a dim glimpse of the shore through the rain. Our schooner bent to the wind, and cut the water so swiftly, that it fairly whistled under her sharp prow. The spray dashed over the deck and the large sails were motionless in their distension, as we ran before the gale, at a most exhilarating speed. A very good dinner at $1, was served up in the eight-by-ten cabin and there was quite a run upon the cook's galley, for pies, at $1 apiece.

We speedily made the entrance to the Straits of Carquinez, where the mountains approach to within three-quarters of a mile. Several of the newly-arrived emigrants expressed themselves delighted with the barren shores and scanty patches of chapparal. It was their first view of the inland scenery of California. The rain had already brought out a timid green on the hills, and the soil no longer looked parched and dead. "Ah!" said one of the company, "what beautiful mountains! this California is really a splendid country." "Very well," thought I, "but if you dig less gold than you anticipate, catch the ague or fail in speculation, what will you say then? Will not the picture you draw be as dark and forbidding as it is now delightful?"

We passed a small sail-boat, bound for Sacramento and filled with emigrants. Half of them were employed in bailing out the scud thrown over the gunwale by every surge. We shot by them like a flash, and came in sight of Benicia, once thought to be a rival to San Francisco. In a glen on the opposite shore is the little town of Martinez.

Benicia is a very pretty place; the situation is well chosen, the land gradually sloping back from the water, with ample space for the spread of the town. The anchorage is excellent, vessels of the largest size being able to lie so near shore as to land goods without lightering. The back country, including the Napa and Sonoma valleys, is one of the finest agricultural districts of California. Notwithstanding these advantages, Benicia must always remain inferior, in commercial importance, both to San Francisco and Sacramento City. While in the country, I was much amused in reading the letters respecting it, which had been sent home and published, many of them predicting the speedy downfall of San Francisco, on account of the superior advantages of the former place. On the strength of these letters vessels had actually cleared for Benicia, with large cargoes. Now, anchorage is one thing, and a good market another; a ship may lie in greater safety at Albany, but the sensible merchant charters his vessel for New York. San Francisco is marked by Nature and Fate (though many will disagree with me in the first half of the assertion) for the great commercial mart of the Pacific, and whatever advantages she may lack will soon be amply provided for by her wealth and enterprise.

Benicia—very properly, as I think—has been made the Naval and Military Station for the Bay. Gen. Smith and Commodore Jones both have their headquarters there. The General's house and the military barracks are built on a headland at the entrance 217 of Suisun Bay—a breezy and healthy situation. Monte Diablo, the giant of the Coast Range, rises high and blue on the other side of the strait, and away beyond the waters of the Bay, beyond the waste marshes of Tulé and the broad grazing plains, and above the low outlines of many an intermediate chain, loom up faint and far and silvery, the snows of the Sierra Nevada.

We came-to off New-York-of-the-Pacific in four hours after leaving San Francisco—a distance of fifty miles. The former place, with its aspiring but most awkward name, is located on a level plain, on the southern shore of Suisun Bay, backed by a range of barren mountains. It consists of three houses, one of which is a three-story one, and several vessels at anchor near the shore. The anchorage is good, and were it not for the mosquitos, the crews might live pleasantly enough, in their seclusion. There never will be a large town there, for the simple reason that there is no possible cause why there *should* be one. Stockton and Sacramento City supply the mines, San Francisco takes the commerce, Benicia the agricultural produce, with a fair share of the inland trade, and this Gotham-of-the-West, I fear, must continue to belie its title.

We anchored, waiting for the steamer *Sacramento*, which was to meet the schooner and receive her passengers. She came along side after dark, but owing to the violence of the rain, did not leave until midnight. She was a small, light craft, not more than sixty feet in length, and had been shipped to San Francisco around Cape Horn. She was at first employed to run between Sacramento City and San Francisco, but proved insufficient to weather the rough seas of the open Bay. The arrival of the steamer *McKim*, which is a good sea-boat and therefore adapted to the navigation of the Bay, where the waves are little less violent than in the Pacific, drove her from the route, but she still continued to run on the Sacramento River. Many small steamers, of similar frail construction, were sent around the Horn, the speculators imagining they were the very thing for inland navigation. The engine of the *Sacramento* was on deck, as also was her den of a cabin—a filthy place, about six feet by eight. A few berths, made of two coarse blankets laid on a plank, were to be had at $5 each; but I preferred taking a camp-stool, throwing my sarape over my shoulders and sleeping with my head on the table, rather than pay such an unchristian price.

As the day dawned, gloomy and wet, I went on deck. We were near the head of "The Slough," a broad navigable cut-off, which saves twenty miles in making the trip. The banks are lined with thickets, behind which extends a narrow belt of timber, principally oak and sycamore. Here and there, in cleared spots, were the cabins of the woodmen, or of squatters, who intend claiming preemption rights. The wood, which brings $12 or $15 a cord, is piled on the bluff banks, and the steamers back up to it, whenever they are obliged to "wood up." At the junction of the slough with the river proper, there is a small village of Indian huts, built of dry Tulé reeds.

The Sacramento is a beautiful stream. Its width varies from two to three hundred yards, and its banks fringed with rich foliage, present, by their continuous windings, a fine succession of views. In appearance, it reminded me somewhat of the Delaware. The foliage, washed by the rain, glistened green and freshly in the morning; and as we advanced the distant mountains on either hand were occasionally visible through gaps in the timber. Before reaching the town of Sutter, we passed a ranch, the produce of which, in vegetables alone, was said to have returned the owner—a German, by the name of Schwartz—$25,000 during the season. Sutter is a town of some thirty houses, scattered along the bank for half a mile. Three miles above this we came in sight of Sacramento City. The forest of masts along the embarcadero more than rivalled the splendid growth of the soil. Boughs and spars were mingled together in striking contrast; the cables were fastened to the trunks and sinewy roots of the trees; sign-boards and figure-heads were set up on shore, facing the levee, and galleys and deck-cabins were turned out "to grass," leased as shops, or occupied as dwellings. The aspect of the place, on landing, was decidedly more novel and picturesque than that of any other town in the country.

The plan of Sacramento City is very simple. Situated on the eastern bank of the Sacramento, at its junction with the Rio Americano, the town plot embraces a square of about one and a-half miles to a side. It is laid out in regular right-angles, in Philadelphia style, those running east and west named after the alphabet, and those north and south after the arithmetic. The limits of the town extended to nearly one square mile, and the number of inhabitants, in tents and houses, fell little short of ten thousand. The previous April there were just four houses in the place! Can the world match a growth like this?

The original forest, trees, standing in all parts of the town, give it a very picturesque appearance. Many of the streets are lined with oaks and sycamores, six feet in diameter, and spreading ample boughs on every side. The emigrants have ruined the finest of them by building camp-fires at their bases, which, in some instances, have burned completely through, leaving a charred and blackened arch for the superb tree to rest upon. The storm which occurred a few days previous to my visit, snapped asunder several trunks which had been thus weakened, one of them crushing to the earth a canvas house in which a man lay asleep. A heavy bough struck the ground on each side of him, saving his life. The destruction of these trees is the more to be regretted, as the intense heat of the Summer days, when the mercury stands at 120°, renders their shade a thing of absolute necessity.

The value of real estate in Sacramento City is only exceeded by that of San Francisco. Lots twenty by seventy-five feet, in the best locations, brought from $3,000 to $3,500. Rents were on a scale equally enormous. The City Hotel, which was formerly a saw-mill, erected by Capt. Sutter, paid $30,000 per annum. A new hotel, going up on the levee, had been already rented at $35,000.

Two drinking and gaming-rooms, on a business street, paid each $1,000, monthly, invariably in advance. Many of the stores transacted business averaging from $1,000 to $3,000 daily. Board was $20 per week at the restaurants and $5 per day at the City Hotel. But what is the use of repeating figures? These dead statistics convey no idea of the marvelous state of things in the place. It was difficult enough for those who saw to believe, and I can only hope to reproduce the very faintest impression of the pictures I there beheld. It was frequently wondered, on this side of the Rocky Mountains, why the gold dust was not sent out of the country in larger quantities, when at least forty thousand men were turning up the placers. The fact is, it was required as currency, and the amount in circulation might be counted by millions. Why, the building up of a single street in Sacramento City (J street) cost *half a million*, at least! The value of all the houses in the city, frail and perishing as many of them were, could not have been less than $2,000,000.

It must be acknowledged there is another side to the picture. Three-fourths of the people who settle in Sacramento City are visited by agues, diarrheas and other reducing complaints. In summer, the place is a furnace, in Winter little better than a swamp; and the influx of emigrants and discouraged miners generally exceeds the demand for labor. A healthy, sensible, wide awake man, however, cannot fail to prosper. In a country where Labor rules everything, no sound man has a right to complain. When carpenters make a strike because they only get *twelve dollars* a day, one may be sure there is room enough for industry and enterprise of all kinds.

The city was peopled principally by New-Yorkers, Jerseymen and people from the Western States. In activity and public spirit, it was nothing behind San Francisco; its growth, indeed, in view of the difference of location, was more remarkable. The inhabitants had elected a Town Council, adopted a City Charter and were making exertions to have the place declared a port of entry. The political waters were being stirred a little, in anticipation of the approaching election. Mr. Gilbert, of the Alta California, and Col. Steuart, candidate for Governor, were in the city. A political meeting, which had been held a few nights before, in front of the City Hotel, passed off as uproariously and with as zealous a sentiment of patriotism as such meetings are wont to exhibit at home. Among the residents whom I met during my visit, was Gen. Green, of Texas, known as commander of the Mier Expedition.

The city already boasted a weekly paper, the *Placer Times*, which was edited and published by Mr. Giles, formerly of the Tribune Office. His printers were all old friends of mine—one of them, in fact, a former fellow-apprentice—and from the fraternal feeling that all possess who have ever belonged to the craft, the place became at once familiar and home-like. The little paper, which had a page of about twelve by eighteen inches, had a circulation of five hundred copies, at $12 a year; the amount received weekly for jobs and advertising, varied from $1,000 to $2,000. Tickets were printed for the different political candidates, at the rate of $20 for every thousand. The compositors were paid $15 daily. Another compositor from the Tribune Office had established a restaurant, and was doing a fine business. His dining saloon was an open tent, unfloored; the tables were plank, with rough benches on each side; the waiters, rude Western boys who had come over the Rocky Mountains-but the meals he furnished could not have been surpassed in any part of the world for substantial richness of quality. There was every day abundance of elk steaks, unsurpassed for sweet and delicate flavor; venison, which had been fattened on the mountain acorns; mutton, such as nothing but the wild pastures of California could produce; salmon and salmon-trout of astonishing size, from the Sacramento River, and now and then the solid flesh of the grizzly bear. The salmon-trout exceeded in fatness any freshwater fish I ever saw; they were between two and three feet in length, with a layer of pure fat, quarter of an inch in thickness, over the ribs. When made into chowder or stewed in claret, they would have thrown into ecstasies the most inveterate Parisian gourmand. The full-moon face of the proprietor of the restaurant was accounted for, when one had tasted his fare; after living there a few days, I could feel my own dimensions sensibly enlarged.

The road to Sutter's Fort, the main streets and the levee fronting on the Embarcadero, were constantly thronged with the teams of emigrants, coming in from the mountains. Such worn, weather beaten individuals I never before imagined. Their tents were pitched by hundreds in the thickets around the town, where they rested a few days before starting to winter in the mines and elsewhere. At times the levee was filled throughout its whole length by their teams, three or four yoke of oxen to every wagon. The beasts had an expression of patient experience which plainly showed that no roads yet to be traveled would astonish them in the least. After tugging the wagons for six months over the salt deserts of the Great Basin, climbing passes and cañons of terrible asperity in the Sierra Nevada, and learning to digest oak bark on the arid plains around the sink of Humboldt's River, it seemed as if no extremity could henceforth intimidate them. Much toil and suffering had given to their countenances a look of almost human wisdom. If their souls should hereafter, according to the theory of some modern philosophers, reappear in human frames, what a crowd of grave and reverend sages may not California be able to produce! The cows had been yoked in with the oxen and made to do equal duty. The women who had come by the overland route appeared to have stood the hardships of the journey remarkably well, and were not half so loud as the men in their complaints.

The amount of gambling in Sacramento City was very great, and the enticement of music was employed even to a greater extent than in San Francisco. All kinds of instruments and tunes made night discordant, for which harrowing service the performers were paid an ounce each. Among the many drinking houses, there was one called "The Plains," which was much frequented by the emigrants. Some western artist, who came across the country, adorned its walls with scenic illustrations of the route, such as Independence Rock, The Sweet-Water Valley, Fort Laramie, Wind River Mountains, etc. There was one of a pass in the Sierra Nevada, on the Carson River route. A wagon and team 224 were represented as coming down the side of a hill, so nearly perpendicular that it seemed no earthly power could prevent them from making but a single fall from the summit to the valley. These particular oxen, however, were happily independent of gravitation, and whisked their tails in the face of the zenith, as they marched slowly down.

I was indebted for quarters in Sacramento City, to Mr. De Graw, who was installed in a frame house, copper-roofed, fronting the levee. I slept very comfortably on a pile of Chinese quilts, behind the counter, lulled by the dashing of the rain against the sides of the house. The rainy season had set in, to all appearances, though it was full a month before the usual time. The sky was bleak and gray, and the wind blew steadily from the south, an unfailing sing to the old residents. The saying of the Mexicans seemed to be verified, that, wherever *los Yankis* go, they take rain with them.

It was therefore the more necessary that I should start at once for the mountains. In a few weeks, the roads would be impassable, and my only chance of seeing the northern rivers be cut off. The first requisite for the journey was a good horse, to procure which I first attended the horse-market which was daily held towards the bottom of K street. This was one of the principal sights in the place, and as picturesque a thing as could be seen anywhere. The trees were here thicker and of larger growth than in other parts of the city; the market-ground in the middle of the street was shaded by an immense evergreen oak, and surrounded by tents of blue and white canvas. One side was flanked by a livery-stable—an open frame of poles, roofed with dry tulé, in which stood a few shivering mules and raw-boned horses, while the stacks of hay and wheat straw, on the open lots in the vicinity, offered feed to the buyers of animals, at the rate of $3 daily for each head.

When the market was in full blast, the scene it presented was grotesque enough. There were no regulations other than the fancy of those who had animals to sell; every man was his own auctioneer, and showed off the points of his horses or mules. The ground was usually occupied by several persons at once,—a rough tawny-faced, long-bearded Missourian, with a couple of pack mules which had been starved in the Great Basin; a quondam New York dandy with a horse whose back he had ruined in his luckless "prospecting" among the mountains; a hard-fisted farmer with the wagon and ox-team which had brought his family and household gods across the continent; or, perhaps, a jocky trader, who understood all the arts of depreciation and recommendation, and invariably sold an animal for much more than he gave. The bids were slow, and the seller would sometimes hang for half an hour without an advance; in fact, where three or four were up at once, it required close attention in the buyer to know which way the competition was running.

I saw a lean sorrel mule sold for $55; several others, of that glossy black color and clean make which denote spirit and endurance, were held at $140, the owner refusing to let them go for less. The owner of a bay horse, which he rode up and down the market at a brisk pace, could get no bid above $45. As the animal was well made and in good condition, I was about to bid, when I noticed a peculiar glare of the eye which betrayed suffering of some kind.

"What kind of a back has he?" I inquired.

"It is a very little scratched on the top," was the answer; "but he is none the worse for that."

"He'll not do for me," I thought, but I watched the other bidders to see how the buyer would be satisfied with his purchase. The horse was finally knocked off at $50: as the saddle was not included the new owner removed it, disclosing a horrible patch of raw and shrinking flesh. An altercation instantly arose, which was not settled when I left to seek a horse elsewhere.

The owner of a stack of hay near at hand desired to sell me a mule out of a number which he had in charge. But one which he recommended as a fine saddle-mule would not go at all, though he wounded her mouth with the cruel bit of the country in the effort to force her into a trot; another, which was declared to be remarkably gentle, stumbled and fell with me, and a third, which seemed to really a good traveler, was held at a price I did not desire to pay. At last, the proprietor of a sort of tavern adjoining the market, offered to sell me a gray mare for $100. Now, as the gray mare is said to be the better horse, and as, on trial, I found her to possess a steady and easy gait, though a little lazy, I determined to take her, since, among so many worn-out and used up animals, it seemed a matter of mere luck whether I would have selected a good one. The mare was American, but the owner assured me she had been long enough in the country, to travel unshod and keep fat on dry grass. As saddles, blankets, and other articles were still necessary, my outfit was rather expensive. I procured a tolerable saddle and bridle for $10; a lariat and saddle blanket for $5; a pair of sharp Mexican spurs for $8, and blankets for $12. With a hunting-knife, a pair of pistols in my pocket, a compass, thermometer, note-book and pencil, I was prepared for a tour of any length among the mountains.

Samuel Clements, Reporting for the *Call*

[Editor's note: Samuel Clements, reporting for the San Francisco *Call* in Edgar M Branch, editor, *Clemens of the Call* (Berkeley: University of California, 1969). pp. 117–121. (*By permission*) Clements (Mark Twain) shows great sympathy for the ship's captain but does not underplay the extent of the tragedy. Technology here cannot overcome the natural hazards which the river holds. See Fig. 13.]

Explosion of the steamer *Washoe's* boilers—supposed killed one hundred—wounded and missing seventy-five—several San Franciscans among number—attention paid by the Sacramentans to the wounded—the cause of the calamity—scenes and incidents etc., etc.

We compiled an account of this terrible disaster from dispatches published in the evening papers. The explosion of the boilers of the *Washoe* took place at ten o'clock, at a point just above the Hog's Back, about ten miles above Rio Vista, on her up-trip on Monday night. One of the boilers collapsed a flue. and, it is said, made a clean sweep aft, going overboard through the stern of the boat. The cause of this dreadful calamity, according to D. M. Andeson, the engineer, (who died at the Sacramento hospital just after he made the statement,) was rotten iron in the boiler. At the time of the explosion there were one hundred and twenty-five pounds pressure on the boiler, with two cocks of solid water. The engine was high pressure. The upper works of the boat aft were completely shattered, some portions of them, with the staterooms being blown overboard. The boat had passed the log's Back about four or five minutes before the explosion. She was about twenty yards off the left bank at the time, and the whole steering gear being destroyed, she took a sheer and ran ashore, her bow providentially touching a tree, to which those not injured fastened the boat. Had she not run ashore, almost everybody on board would have been lost, as they could not steer the wreck, and they had no boats, the steamer sinking gradually astern. The boat was set on fire in three places, which added the horror of the scene. The fire, however, was put out by the few who were uninjured. the *Chrysopolis* was a long way ahead, and knew nothing of the matter. The *Antelope* coming behind, came up and took off the wounded and a large number of the dead, and brought the first news of the sad affair to Sacramento.

Measures for Relief of the Wounded, and Taking off the Dead

On the arrival of the *Antelope* at Sacramento, about half-past five o'clock yesterday morning, with the terrible news, the alarm bells of the city were rung, and the Howard Association turned out to attend to the wounded the steamer had brought up. The scene for the three hours that elapsed before the *Antelope* reached the steamer *Washoe* is described most horrible. All who were alive had been taken ashore, but there was no shelter for them. Those of the wounded who were able to move sought shelter in the sand and brush, groaning and screaming with pain. One man, who was scalded from head to foot, got ashore, and in a nude state stood and screamed for help, but would not allow any covering to be put on him. A woman in a similar condition was brought up on the *Antelope*. The steamer carried only the wounded to Sacramento. A large number of the slightly wounded, who could walk or ride, were taken to the rooms of the Howard Association. The Association hired the Vernon House for hospital for the sufferers. On board of the *Antelope* the scene was a most dreadful one. Her entire upper cabin, with the exception of the passage-ways, was covered with mattresses, on which the injured were lying, sixty-three in number. Others were in the Indies' cabin, and still others in the dining-room. Four are reported to have died on the way up, and at the time of landing others were gasping their last on the levee. At the Vernon House the Howard Association have a large number of members, who, with a large force of ladies, are doing all that can be done for the sufferers, The Association also has committee out collecting, who have so far met with good success. Immediately on the arrival of the *Antelope*, the steamer *Visalia* fired up and went down to the wreck to bring the bodies of the dead left there by the A., and also such others as may be recovered while she is there. Flags were at half-mast yesterday, on the Masonic Temple and most of the engine houses, and on number of private buildings in Sacramento. The entire medical fraternity were in attendance on the sufferers, as well as the clergy of all denominations. The opinion is now that the total dead will exceed ninety, if not one hundred. Too much praise cannot be awarded the members of the Howard Association, who almost to man were engaged in behalf of the sufferers after the arrival of the *Antelope*. A large number of ladies were in constant attendance also the Vernon House, doing all that they could do to alleviate pain. The collections in Sacramento have been quite liberal.

Captain Kidd's Statement, 8 September, 1864

Captain Kidd, of the ill-fated and steamer *Washoe*, has been accused, according to telegraphic reports from Sacramento, of ungenerous and unfeeling conduct, in remaining with the wreck of his boat after the explosion, instead of accompanying maimed and dying sufferers by the catastrophe to Sacramento. In two defense of himself, he says he was satisfied that the wounded would be as well and kindly cared for on the *Antelope* as if he were present himself, and that he thought the most the humane course for him to pursue would be to stay behind with some of his men and search among the her ruins of his boat for helpless victims, and rescue them before they became submerged by the gradually sinking vessel; he believed some of the scalded and frantic victims had as wandered into the woods, and he wished to find them also. He says that his course was prompted by no selfish or heartless motive, but he acted as his conscience told him was for the best. We heartily believe it, and we should be sorry to believe less of any man with a human soul in his body. His search resulted in the finding of five corpses after the *Antelope* left, and these he sent up on the small steamer which visited the wreck on the following day. However, he need not distress himself about the strictures of a few thoughtless men, for that class of people would have blamed him just as cordially no matter what course he had pursued. Whether one or more flues collapsed, or whether one or more boilers exploded, or whether the cause of the accident was that too much steam was being carried, or that the iron was defective or the workmanship bad, are all questions which must remain unsolved until the *Washoe* is raised. At present, and so far as anything that is actually known about the matter goes, one of these conjectures is just as plausible as another. Captain Kidd thinks the cause lay in the inefficient workmanship of the boiler-makers. The surviving engineer says he looked at the steam-gauge scarcely two minutes before the explosion, and it indicated 114 pounds to the square inch (she was allowed to carry 140;) he tried the steam cocks at the same time, and found two of them full of water. The boat carried 120 to 125 pounds of steam from San Francisco to Benicia, and from here to where the accident it occurred, was customary to carry less, as the water grew shoaler, because, as every boatman knows, a steamer cannot make as good time, or steer as well, in shoal water with a full head of steam as she can with less; from Rio Vista to Freeport, it was customary to carry about 110, and above Freeport about 70 pounds of steam. The *Chrysopolis* was far ahead, and had not been seen for more than half an hour; and since the last collision Captain Kidd had given orders that the *Washoe* should be kept behind the line boats and out of danger; he was making no effort to gain upon the *Chrysopolis*, and had no expectation of seeing her again below Sacramento. Gass & Lombard, of Sacramento, contracted to build boilers for the *Washoe* which would stand a pressure of 225 pounds, and secure the inspector's permission to carry 150; Captain Kidd appointed Mr. Foster, one of the best engineers on the coast, to stay at the boiler works and personally superintend the work. The workmanship was bad; the boilers leaked in streams around the flues, and the Inspector would only allow a certificate for 113 pounds of steam. The boat made seven trips, but the leaks did not close up, as was expected. Gass & Lombard then contracted with boiler makers here to take out the flues and make the boilers over again, so that they would stand 140 pounds, Captain Kidd relinquishing 10 pounds from the original contract. It was done, at a cost of $7,000-about what a new set would have cost—and, after a cold-water test of 210 pounds, the Inspector cheerfully gave permission to carry 140. With a margin like this, the boilers could hardly have exploded under a pressure of 114 pounds unless the workmanship was in some sort defective, or the severe test applied by the Inspector had overstrained the boilers; or unless, perhaps, a rivet or so might have been started on some previous trip, under a heavier head of steam, and this source of weakness had increased in magnitude until it finally culminated in a general let-go under a smaller head of steam. The sinking of the boat is attributed to the breaking off of the feed pipes which supply the boilers with water, and which extend through the bottom of the boat; and as the wreck settled and careened, a larger volume of water poured in through the open ash ports forward of the fire doors. The boat sank very gradually, and had not settled entirely until nearly three hours had elapsed. But as we said in the first place, the real cause of this dreadful calamity cannot be ascertained until the wreck is raised and the machinery exposed to view. Captain Kidd leaves today with the necessary apparatus for raising his boat, and Mr. Owens, who built her, will accompany him and superintend the work. It will be several months, however, before the *Washoe* will be in a condition to resume her trips. Captain Kidd says he would raise the boat, anyhow, to satisfy himself as to the cause of the accident, even if he never meant to run her again. Capt. Kidd feels the late calamity as deeply as anyone could, and as anyone not utterly heartless, must. That his impulses are kind and generous all will acknowledge who remember that he kept his boat running night and day, in time of the flood, and brought to this city hundreds of sufferers by that misfortune, without one cent of charge for passage, beds or food.

Tensions Over the Rivers
and the Fertile Lands

[Editor's note: As William Brewer notes, the land that bordered the Sacramento and the San Joaquin Rivers was remarkably rich and physically beautiful to the eyes of mid-nineteenth century visitors. John Muir recounts his enthusiasm for the region while boating down the Sacramento River after a visit with the Bidwells. Jerry MacMullen and Mary Jane Barnes call attention to the social life generated aboard the steam boats that were the focus of Sacramento–San Joaquin River Delta social life at the time. Royce and Norris fictionalize the struggle over control of the rich agricultural land between investors and farmer/ranchers. Both authors focus on an incident that occurred near Tulare, in which those who actually farm violently conflict with those who speculate. These authors see such universality in this story that they move its location further north so it symbolizes the tensions of the Sacramento–San Joaquin River Delta as well as the southern part of the Central Valley. Then, Rockwell Hunt recalls that small town life that grew around wharves and between farms even before 1900 provided the context for his coming of age. Rather than simply a highway to the mountains and gold, the Sacramento–San Joaquin River Delta had, in this period, come into its own as an agricultural mecca.]

William Brewer, from *Up and Down California in 1860–1864*

[Editor's note: *Up and down California in 1860–1864: The Journal of William H. Brewer*, edited by Francis P. Farquhar, (New Haven: Yale, 1930), pp 263–66. Library of Congress, loc.gov/resource/calbk.142 See Fig. 15.]

Wednesday, May 7, dawned and all bid fair. We were off in due season. I doubt if there are half a dozen days in the year so favorable—everything was *just right*, neither too hot nor too cold, a gentle breeze, the atmosphere of matchless purity and transparency. Five of our party, Professor Whitney, Averill, Gabb, Rémond, and I, accompanied our visitors. They rode mules or horses; we (save Averill, who was to see to the ladies) went on foot. First, up a wild rocky canyon, the air sweet with the perfume of the abundant flowers, the sides rocky and picturesque, the sky above of the intensest blue; then, up a steep slope to the height of 2,200 feet, where we halted by a spring, rested, filled our canteens, and then went onward.

The summit was reached, and we spent two and a half hours there. The view was one never to be forgotten. It had nothing of grandeur in it, save the almost unlimited extent of the field of view. The air was clear to the horizon on every side, and although the mountain is only 3,890 feet high, from the peculiar figure of the country probably but few views in North America are more extensive—certainly nothing in Europe.

To the west, thirty miles, lies San Francisco; we see out the Golden Gate, and a great expanse of the blue Pacific stretches beyond. The bay, with its fantastic outline, is all in sight, and the ridges beyond to the west and northwest. Mount St. Helena, fifty or sixty miles, is almost lost in the mountains that surround it, but the snows of Mount Ripley (northeast of Clear Lake), near a hundred miles, seem but a few miles off. South and southwest the view is less extensive, extending only fifty or sixty miles south, and to Mount Bache, seventy or eighty miles southwest.

The great features of the view lie to the east of the meridian passing through the peak. First, the great central valley of California, as level as the sea, stretches to the horizon both on the north and to the southeast. It lies beneath us in all its great expanse for near or quite *three hundred miles of its length!* But there is nothing cheering in it—all things seem blended soon in the great, vast expanse. Multitudes of streams and bayous wind and ramify through the hundreds of square miles—yes, I should say *thousands* of square miles—about the mouths of the San Joaquin and Sacramento rivers, and then away up both of these rivers in opposite directions, until nothing can be seen but the straight line on the horizon. On the north are the Marysville Butters, rising like black masses from the plain, over a hundred miles distant; while still beyond, rising in sharp clear outline against the sky, stand the 265 snow-covered Lassen's Buttes, *over two hundred miles in an air line distant from us*—the longest distance I have ever seen.

Rising from this great plain, and forming the horizon for three hundred miles in extent, possibly more, were the snowy crests of the Sierra Nevada. What a grand sight! The peaks of that mighty chain glittering in the purest white under the bright sun, their icy crests seeming a fitting helmet for their black and furrowed sides! There stood in the northeast Pyramid Peak (near Lake Bigler), 125 miles distant, and Castle Peak (near Lake Mono), 160 miles distant, and hundreds of other peaks without names but vying with the Alps themselves in height and sublimity—all marshaled before us in that grand panorama! I had carried up a barometer, but I could scarcely observe it, so enchanting and enrapturing was the scene.

Figures are dull, I admit, yet in no other way can we convey accurate ideas. I made an estimate from the map, based on the distances to known peaks, and found that the extent of land and sea embraced between the extreme limits of vision amounted to eighty thousand square miles, and that forty thousand square miles, or more, were spread out in tolerably plain view—over 300 miles from north to south, and 260 to 280 miles from east to west, between the extreme points.

We got our observations, ate our lunch, and lounged on the rocks for two and a half hours, and then were loath to leave. We made the descent easily and without mishap or accident—a horse falling once, a girth becoming loose and a lady tumbling off at another time, were the only incidents. The shadows were deep in the canyon as we passed down it, but we were back at sunset. Our friends were tired, some of them nearly used up. With us, the day was not a hard one.

John Muir, Letter to Mrs. Bidwell

[Editor's note: John Muir explores the Sacramento River. Letter to the Bidwell Family, William Frederic Bade, *The Life and Letters of John Muir* (Boston: Houghton Mifflin, 1924), pp. 73–80. See Fig. 14.]

To General John Bidwell, Mrs. Bidwell, and Miss Sallie Kennedy
    Sacramento, *October* 10*th*, 1877
    Friends three:
    The Chico flagship and I are safely arrived in Sacramento, unwrecked, unsnagged, and the whole winding way was one glorious strip of enjoyment. When I bade you good-bye, on the bank I was benumbed and bent down with your lavish kindnesses like one of your vine-laden willows. It is seldom that I experience much difficulty in leaving civilization for God's wilds, but I was loath indeed to leave you three that day after our long free ramble in the mountain woods and that five weeks' rest in your cool fruity home. The last I saw of you was Miss Kennedy white among the leaves like a fleck of mist, then sweeping around a bend you were all gone—the old wildness came back, and I began to observe, and enjoy, and be myself again.

My first camp was made on a little oval island, some ten or twelve miles down, where a clump of arching willows formed a fine nest like shelter; and where I spread my quilt on the gravel and opened the box so daintily and thoughtfully stored for my comfort. I began to reflect again on your real goodness to me from first to last, and said, "I'll not forget those Chico three as long as I live."

I placed the two flags at the head of my bed, one on each side, and as the campfire shone upon them the effect was very imposing and patriotic. The night came on full of strange sounds from birds and insects new to me, but the starry sky was clear and came arching over my lowland nest seemingly as bright and familiar with its glorious constellations as when beheld through the thin crisp atmosphere of the mountain-tops.

On the second day, the Spoonbill sprang a bad leak from the swelling of the bottom timbers; two of them crumpled out thus [sketch] [After Mrs. Bidwell's death, the writer unfortunately was unable to obtain from her relatives the loan of this letter for the reproduction of the two included sketches.] at a point where they were badly nailed, and I had to run her ashore for repairs. I turned her upside down on a pebbly bar, took out one of the timbers, whittled it carefully down to the right dimensions, replaced it, and nailed it tight and fast with a stone for a hammer; then calked the new joint, shoved her back into the current, and rechristened her "The Snag Jumper." She afterwards behaved splendidly in the most trying places, and leaked only at the rate of fifteen tin cupfuls per hour.

Her performances in the way of snag-jumping are truly wonderful. Most snags are covered with slimy algae and lean downstream and the sloping bows of the Jumper enabled her to glance gracefully up and over them, when not too high above the water, while her lightness prevented any strain sufficient to crush her bottom. [Sketch of boat.] On one occasion, she took a firm slippery snag a little obliquely and was nearly rolled upside down, as a sod is turned by a plow. Then I charged myself to be more careful, and while rowing often looked well ahead for snag ripples—but soon I came to a long glassy reach, and my vigilance not being eternal, my thoughts wandered upstream back to those grand spring fountains on the head of the McCloud and Pitt. Then I tried to picture those hidden tributaries that flow beneath the lava tablelands, and recognized in them a capital illustration of the fact that in their farthest fountains all rivers are lost to mortal eye, that the sources of all are hidden as those of the Nile, and so, also, that in this respect every river of knowledge is a Nile. Thus, I was philosophizing, rowing with a steady stroke, and as the current was rapid, the Jumper was making fine headway, when: with a tremendous bump, she reared like "Lize in Jackets," swung around stern downstream, and remained fast on her beam ends, erect like a coffin against a wall. She managed, however, to get out of even this scrape without disaster to herself or to me.

I usually sailed from sunrise to sunset, rowing one third of the time, paddling one third, and drifting the other third in restful comfort, landing now and then to examine a section of the bank or some bush or tree. Under these conditions the voyage to this port was five days in length. On the morning of the third day I hid my craft in the bank vines and set off cross-lots for the highest of the Marysville Buttes, reached the summit, made my observations, and got back to the river and Jumper by two o'clock. The distance to the nearest foothill of the group is about three miles, but to the base of the south most and highest butte is six miles, and its elevation is about eighteen hundred feet above its base, or in round numbers two thousand feet above tidewater. The whole group is volcanic, taking sharp basaltic forms near the summit, and with stratified conglomerates of finely polished quartz and metamorphic pebbles tilted against their flanks. There is a sparse growth of live oak and laurel on the southern slopes, the latter predominating, and on the north quite a close tangle of dwarf oak forming a chaparral. I noticed the white mountain *spiraea* also, and *madroña,* with a few willows, and three ferns toward the summit. *Pellaea andromedoefolia, Gymnogramma triangularis,* and *Cheilanthes gracillima;* and many a fine flower—*penstemons, gilias,* and our brave *eriogonums* of blessed memory. The summit of this highest south most butte is a coast survey station.

The river is very crooked, becoming more and more so in its lower course, flowing in grand lingering deliberation, now south, now north, east and west with fine un-American indirectness. The upper portion down as far as Colusa is full of rapids, but below this point the current is beautifully calm and lake-like, with innumerable reaches of most surpassing loveliness. How you would have enjoyed it! The bank vines all the way down are of the same species as those that festoon your beautiful Chico Creek (*Vitis californica*), but nowhere do they reach such glorious exuberance of development as with you.

The temperature of the water varies only about two and a half degrees between Chico and Sacramento. a distance by the river of nearly two hundred miles—the upper temperature 64 degrees, the lower 66.5 degrees. I found the temperature of the Feather [River] waters at their confluence one degree colder than those of the Sacramento, 65 degrees and 66 degrees respectively, which is a difference in exactly the opposite direction from what I anticipated. All the brown discoloring mud of the lower Sacramento, thus far, is derived from the Feather, and it is curious to observe how completely the two currents keep themselves apart for three or four miles. I never landed to talk to anyone, or ask questions, but was frequently cheered from the bank and challenged by old sailors "Ship ahoy," etc., and while seated in the stern reading a magazine and drifting noiselessly with the current, I overheard a deck hand on one of the steamers say, "Now that's what I call taking it easy."

I am still at a loss to know what there is in the rig or model of the Jumper that excited such universal curiosity. Even the birds of the river, and the animals that came to drink, though paying little or no heed to the passing steamers with all their plash and uproar, at once fixed their attention on my little flagship, some taking flight with loud screams, others waiting with outstretched necks until I nearly touched them, while others circled overhead. The domestic animals usually dashed up the bank in extravagant haste, one crowding on the heels of the other as if suffering extreme terror. I placed one flag, the smaller, on the highest pinnacle of the Butte, where I trust it may long wave to your memory; the other I have still. Watching the thousand land birds—linnets, orioles, sparrows, flickers, quails, etc.—Nature's darlings, taking their morning baths, was no small part of my enjoyments.

I was greatly interested in the fine bank sections shown to extraordinary advantage at the present low water, because they cast so much light upon the formation of this grand valley, but I cannot tell my results here.

This letter is already far too long, and I will hasten to a close. I will rest here a day or so, and then push off again to the mouth of the river a hundred miles or so farther, chiefly to study the deposition of the sediment at the head of the bay, then push for the mountains. I would row up the San Joaquin, but two weeks or more would be required for the trip, and I fear snow on the mountains.

I am glad to know that you are really interested in science, and I might almost venture another lecture upon you, but in the meantime forbear. Looking backward I see you there in your leafy home, and while I wave my hand, I will only wait to thank you all over and over again for the thousand kind things you have done and said—drives, and grapes, and rest, "a' that and a' that."

Jerry MacMullen, from *Paddle-wheel Days in California*

[Editor's note: Jerry MacMullen, *Paddle-wheel Days in California* (Stanford: Stanford University Press, 1944). Chapter 12 provides a sense of the social life engendered by the boats that plied the Sacramento and San Joaquin rivers into the twentieth century. (*By permission*). See Fig. 16.]

"You Get Off Here, Mister"

THERE WERE literally hundreds of landings on the Sacramento and the San Joaquin during the later days of steam boating, landings, in fact, where a boat would stop for as little cargo as a lug of peaches.

Modern charts of the rivers still show, in addition to the named landings, many which were merely numbered. What probably is the record for the number of stops to lift merchandise was a run by the Isleton shortly after the turn of the century; on one trip, she made forty-six landings on her way from San Francisco up to Sacramento, and touched at seventy-six on her way back down-river. Most of those landings are gone now; sheds have been pulled down or have collapsed, and of the landings themselves little remains.

Many of the stops, especially on the Sacramento, were made at what were known as "brush landings" -that is, instead of being wharves, they were merely masses of brush, fruit-tree prunings, asparagus roots, and similar waste, dumped into the water at the river's edge. A steamboat would nose up to one of these landings, swing out her gangplank, lay planks across the brush, and trundle cargo aboard or ashore with hand trucks; sometimes, if the cargo offering consisted only of a lug or so of vegetables or fruit, the deck hands would merely toss it up on their shoulders and trot aboard. The engineer, while this was going on, was as important as the pilot. Looking out through the engine-room windows to judge his position, he would handle the throttle with such nicety—and without any bells from the pilot—that he kept her in just the right position, without the use of mooring lines, until cargo operations were completed. He was a peaceful counterpart—without the accompanying holocaust—of the legendary and heroic Jim Bludso, who swore to "hold her nozzle again the bank 'till the last galoot's ashore!"

If a farmer had cargo for a Southern Pacific boat he would hang out a white flag by day, a white lantern by night. If his cargo, on the other hand, were intended for a member of Sacramento Transportation's fleet, he indicated it by displaying a red flag or l red lantern to call in the passing steamboat. The same signals would get you passage for yourself and your hand luggage.

Before the advent of buses, ranch hands destined for river points traveled chiefly by boat. Many of these farm laborers were Chinese, and the mates of the steamers grew old before their time trying to figure just where to stop for an Oriental who could not speak enough English to make his destination known. Finally, the operators hit upon the scheme of putting Chinese "runners" aboard the boats, and this task became simpler. The mate would tell the Paintersville runner that they were approaching, let us say; the runner would then round up the clients for that community, and they would all be out on deck and ready to go when the boat came alongside the landing.

For the isolated farm landings, the routine was a bit more rugged. If there was but one passenger, and he a farm hand or a bindle stiff, the mate would have the gangway rigged out as they came up to a brush landing which served whatever farm he desired. Then—"You get off here, mister"—and the unsuspecting passenger would be motioned out onto the gangway. Close behind him, and politely carrying his suitcase or bedroll, would a be a deck hand-a big one. The passenger, seeing that there was nothing on which to step but the uninviting mass of brush, would try to get back; this was where the deck hand came in. A large foot, planted in the seat of the victim's pants, was all that was needed. Over he went, frequently to disappear to his armpits in the brush. His luggage was tossed after him, and the boat went on about its business.

But it was good service-so good, in fact, that the farmers rode it to death. As operating costs slowly rose, it became more and more apparent that this business of stopping for a basket of peaches at one landing and for a crate of asparagus at one a hundred yards farther on would have to that stop. For this reason, the operators ruled no steamer would stop for less than $1.25 worth of business. Although this idea was financially sound, it was resented by the farmers, who were not slow to turn to the truck concerns. The latter lost no time in selling the agriculturists the idea that it was better to have the trucks come right into their fields to pick up the cargo for San Francisco direct than it was to cart it along to the next landing to meet the tariff requirement. That was, generally speaking, the end of the pick-up trade along the river.

Along the San Joaquin there were fewer stops, and most of the tonnage among the Delta islands was on the basis of carload or two—carload lots; there was little of what is known to the trade as "LCL," or "less than carload lots." Among these islands the Chinese grew potatoes, the Italians specialized in beans, and the Japs went in for onions in big way. A stop at a potato landing was always an adventure. The steamer would come in, perhaps in the middle of the night, and find not a living soul in sight. Muttering his opinion of farmers in general and potato-growers in particular, the pilot would yank lustily on the whistle-pull. If this brought no results, the vessel's officers would go over the side and head for the bunkhouse, pounding on the door and shouting until they got an answer and a string of sleepy and half-clad Chinese came out.

At these farms, the Chinese all worked on a partnership basis, and the final settling of the cargo tally was not without discussion. Some would be checking off the sacks of potatoes by marks scratched in the dust with a stick; others, more advanced in learning, would be busy with the abacus, and the pilot and mate of the steamer would be making their own count at the same time. No two of the farmers ever came up with the same answer; but the minute any one of them agreed with the figure arrived at by the freighter's officers the rest of the crew would brush the gesticulating Orientals aside and start bringing the potato sacks aboard. When the job was done, the steamer took in her plank, backed out into the slough, and with a cheery toot from her whistle, went on to the next stop, leaving the consignors of her cargo to argue it out among themselves.

All this time improvements were being made in the river vessels. The Fort Sutter and the Capital City startled the world by coming out with staterooms which had private baths; they may have caused no great ripple of excitement among the bindle-stiff clientele, who were allergic to soap anyhow; but the innovation immediately caught the fancy of the more polite travelers topside, and these boats got the cream of the business until the huge *Delta King* and *Delta Queen* came out.

Along in the 'nineties the Union Transportation Company operated the *Dauntless* and the *Captain Weber* on the Stockton run. Mrs. Sarah Gillis, a leader in the Stockton local of the W.C.T.U., became controlling factor in this line upon the death of her husband, who had been its president. As a result, these two were the only dry steamers on the rivers, all of the rest being equipped with well-stocked "buffets," as they called them in those days; the modern appellation of "cocktail lounge" for a blacked-out saloon in which anything can happen was a pitfall of civilization yet to come. The *Captain* was considered the fastest of the Stockton boats, and indeed her hull lines were nothing if not sweet. Her only rival in speed was the two-stacker *H. J. Corcoran*, which later was to achieve wide publicity by mortally wounding the *Seminole* when she crashed into her during a dense fog near Angel Island in 1913. Later, the California Transportation Company bought out the Union Line and the *Captain Weber* was rebuilt. Had Mrs. Gillis lived to see it, she would have been a most unhappy lady indeed; for the first thing, the new owners did was to put in a bar. However, they made another improvement of which no one could complain—they widened the vessel's dining room to the entire width of the cabin. Previously the river steamers' dining rooms had been tunnels down the center of the deck-houses from which you could see nothing but the doors of the staterooms. The new idea caught on at once; the *Captain Weber* got the pick of the passenger trade; and, as new vessels were built or old ones overhauled, the dining room with a view came in.

In their later years the steamboats ran at night; you left San Francisco about six o'clock in the evening, and were at Sacramento or at Stockton in the morning with the whole day before you; then, back aboard as night approached, you returned to "The City" (San Francisco) by morning. For the majority of travelers, it was a straight business proposition, plus rest and relaxation in route. For others, a night trip on the river boats was an adventure and you may interpret that remark in any way you choose. While it would be grossly unfair to characterize the night boat as a floating bagnio, there frequently were among the more playful passengers those who, let us say, looked upon the proprieties with perhaps undue breadth of mind. It was not always safe, therefore, to assume that the charming companion of Mr. X was, in fact, Mrs. X. Regarded with much more alarm by the crew members of the steamboats were large groups bound enmasse for a convention or a football game, or—worst of all—an excursion of flaming youth of high school age. They were the ones who gave the mates and pursers and stewards a need for aspirin in case lots and made replacements for pilferage and broken windows a real item in operating costs.

As respects conventions, the river-boat people may have had in mind what the Emmett Guards did to the poor old *Chrysopolis*, when some nameless saboteur suggested, in 1891, an excursion up to Sacramento to see that Governor H. H. Markham was properly inaugurated. For then the celebrators—a crowd of several hundred San Francisco politicos and hangers-on, accompanied by a brass band, a more than ample supply of hard liquor, and a small cannon-wound up by making the voyage in the ferryboat *Bay City*. She got them to the state capitol in fair shape, their arrival at a point below the old M Street bridge being announced by the booming of the cannon and by band music which was neither too good nor outstandingly bad. At the conclusion of the day's ceremonies the San Francisco delegates either walked or were carried back aboard the *Bay City*, and were off for home. It is not recorded that they did the fine old double-ender any lasting harm, for she continued to serve the commuters of San Francisco Bay for many years afterward.

A variation from the almost universal custom of running the river boats at night was furnished by the Southern Pacific veteran *Apache* and *Modoc*, which, about 1912 and for several years thereafter, left San Francisco and Sacramento in the morning. Incidentally, the company made use of the annual Fourth of July picnic at Rio Vista to give the crews of these boats a bit of a change. Normally, of course, the boat which left San Francisco on Tuesday, Thursday, and Saturday would continue to do so indefinitely, and her week-end layover always would be at Sacramento. To vary this monotony, the boat leaving Sacramento on the morning of stopped at Rio Vista, where she met the July 4 up-boat from San Francisco; after the picnic, she doubled back to Sacramento with the returning picnickers, while her through passengers went on to San Francisco in the other boat. Thus, the two schedules were reversed. Two other well-known Southern Pacific boats were the *Navajo*, which came out in 1909, and the *Seminole*, which followed her two years later; both were night boats and these two comfortable and well-appointed craft were in service until the railroad line went out of the river-passenger business, about 1918.

While the river boats had their lighter moments, and there may have been occasional strayings from the straight and narrow path by some of their customers, there were, for the boats and their own people, more than enough of outstanding virtues-friendly cooperation, absolute honesty, and famous meals, to name but a few. Up-river banks shipped thousands of dollars in gold to San Francisco, in little iron boxes. At times, these precious bits of cargo would lie for hours on a wharf, completely unguarded. Everyone knew what the boxes contained—but none of them was ever touched. Just try that sort of thing today and see what happens. And characteristic of the little things which the steamer people did for their customers was the service of Johnny

Myrick, one of the famous pilots. Sacramento housewives, unable themselves to get to San Francisco, would make out shopping lists and hand them to Myrick, together with the funds necessary for their purchases. The spectacle of hard-boiled river pilot buying corsets or other feminine impedimenta in San Francisco stores no doubt brought raised eyebrows among those who did not know what was going on; but he didn't mind. Had he charged for his services in this trade-which he did not-he could have made a neat little sum on the side. It is small wonder that the name of the kindly and obliging pilot is remembered on the river to this day.

As Chinese living along the rivers died, it was customary, whenever possible, to send the bodies back to China for burial. A certain amount of down-river tonnage to San Francisco hence consisted of the grim pine boxes in which the caskets were encased for the long voyage home. Down-to-earth dock clerks, however, were unimpressed by the solemnity of the occasion; some would stand with one foot on the box while making out bills of lading, while others found them handy places on which to sit during the lunch hour. But then-you'll find that sort of thing anywhere.

Mary Jane Barnes, "Tall Tales of the Delta"

[Editor's note: Mary Jane Barnes was a poet laureate of Brentwood. In this poem from her self-published book, *The Opposite Shore* (1961), she is looking back to a time when riverboat captains invented tales to glorify their experiences. (*By permission*). See Fig. 17.]

Riverboat captains tell:
That winds in the sloughs are so strong
that they pull your hair out by the roots;
That mosquitoes are as a big as river rats;
That a faithful little ship exploded one day,
skyrocketed clear out of sight, and landed
in the Big Dipper where she still is floating;
That all good ships snuggle under the boughs
of the Tree of Heaven after faithful service;
That cottonwoods, willows and sycamores
are giant toothpicks used to pick the water out of the river's teeth;
That once there was a riverboat that could run anywhere,
even if the ground were covered with nothing but fog;
That the big "norther' wind was so strong
that it lifted the sloughs right out of their beds
and tied knots around their necks;

That once there was a padre so good that
when he met a bear on the mountain one day,
he prayed for deliverance; he changed himself
into the wind and swept the bear off the mountain.
That there was a mountain that vomited fire and smoke that turned into gold.

If you don't believe the captain himself
Come and find out these things for yourself

Josiah Royce, from *The Feud of Oakfield Creek*

[Editor's note: Josiah Royce's *The Feud at Oakfield Creek* (Boston: Houghton Mifflin, 1887) is his only novel. It is the least recognized of his books; rather he is best known for his history of California and his philosophical writings. The story takes place in Oakland, San Francisco, and what is today Contra Costa County. He portrays two successful men, one (Alfonzo Eldon) who values his heritage and his wealth and the other (Alf Escott) who values nurturing community. Both take seriously making their mark, but they treat others very differently. Editing of the last chapter of the novel has been done to focus the conflicting perspectives between these two men. See Fig. 18.]

When the Last Lamp is Shattered

Very early one morning, not long afterwards, two horsemen were riding on a road east of the Contra Costa hills. The dawn light was growing clear. The air of this inland valley, some miles from Oakfield Creek, was crisp and cool. The last stars were fading. Mount Diablo, rising towards the east and southeast, had just ceased to seem so much like a vast and shapeless monster. Its outlines were sharp against the faintly rosy sky far above the horizon. The meadowlarks and the grosbeaks had begun to sing. A rabbit was busy in the road; and as the two horsemen rounded the curve, it dashed into the long, green grass. Beyond it, as it fled, the horsemen could not have failed to see, had they looked up, the seemingly endless fields, covered with grain or with wild-flowers, and dotted with oaks. These oaks grew with a singular precision of arrangement, as if somebody had long since laid out this but recently wild region as a great park. For many miles, there were almost regular intervals between the separate trees—intervals of about twenty or thirty yards. One could hear occasionally, this morning, as one rode, the musical sound of some wild dove's wing, as the bird flew from one tree to another. Just here, on the road, there were no houses to be seen. Before very long, however, one would reach the settlement Oakfield Creek. The spring had dealt kindly, so far, with this region. The road was, indeed, already dusty; the drought was coming; the perfect sky overhead meant, before many hours should pass, a hot sun, parching air, a dreary and dying look in the grass on the higher hill-slopes. Yet, at this moment, one could imagine one's self in an earthly paradise, so full of life, so placid, so maturely vigorous, all nature appeared in this hour before sunrise.

The two horsemen were Escott and Harold. They had ridden as rapidly, during the earlier part of the journey, as the steep hills, now behind them, and the dimness of the night had permitted. Once they had missed their way, by trying to take a shorter road. They had with difficulty found their path again, full of shame that they had so easily lost themselves in what they had supposed to be familiar country. They had then hurried on once more, faster than was actually necessary for their purpose. They must be in Oakfield Creek shortly after sunrise, but why sooner? And now that they were at last sure of being in season, they had slackened their pace, and were giving their weary horses a little indulgence. For the first time during the long ride they had begun to talk together freely. They looked down at the way just before them, as they went, taking little or no notice of the dawn, the birds, the flowers, the vast natural park, the oaks, the noble mountain. They showed no signs of weariness, indeed ...

The sun was now just coming over a northern spur of Mount Diablo. The shadow of the mountain covered the hills and plains to the southwards of the travelers. The morning had lost its first bloom and its heart-compelling charm. The time for confessions was over. This was a very matter-of-fact place, after all. The fences were worn, and often broken down. A stray cow was wandering along the road. She had a wicked look and a broken horn. The stream-beds, as one passed near them, were hereabouts already dry. The smoke from the chimneys of the hamlet at Oakfield Creek was, at length, plainly visible. The oak-trees clustered more thickly just ahead, as one approached the banks of the creek. Harold gave a new turn to the conversation: "You were saying something awhile since, Escott, about your talk with Alonzo Eldon, and about his rage and his illusions. How incredible it seems that a man of so much business skill and sagacity should have become so fast bound in the meshes this time!"

"A great man is doomed to be once in his life blind, as the old stories always have it. The situation is simply absurd, at the Creek. But Alonzo tried to do too many things. First, he somehow got into the quarrel with the settlers. Then I heard of the thing, and, being in love with justice and in trouble with Alonzo, I invested my all hereabouts. Then the trouble went on, until Alonzo resolved to be reconciled to the settlers and to save his soul. That thought was desperately unbusinesslike, and the consequences have been fatal to poor

Alonzo's peace of mind. He couldn't well use his mere fiat, and say, 'Let this trouble end.' It was now the company's affair, not his. Therefore, he must buy out the other shareholders, or give up his new plan. He could not at once do the former thing; so, he undertook this most unsatisfactory of all compromises. What confusion of interests and of events has since disturbed poor Alonzo's purposes we know. But just now, the position of things is, I declare, almost unprecedented. Alonzo thinks himself and his son wronged by you. I persist, of course, in standing up for you. So, then he also thinks himself wronged by me. He even fancies it must be all my deep plot to avenge myself for long past injuries. Therefore, he tears up and throws away all his private agreements with me. I'm a traitor, he says. He owes me nothing! As the court has meanwhile decided against me, he has nothing to do but to call for execution of judgment, and then eject me, or rather my caretakers, from my tracts of land. So far again, to be sure, it's once more a private fight between Alonzo and me. But there, of course, the poor settlers enter afresh. An ejection of me, after the decision of the test cases (which were my own cases), means, the settlers are sure, a coming ejection of all of them. Accordingly, they want to fight. Hence the absurdity of this moment. Alonzo, with the United States government behind him, is on one side; the moral law sits there quietly on the other side, and won't budge. The settlers, with their shotguns, are meanwhile trying to hide behind that moral law, but even they can't. And you and I ride along here at sunrise, intending to see whether we can find some way to keep the peace in the Oakfield Creek region. The whole thing, in one sense, is confoundedly funny. I'm almost disposed to sit down by the roadside here and laugh at it" ...

"Now that we're coming into the settlement, you'll also see that I'm a true orator, too, though in a funny way. The settlers for the last day or two have been wholly idle and very excited, because they've been expecting the marshal at any minute, who will, so we know, actually come about noon to-day. So, instead of minding their regular business, they've been under arms, holding sessions, making speeches, and otherwise behaving like asses. If this thing only blows over, they'll go back to work to-morrow like honest men. We shall find them, just at this hour of the day, all cross and sleepy. Besides, they think I've sold out to Alonzo. If they don't shoot us off hand as traitors, Harold, I want to make 'em a speech. They'll first treat us with the cussedest impoliteness in any case; but we 've got to keep cool. I'll do all the talking, my boy; you look out for the horses. My talk, however, won't be precisely of a classical sort: it won't even begin with 'Fellow citizens,' nor make any references to the bird of liberty. It must be judged, Harold, by no academic standard. In fact, what orator ever tried before to move the multitudes at that sacred hour of the rosy morn when the head feels biggest? Not even Demosthenes, I take it. I'm proud of the opportunity. How I wish

Sam Paddington were here! But speech, I'm afraid, wouldn't bear reporting. It will be an old man's plain words to a pack of amateur loafers, and I'm afraid it may be profane. The effects, you know, have to be a little startling on such occasions. Well, we shall see."

The reader would in vain hunt upon the defective maps of this generation to find marked the position of this Oakfield Creek. But at all events, after passing a few houses, as you entered the place, you came to Spofford's hotel, where, of course, there was a large bar-room. But this morning there were collected about the tavern door, even at this early hour, a number of the Brotherhood of Noble Rangers. Several had their horses tied to fences close by. Two or three of the men sat and sulked on the low front steps; more leaned back in chairs on the hotel porch; one supported himself against post of the porch; others, as Escott and Harold rode up, peered through the door and from the windows of the bar-room. Somebody, at the same time, kicked a lazy dog down the steps, between the men there, and almost under the feet of the horses. The chickens about the front of the tavern cackled and fled in dismay; a frightened woman looked out of a second story window, and then drew back suddenly. Meanwhile a dirty child stared steadily and with fascination from the ground at the corner of the hotel building, admiring all that went on. It had been for the last half hour taking its chance to throw an occasional stone at the legs of some one of the horses tied nearby. The building was of a dirty white color, with green blinds and a peaked roof. In front were a pump, a dirty horse-trough, and many empty tin cans.

These Noble Rangers had but few firearms in sight just now. Most of the men must, indeed, have been drinking the whole night; but, however they felt, they looked as sober and stern as Mount Diablo itself. This was not a moment when a resolute man very willingly confessed to the effects of his rum. Some of the Rangers, moreover, were, no doubt, temperance men. Save for the act of kicking the dog, nobody seemed disposed to move for our two travelers. To Escott's greeting there was a poor response. Peterson, who was leaning against the post, answered most noticeably, but still very sulkily. Collins, who stood in the doorway, was even less cordial. Nobody seemed willing to look at Harold. The two friends were plainly in disgrace hereabouts. Escott made not the slightest delay in getting off his horse as well as his feebleness permitted, and found his way up the steps, between the curious but almost motionless men there. Harold, springing lightly off his own horse, took the reins of both, and looked about for place to fasten them. None was near. Nobody helped or directed him and so he stood still, and awaited Escott's next action. By the time Escott had reached the top of the steps, a young man, holding high over his head a light chair, pushed through the doorway, past the unwilling Collins, and offered the chair to Escott. Escott greeted him cordially, thanked him, and laid his hand on the chair, but did not sit down.

"Johnny," said Escott to the young man, very quietly, "would you mind just taking our horses round and giving them to the man at the stable? There seems to be no great flourishing about here this morning to help a newcomer. I suppose Spofford isn't on hand yet, nor his son either, or else we should have seen them here, by this time. I wish, too, you 'd wake up Spofford, if you can, want to talk with him."

"I'm awake enough," said Spofford, making his appearance at the door. "I dunno, Escott, why you need ask Johnny Milliken to do my work, nohow."

"Johnny and I are very old friends, Spofford," said Escott, coolly. "By the way, allow me to introduce my friend, Mr. Harold. Mr. Harold, Mr. Spofford."

"I know Mr. Harold, I think," replied Spofford, gloomily. "He was here before. Johnny, by the way, I think you needn't take Escott's horse to my stable. Plenty of other stables in town. Escott, I'm sorry to be rude, as it were, to an old friend, but the fact is, the gentlemen of the Brotherhood of Noble Rangers has taken possession of this here hotel this mornin', 'nd I'm darned if there's any room in it for another man. I guess you'll find house-roIIom down to your old tract."

"If old Alonzo's right, there's to be lots of room down there before long, and nobody knows it, Escott, better than you and this friend of yours." It was Collins who spoke these last words.

"It's to tell you a little about Alonzo that we've come today, if you please," began Escott, calmly drawing a long breath, as if he expected to speak at some length, "and it's the whole Brotherhood that I want to find, right here and now, so that they may learn what we've got to tell. And what's more, Spofford, I want first of all to remark that I don't care for any of your blarsted airs, anyhow. If you choose to stand there so glum, you and these other Rangers, you may. I don't mind how you look. Harold, here, and I have ridden all night to come to this very place, and to talk to you like men, before you get misled any more by some ghastly nonsense or other, and so fall into a mess with better people than Alonzo's crowd. As for Alonzo, nobody's in a worse row with him than we are ourselves, think what you will. And you needn't look so sulky, either. You must know that I sha'n't greatly worry, Spofford, whether any body believes my story or not. For the fact is, I've come here to say just whatever I choose, so long as it concerns you fellows to hear it. When you've heard, believe it, or call me a liar, or do any other square and polite thing, and I'll not blame you. But what I do want is, I say, to talk with men, not with sickly-looking, half-awake fellows that roost on doorsteps, and hold up posts, and look as sulky as that youngster yonder, that's throwing pebbles at horses' legs for its living. Hang you, man, if you want to sulk, go over to Alonzo's crowd! The sulking there's been this spring in the camp of Boscowitz and of the other boon comrades of that great American land grabber beats all that I see in this crowd even now. And now, Spofford, what do you want to do about it? If you choose to be civil, and rouse up such of your Rangers as have a grain or two of decent courtesy about them, fellows who'll talk squarely to old man like me,—if you'll do that, Harold and I won't make any ceremony. We'll speak our piece, and you can speak yours, and when you're through we'll all think it over. After that, if you have any confounded grudges left, and you call it worthwhile to have 'em out with either of us, why, blaze away, or do whatever else you darn choose. But if, Spofford, you aren't man enough for that, and if your crowd is to go on sulking at this rate until the next rain, why, then, we'll leave the men of this district, Harold and I will, and we'll call a public meeting of children under five years. They, sir, would be at least honest with us, and they 'd speak their minds. So that's my little speech for now, Spofford. take it you and the rest of this darned statuary hereabouts have heard Alf Escott talk before, and perhaps you know how to treat him on this present occasion."

"But see here, Alf," replied Spofford, rather weakly, "I tell you my house is under the control, at present, of a sort of general extra session of the Brotherhood of Noble Rangers. Your approach just now, as I may say, was seen by our patrol about two miles out. A resolution had already been taken last night that, in the now present state of our affairs and controversies, we preferred neither to oppose your coming, if you'd come, nor to precisely, as I may say, welcome it. We'd deal with you through a sort of a delygation, Escott. We'd prefer to send a delygation to kind of interrygate you as to certain dubyous points; and it was meanwhile resolved and accorddin'ly ordered that it wasn't right, you bein' a little under cloud, for us here to, as it were, welcome you to this hospitable roof. Now this isn't my work, Alf, not exactly. It's the Brotherhood that orders it. I don't say I don't approve it. I only say I don't know no ways bear the sole and individual responsibility, Alf. So, I'll ask you to pardon me for my seemin' unkindness, and regard this here that I say as, as it were, final." Spofford spoke all this with the air of one who had prepared himself as well as possible beforehand for this scene.

Escott, still standing, measured him quietly as he spoke, and then said, "Is this all?"

"Yes, Alf, it is."

"How much do you mean to say the Brotherhood here paid you for learning this little oration?"

"I as the owner of this house, Alf."

"How much would you own of this house now, Spofford, if it hadn't been for me?"

"But, Alf, I don't mean to imply anything personal. It's the Brother—"

"Personal be hanged! I asked for a man that could talk, not for this kind of stuff. What have I to do here with your resolutions, and the rest? I know them. They begin, 'Whereas, Alf Escott,' and they go on with a long rigmarole that not one sinner here and now chewing the cud of bitterness about this doorstep can remember or repeat. As for your orders, and your delegations, and the rest, they can go bang. Try that game on Alonzo. He deserves it, and he 'll think it's dignified. But as for Alf Escott, you know him well. He's pulled several of you boys out of the mire in various ways. You, Spofford, he cleared from a disagreeable charge before the Vigilance Committee, twenty-seven years ago; and every man here knows that. And he helped you out of one deucedly bad money-scrape; that, too, you know. You, Peterson—but won't particularize. You all know the facts. Now, why do I come here, where I'm not wanted? Why do persist in staying? Why do say now, this very instant, to the face of all of you, that I won't go till you 've heard me out? Why? Because I shall speak for your good, not for mine. What can a miserable delegation do that you can't do now, if you'll only wake up some man with blood and brains in him to talk to me? To be sure, I've not ridden all night to hold forth here to crowd as dull as this one is, so long as your chiefs don't come out. See here! Where 's McAlpin? If there's anybody in all your Brotherhood that I ought to fear, if I've any way betrayed you, it's McAlpin. As for you, Collins, I know you're a leader, but you always take until tomorrow to hear what's said to you today, and I want a man with quick wits. Bring out McAlpin."

The settlers were evidently staggered by their old leader's vigor. He stood leaning on the chair, as feeble, as clear-voiced, as fiery, as ever. But a short time since, despite some doubtful appearances, they had, nearly all of them, worshiped him. Yet they had just been spending half the night in voting him a traitor, in threatening to slay him, and in preparing an open letter to voice their opinions of him in the public press. They had dreaded his coming, as possibly meaning an effort on his part to win them over afresh, and so to betray them yet again. The notion of a delegation, with set questions, had been hit upon as the best for their purpose. They desired, namely, to get all they could from Escott, in the way of information, and they feared his blunt persuasiveness if used a upon a large company. The night ride and this early appearance had surprised them. They were well on the lookout for the expected marshal; but that an old man like Escott should arrive on his weary horse at sunrise, after so long a journey, they had not thought possible. Spofford's effort to carry out the purposes of the Noble Rangers was therefore a little weak, and was certainly doomed to failure. Escott had not even fairly finished his last appeal before Peterson turned about sharply and spoke. He was a tall, intelligent-looking man, with gray eyes and a hooked nose.

"Boys," he said, "I'm not in favor, now that Escott comes to us in this way, I'm not in favor of sending him off till the whole body has seen him right here, and voted on the thing again. If he's got anything to say, we ought to hear him out. There's been no alarm this past night. The marshal may get here today, and may not; but any rate, there'll be no such hurry before he comes that we can't talk things over. I move, Spofford, that we here, now on guard and awaiting news, receive Escott into this house on our own responsibility, until the boys are all awake. That Alf Escott should be sent off when he comes to us at this hour, it isn't noways fair, nor right. And it's so with Mr. Harold, too. You see, Escott, McAlpin and the others that were looking out for our affairs early in the night are sleeping now in the further wing of the house. We're looking out for that marshal, to whom we mean to show our teeth when he comes. As for you, I think things have looked black for you lately over here. And it's odd. You're in trouble. You're the one against whom the writs are issued. Yet it looks to us as if you'd sold us out, for all that, because yours was the test-case, and you defended it ill, and let the story get abroad that you had private dealings with Alonzo Eldon. Now, though, you've thus let all the main points come to decision in the courts, and they've gone against us; and it seems that your private arrangement is worthless, at least for our interests. We believe you've been bought out, and that your ejection is only good to show Alonzo's triumph and to bring us to his feet. We mean to have something to say about that ourselves, though; and, all the while, we suspect you very seriously. That's our meaning this morning, and it's Spofford's place, of course, to give it vent in this way. But when the boys voted not to receive you here, they didn't know you were coming at this hour. I vote to receive you now, and to put off action about your case until, say, nine o'clock. In the meanwhile, you and Mr. Harold can rest, and your horses. That's my notion about Escott, boys. What do ye say?"

Peterson's words met a general assent now, and Spofford rather gladly sacrificed his dignity, and retracted his former speech.

"Well, boys," said Escott, "if you'll promise us a hearing by and by, I'm content to have no more talk now. Maybe I need rest. But there's one bit of news that you doubtless haven't heard yet. I know for a certainty that the marshal is this side the Contra Costa hills, that he has quite a party with him, and that Alonzo Eldon and his son are of that party. You may say that I know this because I'm on their side. I'm not on their side, though, and I prove it to you by coming and telling you this, which they 've done all they could to keep secret. Alonzo thought, boys, that the sudden appearance here of a larger band than you expected, with his big and wonderful self at the head of it, would scare you to death. I've taken the edge off this surprise, boys, by riding over in the night, and letting you know. But that, as you'll by and by see, isn't my main purpose in coming here now. I want to develop to you a plan by which you can so take advantage of Alonzo's presence as to secure, boys, all the guarantees from him that you like, as touching your own interests. I myself, as you will see, am to gain nothing by that. You are to get what you demand, and my tract will be lost to me, as, perhaps, I deserve to lose it. Before sundown, boys, if you take the thing rightly, the controversy may be ended in your favor,—not, to be sure, in mine. I shall be the only sufferer. Well—no matter now, can't develop my plans yet. Wait until nine o'clock. Only I'm in earnest, as you'll see."

Escott's manner went far to restore confidence in him, despite all the suspicion and the sullenness of this early morning detachment of the Noble Rangers. Their whole life during the forty-eight hours since their "extra session," as Spofford had called it, had begun, seemed to them already like a troubled dream. They had been waiting for the marshal, disputing what to do next, passing resolutions, discussing Escott's betrayal of their interests, planning publications in the newspapers, swallowing many drinks and many big stories, and breathing out threatenings and slaughter. Escott's coming seemed to them now, after all, like an awakening voice. They began to hope that he would set all right, and become their trusted friend again. They had, at least, no real desire to begin war against the national government. They only knew that, somehow, they were being cruelly wronged, and that they were determined to make life impossible for any "jumper" in this region. They still hoped not to be led into any direct contest with the marshal himself. If he came, they meant to turn out in full force. to threaten violently any jumpers who might be in his company, and to induce these jumpers to retire from the contest. As for the marshal himself, well, if he grew troublesome, they might have to surround him, and quietly to disarm him! All must be done, however, decently and in order. A moral victory at least, they fancied, must result, such as to make Alonzo feel that there was no room for him and his jumpers hereabouts. Then, perhaps, he might be induced erelong to settle his cases in a favorable way to them.

When Escott made this startling announcement about Alonzo's coming, and also said that he himself had a new plan to propose, the result, as far as it went, was very much what he had desired. Curiosity was aroused, new excitement was created, other Rangers, on awaking, were erelong informed of the new turn of affairs; and, while Escott and Harold were resting from the ride, taking a little breakfast, and even trying to nap for brief space, the Rangers outside their room were awaiting eagerly the meeting at nine o'clock, when they would assail Escott with reproaches and questions, and would have a chance to find whether there was really, as he had promised, any escape from this fatal downhill course of threats, of recriminations, and of violence.

Escott, meanwhile, was trying to prepare his energies for what he looked forward to as one of the greatest efforts of his life. He must quiet the suspicions of these angry men; he must divert their minds from their dangerous purposes; he must propose to them an armed negotiation with Eldon; he must be ready to offer himself in every sense as a personal sacrifice to their cause; and, above all and in the midst of all, he must keep the peace. Escott was very sanguine of success. Harold was more doubtful and anxious; but he, too, was fully devoted to the undertaking. If only Alonzo and the marshal did not come too early! Escott had mentioned nine o'clock, because the old man believed, from his present sensations, that, after the toils of the night, he could not venture on his task any sooner. Besides, he felt sure, from his information, that the marshal could not arrive before noon.

But Escott's information was, in this respect, mistaken.

At about half past eight o'clock that morning, a young man who had been acting as patrol came in with the news that the marshal's party were in sight. The young man who brought in this news had ridden far out, had met the party, had seen the marshal, Alonzo Eldon, Tom Eldon, Foster, and Buzzard, had recognized all of them, and had then put spurs to his horse and galloped across fields to the settlement, jumping two or three ditches by the way, and taking advantage of broken fences. The youth himself was very proud of his success so far. He was a truant from the city, who had been for some time trying to avoid letting his father hear of his whereabouts. He was much surprised to learn now that his father was in the hotel. The young patrol's name was Sam Escott.

Sam's honesty was so obvious, his simplicity was so engaging, his frequent quarrels with his father were such familiar facts at the Creek, that when he had come to the settlement, a few days ago, nobody had thought of fastening upon him any of the suspicions to which Alf Escott was subject. His services had been cheerfully accepted. He was a good rider, a dead shot, an enthusiastic and boyish young fellow. For the last two days, he had been in the saddle almost all the time, riding about on errands for the Rangers, and acting as a patrol. Of what the people now said about his father Sam had heard little and understood nothing. He loved this exciting moment, with its suggestions of warfare. He hoped that it would not all end in mere talk. He longed for a chance to stand under fire, and to shoot someone. As for the consequences of resisting the law, Sam had no special concern about them. Nor had he any heart-searchings as to the right and wrong of this affair. The Eldons were old enemies. Especially Tom was hateful to Sam, who had never for an instant forgotten Ellen. The thing was a family feud. Sam wished to have a hand in it. Of the immediate causes of the present crisis he had, however, no idea.

What Sam witnessed of the scene that followed was, with a very few additions, something like this. When Sam had shouted out his news at the top of his voice, he rejoiced to see that he was at once the centre of observation. The windows were full of faces, the steps were crowded, and Collins, Peterson, and the others, men who had usually snubbed Sam of late, and ordered him about harshly, were listening respectfully. Then there arose a general call for McAlpin. McAlpin did not appear. "Who saw him last?" "Where is he?" asked various voices; but there was no satisfactory answer. He had ridden over to Murphy's saloon, at the other end of the town. He was sleeping in the attic at Spofford's. He was here a moment since. He had not been here since midnight. Such were the opposing views. But McAlpin responded to the many calls no more than if he were Baal. Nobody could find him. Then somebody called upon Collins, as nominally the next in command among the Rangers, to take the lead. Collins looked sullen, and said that he had resigned last night, as they all knew, after that quarrel with McAlpin. He would follow anywhere, but Peterson must lead. Peterson was, therefore, really the next in command. And so he was called upon. "Well, boys," he said, "if I undertake this affair, I want order. We intend to give old Alonzo an infernal scare, if we find him, but we don't want no powder wasted. I wish somebody else could take charge of this thing, do, because I'm no leader, if I am Second Grand Chief of the Brotherhood. But I'll do my best, and I won't I shirk. Every man to his horse! And then we'll ride out to meet Alonzo in good shape."

Hereupon there was more rushing about after the horses, and much confusion, and good deal of swearing. The women of the house, as Sam saw, were crying. In the midst of all this, however, Escott and Harold appeared, and Sam quailed before his father's eye.

"Well, Sam," said Escott, however, good-humoredly enough, "we haven't met for some days, my boy. How is everything with you? I hope, my dear chicken, you won't get hurt today. Look out for yourself, Sam. Keep cool. Obey orders."

Sam had been sure of an angry outburst, after their last quarrel; for that had been quite a serious one. Escott's voice gave Sam a glad sense of reassurance. He looked very sullen and proud, however, and replied that he had for some time been here on business of his own.

"But what's the price of your pony, Sam? You'll go to the dogs before long, if you indulge in such extravagance as this."

Sam's pony was a sorry mustang, and was now quite hot and worn out. Sam resented the pleasantry a little, and began to tell Escott the news afresh. "Fiddlesticks, my boy, you needn't describe the party. I didn't expect them so early, but know all about how they look. They meant to scare us by the bare sight of 'em. See here, Peterson," continued Escott, turning to the leader, "I understand you're the captain now. I'm no fighter, you know, but we want, my friend Harold and I, to join on to this army of yours in the character of special war correspondents, as it were. We shall hide behind the fence posts while the shooting is going on, and write up the campaign afterwards, with eulogies on the heroes, and so forth. Won't you let us! I've no doubt that Boscowitz is retained to write up the other side. I believe in giving every man a chance. We're ready to obey orders, if you'll let us go along. I believe Harold has a pistol. I am unhappily weaponless myself, but if any man has spare pitchfork about his clothes, I'd be glad of chance to carry it, so that may prod Alonzo a little somewhere about the fifth rib, if he shows any sign of going to sleep while you fellows make your set speeches to him before you begin the war. I believe in giving every man a hearing, I do."

Peterson was looking very anxious as he sat there on his horse, amid the confusion of the men preparing their arms and their beasts. Fresh news bad just come in that Alonzo's party were pausing in a field outside the town, apparently for the sake of reconnoitering. They numbered only some fifteen, all told, whereas there were now about forty Noble Rangers in sight, and armed. Peterson seemed not to enjoy Escott's fashion of talk: nor could Sam make out his father's purpose in treating the affair as a farce. Sam wanted to hear a few glowing words about courage, and the defense of home, and the cruelty of the oppressors, and all that. But still, if Peterson was offended at Escott's manner, he was probably less disposed to think the old man a false friend than he would have been if Escott had now chosen a more unnatural and eloquent strain. He answered rather sternly.

"I thought, Alf, that you'd come here to look at this business like a man. I don't see as this is any time for infernal nonsense, especially from a man in your place."

"Well, Peterson, if I didn't talk nonsense, you'd doubtless just now believe me lying. There's no time to hear my speech to the boys, for I, too, had very carefully prepared a speech. But what I really do want of you, Peterson, is your attention for one instant to a request. It's a personal favor to me. Let me speak three words to these fellows here before we go. Grant it, man! It may prevent bloodshed!"

Peterson was plainly moved by the sudden change in Alf's manner. His face softened. At the earliest chance he called order, and began in a good but artificially emphatic voice, to address his mounted men: "Boys,—I should say Noble Brothers (but, darn it! that's no matter), news has just come that Alonzo Eldon, with his whole pack, has stopped outside in Carson's field. They're reconnoitering. Now, we mean to go out and meet 'em square and in full force, and show 'em what stuff we're made of. I say we're made of peaceable stuff, and have been all along; I say we aren't going to give up our rights; and I also say that we here are the last men in the State of California to violate the laws, unless we're driven to the wall. But if we are, boys, then the law of God is higher than that of man, and even the crushed worm will turn again and—rend you." This last doubtless trite allusion met exactly the feelings of the assembled Rangers, who interrupted the stern and honest voice of Peterson by a torrent of approving shouts, such as seriously frightened some of the more nervous and ill fed of the mustangs. The terrified women at the upper windows gazed tearfully and silently down; a turkey-cock nearby loudly expressed his customary feelings in number of successive outbursts; while the lazy dog rose from his latest resting place, put his tail between his legs, and chased the dirty child once more round the corner of the house. Collins, however, who had been standing on the ground, very busy with his saddle -girth, looked more ill-humored than ever, as he quieted his beast during the applause. At the close of the disturbance, Collins took the first opportunity to remark, in a loud voice, to his next neighbor, "Darn the old thing, it's busted." This remark referred to the saddle-girth.

"Never mind, Collins," began Peterson, in a conciliatory tone. "Take my horse, and I'll ride yours barebacked myself."—

"But, boys, as I was saying, we here don't want to shed no drop of useless blood."

"Useless blood is good, of Tom Eldon, for instance," muttered Escott to Harold, by way of comment. Sam thought this fine joke as he overheard it. He chuckled softly until his face was crimson.

"We want, say, to shed not one God-forsaken drop. We only want to overawe our foes by the irresistible force of him who is thrice-armed, because his quarrel is just and his powder is dry. We want to send Alonzo peacefully and irrevocably home to his own vine and his own potato-patch."

"I'm darned if I think he owns any potato-patch,—by rights, that is," said Collins. There was a laugh.

"No," admitted Peterson, more cheerfully. "I think we shall really have to send him home to some other man's potato-patch that Alonzo's stolen. But no matter. We're brave. We're willing to shed the last drop of our blood in defense of our homes, but we don't want no cuss to say in the newspapers that we began the fight." The mention of newspapers attracted attention once more to Escott. "But now," said Peterson, "we have a minute before we go out, and Alf Escott asks to be heard for that minute. I'm in favor of granting this to him. We have believed in him, boys, we all know how much. He's under a cloud now, but he's come in among us frankly, with every show of honesty, and I move he be heard. Alf Escott, speak up. 'Well, boys,' began Alf, as he sat on his horse near Peterson, I had a speech ready, but there is no time for that. I was going to vindicate myself to this crowd, that I have loved a good deal, after all, and that has turned against me for poor reasons. No matter. I don't ask you now to think well of me, nor to believe a word I say. I only want to propose a plan, as a sensible man, talking to sensible men. If you think there's no good in it, we'll say no more of it. If you think well of it, I'm at your service. You'll ride out here, and meet Alonzo. Well and good! Now, what has Alonzo come for? To eject my caretakers from my land. You think that he's in collusion with me when he does this. He isn't, mind you, but no matter. Suppose he was, or suppose he wasn't, my plan is good all the same. Let me go with you, and let me, first of all, before anything else happens, walk right out in front of you, and then, in plain sight, and where all can bear me, I'll address Alonzo thus. 'Alonzo!' I'll say, 'you come here, armed with processes of the courts, to take my land. So far as I now am concerned, Alonzo,' I shall say, 'take it and be damned. But so far as these men here behind me are concerned, men who have trusted in your solemn promises to me, you shall not take my land until here, openly, in the presence of all, you solemnly renew your undertakings on their behalf, and promise that this ejectment business shall end with me.' That's what we shall say to Alonzo, boys. And I shall say it while I'm standing in fair line of fire from both sides, and my friend Harold will stand there beside me. And if we play you false, you can shoot us dead right on the spot. And so, if you let us do this, and if you wait till we are done, Alonzo will show what he means, fast enough. Thus, again, we'll put the responsibility of the first blood-letting (if there's to be any) upon him for if he's disposed to keep his word to you, and will enter into fresh agreements right there, you can afford to see me lose my land. But if he is playing you false, then the consequences are his own, to take as he wants to. That, boys, is as square as I can make it. This is no speech, but it's a fair business proposition, at any rate."

A general murmur of approval greeted Escott's words. Peterson began to consult anxiously with Collins and with one or two others, and after a general hum of conversation had filled the air for a few moments Peterson once again called order. The more Peterson talked as the leader of the assembled Rangers, the more anxiously dignified this man became, who had begun the discussions of the morning with such a quiet and manly simplicity of bearing.

"Noble Brothers," he said this time, "I've heard with unmixed admiration this proposal of old Alf's. It's worthy of him, I say worthy of his old self. As I understand his meaning, he predicates this now imminent row be a private controversy of him and old Eldon, founded on some difference now in process of going on behind the scenes. And he undertakes to prove this before us all, and to meanwhile serve our cause by this proposition of his. I believe in accepting of his notion. We can't lose anything by it. What do you say? Shall we vote?"

The Rangers were in a hurry. They called for the question at once, allowed no discussion, and accepted the proposition.

"Why," asked Peterson the next moment, privately, of Escott, "do you want Mr. Harold to go beside you, when you ride out in front to talk to Alonzo. One is better than two for such a thing."

"Harold and I want to show, sir, that we two are the really hated ones in this business. Bring us out there alone together, and Alonzo will quickly say whether we are the men he means. If we skulk, when the parties meet, Alonzo will be only the worse, and there'll be a fight. If he sees us, if we demand a parley, then we can ask him to say squarely that we are the only ones he has a fight with. Thereafter you fellows won't care to sympathize with us very much. You'll see, from what he says, that it's a personal and private fight. You'll be disposed to draw out of it. And he observes that fact, he'll be disposed to let you do so. Anyhow, this is our forlorn hope, Peterson, to prevent this trouble. Our plan isn't exactly legal, I know, any more than yours: but neither Harold nor I can skulk just now, if there's to be a clear understanding of this business all around. And only a clear understanding can possibly prevent bloodshed this day. We may fail, but as you fellows feel, there's no other plan. If we don't both go out in front, you fellows won't believe us. and you won't believe Alonzo even if he says that we are the sole men that he's trying to hurt; and, again, you won't know how to deal with him as I do; and so, altogether, you'll be sure to blunder into a battle. We may do the same thing, but, as I say, it's a forlorn hope."

This last decision of Escott's life seems, when judged by the sequel, to have been a blunder.

A few moments later, Sam, who had ridden beside his father and Harold as long as he was allowed to, was watching the scene from the front rank of the irregular line of settlers, while Peterson, Escott, and Harold, a little in advance of the main body, were confronting the marshal's armed men. These were drawn up in a field near the roadside; they were clustered under an oak tree, and about the wagon in which they had been carrying their arms and equipment. The marshal was calling out in a loud voice to the newcomers: "I want to hear no word from you men. I am doing my duty. I cannot parley with armed bands. I have no quarrel with any of you. I have come to put these here parties in possession of certain tracts. You must not bar my way. Disperse, I tell you, disperse." The marshal was a great heavy man, like Alonzo, but his face was red, smooth, dull, and fat, and his little black eyes looked mean and wicked. Yet he was plainly a brave fellow, who meant to do his official duty. Beside him, just in front of the wagon, Alonzo and Tom, both on horseback. Buzzard and Foster, armed with repeating rifles, stood up in the wagon, behind the other men. Sam, who himself had a rifle slung over his shoulder, found himself uneasily fingering it, as he looked at Tom. "That is my sister's murderer," he said to himself. But now Escott was speaking.

"Alonzo Eldon," he said, "it's with you that I want word here, before all these people; and not on my behalf, but on theirs. You don't want the shedding of innocent blood, man, and so—"

"That's a brave word there, Escott!" shouted out with a harsh and unnatural exertion the usually so soft voice of Tom Eldon. Tom was terribly excited. His black eyes flashed, his body quivered with rage; the horse on which he rode took impatiently a step or two forwards, as Tom spoke. "It's a brave word that, about innocent blood, when you lead here these innocent men armed for fight in your own cause. Disperse them first, and then there'll be no blood shed here, at least no innocent blood."

"Tom Eldon," said Escott sternly, "with you I've no reckoning now, nor do I come here to talk to any but men who can hear a fair speech to its end. To you, Alonzo Eldon, I have something to say that may end this land trouble at once. Will you hear me, I ask you again? Will you hear me on behalf of these innocent men, whose property you seem to be threatening?"

"Your own bogus property, Escott," answered Alonzo sternly, "is what's now in danger. For today I have come here to dispossess traitors. Innocent men and quiet citizens have nothing to do but stay at home."

"I'm glad to hear you say that, Alonzo. I don't come here on my own account. Take my property if you will. Call me traitor if you must. my What I ask is a word on behalf of these men."

"Not a word, sir, until you and they lay down your arms."

"I myself have not asked them to arm and come here, Eldon. Finding them armed, I have joined them, unarmed myself, to intercede with you, and plead for a prevention of bloodshed."

"Fine interceders you and Harold make, sir!" Tom again broke in.

"If Mr. Eldon," said Harold now, and in his clearest tone, "if, as I well know, you and your son have come here today more on my account than on that of any other man living, I may join my voice to ask that you should behave like honest men, and that you should fight out your quarrels elsewhere with me whom you call your enemy. But don't come here to vex the peace of this place merely because you hate me. You know what you are here for. You are here because you believe that I have wronged you, so, meet me as you will and where you will; I am ready for you. But, now that you are here, say plainly to this company that your fight isn't with them, but with Escott on my sole account, and with me for myself. Then, when you have pledged your word not to molest them, take Escott's land as you will, and leave the settlers in peace. He and I can be ready for you elsewhere."

"Our fight," came back Tom's voice, "is with traitors, old and young, and with all who follow them, and bear arms here to help them against the law and the courts of the land."

"I'll not hear my father called traitor!" cried Sam Escott. as he spoke, his horse was becoming very restive. Peterson roughly ordered silence, and Alf Escott's stern voice joined itself to Peterson's. But a certain confused murmur from behind encouraged Sam. The marshal had been, meanwhile, very quietly removing his hat and wiping his forehead, for the sun was hot and the marshal's courage was cool; but at Sam's words the marshal was once more on the alert. His hand seized the bridle, which had fallen on his horse's neck. He laid his other hand by his belt.

"Steady here, all of you!" he shouted to his own men, perceiving that they were excited. The two main bodies were not more than fifteen or twenty paces apart, and the situation was growing momentarily worse. Nearly every one heard all that was said at the front, for the speaking was loud and clear, and an almost perfect silence had prevailed in the main bodies. Sam, however, went on: "You, Tom Eldon, are no man to call Alf Escott traitor, you, whose whole soul is nothing but an accursed lie." Sam had once heard his father use this expression, and it pleased him now in his rage. Alf and Peterson vainly tried to quiet the young man or to drown his voice. As for Tom Eldon, his Spanish eyes glowed none the less for this word. He drew his pistol.

The next instant firing began. Nobody could ever afterwards be sure whence came the first shot. Most witnesses declared that Buzzard fired first from the wagon, over Tom Eldon's head. There was, however, much conflict of testimony; and Sam, who was indicted later for murder, was never tried on that charge, just because of this conflict of testimony. At all events, he himself was sure that he heard several bullets whiz by him, and at least a dozen shots fired, before he did more than to try to control his terrified horse. But thereafter, as soon as he realized what it all meant, he sprang from the saddle, let the horse go, raised his own rifle deliberately, and shot full at Tom Eldon. By that time more than half of the marshal's party were in flight, the settlers were discharging their guns from all sides, and a number of settlers also had either fallen or fled. Buzzard, a tall, fierce, dark, heavily bearded man, fired steadily and coolly with his repeating, rifle from his standing place in the wagon. Alonzo Eldon, like Escott, had carried no arms to the battlefield, and at first sat, grim and stiff, on his great black horse, which seemed as cool as himself.

All these things Sam saw, but like a man in dream. He seemed, after his one shot, to stand for a moment paralyzed, not with fear, for he positively amused at the sights before him, but with a numb sense of wonder, and feeling that something unheard of had happened. What! had he actually shot his man? And Tom Eldon? The ancient wrong avenged! For Tom had fallen. The next moment, however, Sam saw his own father close by his side, felt that he himself was staggering, saw strange colors before his eyes, and then knew no more for a long time.

Harold, five minutes later, found himself at the centre of the excited group. The firing had ceased. Buzzard lay dead where the wagon had left him, when the horses at last grew unmanageable and ran away. Tom Eldon was close beside him, whether dead or alive could not be told as yet. Escott and his son were just being carried off by some settlers. Alf Escott was not senseless, but had received two or three ugly looking hurts. Alonzo Eldon, uninjured, was kneeling beside Tom. The marshal, also unhurt, was now disarmed, and a prisoner in the hands of the score of Rangers who, with shogun, pistol, and rifle, had borne the brunt of the battle. These men also surrounded Alonzo. The firing had been remarkably effective, owing to the very short range. Somewhere between two and three hundred shots had been fired, and, on both sides, as many as sixteen men had been struck. Of these, five were already certainly dead, among them Collins. Peterson was helpless with a bad wound. The most effective work, during the skirmish, had been undoubtedly done by Buzzard's repeating rifle. Six or eight men must have been struck by him. How Alonzo Eldon had escaped unhurt was thenceforth a mystery.

Alf Escott and Harold never spoke to each other again. During the day Harold, at his own serious peril, was first busy in saving Alonzo's life from the fury of the settlers, who had taken the old man prisoner; and, having succeeded in this, was then seeking to get Alonzo and the unconscious Tom to a place of safety. But Escott, his wounds ill cared for, his mind anxious about his son, his bed hard and uncomfortable, was slowly dying, through loss of blood and through an old man's weakness, at the house of the nearest settler. He lived until about sunset. He was very cheerful, save for his anxiety about Sam. He could not be persuaded, even by Bertha Boscowitz, to spare himself. He much hastened his death by restlessness and by talking. When they told him about Alonzo's peril, and that the settlers were threatening to hang the old man, Escott could hardly be prevented from going out to speak against the atrocity. As it was, he sent Bertha with a message to Harold. When they told Escott how Harold had taken advantage of a lull in the storm of indignation to speak on Eldon's behalf, how Harold had openly and with reckless courage taken the blame of all that day's bloodshed upon his own shoulders, had insisted that he himself, by some unexplained act of treason to Eldon, was the cause of this scene, and was alone the murderer, and had then used the dying Escott's name as a last and highest ground of appeal, Escott applauded the news rapturously. Just then Sam seemed much better, too, and Escott fell thereupon to joking. "I don't want old Alonzo to die before old Chrysostom Hahn," he said, "because it isn't fair to Alonzo that Chrysostom should preach the funeral sermon. Alonzo deserves better of the world than that."

When he later heard that Alonzo had really managed to convey his sorely wounded son out of the town, Escott expressed yet more satisfaction. "Poor Harold," said he, as if to himself. "It's a lonely life before him, whoever lives or dies. He'll see but few friends in the world from henceforth." Late in the afternoon, Sam improved so much that the one doctor, who at last, in his slow rounds among the wounded, bad come here, assured Alf that the boy was in no danger. "You needn't say anything about whether I am myself or not," said Escott. "I know all about it."

The last hour or two Escott employed, when his voice would let him, in giving messages and directions to Bertha, who bore up wonderfully on this day for one who was in such poor health. He had good advice for Bertha herself; messages for his wife, for Emily, for Harold, and, last of all, one for Alonzo. "Tell Alonzo," he said, "be sure to tell Alonzo that if he's satisfied now on thinking over what Harold has done to see that this is all an infernal mistake, and that I've never betrayed him well, then, I don't, as I die, care for the mistake any more. Tell him I die his friend, Bertha. And tell him, too as my dying declaration, that there is, as I solemnly believe, no cause why he should not be reconciled to his daughter-in-law. Tell him that last in secret, Bertha, and from me. Don't neglect it. As for me, Bertha, my last lecture is about done. Class is excused!"

Escott died very quietly, and he now lies buried in the shadow of Mount Diablo. The settlers honor his grave. Nearly everyone in San Francisco has by this time forgotten him.

But Sam lived to be tried, with others, for conspiracy to defeat the processes of the courts. The ingenuous fellow was acquitted. And today he is his mother's only comfort.

There is little more to tell. All these events are so recent! What can have happened since? Tom Eldon was brought to Martinez, where he soon afterwards died. Margaret was with him at the last. He probably never recognized her as he lay there. She and Alonzo were later, though very imperfectly, reconciled. Harold's bearing that day had put him and the past in a new light before Alonzo's mind. But what would have taken place between them had they ever met afterwards does not appear. Harold waited long enough in the State to find that no prosecution would be begun against him for his share in the affair at Oakfield Creek. Then he vanished.

Frank Norris, from *The Octopus*

[Editor's note: Frank Norris ends his famous novel, *The Octopus* (New York: Doubleday, 1901), in Port Costa, at the point where the Sacramento–San Joaquin River Delta empties into San Francisco Bay. Earlier in the novel, he describes a confrontation between rancher/farmers and investors similar to the confrontation Royce details. Both are retellings of the actual event that occurred near Tulare. However, in addition to the tensions between those who work the land and those who invest, Norris is sensitive to the role agriculture grown in the Sacramento–San Joaquin River Delta and Central Valley plays in the world beyond California. He appreciates the involvement of the region in the world market. See Fig. 19.]

Excerpts from Chapter 9

Upon descending from his train at Port Costa, S. Behrman asked to be directed at once to where the bark "Swanhilda" was taking on grain. Though he had bought and greatly enlarged his new elevator at this port, he had never seen it. The work had been carried on through agents, S. Behrman having far too many and more pressing occupations to demand his presence and attention. Now, however, he was to see the concrete evidence of his success for the first time.

He picked his way across the railroad tracks to the line of warehouses that bordered the docks, numbered with enormous Roman numerals and full of grain in bags. The sight of these bags of grain put him in mind of the fact that among all the other shippers he was practically alone in his way of handling his wheat. They handled the grain in bags; he, however, preferred it in the bulk. Bags were sometimes four cents apiece, and he had decided to build his elevator and bulk his grain therein, rather than to incur this expense. Only a small part of his wheat—that on Number Three division—had been sacked. All the rest, practically two-thirds of the entire harvest of Los Muertos, now found itself warehoused in his enormous elevator at Port Costa.

To a certain degree it had been the desire of observing the working of his system of handling the wheat in bulk that had drawn S. Behrman to Port Costa. But the more powerful motive had been curiosity, not to say downright sentiment. So long had he planned for this day of triumph, so eagerly had he looked forward to it, that now, when it had come, he wished to enjoy it to its fullest extent, wished to miss no feature of the disposal of the crop. He had watched it harvested, he had watched it hauled to the railway, and now would watch it as it poured into the hold of the ship, would even watch the ship as she cleared and got under way.

He passed through the warehouses and came out upon the dock that ran parallel with the shore of the bay. A great quantity of shipping was in view, barques for the most part, Cape Horners, great, deep sea tramps, whose iron-shod forefeet had parted every ocean the world round from Rangoon to Rio Janeiro, and from Melbourne to Christiania. Some were still in the stream, loaded with wheat to the Plimsoll mark, ready to depart with the next tide. But many others laid their great flanks alongside the docks and at that moment were being filled by derrick and crane with thousands upon thousands of bags of wheat. The scene was brisk; the cranes creaked and swung incessantly with a rattle of chains; stevedores and wharfingers toiled and perspired; boatswains and dock masters shouted orders, drays rumbled, the water lapped at the piles; a group of sailors, painting the flanks of one of the great ships, raised an occasional chanty; the trade wind sang aeolian in the cordages, filling the air with the nimble taint of salt. All around were the noises of ships and the feel and flavor of the sea.

S. Behrman soon discovered his elevator. It was the largest structure discernible, and upon its red roof, in enormous white letters, was his own name. Thither, between piles of grain bags, halted drays, crates and boxes of merchandise, with an occasional pyramid of salmon cases, S. Behrman took his way. Cabled to the dock, close under his elevator, lay a great ship with lofty masts and great spars. Her stern was toward him as he approached, and upon it, in raised golden letters, he could read the words "Swanhilda—Liverpool."

He went aboard by a very steep gangway and found the mate on the quarter deck. S. Behrman introduced himself.

"Well," he added, "how are you getting on?"

"Very fairly, sir," returned the mate, who was an Englishman. "We'll have her all snugged down tight by this time, day after tomorrow. It's a great saving of time shunting the stuff in her like that, and three men can do the work of seven."

"I'll have a look 'round, I believe," returned S. Behrman.

"Right oh," answered the mate with a nod.

S. Behrman went forward to the hatch that opened down into the vast hold of the ship. A great iron chute connected this hatch with the elevator, and through it was rushing a veritable cataract of wheat.

It came from some gigantic bin within the elevator itself, rushing down the confines of the chute to plunge into the roomy, gloomy interior of the hold with an incessant, metallic roar, persistent, steady, inevitable. No men were in sight. The place was deserted. No human agency seemed to be back of the movement of the wheat. Rather, the grain seemed impelled with a force of its own, a resistless, huge force, eager, vivid, impatient for the sea.

S. Behrman stood watching, his ears deafened with the roar of the hard grains against the metallic lining of the chute. He put his hand once into the rushing tide, and the contact rasped the flesh of his fingers and like an undertow drew his hand after it in its impetuous dash.

Cautiously he peered down into the hold. A musty odour rose to his nostrils, the vigorous, pungent aroma of the raw cereal. It was dark. He could see nothing; but all about and over the opening of the hatch the air was full of a fine, impalpable dust that blinded the eyes and choked the throat and nostrils.

As his eyes became used to the shadows of the cavern below him, he began to distinguish the grey mass of the wheat, a great expanse, almost liquid in its texture, which, as the cataract from above plunged into it, moved and shifted in long, slow eddies. As he stood there, this cataract on a sudden increased in volume. He turned about, casting his eyes upward toward the elevator to discover the cause. His foot caught in a coil of rope, and he fell headforemost into the hold.

The fall was a long one and he struck the surface of the wheat with the sodden impact of a bundle of damp clothes. For the moment, he was stunned. All the breath was driven from his body. He could neither move nor cry out. But, by degrees, his wits steadied themselves and his breath returned to him. He looked about and above him. The daylight in the hold was dimmed and clouded by the thick, chaff-dust thrown off by the pour of grain, and even this dimness dwindled to twilight at a short distance from the opening of the hatch, while the remotest quarters were lost in impenetrable blackness. He got upon his feet only to find that he sunk ankle deep in the loose packed mass underfoot.

"Hell," he muttered, "here's a fix."

Directly underneath the chute, the wheat, as it poured in, raised itself in a conical mound, but from the sides of this mound it shunted away incessantly in thick layers, flowing in all directions with the nimbleness of water. Even as S. Behrman spoke, a wave of grain poured around his legs and rose rapidly to the level of his knees. He stepped quickly back. To stay near the chute would soon bury him to the waist.

No doubt, there was some other exit from the hold, some companion ladder that led up to the deck. He scuffled and waded across the wheat, groping in the dark with outstretched hands. With every inhalation he choked, filling his mouth and nostrils more with dust than with air. At times he could not breathe at all, but gagged and gasped, his lips distended. But search as he would he could find no outlet to the hold, no stairway, no companion ladder. Again and again, staggering along in the black darkness, he bruised his knuckles and forehead against the iron sides of the ship. He gave up the attempt to find any interior means of escape and returned laboriously to the space under the open hatchway. Already he could see that the level of the wheat was raised.

"God," he said, "this isn't going to do at all." He uttered a great shout. "Hello, on deck there, somebody. For God's sake."

The steady, metallic roar of the pouring wheat drowned out his voice. He could scarcely hear it himself above the rush of the cataract. Besides this, he found it impossible to stay under the hatch. The flying grains of wheat, spattering as they fell, stung his face like wind-driven particles of ice. It was a veritable torture; his hands smarted with it. Once he was all but blinded. Furthermore, the succeeding waves of wheat, rolling from the mound under the chute, beat him back, swirling and dashing against his legs and knees, mounting swiftly higher, carrying him off his feet.

Once more he retreated, drawing back from beneath the hatch. He stood still for a moment and shouted again. It was in vain. His voice returned upon him, unable to penetrate the thunder of the chute, and horrified, he discovered that so soon as he stood motionless upon the wheat, he sank into it. Before he knew it, he was knee-deep again, and a long swirl of grain sweeping outward from the ever-breaking, ever-reforming pyramid below the chute, poured around his thighs, immobilizing him.

A frenzy of terror suddenly leaped to life within him. The horror of death, the Fear of The Trap, shook him like a dry reed. Shouting, he tore himself free of the wheat and once more scrambled and struggled towards the hatchway. He stumbled as he reached it and fell directly beneath the pour. Like a storm of small shot, mercilessly, pitilessly, the unnumbered multitude of hurtling grains flagellated and beat and tore his flesh. Blood streamed from his forehead and, thickening with the powder-like chaff-dust, blinded his eyes. He struggled to his feet once more. An avalanche from the cone of wheat buried him to his thighs. He was forced back and back and back, beating the air, falling, rising, howling for aid. He could no longer see; his eyes, crammed with dust, smarted as if transfixed with needles whenever he opened them. His mouth was full of the dust, his lips were dry with it; thirst tortured him, while his outcries choked and gagged in his rasped throat.

And all the while without stop, incessantly, inexorably, the wheat, as if moving with a force all its own, shot downward in a prolonged roar, persistent, steady, inevitable.

He retreated to a far corner of the hold and sat down with his back against the iron hull of the ship and tried to collect his thoughts, to calm himself. Surely there must be some way of escape; surely he was not to die like this, die in this dreadful substance that was neither solid nor fluid. What was he to do? How make himself heard?

But even as he thought about this, the cone under the chute broke again and sent a great layer of grain rippling and tumbling toward him. It reached him where he sat and buried his hand and one foot.

He sprang up trembling and made for another corner.

"By God," he cried, "by God, I must think of something pretty quick!"

Once more the level of the wheat rose and the grains began piling deeper about him. Once more he retreated. Once more he crawled staggering to the foot of the cataract, screaming till his ears sang and his eyeballs strained in their sockets, and once more the relentless tide drove him back.

Then began that terrible dance of death; the man dodging, doubling, squirming, hunted from one corner to another, the wheat slowly, inexorably flowing, rising, spreading to every angle, to every nook and cranny. It reached his middle. Furious and with bleeding hands and broken nails, he dug his way out to fall backward, all but exhausted, gasping for breath in the dust-thickened air. Roused again by the slow advance of the tide, he leaped up and stumbled away, blinded with the agony in his eyes, only to crash against the metal hull of the vessel. He turned about, the blood streaming from his face, and paused to collect his senses, and with a rush, another wave swirled about his ankles and knees. Exhaustion grew upon him. To stand still meant to sink; to lie or sit meant to be buried the quicker; and all this in the dark, all this in an air that could scarcely be breathed, all this while he fought an enemy that could not be gripped, toiling in a sea that could not be stayed.

Guided by the sound of the falling wheat, S. Behrman crawled on hands and knees toward the hatchway. Once more he raised his voice in a shout for help. His bleeding throat and raw, parched lips refused to utter but a wheezing moan. Once more he tried to look toward the one patch of faint light above him. His eyelids, clogged with chaff, could no longer open. The Wheat poured about his waist as he raised himself upon his knees.

Reason fled. Deafened with the roar of the grain, blinded and made dumb with its chaff, he threw himself forward with clutching fingers, rolling upon his back, and lay there, moving feebly, the head rolling from side to side. The wheat, leaping continuously from the chute, poured around him. It filled the pockets of the coat, it crept up the sleeves and trouser legs, it covered the great, protuberant stomach, it ran at last in rivulets into the distended, gasping mouth. It covered the face. Upon the surface of the Wheat, under the chute, nothing moved but the wheat itself. There was no sign of life. Then, for an instant, the surface stirred. A hand, fat, with short fingers and swollen veins, reached up, clutching, then fell limp and prone. In another instant, it was covered. In the hold of the "*Swanhilda*" there was no movement but the widening ripples that spread flowing from the ever-breaking, ever-reforming cone; no sound, but the rushing of the Wheat that continued to plunge incessantly from the iron chute in a prolonged roar, persistent, steady, inevitable.

Excerpt from Chapter 10, Conclusion, *The Octopus*

The "*Swanhilda*" cast off from the docks at Port Costa two days after Presley had left Bonneville and the ranches and made her way up to San Francisco, anchoring in the stream off the City front. A few hours after her arrival, Presley, waiting at his club, received a dispatch from Cedarquist to the effect that she would clear early the next morning and that he must be aboard of her before midnight.

He sent his trunks aboard and at once hurried to Cedarquist's office to say good-bye. He found the manufacturer in excellent spirits …

"The '*Swanhilda*' is the mother of the fleet, Pres. I had to buy her, but the keel of her sister ship will be laid by the time she discharges at Calcutta. We'll carry our wheat into Asia yet. The Anglo-Saxon started from there at the beginning of everything and its manifest destiny that he must circle the globe and fetch up where he began his march. You are up with procession, Pres, going to India this way in a wheat ship that flies American colors. By the way, do you know where the money is to come from to build the sister ship of the '*Swanhilda*'? From the sale of the plant and scrap iron of the Atlas Works. Yes, I've given it up definitely, that business. The people here would not back me up. But I'm working off on this new line now. It may break me, but we'll try it on. You know the 'Million Dollar Fair' was formally opened yesterday. There is," he added with a wink, "a Midway Pleasance in connection with the thing. Mrs. Cedarquist and our friend Hartrath 'got up a subscription' to construct a figure of California—heroic size—out of dried apricots. I assure you," he remarked with prodigious gravity, "it is a real work of art and quite a 'feature' of the Fair. Well, good luck to you, Pres. Write to me from Honolulu, and bon voyage. My respects to the hungry Hindoo. Tell him 'we're coming, Father Abraham, a hundred thousand more.' Tell the men of the East to look out for the men of the West. The irrepressible Yank is knocking at the doors of their temples and he will want to sell 'em carpet-sweepers for their harems and electric light plants for their temple shrines. Good-bye to you."

"Good-bye, sir" ...

The *"Swanhilda"* lifted and rolled slowly, majestically on the ground swell of the Pacific, the water hissing and boiling under her forefoot, her cordage vibrating and droning in the steady rush of the trade winds. It was drawing towards evening and her lights had just been set ...

Those were the mountains of the Coast range and beyond them was what once had been his home ...

The drama was over. The fight of Ranch and Railroad had been wrought out to its dreadful close. It was true, as Shelgrim had said, that forces rather than men had locked horns in that struggle, but for all that the men of the Ranch and not the men of the Railroad had suffered. Into the prosperous valley, into the quiet community of farmers, that galloping monster, that terror of steel and steam had burst, shooting athwart the horizons, flinging the echo of its thunder over all the ranches of the valley, leaving blood and destruction in its path.

Yes, the Railroad had prevailed. The ranches had been seized in the tentacles of the octopus; the iniquitous burden of extortionate freight rates had been imposed like a yoke of iron ... What then was left? Was there no hope, no outlook for the future, no rift in the black curtain, no glimmer through the night? Was good to be thus overthrown? Was evil thus to be strong and to prevail? Was nothing left?

Then suddenly Vanamee's words came back to his mind. What was the larger view, what contributed the greatest good to the greatest numbers? What was the full round of the circle whose segment only he beheld? In the end, the ultimate, final end of all, what was left? Yes, good issued from this crisis, untouched, unassailable, undefiled.

Men—motes in the sunshine—perished, were shot down in the very noon of life, hearts were broken, little children started in life lamentably handicapped; young girls were brought to a life of shame; old women died in the heart of life for lack of food. In that little, isolated group of human insects, misery, death, and anguish spun like a wheel of fire.

But the wheat remained. Untouched, unassailable, undefiled, that mighty world-force, that nourisher of nations, wrapped in Nirvanic calm, indifferent to the human swarm, gigantic, resistless, moved onward in its appointed grooves. Through the welter of blood at the irrigation ditch, through the sham charity and shallow philanthropy of famine relief committees, the great harvest of Los Muertos rolled like a flood from the Sierras to the Himalayas to feed thousands of starving scarecrows on the barren plains of India.

Falseness dies; injustice and oppression in the end of everything fade and vanish away. Greed, cruelty, selfishness, and inhumanity are short-lived; the individual suffers, but the race goes on. Annixter dies, but in a far distant corner of the world a thousand lives are saved. The larger view always and through all shams, all wickednesses, discovers the Truth that will, in the end, prevail, and all things, surely, inevitably, resistlessly work together for good.

Rockwell Hunt, from *Boyhood Days of Mr. California*

[Editor's note: Rockwell Hunt was called "Mr. California" because of his contributions to the history of California. In *Boyhood Days of Mr. California* (self-published, 1965), he recalls his coming of age in a small Sacramento–San Joaquin River Delta community, Freeport (Chapters 4 and 5). His recollections here are of small town life, on the edge of the agribusiness struggles taking place at the same time in the Sacramento–San Joaquin River Delta. Life was, however, dependent on the railroad and steamboats. (*By permission*). See Fig. 20.]

Chapter 4: The Little Village Called Freeport

Freeport is a tiny village situated on the east bank of the Sacramento River, about eight miles south of the Capitol Building and business center of the city of Sacramento. It is not really a ghost town, for two reasons: first, it was never large enough to deserve the name of town; second, it has always been active, as a village, and even now does not show very great change in appearance from that of early days. But Sacramento, the capital of California, has grown to be one of the large cities of the state since, was born there in 1868; and it is expanding rapidly in all directions at the present time.

But little Freeport does have an interesting history. It was founded in 1862 by the Freeport Railroad Company, which intended it to be a "free port"— Sacramento was not a free port at that time. And besides, the name fits in well, at the time of the Civil War. The Sacramento River, its border on the west, has always been the principal feature, though now the Freeport Boulevard, with all of its automobiles, has become very important.

Freeport took its beginning from a dispute between some railroad men and the city of Sacramento. For a little while it looked like Freeport might even become the chief shipping port. I can still remember some of the big wooden piles, used for a pier, that remained for years, in the river, of the port or wharf, and how they swayed back and forth when the water was high, at the O'Toole place, all gone, a long time ago. In 1866 the railroad men built a branch line from Freeport that connected with the main line near Brighton, nine miles to the east, and not touching Sacramento at all.

A few years later the Central Pacific Company bought the Freeport Road and tore up the rails, almost before they ever came into general use. I'm old enough to remember what we boys called the "First Hill" on the road to Sacramento, less than half a mile north of our home: it was simply the grade crossing for the railroad—a lot of gravel had been hauled in for that purpose. Many a time did we boys go up to the "First Hill" to get a supply of stones for our slings and to throw at birds and other targets. There was no gravel around our home. I can remember when father drove a good long distance in Yolo County, across the river, to a bed of gravel, maybe in a branch of Putah Creek to the first gravel bed I ever saw, for a load of scratch gravel for our chickens. We boys made a good many trips to the "First Hill," with an empty soap-box to fill it with good stones to throw, and then drag it back home, with a piece of "baling rope."

During those very early days the village grew rapidly, until it had a population of almost 400 people. There was a general store, a Wells Fargo Express office, blacksmith shop, hotel, and saloon; and the flat-bottom ferryboat across the river was started. But after the railroad was taken away, the village has never been so large again—the present population is about 125.

The first white child born in Freeport we knew by the name of Pete Frick; but his full name was Henry Clay Freeport Frick, and for a while some of the grown-ups teased him by calling him "Henry Clay Freeport Mowe Robinson Pete Frick." I never knew why all that name was given.

He was born in 1863, while the railroad was being built. He said he had been christened at one of the camp meetings that used to be held at Freeport. Of course, we all knew Pete well when we were boys together, he was a little older than my brother Mark, and was one of our constant companions, everybody seemed to like him. For most of his life Pete lived at Freeport, but he moved to Sacramento for his later years.

The first store in Freeport was built by A. J. Bump, in 1863; and the first, and only, hotel—a very small one two stories high, was opened the same year. Then came the blacksmith shop and other buildings.

Now I want to tell you about the flagpole; for it was the chief landmark for miles around Freeport, and one of the first things to be noticed, coming from either direction. It was raised at the time of the U. S. Grant campaign for president, about the time I was born. The beautiful pole was made of three pieces, each piece from a straight fir tree, and all perfectly spliced together and bound by two sets of iron rings, making it look like a single piece, trimmed to be round and smooth, gradually tapering from bottom to top, in all 135 feet tall.

But how could such a pole ever be raised by the farmers of Freeport? It must have been a very hard job. But it was done with success by using what is called a block-and-tackle and the strength of a yoke of oxen and span of mules, handled by a skillful driver. On its very top was a big red rooster, made of metal, which made a good weather vane.

The pole stood just at the corner of the Freeport Road and the Ferry Road, only a few feet away from our fence, near the first big fig tree. Sometimes, on special occasions, like the Fourth of July, a large flag was hoisted to the top and unfurled. When the flagpole needed a fresh coat of paint, "Skysel" Jack was ready for the job. All the boys envied him because he was such an expert climber. He did not live in Freeport. I don't know how he got that strange nickname.

One thing I remember so well; we often tested our ability to throw stones up alongside the pole. I felt good when I could throw a stone, or green apple, above the "first rings"; only the bigger boys could throw up to the second rings. And I don't think any of us could throw clear over the red rooster at the very top.

One other thing it is pleasant to remember was that when we were riding down the river in our wagon, we would look back every now and then to see the flag-pole; and because of the bends in the river we had to look for it in different directions, this seemed odd to us. We were just following the river bends in the winding road. When that tall pole had to come down, Freeport lost its best landmark; it was never quite the same any more.

What might be called the center of the village was the general store, with saloon in the back part, first owned by Mr. Bump. Of course, the stock of cloth and other dry goods was not large; but there always seemed to be plenty of liquor.

Many of the farmers stopped there to give their horses a good drink, at the water trough, while they stepped inside to make some small purchase. In the saloon there was also some gambling; but not one of us five brothers went into the saloon or formed the habit of gambling, and that was because our mother was very strict about such things. For this we could never be too thankful. She had seen the evil of such things.

When we said we were "going to town" that meant going to Sacramento, a ride of about eight miles. Along the road were located a few "road houses," where drivers often stopped to give their horses a drink, and where liquor and tobacco were the chief things to sell. They were really saloons: by many they were given the name "dead falls."

The Freeport Post Office was in the front part of the store, on the right side as you entered from the wide plank porch, with its wooden bench. For years the mail came only once a week, but later twice a week, brought down from Sacramento in an express wagon. "Going to the Post Office" to get the mail was one of the real events of the week; several of us used to go together. But we never received much mail, except the Sacramento Union, the Pacific Rural Press, and especially the Youths' Companion. One day we broke the family record by receiving in all, nine letters-that was so unusual that I never forgot it!

The village store keeper, who was usually postmaster, too, and owner of the saloon, was thought of as the most important man in the community. To some it almost seemed that what he said was the law. D. G. Webber was the principal owner of the store when we were young boys -Fred Webber was one of my first playmates. When his older brother Lew was drowned in the river, all the young people were made very sad.

For a good while Webber's Store was a kind of natural place for a group of men of the community to get together and sit around the pot-bellied stove of an evening, a sort of town meeting only there was no town, and no head to the group; just a bunch of what you might call old cronies. It was commonly a "Gas Fest," where they could let off steam and "chew the rag."

But the big questions they tackled at times would be fit for elder statesmen, like Bismarck and Gladstone. Someone who agreed with what was being said interrupted now and then with an emphatic "eggsactly"! [*sic*.] But from another quarter came this retort, in a high pitch, "Not on your tintype!"

One night they got into a dispute about what cabinet officers the new President should choose, Grant, I think it was. There were about as many different opinions as men present, with very little agreement: everyone seemed to know just what the President should do. When my father had "got his fill" of that, he, so to speak, took the floor, and in a very solemn voice declared: "I'll tell just what the President ought to do: he ought to come out here to Freeport and pick his cabinet right here!" The meeting soon adjourned.

Later, the store was bought by Phil G. Riehl, a farmer further down the river. We did not know it then, but years later we could see that our own father and Phil Riehl came to be rivals as leading men of Freeport. They did not see things alike. Father did not like the saloon in the back part of the store; but Mr. Riehl worked to increase its business. The difference between them also showed itself in the election for school trustees.

Even our dogs took a part in the rivalry. We had two dogs, and the store keeper had two; they were always looking for a fight. We boys sometimes would "sic" our dogs on the Riehl dogs. Maybe it's only my imagination, but it seemed that every time the fight took place in our yard, the store dogs got licked; but when the fight was in front of the store, the store dogs got the best of it. There were some mighty lively and noisy "scraps" in both places. Anyway, the time came when the store keeper was not able to have his own way about everything in Freeport.

Across the road from the store was the blacksmith shop, and the blacksmith's name was Tom Kirtlan. When father heard me say "Tom" he quietly remarked, "Rock, when you use his name, I wish you would say 'Mr. Kirtlan'". He had large family of boys and girls. I remember Lavina (we always called her "Vine"), Allie, Frank, Fred, Lizzie, Maggie, Arthur—a later one (Elmer) was called "Babe" until another brother was born

(Clarence), who for a while was called, "Little Babe." Among all the boys of Freeport Fred Kirtlan was my chief playmate and schoolmate, he was my classmate, though a little older than I. One day Fred told me that his father had $63, all in the house. I wondered if my father ever had that much money!

I couldn't say how many times I stood there with my hands behind me, watching the blacksmith as he blew the big old-fashioned leather bellows and heated the iron rods and horseshoes in the coal fire to almost white heat, then made the heavy anvil ring and ring with the merry strokes from his swift-moving hammer, which seemed to be a living thing. Then he would seize the iron with his tongs and dip it into the end of the little trough of water at the forge, as it cooled off with a "sizzing" sound.

One of the most interesting things to watch was setting the tires of a big wagon wheel. Very few boys of today, with our rubber tires and free air, ever saw a good country blacksmith set an iron tire on a big wagon wheel. Let me tell you how that was done.

The tire had been taken off from the felloe, or wooden rim, and was then heated in a circle of fire of the same size. Because the spokes and other wooden parts had been shrinking, there had to be a good deal of measuring, so that when the hot iron tire was fitted onto the felloe it was exactly the right size all the way around. After being carefully prepared, it was riveted into place, then cooled by dipping into the water trough, so as to reduce it to be the exact fit for that wheel. A good job of tire setting took a good deal of skill, but it lasted for months, sometimes years.

In the back part of the blacksmith shop was a place for making carriages and cabinet work, with a small paint shop. This was in charge of Jim Lee, an old bachelor, who was known by everybody in the community, including the boys and girls.

But James W. Lee was more than a carriage maker. He could do almost all kinds of jobs, like cutting boys' hair, just as a good neighbor, and making row boats during floods, and sometimes making a fine bow when he had a good piece of hickory wood, as favor for some lucky boy. He was bald-headed but had a long black beard, and always wore fancy boots that tightly fitted his small feet. As near as anybody else, when dressed in his "Sunday best," he was the village dandy, and he didn't seem to have an enemy.

Andy Greer, boot and shoe maker, had his cosy shop just across from the blacksmith shop, near the store. It was shaded by a silver poplar tree. In all these years I never heard of another man quite like Andy. We of course knew the Greer children, who lived a small distance back of the shop—Emma, Ed, and Charley. His regular seat while at work was a piece of strong leather nailed with a row of brass-headed tacks over a good-sized hole cut in his little bench. It seemed to us that he could sit there in that hollowed out seat all day, pegging away and sewing with his waxed ends that is, tough thread that had been properly waxed.

In spite of his bright red whiskers and the pits from smallpox in his face, Andy was a friend of us boys. He told us many strange stories and sang plenty of funny songs. One I remember began this way: "Punkin' pie and a bottle of gin/Got so hot the head fell in."

Sometimes he treated us to a little candy, but more often to a piece of black sewing wax, to use as gum. He knew how to make a fine whip lash. He would stick his sharp knife blade into a piece of waste leather on his cutting board and draw it by the edge of the blade with rapid motion, round and round, till the whole piece was changed into a fine long lash, which would make any boy proud to own.

When we found out that it didn't take much to disturb him, we played some practical jokes on him. I'll tell you about one.

Some of us boys arranged a heavy weight held by a wire, directly over the shop, by a branch of the tree, and the wire was stretched across the road and brought down along a tree to the ground, where the boys, hidden from sight, could control the weight without being seen. When everything was ready, about dark, the weight suddenly dropped on the roof of the shop. Andy rushed out, looked up and all around, but couldn't see anything, returned to his work. Again, came the pounding on the roof: again, the excited cobbler rushed out, this time with his hammer in his hand. The boys kept still as death. After the noise was repeated a few times, Andy went over to the store and returned with a lantern; he finally discovered the weight up in the tree; but by that time the boys had made tracks to places of safety; so Mr. Greer never found out who the guilty boys were.

In my boyhood days no one ever dreamed of such a thing as a modern supermarket, which are now spreading in all directions -and the same about buying things by the self-service method. Take a look at the butcher wagon, for instance, that used to come along the road, once or twice week, loaded with an assortment of different kinds of meat for sale.

The meat man never seemed to be in a hurry. Mother went out to make purchases for a few days ahead; there then being no ice or Frigidaire; the meat wouldn't "keep" very long. You would hardly believe the prices could be so very low-far lower than now. For 25 cents enough round steak could be bought to last a family of six or eight two days. A good mess of stew meat cost 10 to 15 cents. The customer could get a soup bone or a piece of liver simply for the asking, as well as some bones for the dog.

The meat man had scales, hanging out of the rear of the wagon, for weighing the purchases. But we never bought much at one time, since we had lots of salt pork on hand—after the fresh pork was gone; we always had chickens, and in season we had a good deal of wild game, especially ducks. I remember how tired I got of having salt pork so often.

In very early days, wild game—ducks, geese, hares, etc.—could be bought in Sacramento and San Francisco; but we, of course, never thought of buying such things in the market; didn't we have enough right at home?

The only hotel in the village, hardly a hotel at all, was run by a German lady, Mrs. Eilbach. It was a short distance north of the store, on the same side of the road. Its windows had old-fashioned blinds, and there were long front porches for both floors. In our time only a few persons lodged there. For years Jim Lee was the only man that stayed there regularly.

While I used to hear about "shivarees" now and then as a boy, I never took part in one of them. They seemed to be more common among the Portuguese living across the river. The hilarious practice followed the wedding of young couple, a very noisy occasion, sometimes rather rough, a kind of serenade, in which things like big kettles, pans, shotguns were used. Those who took part were usually young men young boys were merely lookers-on. It was practice that would not be considered refined today.

The ferryboat was a broad, flat-bottomed boat, held in place against the current by a big hemp rope, later by a wire cable, made fast to a heavy anchor in the middle of the river, two or three hundred yards upstream, to which were attached a series of buoys. The current of the river forced the boat, properly guided, across the river.

Tied to the ferry-boat was always a small skiff, or row boat, to be used for foot passengers and other purposes.

I recall that a few times, during high water when the current was very swift, the ferry-boat broke loose, and was swept down-stream at a dangerous speed. It was a hard job to bring it to a stop, maybe miles below Freeport, by means of a strong rope tied to a big tree. Then it took at least four or five days to tow the heavy boat back by main force to its regular place, using trees on the bank as hitching posts on the way.

Here I must tell you of one funny little incident, when Manuel Rose, a Portuguese, was ferryman. Two teams were on the boat when there came a break. Rushing about the boat, much confused, Manuel shouted to the drivers to seize the anchor and cast it overboard. In his excitement he yelled (in his poor English), "Throw off the honker-the honker!" The drivers finally understood what he was trying to say, and threw the heavy anchor free from the deck into the river, only to discover when it was too late that no chain or rope was attached to it! There was no gain; even the anchor was lost!

Another incident had an element of sadness. One day a runaway horse, hitched to an empty cart, wildly dashed onto the ferryboat, never stopping till he bad leaped off the outer apron of the boat into the river. A day or two later the dead horse and the cart were found several miles down the river, carried down by the current.

Freeport has always been and is today a little bit of a village; you can't even find the name on some of the maps. And now it looks like it may be swallowed up almost any day by the capital city, Sacramento, whose southern limit has reached to the old north fence of the Hunt Ranch. But that little village means a lot to me.

It's where I lived the first nine years of my life, then later years, and where I learned to swim, and row a boat, wade in the soft mud, and go a-fishing. Also, it's where I learned to milk cows and feed calves, to ride a horse bareback, and follow a harrow. It's where I first went to school, a mile from home, and to church in that one-room schoolhouse. It's where my mother had her beautiful flower garden, just next to the Sacramento River; where my father had his dairy, and made butter. It's where I looked at the big steamboats going up and down the river, and at fishermen hauling in their nets with now and then fine big salmon. It's where I saw great flocks of wild geese flying overhead, lined up like an army, going north to Canada, and lots of pelicans, and swans, and sandhill cranes. It's where I really became acquainted with the Sacramento, "River of Gold," in low water time and in flood time, and almost felt that it was my river.

Yes, Freeport was a little bit of a village, but it has meant a lot to me.

Chapter 5: The Sacramento—"River of Gold"

My own childhood days-and those of my four brothers—were so closely linked to the grand old Sacramento River that I decided to write a separate chapter about that river. Our early home was on its eastern bank; every day we saw it, just flowing quietly along during the hot summer days, giving to us some of its coolness, and rushing swiftly by on its way to the Golden Gate in the wet season. It was our constant companion, whatever season it might be. It was there long before there were any Americans, or even Indians; it is still there—the largest river in California—and it will be flowing for centuries to come.

I have a copy of Julian Dana's book, *Sacramento, River of Gold*, which tells us a great deal about the river, and which, in one chapter, describes my own boyhood days there on its banks.

General Mariano G. Vallejo said this river was discovered on the anniversary of the "Lord's Supper," and because of that it was given the beautiful name "Rio Sacramento," which means the river of the holy sacrament. Joaquin Miller, the "Poet of the Sierras," called it the most classic storied as well as most beautiful of all the rivers of this continent." "Here," he continued, "story and glory, golden and glittering harvest are and have been from the first and must remain to the end of time."

Just as Egypt has been called "the gift of the Nile," so our own great northern valley may be called the gift of the Sacramento. In the year 1839 Captain John A. Sutter sailed a schooner, named Sacramento, up the river, and founded Sutter's Fort, which has been restored and is now one of the chief historic landmarks of all California. In the golden days of '49, all kinds of boats—steamboats, ships, schooners, small sail boats—went up and down the river. People from all parts of the world were coming in search of gold; San Francisco and Sacramento became the most important cities in the newly created state.

It was along the branches of the Sacramento, like the American River and the Feather and Pit Rivers, and their many forks, that many of the gold mines were located. But the Sacramento River itself has its beginning far to the north, near the base of Mt. Shasta, which I admire so much that I call it my "favorite mountain" of California, majestic guardian of the north.

In early days, the water in the river was clear, like a mountain stream; and it was deep, so that big steamboats and ocean ships could go clear up to Sacramento; and smaller steamers could go up to Marysville, and even to Red Bluff. Let me give you the names of some of the grand steamboats of my childhood days: *Senator, New World, Capitol, Chrysopolis, Amador, and Yosemite*. Many of the boats were side-wheelers; some had great walking-beams, which were interesting to us boys, as we could see them working up and down, up and down.

But the favorite with us boys was the *S. M. Whipple*; it was beautiful steamboat, all the more wonderful to us because it had what was called a steam calliope on its deck, with its series of loud whistles, something like a big pipe organ.

Sometimes, when we could see the smoke from a steamboat more than mile away, we would rush to the levee and climb up on the windmill tower to get the first sight of it as it came around the "bend," beyond the O'Toole place. And then, if it was the *Whipple*, we were filled with delight; for when it came near we would shout to the men on deck, "Give us a tune! Give us a tune!" and they did that! One of the most popular tunes was "The Girl I Left Behind Me." We could hear the calliope long after it passed our home, maybe a mile or more away. The *Whipple* could beat the other steamboats in a race, too. Of course, they carried passengers in those days; and I know it must have been a very enjoyable ride from Sacramento to San Francisco; the scenery along the shore line was beautiful, with the vine-covered trees and natural plant life of great variety.

For a while the *Sacramento* carried a brass band on its trips, to compete with the *Whipple*: the competition for passengers among the steamers became so sharp that for a short time the "rate war" brought the fare between Sacramento and San Francisco (nearly 100 miles) down to "two bits" (twenty-five cents) with dinner thrown in! That made it cheaper to travel on the steamboat than to stay home!

When hydraulic mining grew to a very large scale, that is, forcing great streams of water through a wide nozzle against the mountain sides in the search for gold, that resulted in filling the beds of streams with dirt and rocks and all kinds of rubbish, called debris; also there were vast quantities of yellow mud, called "slickens." In some cases the whole side of a mountain was washed away, which destroyed much of its natural beauty.

All this had a very bad effect on the Sacramento River; it was no longer the clear mountain stream it had been before; and besides, the river bed was badly clogged up with rubbish of all kinds, so that the big side-wheelers I saw as a young boy could no longer reach Sacramento; the water in the river was too shallow. Stern wheelers, which did not require such deep water, took their place.

Of all the many steamboats we used to see, the *San Joaquin No. 2*, a freight boat, was the one we saw most often. It was a fine sight to see it on the way to San Francisco tugging behind a string of three large barges, all loaded with tier on tier of sacks of wheat. I remember when the fine passenger steamers *Modoc* and *Apache* first began to go up and down the river; but the *Delta King* and *Delta Queen*, which came still later, were the most beautiful of all the stern wheelers.

The first stern wheeler that carried passengers was the *Continental* this was one of the few steamboats that had two tall smoke stacks. The names of some of the other stern wheelers were the *Julia, Cora, Chin du Wan, San Joaquin No. 1*; many others came later. *San Joaquin No. 2* seemed to be the busiest of all. I'd like to know just how many trips between San Francisco and Sacramento that steamer really made; must be a good many hundreds.

Some of the first money-small money it was-we ever earned as small boys was received from bottles, corks, and driftwood collected along the river bank. We liked very much, during summer time when the water was low, to go wading in the "slickens" along the edge of the river, with pants rolled up above our knees, looking for little things that had drifted in from the current; some things we could sell or trade, and just for the fun we got out of it.

Of course, anything we picked up was not usually worth as much as a dime, and at that time there were no nickels. But at the store, we could exchange bottles and good corks for what were really little prize boxes, called "King William." Each was a small paper box, with the picture of a prince or king on the outside, and about a dozen little pieces of candy inside; but also a cheap prize in every package. These prize boxes were very popular in those days; but I have never seen one for many years. Sometimes they had mottoes printed on the outside, like this one: "Here you go-try box,/Before you go, buy a box."

Every boy will understand that we thought one of the principal uses of the river was as a place to go in swimming. What's the use of a big river like that if not a place in which to go swimming, just as soon as the water was warm enough for comfort? I have told about our favorite swimming hole in another chapter.

But the river was not very safe for little boys: most of us first learned to swim out in the canal or the "back water," before going in the river. I shall never forget the time when was able to swim clear across the river. It made me feel big and proud. When a dozen of us boys, of different ages, went in swimming together, we had fun in the good old Sacramento.

It was along the beautiful river bank, before the great trees were chopped down, or up-rooted by the giant dredger, destroying the beauty of the scenery, that we used to go "wild-graping." Here and there the vines hung in graceful festoons upon the lofty sycamore trees and the giant oaks and certain kinds of willows. In the fall we could gather enough wild grapes for the winter's supply of jelly—and they made good jelly too.

But going wild blackberrying, on the Yolo side of the river, was a still bigger event. The best places were a half mile or more back from the river. Sometimes a dozen or so of us went together-boys and girls of different ages-taking our lunches and our little pails. In just a short time, we were in a real jungle, looking for the best places for the ripening berries.

And what is more fragrant than a pail-full of wild blackberries! Many times I would press the top of my face into my little pail—it seemed to me nothing ever smelled better. And I could not wish for a better-tasting pie than the big, thick wild blackberry pies my mother knew how so well to make. But besides that, the jam and jelly were wonderful.

These happy berrying parties were often filled with childish adventures for us youngsters. Now and then a new kind of bird's nest was found; somebody might get stung by bumble-bee, or be frightened by a big water snake; once in while some youngster would stray too far away and get lost in the wilderness; and, most exciting of all, strange cattle might discover us, and from all sides come closer and closer to us, when a few of the boys started to climb trees, and the younger children became more and more scared. The cattle seemed very wild, and surprised to see us there; but when one of the big boys made a sudden lunge at them and threw a club at the closest cow, they took to their heels with tails in the air, and disappeared from sight. Nobody really got hurt by the cattle that seemed to be so wild.

There were a great many fish, of different kinds, in the Sacramento River. What were called the common white fish were full of little bones; but the perch were very good to eat. In those days there were no catfish and no bass in the river; but there were suckers and pike, as well as other kinds. But the large fish were the fine salmon and the sturgeon. The sturgeons grew to be very big, sometimes more than six feet long; nobody would fish for them or think of eating them; they were a nuisance to the salmon fishermen, who always caught them in their nets, killed them when caught, and threw them overboard. It will surprise you to learn that we could buy a fine big salmon for twenty-five cents.

Sometimes we used circular nets near the shore in fishing for the market. Every morning we would go in our rowboat, lift up the net, with different kinds of fish—sometimes maybe turtle—and dump them into the boat.

The way we boys fished was very simple-no fancy rod, no reel, but a pole from a willow tree, with common line, hook, sinker, and cork. But we knew the difference between a "nibble" and "bite," and we did catch fish.

The greatest excitement of all about the Sacramento River came in the winter times, especially when there was "high water," or a real flood. We know there were sometimes floods even before California became a state; and many a flood did we see in our own time. But the great floods of the Sacramento are a long story by themselves.

In every season of the year, we boys, back in the 1870s, found adventure and learned many things from the "River of Gold." It was a constant companion.

I have the book about that big, grand river, written by Julian Dana, who gave me a copy many years ago. He says in that book; "It runs through the land like a bright tree of life." He tells of the changes in the river people and their homes; then he adds; "The tide of progress has made a pioneer way of life only a memory on the Sacramento and in the Great Valley."

Who could be a healthy boy and son of California pioneers, living right there on the bank of that wonderful river, and not find lots of enjoyment every day of the year? Is it any wonder that we came to have a kind of feeling that we were some way related to the river itself?

6

Agricultural Technology

[Editor's note: Its soil and the water has made the Sacramento–San Joaquin River Delta an ideal agricultural region, but the raising of food beyond the diet and demands of Native Californians required drainage, and later special equipment to harvest crops in soggy fields. The story of the development of ever more efficient dredging equipment and the role of Sacramento–San Joaquin River Delta inventors has been well told in John Thompson and Edward A. Dutra, *The Tule Breakers: The Story of the California Dredge* (Stockton: The University of the Pacific, 1983). However, in the late nineteenth and early twentieth centuries, Stockton and Rio Vista became hubs of agricultural mechanization, including the development of the tractor, scraping (leveling) machines, and a variety of harvesting equipment. The Sacramento–San Joaquin River Delta was also a center for canning and packing, which resulted in social as well as machine innovations.]

Benjamin Holt from Walter Payne, *Benjamin Holt: The Story of the Caterpillar Tractor*

[Editor's note: Walter Payne, *Benjamin Holt: The Story of the Caterpillar Tractor* (Stockton: University of the Pacific, 1982), pp. 83–98. (*By permission*). See Fig. 21.]

Benjamin Holt: The Man

By the end of hostilities in World War I, Benjamin Holt, the last surviving member of the Holt brothers of California, had achieved great recognition and world-wide renowned for his many mechanical inventions and improvements in the field of agricultural, transport, and earth-moving machinery. In fact, he and the Holt Manufacturing Company were at a peak of growth, creative invention, productivity, and importance as a result of meeting the challenge to forward the cause of the Allied powers in that "Great War" through the production of Caterpillars and other equipment after August, 1916.

By January, 1919, Holt had reached his seventieth birthday, and he could look back with immense satisfaction to the thirty-six years of innovative and constantly expanding productivity that had marked the period since his arrival at Stockton in 1883. In retrospect, those years had enabled Benjamin Holt and other early local economic leaders to contribute heavily to the opening and settlement of the great Central Valley of California. Through their talents the land was brought under rich cultivation for the United States, and many of their machines and businesses went on to make significant impact on the rest of the country and the world beyond Stockton.

Constant Adaptation and Continuing Expansion

In the case of Benjamin Holt, each successive mechanical innovation brought general acceptance, and each new challenge to derive greater production of food or construction of projects for the improvement of water supply, building of roadways, or the transporting of crops, ore, and lumber led to ever greater growth and further adaptation to human needs. The Stockton Wheel Company of 1883 gave rise to the first Holt combine by 1886, and within four years it was powered by a Holt steam traction engine and adapted the following year to use as a side-hill harvester. In 1892, the Holt Manufacturing Company was born with Benjamin Holt as president, and in the following year the company began to expand sales outside California into Washington State and then to other states. A harvester was shipped abroad—to Australia—in 1894, and more machines went out to Canada, Spain, Mexico, Argentina, Cuba, Europe, Africa, Java, and into twenty foreign lands.

The years from 1904 to 1909 brought deep-seated developments that stimulated and expanded Company operations. The construction and final production model of the steam track-type Caterpillar from 1904 to 1906 gave Holt and the world a remarkable machine that could be used widely over the face of the earth and in its many climates. By 1908, the gasoline traction engine Caterpillar and a newly-designed ore wagon were adopted for hauling equipment, materials, and for earth-moving work on the dry deserts of the Los Angeles Aqueduct Project, and the basically agricultural application of Holt machines moved dramatically into the early and very profitable phase of earth-moving which later was to be its most important use. Another large market was opened with the Los Angeles project too.

Holt already had a production plant at Spokane, Washington, to serve the great Northwest, but, in 1909, the opportunity arose to purchase a second production plant at Peoria, Illinois. This new expansion was initially aimed at making the Holt Company the first large West Coast company to move into the industrial heartland to the east, and it began with relatively little fanfare. The central location in the Midwest gave direct access to the heart of national wheat and grain production, as well as the iron deposits of the nation. The *Stockton Daily Evening Record* (September 25, 1908) was already editorializing on both the potential in expansion and the central importance for Stockton:

> The "Caterpillar" will without question become the greatest advertisement that Stockton has ever had for achievement in mechanics, not excepting the combined harvester, for the new tractor engine will be used in all parts of the world, in the tropics and in the frozen north, and every one of them will bear the label of Stockton manufacture.

The editorial gave the sense of global expectations for the Holt enterprises by 1909, and, of course, these were well advanced by that time.

Production and sales were on the rise on the eve of World War I in Western Europe. Even though the United States entry into the conflict came relatively late, the crawler concept and the durable Holt Caterpillars found a new, unforeseen market in military technology, and once again the Company adapted its product, resources, and pool of mechanical genius to produce a vital product in great number to serve the Allied Powers from 1916 until 1918. By that time, the Holt plant at Stockton had expanded from a building with a small number of workers that would fit into a single photograph to a wartime industry with perhaps 2,500 workers and a payroll of about $2,500,000. Benjamin Holt, president of the Company since 1892, could certainly view that growth with deep pride, and the value to the city and to the employees in Stockton was clear.

The Death of the Patriarch

Benjamin Holt lived out the war years, but his death came at Stockton on December 5, 1920, near the end of his seventy-first year. His death took away the founding leadership of Holt Manufacturing Company, a role that he had filled since 1892 when the Company was organized. Death ended a long and devoted career in the earth—moving and agricultural mechanization fields. It left a great gap in the management of the Caterpillar interests in Stockton, and that loss of "Uncle Ben" was impossible to restore. His most dominant qualities were clear. He was a man dedicated to seeking the means to greater agricultural, transport, and earth-moving production through the use of machines. To do this he embodied a rare genius for problem solving, meeting new natural and human problems with creative ways to adapt machines to man's needs and nature's ways. He seemed to his associates to be single-minded in his ability to perceive a new need and to pursue it to a successful invention or a wise adaptation in the interest of ever more efficient machines. He was a shrewd, lifelong manager who stood for the best in quality and service. Contemporaries recalled that, while he had few illusions about his work, he was a visionary who was prepared to spend huge sums of his own money to perfect his ideas. Above all, he was able to adapt to change, and, in turn, to change his own directions to keep abreast and usually ahead of the times. In earlier days, while his older brother Charles was often judged to be the "brains" of their operations, Benjamin was always considered to be the "heart."

While Benjamin Holt was an outstanding and uncommon individual himself, he had the ability to surround himself with good and loyal managers and workmen. A nephew, C. Parker Holt left a manuscript that detailed key managerial associates who ran their respective functions during the early years and through the rise of the corporation. In the Holt family, three nephews were particularly instrumental: C. Parker Holt excelled as treasurer; Pliny E. Holt was outstanding in engines, motorized military operations, and as a vice president of the company; and, Ben. C. Holt served in sales.

There were other key executives who served from the earliest days too: George H. Cowie was bookkeeper and treasurer, George L. Dickenson served as company secretary at Stockton and continued at Peoria until 1913; Thomas H. Luke rose to sales manager, working up from heading the parts area; Russell S. Springer served from the machine shop to ultimately become a vice president by 1925; Dan N. Gilmore was long recognized as a great salesman and finally as an officer and director of the company; Murray M. Baker headed the Peoria operations and filled a vice-presidency; O.H. Eccleston served the company for forty-eight years as auditor; and Willard E. Shepherd began as an office and mail boy, becoming later a plant manager. Many other leaders, men of inventive capacity and great creativity, talent, and loyalty also served in the ultimate success of the Company.

World War I and the Postwar Era

These men and Benjamin Holt had brought the Company through nearly three exciting decades, but, unfortunately World War I had two faces for the Holt Manufacturing Company. Popular interest is immediately caught up with Holt's contribution to motorized military and transport equipment that was of such basic strategic impact in bringing about an Allied Powers victory. That development brought immense growth, production, employment, and profits, all of which accompanied and benefitted the development of the Stockton community by 1920.

But, the other face of the postwar period was one of the deflation after 1919 when Holt Brothers was confronted once again with an array of new economic challenges arising out of overexpansion of company plant and resources in order to respond to the wartime demands of the Allied nations. At the end of hostilities, the United States government ended its military contracts on the one hand, and it seemed to harm potential tractor sales by disposing of several thousand machines to American road districts as war surplus; fortunately, it appeared later that the tractors did such an exceptional job in roadbuilding work that the net result was to create a new demand for such equipment that probably compensated for any loss of sales. However, there was a general drop in the demand for farm machinery in the agricultural sector, at the same time several hundred new manufacturing companies had appeared on the American industrial scene during the conflict. The Holt people had neglected the home markets and sales and distribution were lacking in the face of this unprecedented competition. The Company was finding difficulty in securing investment capital at that time.

In retrospect, it is tempting to view the war years as a period of time that was unforeseen, but temporary, and to see that period as one of rather spectacular health for the Company. One wonders whether there might not have been change in the national location of tractor headquarters earlier than 1925 had war not artificially provided such an exciting alternative. This view is especially attractive when one adds to it the impact of the death of the founder in 1920 at Stockton.

Any number of fundamental changes had taken place in terms of plant location by that time. Holt machines had been introduced to national markets, and important production plants had been established at Spokane and Peoria. Also, international markets were opened from the turn of the century, and they provided great sales potential for agricultural and earth-moving vehicles. California was a state that sat on the western fringe of American industry and Atlantic-related markets, remote from the industrial and transport centers of the nation. Grain production declined in California in the first decade of the 1900s, but it thrived in the region adjacent to Peoria, Illinois.

At that same time, rail transportation patterns had changed considerably, and transportation costs became more and more important as a factor in the sales and distribution of machines in the United States and abroad. Simultaneously, the new agriculture of the San Joaquin area was changing away from the very base upon which agricultural machinery had first supported the rise of the Company with its harvesting and other grain-related activities before about 1910. And, finally, the death of Benjamin Holt in 1920 removed a great, stabilizing force that had always supported Stockton as the home and headquarters of the Caterpillar Tractor.

By 1925, an entire set of circumstances led to a Company decision to merge the Holt Manufacturing Company of California with the C.L. Best Tractor Company of San Leandro, California. The new company took the Holt name, the Caterpillar Tractor Company, and it was a merger that consolidated several Holt subsidiaries like the plant at Stockton and at Peoria, the Hauser and Haines Manufacturing Company (Stockton), the Aurora Engine Company (Stockton), and the Canadian Holt Company, Limited (Calgary and Alberta). The Company directors under C.L. Best as chairman, decided to center the activities of the new company at Peoria, which had begun in 1909 as an attempt to extend the western Holt Company toward the eastern markets. So, after nearly sixty years, the Stockton interests did not cease, but they did merge with the Best Company and their long and highly productive history at Stockton, like the life of Benjamin Holt, came to an end.

Benjamin Holt and Stockton

Since the founder and heart of the Company had been dead since 1920, Stockton had now lost both its leading industry and its world-famous industrialist within a period of less than five years. Benjamin Holt had liked and boosted Stockton, even though he had for years traveled widely throughout the world and could certainly have felt otherwise had he chosen to do so. Typically, when British General Swinton opened his remarks at Stockton in that famous meeting of 1918 by saying he was glad to be in Stockton and to meet Benjamin Holt, the latter replied: "General Swinton, you couldn't have come to a better country. I've traveled around considerable, and I've come to the conclusion that there's no finer spot. Welcome to California."

Holt came to Stockton as a bachelor in 1883, but on December 18, 1890, he married Anna Brown. She came from a pioneer California family, and her father, Benjamin E. Brown, was a San Joaquin County farmer. The couple lived at Miner Avenue and Aurora Street and then at Miner and Stanislaus Street before settling permanently at the family home at 548 East Park Street in 1895. They raised their five children in Stockton-Alfred Brown Holt, William Knox Holt, Anne Holt Atherton, Benjamin Dean Holt, and Edison Ames Holt. Anna Brown Holt lived until 1952, most of the time in Stockton, where she was known for her charitable and social work and where she was for over a quarter of a century a Regent of the local College of the Pacific, subsequently renamed the University of the Pacific.

Benjamin Holt was a modest and unassuming man who devoted himself to his work. He spent much time in his experimental room at the plant, where he dealt with whatever mechanical problems that faced him at a given time. He kept an eye on the workings of the Company, and he enjoyed his work and his daily contact with employees as he moved about the plant, often in his shirtsleeves and bowler or straw hat. He was considered to be democratic in his dealings with others, and he reportedly treated his men accordingly, calling them by name and welcoming long-standing friendships. With the main exception of a months-long strike in 1904—the workers lost their bid to organize a machinists' union—his relationships with employees were good. In 1921, they honored his memory with a bronze plaque expressing their gratitude:

> BENJAMIN HOLT. Born January 1,1849. Died December 5, 1920. INVENTOR of the CATERPILLAR TRACTOR. One of the Founders and for Twenty-Eight Years the President and Inventive Genius of the Holt Manufacturing Company. This Tablet Erected by Holt Employees ... To Perpetuate His Memory ...

For his part, Holt willed a trust fund of $25,000 to be used to aid former employees who found themselves in distress. The fund was revealed in 1932, when it was formally transferred to the trustees—Anna Brown Holt, O. H. Eccleston, and Holt's lawyer, Charles L. Neumiller. *The Stockton Independent* (February 10, 1932) reported the trust as follows:

> Old and faithful employees of the former Holt Manufacturing Company have been given financial assistance when needed because of sickness or distress during the last eleven years through a $25,000 trust fund left them by the late Benjamin Holt, founder and president of the firm. Holt, who died December 5, 1920, provided in his last testament that use of the fund should begin immediately after his death. During his lifetime, he saw that none of the employees of the firm who had given long years of service went in need. Some of them had been with the concern from its inception, and worked elbow to elbow with Holt.

The Community Heritage of Ben Holt

Stockton mourned his passing, and this is no better illustrated than in a tribute printed in the *Stockton Daily Evening Record* (December 6, 1920), written by A.C. Oullahan, the Mayor of Stockton:

> Benjamin Holt is dead. Stockton mourns the loss of a good and useful citizen, whose genius and industry enriched the community and carried its name

across the mountains and the valleys and the seas to the far places of the earth. He was a man. Fame came to him, but his rugged manhood did not become less rugged; the friends who walked with him when shadows fell athwart the path were yet his friends of his choice. He was still Ben Holt, unchanged under the glamor of renown; plain, honest, industrious and true. In our fancy, a great tree stood yesterday before the House of Stockton. Today it is gone. We look upon the vacant place and contemplate dolefully the irreparable loss. It cannot be put back. It was a landmark that helped to point the way to Stockton, and for it we had deep affection. Ben Holt was such a landmark. Like the great tree, whose sheltering boughs protected many from the heat of summer, he held forth his hands in meting charity to protect many from the blasts of the winter of want. It is fitting that this man, whose modesty forbade us to honor him in life, should honor him in death, I recommend that all business of the city be suspended during the hour of his funeral, and that all flags of the city be displayed at half-mast. Ben Holt was loyal to Stockton. In God's name let us show that Stockton is loyal to his memory.

The San Joaquin County Board of Supervisors also adopted their own resolution and resolved that its contents be delivered to the family. Noting the worldwide fame brought to the county through the harvester, the tractor, and the tank, the supervisors added:

> The deceased was a man of high character, who devoted his entire time to the great industry which bears his name. He became not only a factor but a foundation stone in the building of our resourceful county by the establishment of the large plant, which not only gives employment to thousands of men, but which, in the purchasing of supplies and materials, distributes thousands of dollars monthly in this county. Notwithstanding the success that he achieved, he followed the even tenor of his way, never seeking fame, but satisfied in the accomplishment of that which he believed to be beneficial to mankind. His death leaves a vacancy in our community which will not easily be filled.

At the funeral that week, the surviving relatives and Company officers were pall bearers and honorary pall bearers-the men who had served the Company under Benjamin Holt. Among them were C. Parker Holt, Pliny E. Holt, Ben C. Holt, Russell S. Springer, Thomas H. Luke, Dan N. Gilmore, Murray M. Baker, Willard H. Shepherd, and O.H. Eccleston, along with others. Last rites were conducted by Dr. A.C. Bane at the Central Methodist Church, and, in a lengthy eulogy, he recounted the many and worldwide contributions of Benjamin Holt. As part of his remarks, he also reminded the mourners that:

He lives in the love of his own hometown, because by his brain and brawn he has written the name of "Stockton" across the map of the world and lifted her from the rank of a village to a great, progressive, industrial city. His very life and spirit have been breathed into Stockton until she lives and thrives because of him.

The heritage that Benjamin Holt left to the city of Stockton and to San Joaquin County was rich and sustaining, and the memory of the man has continued to be honored down through the years. Among the main reminders of Holt are Benjamin Holt Drive, which runs through the north section of Stockton and perpetuates his name. The Pioneer Museum and Haggin Galleries of Stockton have an excellent exhibit of machines and memorabilia from Benjamin Holt and his Company displayed for the enjoyment of the public in their Holt Memorial Hall. Stockton's San Joaquin Delta College trains community students in their Holt Center classroom building. The Holt name is perpetuated at the University of the Pacific, which recently named the Holt-Atherton Pacific Center for Western Studies, an archive and special collections library for students and researchers. It is dedicated to Benjamin's wife, Anna Brown Holt, his daughter, Anne Holt Atherton, and his son-in-law, Warren H. Atherton, a distinguished Stockton attorney known as the "Father of the G.I. Bill of Rights."

In 1980, a Caterpillar collector, James Clack of Fresno, California, donated twenty-one Holt tractors to the San Joaquin County Historical Museum at Micke Grove near Stockton. These will be added to other Holt machines and agricultural displays that will serve visitors from the area. Almost all of the tractors were in running condition. The collection is a major one. Early in 1981, the American Society of Mechanical Engineers sent its national president to Stockton to give national recognition to the track-laying vehicle, the Caterpillar Tractor, as a mechanical engineering landmark. Finally, a soon to be built library on the University Campus will memorialize the name of Benjamin Holt's son, William Knox Holt. The heritage of Benjamin Holt to the city, the county, the nation, and to the world of mechanized agriculture, transport, and earth-moving was uncommonly rich. He was, for all his modesty and lack of pretension, a most uncommon man, one whose great contributions continue to be recognized in the years since his death.

R.G. LeTourneau, from *Mover of Men and Mountains*

[Editor's note: A second inventor (of a successful scraper/leveler) from Stockton was R. G. Letourneau, who documents his rise in an autobiography, *Mover of Men and Mountains* (Chicago: Moody, 1967), Chapter 9. (*By permission*). Notice his discussion of Benjamin Holt. Like Holt, Letourneau relocates to the center of the continent to better serve his growing market. The Sacramento–San Joaquin River Delta was fertile for innovation, but too isolated to be a significant center for distribution of equipment. See Fig. 22.]

Chapter 9

In the spring of 1919 I had uncovered the last of the unpaid bills at the garage, the books were in order, and at last we knew where we stood. The picture was both good and bad. On the bad side was the fact that we were still $20,000 in the red. On the good side was the fact that I had reconditioned and sold the glut of used cars Parks had accumulated, recovering about 60 cents on the dollar. Furthermore, my repair business was flourishing, and Parks was staying sober and selling cars. As far as I could see, in another couple of years we would be out of debt and ready to really get going.

I found no comfort in the prospect. Whatever attractions the garage business had held for me before Parks had got us into the mess were now gone, wiped out by the overwork and experiences of the last six months. I had a fierce desire to get out on my own and make a fresh start.

I didn't know how to go about it, so I did the most obvious thing. I just called a meeting of our creditors, and told them I wanted out. I remember Parks was there, and his father, and the real estate man who had built our garage, and our banker, and maybe a dozen others.

"I'm not trying to get out of my half of the debts," I assured them. "At the same time, we've got the garage going again, and I've got a half-interest in it that ought to be worth something. Now my idea is to sell out that half-interest, apply that on my debts, and then pay the balance if it takes me the rest of my life."

"What security have you got for the balance?" asked the banker.

That hadn't occurred to me. I simply held up my two big hands.

To my surprise, the banker nodded as though satisfied. For the next half hour he and the rest went over the books I had worked on so long, while I helpfully pointed out the upward trend of recent months. Then came the decision. "If you will sign over your half interest in the business to Parks, and promise to pay $5,000 to us over the next three years consider it deal."

I accepted at once. I signed a note with the banker, transferred my half of the business to Parks and his backers, and walked out. I was 30 years old, unemployed, and $5,000 in debt.

The next day I met my old friend Ira Guy on the street. "I hear you're out of the garage, he said.

"Yes, I am," I answered.

"What are you going to do now?"

I had the answer for that, too. "I'm going to take the first job I can find that's good enough to pay my debts."

"Good enough," he said. "I know where there's a job to start out on."

And that's how, on that casual meeting, I got my start in the earth-moving business.

Ira Guy and his brother Bill, two chaps only slightly older than I, were big dealers in farm machinery, working both ends against the middle and then some. They had started out about the time I started in the garage business with one old steam tractor and threshing machine, touring the county to thresh grain from farm to farm at so much a bushel. Now they had a fleet of Harris Harvester Company combines and Holt tractors, and contracts to thresh thousands of acres of grain a season, and never let it be said that if a rancher wanted to buy their machines for his own use, they wouldn't sell. They turned their threshing contracts into sales demonstrations, and they were going to town. If one of their machines broke down, I was the one they had called in as doctor, so you could say we were pretty well acquainted.

"What's the job?" I asked.

"Old man Grunaur is so mad he's walking on stilts," said Ira. "Four feet above ground. He claims the tractor we sold him is no good."

I had to admit that was serious. Grunaur, the senior partner of a big land company called Grunaur & Fabian, was one of the biggest customers the Guy brothers had, and if he was really mad, it could cost the brothers plenty. "What seems to be the trouble?" I asked.

"We can't figure it out. Bill has been out there four times, but no matter what he does, the thing breaks down a day or two later. I'd sure like you to run out there to see what you can do. I know you'll be able to find the trouble."

"Okay, I'll try it," I said, and walked on, feeling pretty set up at getting a job, even if it was a small one. I hadn't walked a block when I remembered something. When I left the garage, had taken with me my welding torch and a few tools of my trade. The company car and service truck that I had always used before had been left behind as part of the deal, so I had no way of running down to Grunaur's Whitehall Ranch, some 20 miles away over old dirt roads. I was about to turn around to tell Ira I couldn't take his job after all when an old garage customer hailed me.

"Bob, I've got a deal for you," he said. "You know the Saxon I bought?"

I certainly did. It was a beauty. Bright yellow, with a sport chummy seat, and I knew it was in perfect condition because I had serviced it once a month myself.

"Well, I tried to turn it in to that partner of yours, and he'd only give me $400 for it," he said. "And you know yourself we still owe $400 on it. He'd be getting it for nothing. I don't want that to happen, so why don't you take it over for the payments that are left?"

It was a tempting offer. I knew I couldn't lose, but at the same time my $5,000 debt was so huge I could only look at around the edges. And what would my banker say if he saw his pauper riding around in a Saxon? It hurt me, but I turned him down.

My sister Sarah was visiting us in Stockton, and when I related the day's events that evening, she remembered that just happened to have $400 saved for her return passage to Wei Hai Wei Mission in China.

"That's just too good bargain to miss," she said firmly, "I'll buy it myself. The only thing is, be sure you buy it back from me before I have to buy my ticket."

Evelyn and I looked at her, knowing she was staking us to the car. Nevertheless, I had to protest. "What if we don't have any money?" I said.

"The Lord will provide," she said calmly. I must mention here that there is big difference between faith in the Lord and presumption. Had I made a statement like that at that time, I would have I been presumptuous. Sarah, with her wonderful, serene faith, could say, "The Lord will provide," with absolute conviction. I must also add that her confidence in sailing on schedule was all in the Lord, and not in me.

I was filled with doubt when I took possession of the Saxon. A lot of people, knowing how broke I was, would think was riding pretty high. That the car might create a beneficial impression never occurred to me until after I arrived at the Whitehall Ranch. Grunaur, seeing me drive up in my yellow beauty to repair his Holt tractor, thought it was Mr. Holt himself. I think it was the first time in his life that he ever addressed a mechanic as "Mister".

The ailing tractor was a huge, 30,000-pound, 75 horsepower job that was plain sick all over. The timer had been monkeyed with so often that even after it was adjusted it would hold only for a few minutes and then start drifting off. I solved that problem by simply welding the adjustment bolt in place so it could never drift again. Next, I discovered that Grunaur's gasoline storage tank was so lined with rust that every time he gassed the tractor he poured more iron than gasoline into the carburetor. It took me a week to go over the whole machine, but when I was through it was as good as new.

"Now let's see if it will keep on running like that," Grunaur said. "I've got 40 acres I want leveled for irrigation, so you just go on down there and shave off the hummocks. If the machine is still running a week from now, I'll pay your repair bill and give you a dollar an hour for your work to boot."

The tract he wanted leveled was located in that section of the valley known as The Islands. Today the name is meaningless, but in 1919, before the vast drainage system was completed, the islands were real enough. Each spring the San Joaquin River would flood over hundreds of square miles of land, inundating all but those strange mounds. For the most part, they were composed of sediment and peat, but some of the islands contained the relics of ancient Indian villages. When we land-levelers hit one of them, we called in the archaeologists of the University of California and let them do some of our leveling for us.

Before I could start leveling land, I had to repair the scraper. As I look back on it now, if that scraper had been in perfect working condition, I might never have gone into the manufacture of earth-moving equipment. As it was, there were so many things wrong with that machine that I practically had to rebuild it, and by the time I had it running I thought it was the most fascinating piece of machinery I had ever encountered. I don't know why. Some men go for airplanes, or electronics, or automobiles, or atoms. I went for the ugliest chunk of brute machinery you'd ever want to see.

Several writers have credited me with being the first to build powered scrapers, so right now I want to give that credit to the right man, Mr. T. G. Schmeiser of Fresno. In 1915 he patented a scraper with a blade that could be raised or lowered by compressed air. It was a cumbersome affair, but with one man pulling it with a tractor, and another man on the scraper operating the compressed air valves, it could move three cubic yards of dirt at the rate of about three miles an hour. By comparison, that was about what six mule-skinners driving 24 mules on six big Fresnos could do.

Other manufacturers like Holt then came out with tractor-drawn scrapers, using a variety of belts, pulleys and gears to manipulate the blade. All shared the same weakness. When the blade hit a rock or a tough root, belts would slip, gear teeth would be stripped, or the compressed air system would either bounce the blade or blow out an air hose. As a result, the land being leveled was left about as uneven as a field of drifted snow, and a lot of plowing, harrowing, and hand-shoveling had to be done to get the table-top smoothness required for irrigation. Of course, if they hadn't had this weakness, along with many others, there would have been no room for me to introduce my own scraper when the time came.

The tractor and scraper I used on my first earth-moving job for Grunaur were both made by Holt. I drove the tractor, and Grunaur's foreman operated the scraper. If he's alive, he's still hating me. I claim there is no surer way to turn two friends into enemies than to put one on a tractor and the other on the scraper behind. Every time we hit a root that flipped him off the scraper, he swore I hunted it up on purpose. Every time he socked the blade unexpectedly deep into the ground, stopping the tractor cold and cracking my neck like a whip, I was just as convinced he had done it deliberately.

Maybe I did hit some bumps too hard. By the end of my second day I knew had found a job that satisfied me like none in my life. When I was in dry going, the track-type treads of the Holt threw sand and dust into my face. When I was down in the bottoms, they threw mud, and I loved it. When I saw a hummock ahead to be cut down, I charged it as though I were a knight in a tournament, and if my scraper operator bounced out without slicing off a good cut, I was furious. I wanted to move dirt. Lots of dirt.

Grunaur was so pleased with the job we did leveling his land that he invited me to overhaul all the rest of the land company's equipment. That included a steam tractor, threshing machine, hay mowers, gang plows, irrigation pumps, and several wagons and dump carts. For me it was a holiday. Many of the machines were so old that no spare parts could be found for them, so I had to make my own with my welding torch. By fall, when I completed my work, I knew those machines inside and out, and had learned more about pumps, belts, and gears for heavy equipment than I had learned in all my correspondence courses combined.

I still had a lot to learn the hard way. For my last repair job, I overhauled an irrigation pump and then started it up to fill a reservoir about a quarter of a mile back from the river. Both the six-inch concrete pipe and the reservoir were empty at the time so the water flowed along briskly though I did notice that along toward evening the pump had to work a little harder as the weight of the water in the reservoir built up. I shut it off and returned the next morning, setting the pump at the same speed it had operated at most efficiently the day before.

Right off it began to labor and groan. I couldn't figure that out. I thought maybe the gasoline engine wasn't getting enough gas, so souped it up a little. That only made the groaning louder. Right then had a horrible feeling I was doing something very wrong, but the feeling came too late. Before I could shut off the engine a hundred yards of pipe burst, spraying the countryside with mud and water. While that tremendous geyser was still in the air, out of the shattered pipe poured all the water in the reservoir, cutting a gully all the way down to the river and covering me and the pump with mud.

As any irrigation man could have told me if I'd had enough sense to ask, it is one thing to start a flow of water through an empty pipe, and quite something else to start flow through a full one, especially if there is a reservoir of water standing on top of it. There's a little thing called the inertia of water to be reckoned with. When I started up the pump at high speed that morning the water in the pipe was no longer flowing as it had been the evening before. It was just lying there, and even if it had wanted to move there was all that weight of water in the reservoir holding it back. Thus, when I put the pump into high speed, I was building up an enormous pressure at the pump end of the line long before the water at the reservoir end was even getting ready to move.

I ran into a sign on a safety bulletin board one time that went like this: "Where did you get your good judgment?" "From my experience." "And where did you get your experience?" "From my bad judgment."

I didn't have to write that down to remember it. When you are rebuilding a pumping station and replacing a hundred yards of pipe on your own time, the "inertia of water" has a far deeper meaning than you'll ever find attached to it in a classroom. Just to be sure I never made the same mistake again, I took another correspondence course, this one on hydraulic power, and I doubt that my postal professors ever had a more earnest student.

That doesn't mean that I learned it all. I still had to learn that an expert in one field is no expert if one field is all he knows. There are a lot of angles to hydraulics that have nothing to do with liquids. Cement, for instance. Two years after the pipe-burst for Grunaur, I contracted to build a 4,000-foot pipeline for Carlton Case, a prominent Stockton attorney and rancher. I was so anxious to make good for this influential man that I read all there was to be had on concrete pipe. I surveyed the course from river to reservoir myself. I invented a ditcher and dug my own ditch. As final precaution to insure top quality, I built my own pipe-casting machine and mixed my own cement to meet the highest standards. Then with the assistance of my brother-in-law, Howard Peterson, we started laying pipe.

The pipe was made in two-foot sections, each section having a collar that would tightly enclose the butt end of the next. As fast as the machine turned out the sections, we snugged them into place, it being my idea that if the cement was still a little moist, the joints would be sealed just that much more firmly. I was right as far as I went, but then I had to go ahead and have another idea.

"If we bury the pipe as we go along," I told Howard, one of the requirements being that the pipe be buried two feet below plow level, "we'll be in an awful mess if we have a few leaks and have to do a lot of digging. Let's lay the whole thing, and then test it for leaks before we bury it."

The idea sounded reasonable to him. We built the line, never once thinking of the fact that the bottom half of the pipe lay in the damp, cool soil of the trench while the top half was exposed to the burning California sun. Came the day that I started up the pump, and you can be sure I did it cautiously. I could have spared myself the worry. By the time the water had progressed halfway up the line, the top of every joint along the way was spraying up water as fast as I could pump it in.

Howard did his best. "Maybe we haven't got a pipe line," he said. "But I'll bet we've got the biggest water sprinkler in the world."

I was a long time in figuring out that while the bottom half of my pipe had been curing perfectly on its foundation of moist soil, the sun baked top half had been shrinking at a furious rate.

In mechanics, a nice feature is that once you have found the cause of the trouble, the cure is usually simple; if you have found the right cause. In this case Howard and I had a simple cure. We just got down in that ditch, straddling that twelve-inch pipe with our backs exposed to the sun where not a breath of air could reach us, and plugged the leaks. We had buckets of wet cement with us, and rock drills to punch three-inch holes in the pipe. With the hole punched we'd reach in with a handful of cement and pack the left. Another handful for leaky joint at the right. One punched hole for every two joints, two sealing operations, and then one cement plug for every hole. Today I fly some 200,000 miles a year at better than 300 mph, but don't think I don't know that 4,000 feet of leaky pipe line is the longest distance in the world. I've measured it.

I have introduced these mistakes of mine to keep things in balance because there is an impression around that I was practically forced into becoming a success. "You were the right man in the right place at the right time," I've been told more than once. If I was the right man, I was a long time finding out about it, but I can't deny that I was in the right place at the right time.

California in 1919 was just ready to start its irrigation projects in earnest, not that irrigation was anything new in the state. The ruins of a Spanish irrigation system are still to be seen behind the Santa Barbara Mission, and I've been told that the Indians were irrigating long before the Spaniards arrived. Nevertheless, progress was slow. Only land that was relatively flat and close to water could be worked at all, and even the rancher that lucky stood in annual danger of seeing his laboriously dug ditches washed out by spring floods.

A big step forward was made by old Benjamin Holt when he built his first tractor in Stockton in 1885. Not long after that old Daniel Best started his tractor factory in nearby San Leandro. For some 20 years, using first steam and then gasoline engines, the two rivals turned out immense machines resembling short-line locomotives. Mounted on wide steel wheels and wearing big cleats called grousers, one of these monsters could do the work of 100 mules if the going was good. Unfortunately, as any construction man can tell you, the going is rarely good in the earth-moving business. On even mild hillsides let alone on mountain slopes the tractors were not only dangerously top-heavy, but they needed all their power just to move their own weight. After a rain or in soft bottom land they were helpless. Once the big cleats would throw out drive-wheels started to spin, the mud by the bucketful, and down would settle the machine.

The story is that one day Holt was testing one of his machines in a rain-soaked field when his wheels started to spin. He was a good operator, but in 30 seconds he was dug in to the axles. Tromping back through the mud, tired and discouraged, slipping back two feet for every three he advanced, he felt, he said, "like a hoss on a treadmill."

Some inventions do come in flashes, and the treadmill gave Holt all the flash he needed. Back on his old New England farm the horse on the treadmill walked miles going nowhere, but his plodding turned the gears that ground the corn. Now, figured Holt, if a treadmill could power gears, then gears could power a treadmill, and instead of going no place, the wide, endless belt could be made to roll along the ground at a fine rate. Even over mud like that in which his tractor was stuck fast. By the time he reached his shop, Holt already had in mind a tractor that would be mounted on wide, treadmill type tracks. It was a dazzler of an idea all right. No longer would the tons of tractor weight rest on the of steel wheels that touched the ground. No few square inches longer would two drive wheels spin and dig in. All the weight and drive would be spread evenly from front end to rear of the long, wide tracks.

Holt turned out his first track-type tractor in 1905. "Crawls over mud like a caterpillar," he said, and thus the Caterpillar tractor got its name.

For all that he had a revolutionary idea, public acceptance was slow. Contractors still thought mules were cheaper and more dependable than tractors, and there were very few ranchers big enough, and progressive enough to buy an expensive machine. Then one sale to a gold mining company in South Africa changed the course of history. Quite by chance some British military figures touring the mining property saw the machine in action. No ideas sparked then, but a few years later, when World War I bogged down in the mud of trench warfare, the memory of the old Holt crawling through the mud of the gold mine stirred up some ideas in the British Ministry of War. Things happened fast after that. In a matter of months, the Holt, covered with armor plating and carrying a gun turret resembling a water tank, was on its way to the Western Front. The tank became the decisive weapon of the war. It wallowed through water-filled shell holes and crashed over sand bags to straddle German trenches. It knocked down stone walls and trees, crushed machine gun nests, and blew up ammunition dumps. By war's end there was no longer any doubt about what a track-type machine could do.

Along with having developed the track-type tractor, the war had developed a tremendous demand for foodstuffs that had been in short supply for years. Thus, when at last the tractor factories could return to peacetime production, the real irrigation boom began.

Jobs there were aplenty. Grunaur was loud in his recommendation, selling me as the mechanic who could fix anything with a welding torch. Ira, too, had more work waiting for me than I could handle. The rub was that even if I doubled as cat-skinner, mechanic and welder, I could still only make about $2 an hour. High wages in those days, yes, but ten hours a day on a tractor, and another four or five hours at night as mechanic barely kept me caught up on my debts. Then there was the boat fare I had to return to Sarah, our pledge to the church, food, rent, new welding equipment; the list seemed endless.

Tormenting me was the thought that if I had my own tractor could get my head above water. The tractor operator who supplied his own machine could get $7.50 an hour for himself and machine, or about twice, according to my figures, what I was making as a hired hand.

Evelyn knew how I felt. "I'm going to get a job, too," she announced. "It's the only way we can get ahead."

I didn't like the idea of her going to work, especially with her father still sore at me and ready to claim I couldn't support his daughter. We took our problem to our Lord, and felt better about it. You know, a lot of people take their problems to the Lord, and get up and walk away, carrying their problems back with them. Like those who pray for rain, and then go out without an umbrella. If that's all the faith there is, there is not much point in praying. The Lord can't help you if you insist on carrying your problems with you. Leave them with Him, and they are no longer yours but His.

Shortly after that I went back to leveling more land at the Whitehall Ranch down in The Islands for Grunaur. At almost the same time the rancher just across the Grand Line Canal found himself in urgent need of a nursemaid to help his ailing wife with the children. Not even Oscar could resent his daughter's answering a call for help like that. Evelyn took the job at $40 a month, and with no rent to pay or groceries to buy in Stockton, that made the difference.

The situation was rough on us, however. We were close enough to see each other daily, and wave, but that canal was a quarter of a mile wide with not a bridge for miles in either direction, and no telephone connections between the ranches. Just to complicate matters, I had put the car up for sale, the time being near for Sarah to return to China. The best we could do was on Sunday when I would go down to the canal, put my rolled-up clothes on a raft made of fence posts, and swim across pushing the raft ahead of me. Then, dressed again in a suit somewhat damp from the crossing, I could call on my wife for a few hours while she did the housework and minded the children.

We will never forget the Christmas of 1919. With the recovery of the rancher's wife, Evelyn's job had ended, but I was still leveling land on the Whitehall Ranch. The main point was that we were together again in our own home, and it was quite a place. It was a portable cook shack, mounted on iron wheels, and in its day it had seen the preparation of thousands of meals for migrant sugar beet harvesters. The cook stove was still there, and the kerosene lamps, and a couple of cots, but the walls were cracked and the roof leaked. Every day the hogs would come to scratch themselves on the iron wheels, and then Evelyn would have to rush to catch a falling lamp chimney or save the stove pipe from collapse. When I was leveling land, the December dust would drift across the fields and through the cracks of the shack to pile up in mounds. To keep the dust off the dishes, Evelyn had to turn them face down on the table until the food was served. Water came from a distant pump. Corn cobs fueled the stove. You may not think that was very jolly, we never felt sorry for ourselves. I do remember one plaintive remark of Evelyn's after a particularly dusty day. "I tried to wash the dust off the floor," she said, "but I guess I only irrigated it."

Yet it was a wonderful Christmas. God let us know then that He was gifting us with a second child. Our heads were above water, our faith was stronger than ever, and we were together in person and in prayer. A shack we might be in, but who could be richer than we were?

You might call that an academic question, but in April, 1942, Evelyn and I were housed in [a] leaky trailer in the midst of acres of mud, ten miles south of Vicksburg where I was building a new factory. Our annual report, published a few weeks earlier, had revealed that our company's net earning had topped the two million mark, for the first time. I had some "construction man's" coffee on the gasoline burner—two spoons of coffee per cup of water on Monday, keep adding coffee and water to match the rate of consumption for the rest of the week, but under no circumstances throw away the grounds until Sunday night and we sat chewing on that. It does get a little thick. The rain dripped through, and the winds shook the trailer as the hogs had once done.

Were we happier than we had been that Christmas of 1919? More grateful, perhaps, because God had let us help Him do one of the things we wanted to do then. But happier? We had been in the service of the Lord then, and we were in the service of the Lord now, and there is nothing in that kind of happiness that two million net earnings can add to or buy.

Lloyd Schmidt, "Inventing a Sugar Beet Harvester"

[Editor's note: Lloyd Schmidt, "Inventing a Sugar Beet Harvester," *Schmidt's Short Stories and Poems*, Volume I (Detroit: Harlo Press, 1986), pp. 99–109. (*By permission*). In addition to larger machines, the Sacramento–San Joaquin River Delta also stimulated the creation of more specialized products. With the rise of sugar beets, the need for equipment to harvest them became evident. Again, distribution became a challenge as the company grew and attracted wider attention. See Fig. 23.]

My brother Luke and I invented and built the first commercially successful sugar beet harvester to be used in California. It was not an earthshaking achievement and I was far more impressed by the large number of people the invention influenced than by the invention itself.

The need for a sugar beet harvester became apparent because I had a country welding shop that was practically surrounded by sugar beet fields. When World War II started, the farm labor left for the military service or wartime jobs and the farmers had no way to harvest their beets.

Many people had been working on mechanical beet harvesting machines and I became fascinated by the challenge. Our beet harvester was not a sudden inspiration. I spent about two years tracking down rumors and looking at everything that had been built.

The University of California had grants from many sources and spent years and large amounts of money trying to build a beet harvesting machine. The sugar beet companies brought some experimental machines to California but they would not work in the hard, cloddy conditions.

My welding shop was heated by a large, oil-fired stove. On cold, foggy days, the local farmers gathered around to warm up a little and discuss the topics of the day. The conversation always turned to sugar beet harvesters. I knew little about farming and the direct input of the real farmers was an absolute necessity. We discussed many ways to build a beet harvester and the old stove was covered with soapstone drawings.

All the other machines I had looked at cut off the tops while the beets were in the ground and then scooped up the dirt and beets and shook out the dirt. The California soil broke up into beet -size clods that would not shake out. These machines loaded more dirt than beets. I believed that the beets could be picked up on a spiked wheel without lifting the clods. When the spiked beets reached the top of the wheel, they would be upside down. Knives between the spikes would cut off the tops. The beets would go over the knives and into the truck conveyor. The tops would be scraped from the wheel with strippers and conveyed out the side.

Brother Mick was in the South Pacific fighting the war and Brother Luke was in the Army and stationed 250 miles away so I had no shop help.

One weekend, when Luke was home on leave, I explained my idea and said that was going to build a beet harvester. His analytical mind took control, as always, and he said, "You are not going to build anything because you don't even know if a spike will pick up a beet." That question had to be answered first so we bent a steel band on a four-foot radius. We welded a spike to the middle of the band and took it to the beet field.

The band rolled on the beets until the beet and spike impaled and then we tested the lifting power. It was not good so Luke said, "The straight spike is cutting a slot. If we bend the spike in a progressive curve, it will make a clean hole." He laid out the curve and we carefully bent the spike to the pattern. The test was very satisfactory so we planned to build the beet harvester.

Luke borrowed my motorcycle for the trip back to camp and planned to return on his next leave to see what progress had been made.

The first beet harvester was built from the junk pile and there was not one new piece of steel in it. I welded the spikes onto the rim of an old grain harvester wheel. The frame was made from junk pipe and all the chains and sprockets were from a discarded hay loader. The tractor had no power takeoff so a one cylinder potato digger engine was used to power the beet conveyor. A hand-cranked winch was used to lift the plows and the spike wheel at the end of each row. It was a very junkie machine but it was good enough to prove the point.

Time was running out because the harvest had started and there was no time to waste. I worked days, nights and weekends and Luke made many long trips home to solve the problems as they came up.

We were finally ready for the first actual test but we were not ready for the results. Our first run was about 10 feet and then everything plugged up. We worked from a portable welding truck and chopped and changed as we went. Each trial run we went a little farther and we were finally able to complete a row without a stop. At last! Everything was adjusted and working and we were harvesting, row after row, of beets.

Few farmers in the area were harvesting because they were unable to get the necessary labor. Our truckloads of clean topped beets began to show up at the beet dump and the word spread like wildfire. Beet growers came from miles around to see the operation and we were able to harvest 40 acres with the junkie patch and go machine.

The Dean of the Agricultural College and the Chief Agricultural Engineer came to see the beet harvester. The three of us were walking along behind the machine when the chief engineer said, "That thing can't work; it is too simple." The Dean replied, "It is putting clean beets on the truck." The engineer repeated, "It just can't work." The Dean raised his voice and said angrily, "I learned that educated engineers are not always practical people and I have encountered many of them over the years."

Suddenly, dozens of people, with dreams of wealth and power, got into the act. Some even claimed that they had invented the machine and had it built at my shop. I never could, and never will, understand how some people can achieve satisfaction by lying to themselves about their accomplishments. I now know that they are not unusual and there are many of them.

A small group of local businessmen formed a company to manufacture and sell the beet harvester. I was totally exhausted from the super effort that was necessary to get the machine working before the beet season ended and I wanted a rest.

The local group raised the money and hired a manufacturing company to build prototype of a production machine. I was supposed to oversee the construction but now everyone was an expert and there were too many people and too many ideas. The machine did not work and it was a revolting development. I gave up in disgust and went back to my shop and other projects.

When Luke completed his military service, he went to work for the manufacturer to design and build machines for California conditions. These machines were big and heavy and designed for the extremely hard, dry California soil. They were very successful and many are still in use after more than 40 years of seasonal service.

The amount of effort needed to develop such a machine, under the constant pressure of a passing season, took Luke to the edge of exhaustion and he needed a rest.

The investment group was eager for more patent royalties and decided to invade the Midwest. The manufacturing company built a smaller, lighter machine and it worked fairly well in light California conditions, so a sales promotion plan was worked out.

Luke and I and one of the investment group were to take the new machine to every beet growing area in the United States to demonstrate it. The itinerary was planned by the sugar companies and we drove the truck that hauled the tractor and towed the beet harvester. The trip was a disaster. The machine was not suited to the small farms and conditions of the Midwest and it would not work in the mud. I could see that the California machine would not meet any of the requirements of the mid-west beet grower, and I tried to abort the trip. I was overruled by the investment group and a great deal of time and money were spent was to prove that our machine was for California only.

Luke took the time to learn what was needed and built a very small machine that was designed for the mid-west conditions. A small spike wheel and topping unit were mounted on the side of a wheel tractor and a cart was pulled behind to receive the beets. This machine was very successful and thousands of them were sold.

Mechanizing the sugar beet industry was a constant fight. There were many people who had never grown beets before and knew nothing about machinery. Planting practices were impossible. There were many odd row spacings and every field was different. There was rain and frozen ground and weeds and mud and some operations were a total disaster.

One such disaster took place on our first year in the Midwest. In a frantic effort, one of the little machines was ready for a test at the very end of the beet season. We arrived in Colorado in the middle of beautiful Indian summer and conditions were perfect. The ground was dry and the machine put on an eye-popping demonstration. Forty machines were sold for the next season.

The machines were delivered and when the beet season started, the rain started too and it did not stop for two weeks.

Luke and I, the manufacturers, the group representative and the dealer were trying to get machines started but they would not work in the mud and we did not have the answers. The beet growers were demanding immediate performance or their money back. Forty buyers were in the hotel lobby every evening threatening violence unless we got those machines working. The pressure built to explosive proportions and almost got out of control. Taking the machines back was certain ruin so we fought on.

It was after dark and Luke had not come in from the field so I was very worried. At last! He came dragging in. He was exhausted and covered with mud but he was laughing when he said, "I found the answer."

We were working in teams and each team went to a different machine. We were hoping that we could find dry or sandy conditions so we could get some machines working while we stalled for time and dry weather.

When Luke arrived at his designated machine, it was operating. The farmer's wife was sitting in the beet field reading the instruction book while her husband ran the beet harvester. The conditions were just as wet and sticky as other fields and Luke could not understand why this machine was working while the others would not.

When the machine reached the end of the row he took a very close look at it. He noticed that the plow points were mounted in an unfamiliar position.

Without realizing it the farmer had put the plow points on opposite sides from the way they were intended to be used and he accidentally discovered the solution to our problems. The plow points were copied from the beet lifters that had been used for years. They presented a large, flat surface for the mud to stick to. The mud blocked the flow of beets through the plows and pushed the beets over before they could be spiked. When the plow points were bolted on "farmer style," the bolt holes were such that the points were much more vertical than horizontal. This presents a much smaller surface to the mud and gave the beets a short, quick lift.

Luke was never one to jump at conclusions as he put the plows on the way they belonged. The machine would not work and he knew he had found the answer.

He put the plows back on "farmer style" and adjusted the digging depth and the topping unit. The little machine was doing such a wonderful job that they were all elated and harvested until dark.

The party-line phone service in that area was far more effective than a powerful radio station. That evening the farmer's wife called all her friends to say, "It works! It works just beautiful, and I am never going to pick up another sugar beet!"

Within a few hours the word had spread and the effect was so dramatic that it was unbelievable.

The next evening the hotel lobby was bedlam but the hostility had turned to happiness.

The farmers were bragging about how many tons they had harvested that day and backing it up with their weight tickets. The race for the most tons per day was on.

We finished the season with flying colors and many orders for next season's harvest. For several years the little machine was sold throughout the United States and Canada and it was all because a farmer and his wife were impatient to try their new machine.

The cost of farming was climbing steadily and the growers had to find faster, cheaper methods if they were to survive. They were clamoring for a two-row machine.

Luke did not want to build the two-row machine and said, "You will never be able to pull it." He was overruled again so he built the machine. He was right again and we could not pull it.

The two-row machine was saved by a second generation of wheel tractors that had much more power so the development continued. It was never very successful in muddy ground but it became the machine to beat in the Imperial Valley where the ground can get as hard as the highway.

During the beet season, I worked as a factory representative for the manufacturers and followed the little machine to every beet growing area in the United States and Canada. I could see that tremendous changes were taking place in the beet industry and wanted to build a wheel lifter for the Midwest and the mud and spike wheel machine for California conditions.

I believed that it was necessary to give the growers and dealers what they wanted. I also wanted to preserve the vast sales organization that had been built up by the sales of the small machines.

There were no patent royalties on the sales of the wheel lifter machines so I was overruled by the investment group who wanted to do it their way. They formed a high-pressure sales organization and forced untested machines into areas where they did not belong.

Modifications and changes were needed to fit the new areas and the burden fell on Luke. I went to work to help Luke out but there was no way we could satisfy the claims of the sales department. The sales organization and the two-row machine faded until the only area that was left was the Imperial Valley of California.

My years of experience in the sugar beet industry now led me to some sound conclusions. I believe that all manufacturers of farm machinery and their sales staffs are self-destructive. I know that is very bold statement and requires an explanation.

Manufacturers do not sell to consumers; they sell to dealers. The sales staff assume that the more dealers there are the more sales there will be. Anyone can become a dealer by purchasing the required number of machines. Sales were achieved in this way and the manufacturers were happy. The dealers found themselves in a saturated market and competing with each other for little or no profits. They dumped their inventory in order to get out and the system collapsed.

I saw this happening to dealer after dealer but there were still many thousands of acres of sugar beets in Imperial Valley and a huge parts market existed.

Growers cannot operate with parts that must be ordered so I started a business to manufacture and stock parts for all makes of beet harvesters.

During the next five years we modified and improved parts for the two-row machine to improve its performance and dependability and today it is the overall performance champion of the valley.

The growers liked our "get them and go" parts service and the business expanded very rapidly.

Just about the time it was ready to relax, disaster struck again. The bolt manufacturing company that made our spikes for many years could not get the square steel wire that was needed and would make no more spikes.

I went to a stamping company and the owner said "he could stamp spikes from steel plate faster, better and cheaper." I paid for the stamping dies and had the steel delivered to him. Instead of getting spikes I got excuses. So I went to check it out. I found that the plant owner and his wife were involved in a divorce case.

He left and his wife and her employees tried to stamp the spikes. It was not successful so I had the steel hauled to my shop and called brother Luke for assistance. He made a pattern and burned the spikes from the plate with an automatic profile machine. After many problems and a difficult period of development, we were making spikes but the beet season was only a month away.

Six months had passed while I struggled to achieve spike production and during this time there were other developments.

A sugar beet harvesting contractor went to Mexico and found someone to manufacture spikes for him. It was too soon for me to guarantee delivery or performance for my spikes, so I was happy that there was another source of supply. Many of my loyal customers knew of my efforts and problems and agreed to wait for their spikes.

The day that beet season started, I answered the phone and a furious farmer said, "Those lousy spikes are all bent back like the quills on a porcupine. Have you got any of your spikes?"

Our store began to fill up with people and they were all demanding spikes but I had slowed the operation and was making spikes on order only. I told the growers that I would increase the production but they would have to get by until their name came up on the order list. All my family and relations went to work making spikes. We worked overtime and weekends and the manufacturing process improved as we went along. We were able to supply the demand and finished the season with spikes in stock.

The growers were all looking for the beet contractor to get their money back, but he was long gone. I told them that he had gone away to school to learn about steel and heat treating, but they did not appreciate it.

We developed our spikes until they are, by far, the best spikes we have ever had and we are now in full charge of production and no longer dependent on people who were involved with other suppliers.

Over the years, hundreds of the spike wheel harvesters, changing times, conditions, bad decisions and greed eliminated all of them until I was the sole owner of all that was left. Truly the invention had come full circle.

The real reward was the education that came with the development of the beet harvester and it was far greater than the monetary gain.

I have always been told that properly educated engineers can build anything. That may be true but they can never tell you how long it will take or how much it will cost. They do not understand that there is nothing in farming that is constant and new problems will appear as fast as they are solved.

The manufacturer of the beet harvesters believed that a college degree was necessary to design and build farm machinery. He hired a task force and planned to mechanize all phases of the farm industry. The engineering group spent a lot of time and large sums of money but most of what they built was absurd and unsaleable.

Most of the successful products that kept the manufacturer in business were developed by people with no formal education.

I now know that to be successful in the development of farm machinery, someone has to get dirty, sunburned, bug-bitten, frozen and muddy and they must be fully determined to make it work regardless of conditions. We paid our dues.

I now dream of a second-generation sugar beet harvester that could solve all the problems that remain. Years of experience and modern technology would make it possible.

I am retired now so the dream of a self-propelled, four-wheel drive, three row beet harvester will remain just a beautiful dream. My nephew John and his wife Kathy now operate the parts business and I believe that spike wheel machines will be rolling in the harvest as long as there are beets in Imperial Valley.

Lloyd Schmidt, "California Packing Corporation, #22"

[Editor's note: Lloyd Schmidt, "California Packing Corporation Plant #22," *Rio Vista Short Stories* (Bend, OR: Maverick Press, 1991), pp 35–40. (*By permission*). Canneries were a critical part of the agricultural success of the Sacramento–San Joaquin River Delta, allowing farmers to grow crops that could perish before they could be brought to market. However, canneries declined once the crops they processed could not be grown as cheaply as in other places. Still, they dominated the social life of towns while they were economically viable. See Fig. 24.]

Rio Vista was known worldwide for California Packing Corporation Plant #22. It was the largest asparagus cannery in the world and was located on forty acres of land that fronted the Sacramento River and was a long asparagus butt throw north of the Rio Vista Bridge.

The rich delta lands were being reclaimed from the tule swamps and the soil, water and weather conditions were favorably suited for the production of asparagus. The roots of the asparagus plants looked like a black mass of interwoven twigs and they were planted in shallow furrows on wide row spacings. Once they were planted the roots remained in the ground and were productive for about ten years. It was necessary to get the rows as straight as possible because repeated cultivations of the rows would take place for many seasons.

A unique "Yuba Tractor," that was manufactured in Benicia had caterpillar tracks that rolled on big ball bearings and it was perfectly suited to the soft delta soil. A steerable front wheel made small steering correction possible and a steel arrow that was mounted above the wheel was used to sight the tractor at a distant target. Perfectly straight rows were possible.

After a couple of years of growth, the asparagus was ready for harvest. The dirt between the wide rows was heaped into beds over the roots and asparagus spears soon grew up out of the beds. Stoop labor from all over the world came to cut the asparagus and the small people from the Philippine Islands were the most numerous and the best. Asparagus cutting was one of the most physically demanding jobs in farming. A knife that resembled a wide wood chisel with a long handle was used to cut the asparagus. One hand lightly grasped the asparagus spear and the knife was plunged into the soil to cut the spear below the surface of the bed. Spears were cut until the bundle got too large to handle and then they were placed in a small cart. A faithful well-trained horse pulled the cart down the rows and the cart was always within a few steps of the cutter. When the cart was full the horse pulled it to the ranch packing shed where the asparagus was washed and put into lug boxes for shipment to the canneries. The asparagus beds were cut over and over again and were productive for about ten weeks. When the harvest was finished the beds were knocked down and the soil was dragged flat. Big, tall, beautiful lacy ferns grew up and the first frost change them from dark green to a fantastic display of beautiful colors.

The ferns were mowed off and raked into piles for burning. This was necessary for insect control and because centipedes have a voracious appetite for asparagus.

The smoke from the burning ferns combined with the tule fog and created an atmosphere of almost zero visibility. The local folks said that the smog was so thick that you could cut it with a knife and stack it like building blocks. The reality was that everything slowed to a snail's pace until the wind blew it away, but the drippy, dreary tule smog could hang in for weeks.

The soil and the asparagus roots were depleted in about ten years and the farmers wanted crops that could be changed on a seasonal basis. It was very difficult to get rid of the vast tangle of tough asparagus roots.

Rio Vista had many machine shops that were left over from the river boat days and an asparagus plow was invented to solve the problem. A big rotating mass of sharp steel blades was mounted on the back of a huge crawler tractor and it chopped the roots into pieces too small for regrowth. It was slow and expensive but it left the land in perfect shape for the immediate planting of other crops.

The roaring asparagus plows crawled slowly up and down the rows chopping the tough roots into small bits. After many years of difficult work most of the asparagus was gone forever. During the heydays the harvested asparagus was shipped to Plant #22 and that triggered a chain of events that were known as "Cannery Season."

In the depression years of the early thirties people of all races, colors and creeds came to find work in the canneries. The population explosion in the small town created many problems but Rio Vista merchants loved it. More school rooms had to be found. The students were an unusual blending of many nationalities and school clothes were a mixed-up mess of foreign influence but were very casual and colorful.

Plant #22 provided row after row of small box like houses. There were public toilets and wash rooms and cannery life, at the very best, was meager and difficult, but it was not all drudgery.

The many young boys met the eager young girls and life swirled in a madness of work and play. There were rivalries and jealousies and romances that often led to marriage. Old cars and motorcycles were a part of the moving scene and car-seat college had many eager students. Motorcycles had no macho image and were used strictly for the economy they could provide.

Boys and girls riding double on motorcycles roared along the narrow winding levee roads but the bikes had lots of roving room and there were few accidents.

Other canneries along the great river were canning pickles, peaches, pears and asparagus and the wealth of the delta was being put into cans. The cars and the bikes cruised the area in a never ending "Hunting Parade." The boys met the girls and dates were made for the local dances. Cannery leisure time could be very exciting and lots of fun.

At Plant #22 the women worked at piece work and sorted the asparagus for size and color. The spears were cut to proper length and placed in the cans. The asparagus butts, which were about two inches long, were simply dumped into the river and that caused another group of problems.

Kids in the snow country had their winter snowball fights but the kids in Rio Vista had their summer asparagus butt wars. The butts gathered in the back waters and were a perpetual supply of ammunition. Whirling butts hit bare skin with stinging results and wars were won and lost by counting the number of red welts inflicted. In the heat of the summer the butts began to decay and the stench was almost unbearable. Flies swarmed for the feast and some cannery days were also very difficult days.

After the women had packed the asparagus in the cans the men filled them with salt water and ran them through the seamer machines. The can lids were sealed on and the trays were then moved to the big steam heated retorts where the asparagus was cooked in the cans. The cooking was a very delicate operation because the pressure in the retort had to exactly balance the pressure in the cans to prevent them from exploding. Each retort load was a batch and each batch was numbered for quality control. Six people in sanitary uniforms came to open and test the asparagus and only the very best was selected to wear the famous "Del Monte Brand," label. The others would be labeled with the brand names of the purchasers when they were sold.

The cannery operated for about ten weeks and the cavernous warehouses were filled from floor to rafters with the stacked cans. The can stackers were also piece workers and were paid by the completed stack. There was always friendly competition to see who was the fastest can stacker. The dexterity they developed was so smooth that it looked like a continuous stream of trays was flying through the air without assistance. Every tray landed in exactly the right spot and the speed and precision was remarkable.

When the cannery season was over most workers left, but a small force of local people continued to work there temporarily. They labeled the cans and got them ready for shipment. The people who were putting the cans into the cases broke the boredom by putting cards asking for pen pals in the cases with the cans. Replies were received from many places. California Packing Corporation Plant #22 that was located at Rio Vista, California, became known to many people all over the world.

The freight boats that arrived to pick up the asparagus used two-cycle, direct reversing diesel engines and it was always exciting to see them come in for a landing. Without hardly slowing down they came in on a long angle. At precisely the right moment the Captain gave the order for full reverse. The engines were stopped and there was dead silence as the injector timing was shifted. A 300-pound blast of compressed air hit the pistons and the engines started in the opposite rotation. There was the rumble of thunder and big cloud of black smoke as the freight boat put on the brakes and then lightly touched the wharf in a perfect landing. Small fork lift trucks scurried in and out of the warehouse like ants working on a sugar sack and the freight boat was soon loaded.

The thunder roared and the black smoke billowed again as the diesels fired up in forward rotation and the freight boat was on her way to far-away places.

The decline in the production of asparagus and competition from Texas and Mexico caused Plant #22 to close and it sat idle for many years. Old age and neglect made the original part of the cannery unsafe so it was torn down. The new warehouses that were in back of the main cannery remained.

The Blackwelder Iron Works bought the property to manufacture a new sugar beet harvester that was invented on near-by Ryer Island. The warehouses were converted to manufacturing shops and the location again provided many jobs for the people of Rio vista. The beet harvesters were sold worldwide and the Blackwelder Manufacturing Company, of Rio Vista, became known everywhere that sugar beets are grown.

The Blackwelder Manufacturing Company makes many other products there now but the old timers cannot pass that location without recalling fond memories of California Packing Corporation Plant #22.

7

Owners and Laborers

[Editor's note: The two classes in the Sacramento–San Joaquin River Delta were the owners and the laborers. The social reality approached what Carey McWilliams called the "factory in the fields." The owners were in a consistent battle with nature (flooding in particular) and global competition. They could adjust crops to respond, but the risks were real. These struggles played out during a period where owners were declining in power at the state level and labor was increasingly restless. Joan Didion captures the psychic cost of this social system in the excerpt from her novel, *Run River*.

The emotional strains on workers is expressed here, from several perspectives. Jack London captures the competition between ethnic fisherman. Edwin Markham senses the degrading social position of the laborer; his poem, "Man with a Hoe," is often said to have been inspired by a French painting, but may also have reflected his experience with laborers in and around the Sacramento–San Joaquin River Delta where he was both raised and worked. Leonard Gardner's *Fat City* is set in Stockton, and the main characters are agricultural workers in the Sacramento–San Joaquin River Delta who underwrite their commitment to boxing by laboring in the fields. *Barrio Boy* by Ernesto Galarza describes the life of Mexican laborers in the Sacramento–San Joaquin River Delta even before the Bracero program was created during WWII. In every case, laborers could count on work in the Sacramento–San Joaquin River Delta, but it was hard and poorly compensated.]

Richard Dillon, from *Delta Country*

[Editor's note: Historian Richard Dillon discusses the stresses, strains and rebounds of Sacramento–San Joaquin River Delta farmers in *Delta Country*

(San Francisco: Presidio Press, 1982), pp. 93–100. (*By permission*). See Fig. 25.]

... By the 1860s, there was such a surplus of vegetables over subsistence needs and local sales that a brisk trade began with the cities. It was the reason for the reclamation of Rough and Ready Island, for one. By 1861, the rich black loam and the sandy loam were found to be so amenable to double-cropping (two harvests a year from the same plot) that a Tyler Island farm, only half rescued from tules, sold for six thousand dollars. In 1869, Chinese lessees were turning the natural levees on the riverside of Roberts Island into long strips of truck and fruit gardens. Eight years later, a string of onion, bean, and blackberry plots reached Rough and Ready Island and spilled over into the old Pescadero Grant.

But the big news of the 1870s was the Delta's harvest of small grains. Both wheat and barley ran from a third to two-thirds higher in yield there than on the plains. That meant a harvest of two tons per acre. The reclaimed Delta was now called San Francisco's Bread Basket. When the wheat boom faded, it came to be called The Garden District of California.

Besides grain and the "trademark" crops that made the Delta world famous—Bartlett pears, asparagus, and Irish potatoes—the land has proven ideal for tomatoes, sweet corn and field corn, beans, melons, squash, sweet potatoes, onions, sugar beets, apricots, peaches, celery, and alfalfa. Less rewarding were experiments with peanuts, rice, jute, ramie, hemp, cranberries, mulberries, peppermint, and spearmint. Pomelos, Chinese grapefruit, were tried, and the federal government experimented with sugar cane (1894–95) on Union Island and the Terminous Tract. Chicory was hardly a wild success, but it was not the soil's fault. It was grown on Roberts Island and in Reclamation District 17, 1860–1914, and there was a factory in Stockton. But San Francisco's coffee roasters could not convert their customers' taste to the continental brew.

At first, settlers cleared peat land by burning off the tules, but all-peat soils smoldered right down to the water table and this wasteful practice was stopped. Burning increased wind erosion, too. From a quarter to a half inch of top soil could be lost each year. Subsidence, accelerated by burning as well as by oxidation and compaction, was destructive of cropland. Ashy dust storms whirled into settlements. The costs of ditching and pumping grew so large that sinking areas, like Franks Tract, had to be abandoned by agriculturalists to yachtsmen, house boaters, fishermen, and the "miners" of peat for gardens.

In great contrast to the disaster of Franks Tract was the rescue of the Pearson District around Courtland. In 1878 the levee gave way and the back country became a lake. So badly hurt were the ranchers that the San Francisco Savings Union found itself the surprised owner of 4,000 acres of submerged land. P. J. Van Loben Sels supervised construction of a great second line of defense. It lay three and a half miles behind the riverside levee and its half-mile-wide belt of Bartletts. This pear paradise extended from Dwight Hollister's place to the W. E. Eastman ranch. The new dike, twenty-three feet high and twelve across at the crown, protected 9,000 acres. The Union paid half of the $180,000 of this walling-off, and the pumping plant ate up $130,000 more. But, by 1889, every acre was ready for cultivation and many were already renting for $14 to $20 a year. When the lake in the lowest part of the district dried up in June, it became a field of beans that produced forty sacks to the acre in September.

Alex Brown, in 1887, leased 3,830 acres still held by the Union and raised two crops a year on what W. J. Davis called the "no longer Dismal Swamp." A 32-acre parcel yielded, in one year, 11,580 sacks of potatoes, 300 of onions, and 50 of sweet potatoes, plus a ton and a half of beans per acre. These yields made the Pearson District, in Davis's words, "a new Land of Goshen." By 1889, three new orchards were planted, the Union put up neat and substantial residences and barns for workers and subtenants, and Alex Brown was giving asparagus a try.

A promotional brochure of 1914 was being modest, not boastful, when it described Delta yields as always bountiful and usually phenomenal. It pointed to crop values of $100 to $200 per acre of asparagus (on 20,500 acres), $100 to $400 for pears, and $50 to $100 for potatoes. Almost seventy years ago, Delta fields whatever the crop, were averaging out at $100 an acre in yield.

In recent years, there has been a shift from such distinctively Deltan crops as pears, potatoes, and asparagus to such mundane crops as field corn, alfalfa, sugar beets, and tomatoes. Today, California produces 80 percent of the nation's canning tomatoes, much of it from the Delta. The five-million-ton crop of 1981 was gathered not by big crews but by UC/Blackwelder harvesters, called "job eaters" by worried critics. These monsters, worth $160,000 each, lumber through the fields at only six miles per hour, but gather in a thousand pounds of ripe tomatoes each minute. No wonder that the Delta's new worry is overproduction and glutting of the market.

Horace ("Go West, Young Man ...") Greeley was right more than once. He also said (in 1859), "Fruit growing is destined to be the ultimate glory of California." The levee corridor from Freeport to Isleton was already growing peaches, apples, nectarines, plums, and even quinces and figs, as Greeley took pen in hand. But pears triumphed over all rivals. The others simply could not handle the seepage and high-water table; they disliked "wet feet." Bartlett pears spread from the east bank to Roberts, Union, Grand, Andrus, and Tyler islands, with sheds being thrown up alongside steamer landings.

Fruit was dried and transported by sea till completion of the transcontinental railroad in 1869. In 1870, 70 cars of fresh fruit were shipped east. It was 115 cars the next year, mostly pears. By 1876, New York and Chicago commission houses were sending purchasing agents into the Delta by riverboat. When "reefers," refrigerated railroad cars, were introduced, the market blossomed.

As early as 1878, owners were offered $1,000 an acre for prime orchard land, though the average price was below that as late as the 1920s. During the decade of the 1870s, a 640-acre farm near Courtland grossed between $5,000 and $10,000 a year from its 60 acres of pears, while only earning a total of $3,000 from all of its other products, butter, beef, and alfalfa seed.

The Bartlett, or "summer pear" (it is the first to ripen), was a European immigrant, like so many Delta agriculturalists themselves. It is the Williams pear of England, *circa* 1770, renamed in Massachusetts. But it found its true and perfect home in the Delta, where it brought wealth to many families because the species adapted itself so well to poorly drained land.

The great horticultural authority, Professor E. J. Wickson, wrote that the Bartlett not only defied excess moisture but "delighted" in soils at which other deciduous fruits would rebel. It withstood neglect as well as thrips, blights, and smuts. Wickson added, "Neither frost nor standing water can avail against it."

The romantic Wickson preferred the peach to the pear because of the former's "dash and spirit." But he considered the Bartlett to be one of California's most profitable fruits, fresh or canned. With its long (July–October), slow-ripening season, in some orchards there were two distinct crops, it was ideal for marketing. It was universally favored for shipping because it not only "carried" well without bruising or spoiling, but ripened during travel.

But the experts slighted the real reason for the Bartlett Boom in the Delta, the eager acceptance of the fruit by consumers. This was partly because of its size (a huge specimen of 1870 weighed in at four pounds, nine ounces) and its beauty. But its sweet aroma and rich flavor were more important than size and color. Wickson was right when he wrote, "The Bartlett is not only the greatest pear in California, but the greatest pear in the world."

In 1914, Wickson estimated that California's 1,751,326 already-bearing trees, of a total of 2,101,236 rooted, were producing 53,483 tons of pears a year. They commanded top prices in the London market, even besting peaches.

Around World War I, the Bartlett Boom peaked. The state produced 48.5 percent of all American pears, and most of that figure belonged to the Delta. About 30 percent of the crop was canned, 50 percent sold fresh, and 20 percent, mostly windfalls, dried. Even the latter brought $35 a ton to the growers, while the overall average was $73. Choice canning fruit was worth a hefty $85 and the contents of the 4,300-plus railroad cars that pulled out of Sacramento in 1919 for the East were auctioned off at $90 to $100 a ton. Early choice Bartletts in dessert-hungry New York City were worth $6.20 a box. By 1923, pear orchards were averaging $250 to $400 an acre and some were producing $800, even $1,200.

Pears are still picked by hand, with skilled Chinese and Japanese Americans preferred. Pay can be either by the hour or by the piece, but dedicated orchardists will tell you that the fruit will be hurt unless pickers are hired by the hour. In such a case, "they will be kind to the Bartletts." The first pears are sent eastward by late June; the crop from later in the season is trucked to canneries or to cold storage in the cities.

Traditionally, pear orchards averaged fifty acres and were owner-operated, though there was some share-cropping, and a few were run for absentee landlords. Most pear growers have been Caucasians, with Asian work crews. An exception to the rule is Lincoln Chan, a Chinese-American of Courtland. Mr. Chan today has a thousand acres (mostly leased) in Bartletts, running from Sacramento's Metropolitan Airport to Walnut Grove.

Pears declined in importance as newly reclaimed lands were opened up, particularly for another bonanza crop, asparagus. The 16,500 acres of pears of 1929 shrank to 4,900 by 1945, before gradually leveling off. By the 1950s, there were some new, modest plantings. Nowadays, pear orchards are irrigated only two to four times a year. This is not only a laborsaving technique, it is ecologically sound. It extends the lives of the trees by not raising the water table and by not hastening the accumulation of salts as, unfortunately, frequent sub-irrigation and check irrigation used to do.

Some anonymous settlers on forty acres of river bank south of Sacramento introduced asparagus to the Delta in the early 1850s. But the first shipments of "sparrow grass, or just grass," were from Stockton, and not till 1880. By 1894, however, Sacramento River growers were netting, not grossing, $100 to $175 an acre from this most profitable of fresh vegetables. The Capital Packing Company had begun canning operations in 1882, but a later improvement in the process led to an explosion in sales. Asparagus became practically synonymous with the Delta. It was called the area's Prima Donna Crop when, by the 1900s, the greatest beds in the world there produced an $11,000,000 harvest, one half of all produced in the United States.

Robert Hickmott planted a cannery as well as asparagus on Bouldin Island in 1892. In just four years, he was shipping carload lots and, by 1900, building a second packing plant. At the century's end, he had half of his six thousand Bouldin Island acres in the new crop. In 1901 his cannery was operating from mid-March to mid-June, putting twenty tons of spears into tins each day.

A rival cannery appeared on Bouldin Island in 1903, and that year, the two of them put up 100,000 cases, for which the world's epicures paid a neat half-million dollars. Asparagus rows and canneries spread to Grand, Andrus, and Jersey islands, and even invaded the Pearson pear paradise (a cannery was set up at Vorden, or Trask's Landing).

Around 1915, about two-thirds of this leading winter vegetable field crop was canned, in 1,031,269 cases. This amounted to 47,747,755 pounds, as contrasted with only 15,915,918 pounds in consignments of fresh asparagus.

Large commercial "plantations" spread through the Delta, since the asparagus plants grow readily from seed and set out new shoots annually. The soft peat soil was ridged up over the root crowns to produce the much-desired white stalks that were a virtual trademark of the Delta's canned spears. Fresh asparagus was usually not blanched, but left in its normal chlorophyllic garb.

The shoots were cut from mid-February to June or July with a long butcher knife or a long-handled gouge. Then the plants were allowed to rest, to "go to fern." Stalks were graded and bunched for marketing, tied with cotton tape raffia, and stood on end so as not to get the bends. The ends were cut off, and the bunches wrapped in oiled paper and packed in crates with a couple of inches of wet moss at the bottom to keep them moist, and an inch or two of space at the top of the crate. This was because, like fingernails, they continued to grow on their journeys and needed headroom.

A scare was thrown into the fields in 1905 when asparagus rust reached the Delta. But the U.C. Experiment Station and Professor R. E. Smith found that it could be controlled by using sulphur to protect the top growth after cutting. However, a real curse came to stay, Fusarium wilt. "Grass" can be counted on for a normal six to ten years of heavy yield and a total commercial life of a dozen years. But replanting is almost impossible because of the wilt.

As early as 1902, asparagus raising was a boom business. The twenty-dollar-a-ton price for it as fresh produce jumped to sixty dollars. Asparagus followed potatoes to the South Delta as land "wore out" on the Sacramento. At first it did not do well there, but then improved between 1909 and 1915. Canneries were soon found at Middle River, Orwood, Holt, and Antioch as well as in Stockton.

Most really productive areas of asparagus were still on the Sacramento when production hit 27,750,000 pounds in 1909–10. But, by 1924, the old fields of Grand, Andrus, Bouldin, Twitchell, and Jersey islands and the Pearson District of the mainland were all past their prime. Ryer Island followed them into defeat, then the Egbert District, and "grass" migrated from tiring soils to new plantings in the Yolo Basin and on Union, Coney, and Lower Roberts islands.

World War II saw a shift of "sparrow grass" to mineral lands, as well as disease free new peat lands. The shift to non-peat soils, by great luck, came just at a time of changing taste, when the blanching by the heaped-up peat was no longer necessary to please buyers.

An overall decline in asparagus set in and the crop almost disappeared from the Sacramento River. Canneries in Walnut Grove, Rio Vista, and Isleton dropped from ten in 1936 to none in 1950. After about 1952, Jersey and Bradford Islands and the Webb Tract had to give up, and the crop barely held on at Staten and Bouldin Islands. But Union, Victoria, and Lower Roberts Islands, and the Fabian, Clifton Court, Byron, Wright, and Shima Tracts on the mainland became preeminent. The San Joaquin area, which had held but 16 percent of the plantings of 1924, held 95 percent by 1952. Asparagus then occupied about 15 to 22 percent of all South Delta farmland.

Labor requirements are high in asparagus growing. The gangs of Japanese, Chinese, and some Hindus are gone, and most of the Filipinos too, replaced by Mexicans. But it remains an important production. The Bank of America reported an actual increase in acreage between 1979 and 1980, from 26,400 to 27,900 acres. Early season stalks are air-expressed to asparagus lovers in the East, followed by bulk shipments by rail within eight to twelve hours after cutting. In mid-April a shift occurs, and the crop is trucked to packers in nearby cities.

Surely, George Shima's is the greatest success story in the Delta. The potato was one of the area's first crops, grown with onions and cabbages in miserable clearings among the tules for sale to Sierra miners, hopeful of a dietetic cure for scurvy when citrus was unavailable. Shima moved the humble Irish "pratie" from the garden patch to vast fields and made it big, big Delta business.

Shima was a young immigrant who had trained at an agricultural school in Japan, but when he began working in the Delta it was as a day laborer for tule farmer Arthur Thornton of New Hope. Thornton is named for him, the Shima Tract for his employee. Soon, Shima was farming a ten-acre plot on shares. He was very shrewd in business matters. By 1906–07, he had cornered the potato market in the Delta. He was soon being called California's Potato King. By 1910, he owned only 420 acres but leased an amazing 8,300 more. And in those days, Delta fields gave up four hundred bushels an acre.

Shima bought 1,500 acres of King Island and spent $75,000 on reclamation just before the Alien Land Law of 1913 went into effect to forbid the ownership of property by alien Orientals. In 1916, he leased another 25,000 acres, including Bacon Island, and in 1922 was still operating more than 12,000 acres, though the "pertater" [*sic.*] boom was now over.

George Shima held stock in a firm founded by local and Oakland capital in 1907, the California Delta Farms Company. It was reminiscent of such great development companies ("land grabbers," cried their opponents) as the Glasgow-California Reclamation Company and George D. Roberts's Tide Lands Reclamation Company. The company was formed to develop the Webb, Holland, Orwood, and Empire tracts and King and Medford islands. For John Herd, Shima's firm leveed Mandeville and Bacon islands and the Shima, McDonald, Henning, and other tracts. Reclaiming was supervised by Lee Phillips, who had only an oral contract with Shima to obtain unreclaimed land, to levee it, and to turn it over to the Issei for clearing and potato planting.

Leases cost Shima $17 an acre the first year and $30 for the next two years. He then would have to move to fresh land because he was limited to three years' occupation by the hostile Alien Land Law. Happily for him, the term coincided exactly with the period of grace extended by Mother Nature before she allowed fungus to enter, and ruin, a productive potato patch.

The Japanese American paid well for his leases of new land, but prospered by his sale of the 35 to 40 per-cent of each crop of spuds that he received from subleases to Japanese, Chinese, Hindu, and Italian farmers. A typical 1916 contract involved a lease of 2,700 acres of the Henning Tract for potatoes and onions at $20 an acre from Weyl-Zuckerman Company. He then subleased for $27.50 cash some acreage, but furnished seed and a foreman or overseer for the gangs of Japanese or Chinese workers. By 1915, 75 percent of all tenant farmers were Orientals. Field hands could each take care of seventy-five acres until digging time, when extra laborers were needed.

In 1918, Shima organized his Empire Navigation Company to manage his holdings, collect his share of crops, and buy and sell his potatoes and onions. He soon had his own fleet of towboats, barges, and gasoline launches to transport his root crops to San Francisco. The wheelhouse of one of his vessels is preserved today as an exhibit on the Hyde Street Wharf of San Francisco's National Maritime Museum.

The year's two potato crops were usually sold in the ground, well before harvesting time. They brought from thirty cents to three dollars a sack, but averaged one dollar. Gunnysack loads were hauled to landings to be picked up by steamboat-freighters or barges for the wholesale produce buyers of San Francisco, Sacramento, and Stockton.

Shima was not only the Delta's first great potato wholesaler, he was the first grower or shipper to adopt a trademark (his red sacks) and to carefully wash and grade his tubers before sacking them. He thus pioneered product standards, or quality control.

Shima learned that peat soils produced light-skinned potatoes. The Early Rose and American Wonder, early favorites, he replaced with the Burbank about 1894. It was later joined by the White Rose variety. With the application of commercial fertilizer, a single Delta area could produce 350 bushels of superb spuds.

A decline in potato culture followed World War, as labor, fertilizer, and farm machinery costs increased and the yield dropped to an average 155 bushels an acre. Still, 95 percent of California's commercial shipment of 6,200 railroad cars in 1919 came from Delta rows. And in the 1920s, when the California Delta Potato Growers Association was doing business at 833 Market in 'Frisco, it is said that ten million pounds of potatoes were still being dug in Delta fields each month.

By 1924, only 7 percent of the Delta's crop total was in potatoes, barely 1.8 percent in 1952. The last strongholds are McDonald and Bacon Islands. Such Stockton names as Zuckerman and Weston have continued the grand old tradition of Delta spuds since Shima's day.

The development of large-scale agriculture in the Delta had its roots in the success of men like Shima. The farming of land in the interior Delta began with the Swamp Land Act of 1850, in which the federal government ceded overflowed lands to the State of California for sale to individuals. The surveyor general planned marsh drainage and the legislature implemented plans by authorizing land reclamation for agriculture (1851) and its sale (1855, 1858) by surveys. A 320-acre limit was dropped in 1868 when reclamation was returned from a (terminated) State Board of Reclamation Commissioners to the counties. Sacramento River ranches grew larger, but they were dwarfed by the family run or corporate owned holdings of the San Joaquin.

The Tide Lands Reclamation Company, 1869, was the greatest of its breed. Its George D. Roberts became the most successful land agent in the history of the West. The company was bought in 1879 by two large-scale Union Island developers, David Bixler and Gen. Thomas H. Williams, the so-called Land Hog. Adjoining them on the old Pescadero properties was Gen. Henry M. Naglee. Other capitalist investors and developers included M. C. Fisher, James Ben Ali Haggin, Lloyd Tevis, and Ross C. Sargent. California's agribusiness, seemingly running amok today in the grape and cotton fields of the southern San Joaquin Valley, alas, had its birth like Moses in the bulrushes of the San Joaquin's sleepy bayous.

The big outfits were a mixed blessing. They did, indeed, hog land. But they also had enough money to build proper levees. When the Land Hog General rebuilt almost fifty miles of Union Island's ramparts, he paid a thousand Chinese fifteen cents a cubic yard of dirt to create fields that would soon yield 26.6 bushels of wheat, grossing thirty-two dollars and netting seventeen dollars per acre. When Roberts teamed up with Williams in reclamation in 1877, they added teams and gangplows and eighty-two horse drawn Fresno scrapers to a small army (three thousand) of Chinese. Then they really went modern and hired Col. Alexis Von Schmidt to build the first of a long line of dredges, starting with *Hercules* and *Thor* ...

Joan Didion, from *Run River*

[Editor's note: In *Run River*, Joan Didion describes the psychological burdens places on a Sacramento–San Joaquin River Delta family by the expectations that they will be successful because of the natural bounty that they have inherited. This is a frequent theme in Didion's work, and here she explores the impact of feelings of entitlement to success on several generations of a family and on the women as well as the men. Joan Didion, *Run River* (New York: Random House, 1991), Chapter 4. (*By permission*). See Fig. 26.]

With faith that troubled Walter Knight even as he encouraged it, Lily believed at sixteen, as firmly as she believed that it was America's mission to make manifest to the world the wishes of an Episcopal God, that her father would one day be Governor of California. It was only a matter of time before he could be rightfully installed in Sacramento in the white Victorian house he still called, in an excess of nonchalance (it had been since 1905 the Governor's Mansion), "the old Gallatin place." Any time Walter Knight spent in town could be explained in view of this end, and he spent, the year Lily was sixteen, a great deal of time in town, more time than he would ever spend again, for 1938 was to be, although they did not then know it, his last year in the Legislature.

Gomez ran the ranch, even bargained with the fruit buyers, while Walter Knight sat in the familiar gloom of the Senator Hotel bar and called at the white frame house on Thirty-eighth Street where Miss Rita Blanchard lived. (Miss Rita Blanchard was, as he so often said, his closest friend in town, a good friend, a loyal friend, a friend whose name could be mentioned in the Senator Hotel bar in the presence of Walter Knight only by Walter Knight.) Gomez was the most dolorous of men; one might have thought him intent only upon disproving the notion that our neighbors from south of the border were so *muy simpatico*. Patiently, he illustrated Walter Knight's contention that honesty could be expected only of native northern Californians. "I pay that bastard more than any Mexican in the Valley gets paid," Walter Knight would say periodically. "Yet he cheats me, finds it necessary steal me blind. Add that one up if you will. Rationalize that one for me." The challenge, although rhetorical, was calculated to lend everyone present a pleasant se noblesse oblige; as Walter Knight was the first to say, he had never hired a Mexican foreman expecting that they would operate under the Stanford Honor Code. Once Edith Knight had taken up the challenge, but the rationale she offered had little to do with Gomez. "Maybe that wouldn't happen," she said one night at dinner, her hands flat on the heavy white linen cloth and her eyes focused at some point away from her husband and daughter, "just possibly that wouldn't if happen if you were to spend, say, one half the time on this ranch that you spend on Thirty-eighth Street."

Walter Knight demanded that Lily observe the delicacy of the asparagus, grown, despite an extraordinarily poor season for asparagus growers in the southern part of the state, not three miles away on the Pierson place.

"Walter." Edith Knight whispered finally, flushed and rigid with regret as if with fever. Without looking at her, Walter Knight reached across the table and touched her hand. "Sarcasm," he said, "has never been your forté." Edith Knight stiffened her shoulders and picked up her water goblet. "The word is forte, Walter," she said after moment, entirely herself again. "Quite unaccented."

Such lapses were rare for Edith Knight; a change for the better was among the prime tenets of her faith. That was the year, Lily's sixteenth, when she tried parties. Through the holidays and late into spring, she entertained as no one on the river had entertained in years, confident that the next party would reveal to her the just-around-the-corner country where the green grass grew. I thought of floating camellias in the silver bowls, she would write to Lily at Dominican, or do you think all violets, masses and masses of violets? P.S. bring someone home if you want but don't come if it's an Assembly weekend, you'll miss meeting great many nice people if you keep on missing those dances. Because Lily would have gone extraordinary to lengths to avoid an Assembly (the sight of the inexorable square envelopes in her mail slot at school turned her faint, chilled her with a vision of herself stranded on a gilt chair at the St. Francis Hotel, her organdy dress wilting and her hands in kid gloves, she always came home for her mother's parties.

She would arrive on the Saturday morning train, and Gomez would meet her in Sacramento. ("*Como esta usted, Señor* Gomez?" she called one morning as she stepped off the train. "I don't get you," he said, picking up her bags and handing her the heavier one.) Although Gomez would sometimes agree to stop at a place in the West End where she could eat tacos with her fingers, he never spoke on those occasions unless Crystal was along. Crystal was his common-law wife by virtue of mutual endurance, and if Gomez brought her into town on Saturday morning it was only to confront her with the scenes of her Friday-night defections. In a moment of misdirected intimacy, Crystal once told Lily that she had worked the whole goddamn Valley in season before Gomez latched on to her in Fresno. "I don't mean picking, honey, you get that," she added, producing as evidence her white hands, each nail filed to a point and lacquered jade green. Ignoring Lily, Gomez would vent his monotonous fury in Spanish, which Crystal pretended not to understand. "You're a nutsy son of a bitch," she would drawl from time to time by way of reply, nudging Lily hilariously and inspecting the dark roots of Jean Harlow hair in her pocket mirror. (Although Crystal had lived with Gomez three months before Walter Knight noticed her presence on the ranch she had become, the moment he did notice her, one of his favorite figures, referred to alternately as "Iseult the Fair" and "that sweetheart.")

About seven o'clock, when the house was full of faint sweet smell of wax and the almost palpable substance of Edith Knight's anticipation, Lily, dressed in the blue crêpe de Chine her mother thought most set off her hair, would take a glass of champagne up the third floor and sit by the front window, watching the cars swing off the bridge and up the road to the ranch. Everyone came to those parties: river people, town people, and, when the Legislature was in session, people from Red Bluff, Stockton, Placerville, Sonora, Salinas, everywhere. Even the people from down South came, proof to the doubtful that Walter Knight was more interested in California than in water rights, than in small disagreements, than in a bill he had once introduced proposing the establishment of two distinct states, the border to fall somewhere in the Tehachapi. "I'll tell the world," lobbyist from down South once said to Lily, "L.A. is God's own little orchard." His wife echoed him: "God's own little orchard." Neither was actually from California; he had met the little lady in a band contest, an all-state high school competition held in the Iowa State football stadium. His band won first prize, her band won third; and three winning bands were awarded all-expenses-paid trips to the Palmer House in Chicago, where he and the little lady had decided, he said, to make it legal. "Came to L.A. with a bride on my arm and a dime in pocket," he added, "but baby won't you look at us now." God's own orchard. "I've got a few of your compatriots in my orchard," Walter Knight said; the Okies were still pitching tents at the far end of the ranch, near the main highway south. Although he said it pleasantly enough, Edith Knight looked at him, reproof in her eyes. That wasn't the way to the green grass.

No matter who came, Rita Blanchard always came. As if she had lain in a dark room for days, conserving all of her animation for this one evening, she smiled constantly, watching Edith and Walter Knight even as she talked to someone else. Her apologetic inattention her face to the world, vital to that air of being irrevocably miscast, fatally unfitted, the kind of woman who appears for dinner a day before or a day after the day appointed, who inevitably arrives dressed for tennis when the game under way is bridge. Her mooring in the world seemed so tenuous that every spring when she went away (to Carmel for the month of April, abroad for the month of May), there were those who said that she had in truth been committed. In spite of what she knew, Lily felt a guilty love for Rita Blanchard: even at thirty-five, Rita seemed always to be sitting on those gilt chairs at the St. Francis. Although she must have known that she was considered something of a beauty in the Valley, the very way she walked into room belied that knowledge, announced her certain faith in her inability to please. She dropped her head forward, brushing her long hair back from her face with nervous fingers; should someone startle her by speaking suddenly, would begin to stutter. Each tale in the folklore of spinsterhood had at one time or another been suggested in explanation of her official celibacy; the secret demonic marriage and subsequent annulment; the dead lover, struck down on the eve of their public betrothal; the father who would allow no suitor close enough. Not even the fact that Rita's father, the gentlest of men when alive, had been dead since Rita's twelfth birthday could abate the popularity of the last theory. The truth was simply that Walter Knight had kept her company for twelve years, and if Rita had once expected something else, her diffidence and Walter Knight's lack of it had combined to dispel those shadows. Although it was rumored that there was not the money there had once been, enough remained of the Blanchard estate to enable Rita to give Lily expensive presents every Christmas ("You be sure now you thank poor Rita," Edith Knight always ordered the adjective "poor" was for her a part of Rita's Christian name, "but French perfume is not what I would call a suitable gift for a *jeune fille*"), to bring home all her clothes from Jean Patou in Paris, and to ask favors of no one but Walter Knight.

So Rita came, along with everyone else, and if everyone had a good time at those parties, who enjoyed them more than the Knights? When the evenings grew warm that year they threw open the French doors and set up the bar in the garden, to catch the first cool wind off the river. "Edie says hot nights make better parties," Walter Knight would say, drawing her toward him, "and Edie's right about most things." There seemed a tacit promise between them, lasting the duration of each party: all they had ever seen or heard of affectionate behavior was brought to bear upon those evenings. One might have thought them victims to twenty-year infatuation. As they said good night at the door, Edith Knight would stand in front of him and lean back on his chest, her face no longer determined but radiant, her manner not dry but almost languorous, her smallness, against Walter Knight's bulk, proof of her helplessness, her dependence, her very love. "Take now," she would say softly, her eyes nearly closed, "we're so happy you came." All the world could see: there was bride's cake under her pillow upstairs, and upstairs was where she wanted to be.

After everyone had gone, she would hum dance music as she and Lily blew out the candles, closed the glass doors, picked up napkins here and there from the floor. Of thee sing, baby, da da da da da da, spring, baby. "Do you know," she would break off suddenly and demand of Walter Knight, "how many times Harry Scott's sister saw Of Thee Sing when she was married to that man who did business in New York City?"

"I can't imagine."

"Fourteen. She saw it fourteen times. With customers."

"I trust she knows the lyrics better than you do."

"Never mind about that."

Still mesmerized by her own performance, she would go then to sit on the edge of Walter Knight's chair. "You go on up, Edith," he said invariably, kissing her wrist. "I'll be along. I want to finish this drink." Embarrassed, Lily would find more ashtrays to empty, more glasses to pick up: she did not want to follow her mother upstairs, to pass her open door and see her sitting by the window in her in violet robe, filing her nails or simply sitting with her hands folded, the room ablaze of light. Of thee sing, baby.

Walter Knight would sit downstairs, looking at the pages of a book until it was time to go to the earliest Mass. He did not, however, go to Mass; only to bed. "I like to watch the sun come up," he explained. "Most people are satisfied to watch it go down," Edith Knight said one morning. "Ah," he answered. "Only California."

Edith Knight spent the day after every party in her room, the shutters closed. Although the doctor had told her she had migraine headaches, she would not take the medicine he gave her: she did not believe in migraine headaches. What was wrong with her, she told Lily and Walter Knight every Sunday morning, was a touch of the flu complicated by overwork and she never should have taken two drinks; what was really wrong with her, she had decided by the end of May, was a touch pernicious anemia complicated by the pollen and she needed a change of scene. She would take Lily abroad. She had always wanted to see Paris and London, and the way they were abroad, you could never tell. It was the ideal time to go.

A week later they left for Europe, and it occurred to Lily later that the highlight of the trip for her mother, who kept her watch all summer on Pacific Standard Time, had been neither Paris nor London but the night in New York, before they boarded the Normandie, when they met Rita Blanchard for dinner at Luchow's. In New York for week on her way home from Paris, Rita looked pale and tired; she dropped a napkin, knocked over a glass, apologized, stuttering, for having suggested Luchow's: possibly Lily did not like German food. Lily loved German food, Edith Knight declared firmly, and it had been an excellent choice on Rita's part. She for one did not hold those who thought that patronizing German places meant you had pro-German sympathies, not at all; at any rate, anyone could see, from Rita's difficulty with the menu, that Rita's sympathies were simply not pro-German, and that was that. The night was warm and the air heavy with some exotic mildew; the weather was what Lily always remembered, and after dinner they walked down a street where sidewalk was lined with fruit for sale. Rita noticed that some of the pears were from the Knight orchards; unwary in her delight, she drew both Lily and Edith Knight over to examine the boxes stamped "CAL-KNIGHT." "Do tell Walter," Edith Knight said to Rita in her dry voice. "Do make a point of ringing him up when you get home. He'll enjoy hearing."

After Walter Knight left the Legislature that fall they did not have as many parties. Possibly due to his failure to comprehend that three speeches at dinners at the Sutter Club in Sacramento and a large picnic attended mainly by various branches of the candidate's family did not in 1938 constitute an aggressive political campaign, he was defeated in the November general election by Democratic candidate, a one-time postal clerk named Henry ("Hank") Catlin. Henry Catlin made it clear that the "Gentleman Incumbent" was in the pay of Satan as well as of the Pope, natural enough *front populaire* since the Vatican in fact the workshop of the Devil. In neighborhoods of heavy Mexican penetration, however, Henry Catlin would abandon this suggestion in favor of another: that Walter Knight had been excommunicated for marrying out of the Church and other sins, and he could send his Protestant daughter to Catholic schools until hell froze over and it wouldn't make a whit of difference. "I don't know how you folks think a family man ought to behave," he was frequently heard to remark at picnics and rallies. Quite aside from Walter Knight's not inconsiderable personal liabilities, he was, as well, the representative of "the robber land barons" and the "sworn foe of the little fellow." Henry Catlin, on the other hand, stood up for up the little fellow and for his Human Right to a Place in the Sun. If he failed to quote Progress and Poverty, it was only because he had not heard Henry George.

On the night of the election, Lily and Edith Knight sat in the living room alone and listened to the returns on the radio. Although the shape of Walter Knight's political future was clear by ten o'clock, Edith Knight waited until the last votes had been reported before she folded her needlepoint and stood up.

"Don't cry," she said to Lily. "It's nothing for you to cry about."

"I'm not."

"I can see you are. It's your age. You're going through that mopey phase."

"He can't be Governor now. He couldn't lose this election and ever get nominated."

Edith Knight looked at Lily a long time.

"He never could have been," she said finally. "Never in this world."

"From the stair landing, she added: "But don't you dare pay any mind to what those Okies said about him. You hear?"

Lily nodded, staring intently at the red light on the radio dial.

She was still crying when Henry Catlin came on the radio to accept his sacred burden. He explained in his Midwestern accent how humbling it was to be the choice of the people—of all the people, you folks who really work the land, you folks who know the value of a dollar because you bleed for every one you get—to be the choice of the people to help lead them into California's great tomorrow, the new California, Culbert Olson's California, the California of jobs and benefits and milk and honey and 160 acres for everybody equably distributed, the California that was promised us yessir I mean in Scripture.

"Well," Walter Knight said, taking off his hat. "Lily."

She had meant to be upstairs before he came, and did not know what say. "I'm sorry," she said finally.

"No call to be sorry, no call for that. We're in the era of the medicine men. We're going to have snake oil every Thursday. Dr. Townsend is going to administer personally, with an unwilling assist from Sheridan Downey."

She could tell that he was a little drunk.

"Snake oil," he repeated with satisfaction. "Right in your Ham and Eggs. According to Mr. Catlin, we are starting up a golden ladder into California's great tomorrow."

"I heard him."

Humming "We Are Climbing Jacob's Ladder," Walter Knight opened the liquor cupboard, took out a bottle, and then, without opening it, lay down the couch and closed his eyes.

"Different world, Lily. Different rules. But we'll beat them at their own game. You know why?" He opened his eyes and looked at her. "Because you've got in your little finger more brains and more guts than all those Okies got put together."

She tried to smile.

"Now. Lily. Lily-of-the-valley. Don't do that. I'm going to have a lot more time to spend on the ranch. We're going do things together, read things, go places, do things. I don't want to think you're crying about that."

"That'll be nice," she said finally, crushing the handkerchief he had given her and jamming it into the pocket of her jumper.

"You're still my princess."

She smiled.

"Princess of the whole goddamn world. Nobody can touch you." He opened the liquor cupboard again, replaced the bottle he had taken out, and picked up instead the squared, corked bottle which held the last of his father's bourbon, clouded and darkened, no ordinary whiskey.

"This is to put you to sleep," he said, handing her a glass. "Now. What you may not have realized is that Henry Catlin happens to be an agent of Divine Will, placed on earth expressly to deliver California from her native sons. He was conceived in order to usher in the New California. An angel came to Mr. Catlin's mother. A Baptist angel, wearing a Mother Hubbard and a hair net. He paused. "Or maybe it was Aimee Semple McPherson. I am not too clear about Scripture on this point."

"He's not at all a nice man," Lily said firmly, encouraged by the bourbon.

"Everything changes, princess. Now you take that drink to bed."

Everything changes, everything changed: summer evenings driving downriver auctions, past the green hops in leaf, blackbirds flying up from the brush in the dry twilight air, red Christmas-tree balls glittering in the firelight, rush of autumn Sundays, all gone, when you drove through the rain to visit the great aunts. "Lily is to have the Spode, Edith, the Spode and the Canton platters Alec brought from the Orient, are you hearing me?" And although Aunt Laura dies neither that year nor the next, she does die one morning, fifteen years later: the call comes from the hospital while you sit at breakfast telling Julie that soft-boiled eggs will make her beautiful and good, and the Spode does pass to you, the Spode and the Canton platters Alec brought from the Orient. (You have seen only one yellowed snapshot of Alec, and that was much later, after he had lost his health and mind and all memory of the Orient. But imagine him a young man, a fine figure of man or so they said, sailing out from

San Francisco and Seattle in the waning days the China trade, touching home once a year with Canton for his sisters and sailing again.) Things change. Your father no longer tells you when to go to bed, no longer lulls you with his father's bourbon, brought out for comfort at Christmas and funerals. Nobody chooses it but nothing can halt it, once underway, you now share not only that blood but that loss. A long time later you know or anyway decide what your father had after all: a nice man who never wanted anything quite enough, an uneven success on the public record and a final failure on his own, a man who liked to think that he had lost a brilliant future, a man with the normal ratio of nobility to venality and perhaps an exceptional talent only for deceiving himself (but never know about that, never know who remains deceived at four o'clock in the morning), good man but maybe not good enough, often enough, to count for much in the long run. When you know that you know something about yourself, but you did not know it then.

Jack London, from *Tales of the Fish Patrol*

[Editor's note: In *Tales of the Fish Patrol*, Jack London describes the lives of fishermen on the confluence of the San Joaquin and Sacramento Rivers with great sensitivity to ethnic tensions. See *gutenberg.org/ebooks/28693*. See Fig. 28.]

Charley's Coup

Perhaps our most laughable exploit on the fish patrol, and at the same time our most dangerous one, was when we rounded in, at a single haul, an even score of wrathful fishermen. Charley called it a "coup," having heard Neil Partington use the term; but I think he misunderstood the word, and thought it meant "coop," to catch, to trap.

The fishermen, however, coup or coop, must have called it a Waterloo, for it was the severest stroke ever dealt them by the fish patrol, while they had invited it by open and impudent defiance of the law.

During what is called the "open season" the fishermen might catch as many salmon as their luck allowed and their boats could hold. But there was one important restriction. From sun-down Saturday night to sun up Monday morning, they were not permitted to set a net.

This was a wise provision on the part of the Fish Commission, for it was necessary to give the spawning salmon some opportunity to ascend the river and lay their eggs. And this law, with only an occasional violation, had been obediently observed by the Greek fishermen who caught salmon for the canneries and the market.

One Sunday morning, Charley received a telephone call from a friend in Collinsville, who told him that the full force of fishermen was out with its nets. Charley and I jumped into our salmon boat and started for the scene of the trouble. With a light favoring wind at our back we went through the Carquinez Straits, crossed Suisun Bay, passed the Ship Island Light, and came upon the whole fleet at work.

But first let me describe the method by which they worked. The net used is what is known as a gill net. It has a simple diamond-shaped mesh which measures at least seven and one-half inches between the knots. From five to seven and even eight hundred feet in length, these nets are only a few feet wide. They are not stationary, but float with the current, the upper edge supported on the surface by floats, the lower edge sunk by means of leaden weights.

This arrangement keeps the net upright in the current and effectually prevents all but the smaller fish from ascending the river. The salmon, swimming near the surface, as is their custom, run their heads through these meshes, and are prevented from going on through by their larger girth of body, and from going back because of their gills, which catch in the mesh.

It requires two fishermen to set such a net; one to row the boat, while the other, standing in the stern, carefully pays out the net. When itis all out, stretching directly across the stream, the men make their boat fast to one end of the net and drift along with it.

As we came upon the fleet of law-breaking fishermen, each boat two or three hundred yards from its neighbors, and boats and nets dotting the river as far as we could see, Charley said: "I've only one regret, lad, and that is that I haven't a thousand arms so as to be able to catch them all. As it is, we'll only be able to catch one boat, for while we are tackling that one it will be up nets and away with the rest."

As we drew closer, we observed none of the usual flurry and excitement which our appearance invariably produced. Instead, each boat lay quietly by its net, while the fishermen favored us with not the slightest attention.

"It's curious," Charley muttered. "Can it be they don't recognize us?" I said that it was impossible, and Charley agreed; yet there was a whole fleet, manned by men who knew us only too well, and who took no more notice of us than if we were a hay scow or a pleasure yacht.

This did not continue to be the case, however, for as we bore down upon the nearest net, the men to whom it belonged detached their boat and rowed slowly toward the shore. The rest of the boats showed no sign of uneasiness. "That's funny," was Charley's remark. "But we can confiscate the net, at any rate."

We lowered sail, picked up one end of the net, and began to heave it into the boat. But at the first heave we heard a bullet zip-zipping past us on the water, followed by the faint report of a rifle. The men who had rowed ashore were shooting at us. At the next heave a second bullet went zipping past, perilously near. Charley took a turn around a pin and sat down. There were no more shots. But as soon as he began to heave in, the shooting recommenced.

"That settles it," he said, flinging the end of the net overboard. "You fellows want it worse than we do, and you can have it."

We rowed over toward the next net, for Charley was intent on finding out whether or not we were face to face with an organized defiance.

As we approached, the two fishermen proceeded to cast off from their net and row ashore, while the first two rowed back and made fast to the net we had abandoned. And at the second net we were greeted by rifle shots till we desisted and went on to the third, where the maneuver was again repeated.

Then we gave it up, completely routed, and hoisted sail and started on the long wind-ward beat back to Benicia. A number of Sundays went by, on each of which the law was persistently violated. Yet, short of an armed force of soldiers, we could do nothing. The fishermen had hit upon a new idea and were using it for all it was worth, while there seemed no way by which we could get the better of them.

About this time Neil Partington happened along from the Lower Bay, where he had been for a number of weeks. With him was Nicholas, the Greek boy who had helped us in our raid on the oyster pirates, and the pair of them took a hand. We made our arrangements carefully. It was planned that while Charley and I tackled the nets, they were to be hidden ashore so as to ambush the fishermen who landed to shoot at us.

It was a pretty plan. Even Charley said it was. But we reckoned not half so well as the Greeks. They forestalled us by ambushing Neil and Nicholas and taking them prisoners, while, as of old, bullets whistled about our ears when Charley and I attempted to take possession of the nets. When we were again beaten off, Neil Partington and Nicholas were released. They were rather shamefaced when they put in an appearance, and Charley chaffed them unmercifully.

But Neil chaffed back, demanding to know why Charley's imagination had not long since overcome the difficulty.

"Just you wait; the idea'll come all right," Charley promised.

"Most probably," Neil agreed. "But I'm afraid the salmon will be exterminated first, and then there will be no need for it when it does come."

Neil Partington, highly disgusted with his adventure, departed for the Lower Bay, taking Nicholas with him, and Charley and I were left to our own resources. This meant that the Sunday fishing would be left to itself, too, until such time as Charley's idea happened along.

I puzzled my head a good deal to find out some way of checkmating the Greeks, as also did Charley, and we broached a thousand expedients which on discussion proved worthless.

The fishermen, on the other hand, were in high feather, and their boasts went up and down the river to add to our discomfiture. Among all classes of them we became aware of a growing insubordination. We were beaten, and they were losing respect for us. With the loss of respect, contempt began to arise. Charley began to be spoken of as the "old a woman," and I received my rating as the "pee-wee kid." The situation was fast becoming unbearable, and we knew that we should have to deliver a stunning stroke at the Greeks in order to regain the old-time respect in which we had stood.

Then one morning the idea came. We were down on Steamboat Wharf, where the river steamers made their landings, and where we found a group of amused longshoremen and loafers listening to the hard-luck tale of a sleepy-eyed young fellow in long sea-boots. He was a sort of amateur fisherman, he said, fishing for the local market of Berkeley. Now Berkeley was on the Lower Bay, thirty miles away. On the previous night, he said, he had set his net and dozed off to sleep in the bottom of the boat.

The next he knew it was morning, and he opened his eyes to find his boat rubbing softly against the piles of Steamboat Wharf at Benicia. Also, he saw the river steamer *Apache* lying ahead of him, and a couple of deck hands disentangling the shreds of his net from the paddle-wheel. In short, after he had gone to sleep, his fisherman's riding light had gone out, and the *Apache* had run over his net. Though torn pretty well to pieces, the net in some way still remained foul, and he had had a thirty-mile tow out of his course.

Charley nudged me with his elbow. I grasped his thought on the instant, but objected:

"We can't charter a steamboat."

"Don't intend to," he rejoined. "But let's run over to Turner's Shipyard. I've something in my mind there that may be of use to us."

And over we went to the shipyard, where Charley led the way to the *Mary Rebecca*, lying hauled out on the ways, where she was being cleaned and overhauled.

She was a scow schooner we both knew well, carrying a cargo of one hundred and forty tons and a spread of canvas greater than any other schooner on the bay.

"How d'ye do, Ole," Charley greeted a big blue-shirted Swede who was greasing the jaws of the main gaff with a piece of pork rind.

Ole grunted, puffed away at his pipe, and went on greasing. The captain of a bay schooner is supposed to work with his hands just as well as the men.

Ole Ericsen verified Charley's conjecture that the *Mary Rebecca*, as soon as launched, would run up the San Joaquin River nearly to Stockton for a load of wheat. Then Charley made his proposition, and Ole Ericsen shook his head.

"Just a hook, one good-sized hook," Charley pleaded.

"No, Ay tank not," said Ole Ericsen. "Der *Mary Rebecca* yust hang up on efery mud bank with that hook. Ay don't want to lose der *Mary Rebecca*. She's all Ay got."

"No, no," Charley hurried to explain. "We can put the end of the hook through the bottom from the outside, and fasten it on the inside with a nut. After it's done its work, why, all we have to do is to go down into the hold, unscrew the nut, and out drops the hook. Then drive a wooden peg into the hole, and the *Mary Rebecca* will be all right again."

Ole Ericsen was obstinate for a long time; but in the end, after we had had dinner with him, he was brought round to consent.

"Ay do it, by Yupiter!" he said, striking one huge fist into the palm of the other hand. "But yust hurry you up with der hook. Der *Mary Rebecca* slides into der water tonight."

It was Saturday, and Charley had need to hurry. We headed for the shipyard blacksmith shop, where, under Charley's directions, a most generously curved hook of heavy steel was made.

Back we hastened to the *Mary Rebecca*. Aft of the great centreboard case, through what was properly her keel, a hole was bored. The end of the hook was inserted from the outside, and Charley, on the inside, screwed the nut on tightly. As it stood complete, the hook projected over a foot beneath the bottom of the schooner. Its curve was something like the curve of a sickle, but deeper.

In the late afternoon, the *Mary Rebecca* was launched, and preparations were finished for the start upriver next morning. Charley and Ole intently studied the evening sky for signs of wind, for without a good breeze our project was doomed to failure. They agreed that there were all the signs of a stiff westerly wind; not the ordinary afternoon sea breeze, but a half gale, which even then was springing up.

Next morning found their predictions verified. The sun was shining brightly, but something more than a half gale was shrieking up the Carquinez Straits, and the *Mary Rebecca* got under way with two reefs in her mainsail and one in her foresail. We found it quite rough in the Straits and in Suisun Bay; but as the water grew more land locked it became calm, though without letup in the wind.

Off Ship Island Light the reefs were shaken out, and at Charley's suggestion a big fisherman's staysail was made all ready for hoisting, and the main topsail, bunched into a cap at the masthead, was overhauled so that it could be set on an instant's notice.

We were tearing along, wing-and-wing, before the wind, foresail to starboard and mainsail to port, as we came upon the salmon fleet. There they were, boats and nets, as on that first Sunday when they had bested us, strung out evenly over the river as far as we could see. A narrow space on the right-hand side of the channel was left clear for steamboats, but the rest of the river was covered with the wide stretching nets. The narrow space was our logical course, but Charley, at the wheel, steered the *Mary Rebecca* straight for the nets.

This did not cause any alarm among the fishermen, because upriver sailing craft are always provided with "shoes" on the ends of their keels, which permit them to slip over the nets without fouling them. "Now she takes it!" Charley cried, as we dashed across the middle of a line of floats which marked a net.

At one end of this line was a small barrel buoy, at the other the two fishermen in their boat. Buoy and boat at once began to draw together, and the fishermen to cry out, as they were jerked after us. A couple of minutes later we hooked a second net, and then a third, and in this fashion, we tore straight up through the center of the fleet.

The consternation we spread among the fishermen was tremendous. As fast as we hooked a net the two ends of it, buoy and boat, came together as they dragged out astern; and so many buoys and boats, coming together at such breakneck speed, kept the fishermen on the jump to avoid smashing into one another.

Also, they shouted at us like mad to heave to into the wind, for they took it as some drunken prank on the part of scow sailors, little dreaming that we were the fish patrol.

The drag of a single net is very heavy, and Charley and Ole Ericsen decided that even in such a wind ten nets were all the *Mary Rebecca* could take along with her. So when we had hooked ten nets, with ten boats containing twenty men streaming along behind us, we veered to the left out of the fleet and headed toward Collinsville.

We were all jubilant. Charley was handling the wheel as though he were steering the winning yacht home in a race. The two sailors who made up the crew of the *Mary Rebecca*, were grinning and joking. Ole Ericsen was rubbing his huge hands in child-like glee.

"Ay tank you fish patrol fallers never ban so lucky as when you sail with Ole Ericsen," he was saying, when a rifle cracked sharply astern, and a bullet gouged along the newly painted cabin, glanced on a nail, and sang shrilly onward into space.

This was too much for Ole Ericsen. At sight of his beloved paintwork thus defaced, he jumped up and shook his fist at the fishermen; but a second bullet smashed into the cabin not six inches from his head, and he dropped down to the deck under cover of the rail.

All the fishermen had rifles, and they now opened a general fusillade. We were all driven to cover, even Charley, who was compelled to desert the wheel. Had it not been for the heavy drag of the nets, we would inevitably have broached to at the mercy of the enraged fishermen. But the nets, fastened to the bottom of the *Mary Rebecca* well aft, held her stern into the wind, and she continued to plough on, though somewhat erratically.

Charley, lying on the deck, could just manage to reach the lower spokes of the wheel; but while he could steer after a fashion, it was very awkward. Ole Ericsen bethought himself of a large piece of sheet steel in the empty hold. It was in fact a plate from the side of the New Jersey, a steamer which had recently been wrecked outside the Golden Gate, and in the salving of which the *Mary Rebecca* had taken part.

Crawling carefully along the deck, the two sailors, Ole, and myself got the heavy plate on deck and aft, where we reared it as a shield between the wheel and the fishermen. The bullets whanged and banged against it till it rang like a bull's-eye, but Charley grinned in its shelter, and coolly went on steering. So we raced along, behind us a howling, screaming bedlam of wrathful Greeks, Collinsville ahead, and bullets spat-spatting all around us.

"Ole," Charley said in a faint voice, "I don't know what we're going to do."

Ole Ericsen, lying on his back close to the rail and grinning upward at the sky, turned over on his side and looked at him. "Ay tank we go into Collinsville yust der same," he said.

"But we can't stop," Charley groaned. "I never thought of it, but we can't stop."

A look of consternation slowly overspread Ole Ericsen's broad face. It was only too true. We had a hornet's nest on our hands, and to stop at Collinsville would be to have it about our ears.

"Every man Jack of them has a gun," one of the sailors remarked cheerfully.

"Yes, and a knife, too," the other sailor added.

It was Ole Ericsen's turn to groan. "What for a Svaidish faller like me monkey with none of my biziness, I don't know," he soliloquized. A bullet glanced on the stern and sang off to starboard like a spiteful bee.

"There's nothing to do but plump the *Mary Rebecca* ashore and run for it," was the verdict of the first cheerful sailor.

"And leaf der *Mary Rebecca*?" Ole demanded, with unspeakable horror in his voice.

"Not unless you want to," was the response. "But I don't want to be within a thousand miles of her when those fellers come aboard," indicating the bedlam of excited Greeks towing behind.

We were right in at Collinsville then, and went foaming by within biscuit-toss of the wharf.

"I only hope the wind holds out," Charley said, stealing a glance at our prisoners.

"What of der wind?" Ole demanded disconsolately. "Der river will not hold out, and then, and then."

"It's heading for tall timber, and the Greeks take the hindermost," adjudged the cheerful sailor, while Ole was stuttering over what would happen when we came to the end of the river.

We had now reached a dividing of the ways. To the left was the mouth of the Sacramento River, to the right the mouth of the San Joaquin. The cheerful sailor crept forward and jibed over the foresail as Charley put the helm to starboard and we swerved to the right into the San Joaquin.

The wind, from which we had been running away on an even keel, now caught us on our beam, and the *Mary Rebecca* was pressed down on her port side as if she were about to capsize.

Still we dashed on, and still the fishermen dashed on behind. The value of their nets was greater than the fines they would have to pay for violating the fish laws; so to cast off from their nets and escape, which they could easily do, would profit them nothing. Further, they remained by their nets instinctively, as a sailor remains by his ship. And still further, the desire for vengeance was roused, and we could depend upon it that they would follow us to the ends of the earth, if we undertook to tow them that far.

The rifle firing had ceased, and we looked astern to see what our prisoners were doing. The boats were strung along at unequal distances apart, and we saw the four nearest ones bunching together. This was done by the boat ahead trailing a small rope astern to the one behind. When this was caught, they would cast off from their net and heave in on the line till they were brought up to the boat in front.

So great was the speed at which we were travelling, however, that this was very slow work. Sometimes the men would strain to their utmost and fail to get in an inch of the rope; at other times they came ahead more rapidly.

When the four boats were near enough together for a man to pass from one to another, one Greek from each of three got into the nearest boat to us, taking his rifle with him. This made five in the foremost boat, and it was plain that their intention was to board us. This they undertook to do, by main strength and sweat, running hand over hand the float-line of a net. And though it was slow, and they stopped frequently to rest, they gradually drew nearer.

Charley smiled at their efforts, and said, "Give her the topsail, Ole."

The cap at the mainmast head was broken out, and sheet and downhaul pulled flat, amid a scattering rifle fire from the boats; and the *Mary Rebecca* lay over and sprang ahead faster than ever.

But the Greeks were undaunted. Unable, at the increased speed, to draw themselves nearer by means of their hands, they rigged from the blocks of their boat sail what sailors call a "watch tackle." One of them, held by the legs by his mates, would lean far over the bow and make the tackle fast to the float-line. Then they would heave in on the tackle till the blocks were together, when the maneuver would be repeated.

"Have to give her the staysail," Charley said.

Ole Ericsen looked at the straining *Mary Rebecca* and shook his head. "It will take der masts out of her," he said.

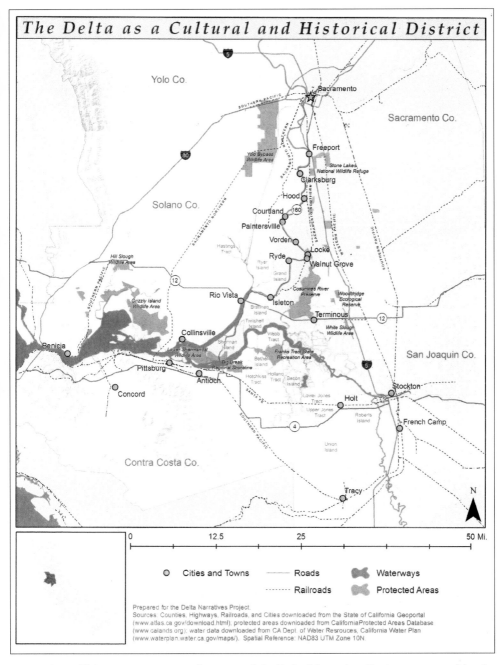

Fig. 1: This map was prepared as part of the Delta Narratives Project sponsored by the Delta Protection Commission. The report is available at scholarlycommons.pacific.edu/cop-facreports/7/. See page 14.

Coiffures de danse des habitans de la Californie.

Fig. 4: Joyce Rummerfield's poem has been posted in the garden at the Blue Mountain Coalition for Youth and Families in West Point, California, as well as at the Calaveras County Government Center. The Miwok peoples who once dwelled along the Sacramento–San Joaquin River Delta and the rivers that were its tributaries were collected and moved to a reservation in the Sierras. Grinding Rock State Park near Jackson, California, has reproduced and preserved some traditional native dwellings here; the photo is from 2012. See pages 28–29. (*Carol Highsmith, Lovelace Collection, Library of Congress*)

Opposite above: Fig. 2: Bridges are the gateways to the Sacramento–San Joaquin River Delta. Here is pictured the bridge at Isleton in 2012. See pages 16–21. (*Carol Highsmith, Lovelace Collection, Library of Congress*)

Opposite below: Fig. 3: The drawing is by Louis Choris who toured Bay Area in 1816, as part of a Russian expedition led by Otto von Kotzebue. During his time in the region, he came in contact with different local triblets including members of the Ohlone, Coast Miwok, and Yokuts linguistic groups. See pages 23–28.

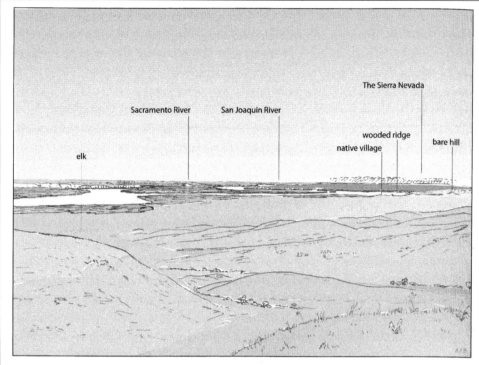

FIGURE 34. A reconstructed sketch of the view from the hills near Willow Pass. The mouth of the San Joaquín ("San Francisco") River is to the left, the low bare hill at Antioch to the extreme right, and the Sierra Nevada in the background. *Drawn by Alan K. Brown.*

Fig. 5: As the citation says, this map was prepared by Alan K. Brown to accompany his translation of *The Journal of Pedro Font*. It depicts the view of the confluence of the Sacramento–San Joaquin Rivers as Font saw it. See pages 30–39.

Opposite above: Fig. 6: Narciso Duran was the rector of the San Jose Mission when he explored the delta. The mission is located near the town of Fremont on the eastern side of San Francisco Bay. More than other area missions, San Jose recruited native peoples from the delta region. In addition to agricultural work, Father Duran organized native choirs and instrumental groups to perform baroque compositions that he arranged. Estanislaus, who was recruited to San Jose and escaped, became notorious for his organizing of native bands who robbed area ranches. Duran arranged a pardon for him from the Spanish governor and brought Estanislaus back to San Jose, where he became a leader among native workers. This photo was taken January 1940 and is part of the William Knowles Collection, Library of Congress. See pages 39–45.

Opposite below: Fig. 7: John Bidwell, an early pioneer and rancher, talks of his stay with John Marsh in the northern portion what is now Contra Costa County. The Marsh House still stands; the photo was taken in 1925. See pages 46–50. (*Survey of Historical Buildings, Library of Congress*)

Fig. 8: Sutter's Fort, is here depicted in an early, probably mid-nineteenth century, drawing. See pages 50–56. (*Library of Congress*)

Fig. 9: This likeness of Theodor Cordua accompanies his memoirs translated by Erwin Gudde (1933). It may have been enhanced by his great-great-great grandson Ted Cordua. See corduan.com/images/Ted_Cordua_Memoirs.pdf. See pages 56–64.

Fig. 10: George Derby came to California to map California after the Mexican War. This picture was published in 1866 and orients toward Mount Diablo. It shows the rather primitive state of much of the community of Benecia at that time. See pages 65–69. (*Lawrence and Houseworth, Library of Congress*)

Above left: Fig. 11: This portrait of Bret Harte was taken in London around 1890 and captures his sense of self as he became a successful author, poet, and editor on the world scene. See pages 69–79. (*Library of Congress*)

Above right: Fig. 12: This portrait of Bayard Taylor is from 1878 when he had moved from journalism to become the U.S. minister to Prussia. See pages 79–86. (*Library of Congress*)

Above left: Fig. 13: Mark Twain served as a journalist for much of his time in California and before he wrote the books about the Mississippi that made his reputation. This is a portrait of him as a relatively young man, taken during a trip to Europe in 1867 by Abdullah Frères. See pages 87–90. (*Library of Congress*)

Above right: Fig. 14: John Muir, the naturalist, enjoyed water of any sort. Here is a portrait originally copyrighted by Edward Hughes. See pages 93–96. (*Library of Congress*)

Fig. 15: In 1860, William Brewer was invited by Josiah D. Whitney to become the chief botanist of the California Division of Mines and Geology. Brewer led field parties in the extensive survey of the geology of California until 1864, when he became the chair of agriculture at Sheffield Scientific School. This photo from 1866 captures the territory around Mount Diablo that Brewer would have seen. See pages 91–93. (*Lawrence and Houseworth, Library of Congress*)

Fig. 16: The Sacramento–San Joaquin River Delta and San Francisco Bay were alive with boats during the latter part of the nineteenth century. Steam-and-sail-powered vessels of all sizes plowed the waters. This painting by Charles Jargensen and etched by A. Drescher in 1887 captures the diversity of craft afloat in these years. See pages 96–101. (*Library of Congress*)

Fig. 17: The steamboats dominated the life of the Sacramento–San Joaquin River Delta through the nineteenth century. The photo captures two steam vessels docking in Stockton on the San Joaquin River in 1886. See pages 101–102. (*Lawrence and Housework, Library of Congress*)

Above: Fig. 18: Josiah Royce, a Harvard philosophy professor, never forgot his Californian roots. While his novel about California has been neglected, his history—*California, from the Conquest in 1846 to the Second Vigilance Committee in San Francisco: A Study of American Character*—is still referenced. This picture, taken by Dorothea Lange, the famous Depression photographer, in 1938, still captures the Contra Costa County landscape that is the subject of Royce's novel. See pages 102–120. (*Library of Congress*)

Left: Fig. 19: This portrait of Frank Norris, taken before his death at thirty-two in 1902, captures his youthful drive. See pages 120–127. (*Genthe's Collection, Library of Congress*)

Fig. 20: Rockwell Hunt taught at the University of Southern California and the University of the Pacific. The photo was taken on the Pacific campus. See pages 127–138. (*Permission given to use this photo by the Holt Atherton Archives, University of the Pacific*)

Fig. 23: Before harvesters, sugar beets were collected by hand. Here is a photo from 1943 of Mexican workers near Stockton topping sugar beets. See pages 157–164. (*Marjory Collins, Library of Congress*)

Opposite above: Fig. 21: Benjamin Holt began a company which has revolutionized agricultural technology. This picture was taken by Dorothea Lange in 1938, after the Holt factory had moved out of Stockton. It illustrates the continuing importance of the Caterpillar tractor to agriculture in the region. Here the farmer is cultivating potato fields. See pages 139–147. (*Library of Congress*)

Opposite below: Fig. 22: Robert Gilmore LeTourneau (November 30, 1888–June 1, 1969), though born in Vermont, developed his earthmoving empire in Stockton. His machines represented nearly 70 percent of the earthmoving equipment and engineering vehicles used during World War II. With his wife, Evelyn, he founded LeTourneau University in Texas. He was a devote Christian and generous philanthropist. This picture documents the significance of his equipment to the war effort as one of his scrappers is being readied for shipment overseas in May 1943. See pages 147–157. (*Ann Rosener, Library of Congress*)

Fig. 24: Asparagus was not the only crop canned in and around the Sacramento–San Joaquin River Delta. Many migrant families would work in the canneries and in the fields to make ends meet. This photo by Dorothea Lange pictures the encampment of such a family on the American River near the Sacramento–San Joaquin River Delta. She writes about the photo," Home of Tennessee family, now migratory workers. Seven in family, came to California July 1935, following relatives who had come in 1933. Father was a coal miner in Tennessee. Reason for coming to California. 'Our neighbors were coming. We only got one or two days' work a week (relief.) Thought we could make it better here.' Since arrival family has worked in walnuts, tomatoes, peaches, and the mother has worked in a fruit cannery." See pages 164–168. (*Library of Congress*)

Fig. 25: Farmers in the Sacramento–San Joaquin River Delta enjoyed success and failure. They stood against nature and profited from nature. Here is one of the out-buildings of a farm constructed along the River Road near Walnut Grove captured in 2012. See pages 169–177. (*Carol Highsmith, Lovelace Collection, Library of Congress*)

Fig. 26: Joan Didion, the famous contemporary novelist and writer of essays, did not live on the Sacramento–San Joaquin River Delta but did swim in the Sacramento River as a child. She lived in Sacramento, which shared with the Sacramento–San Joaquin River Delta a bounty of Victorian and Edwardian homes. One that has been preserved is the Albert Gallatin house. While it is probably more elaborate than any constructed along the Sacramento River, it is not dissimilar from those constructed there in architectural style and pretension. This photo was taken in 1960. See pages 177–185. (*Jack Boucher, Library of Congress*)

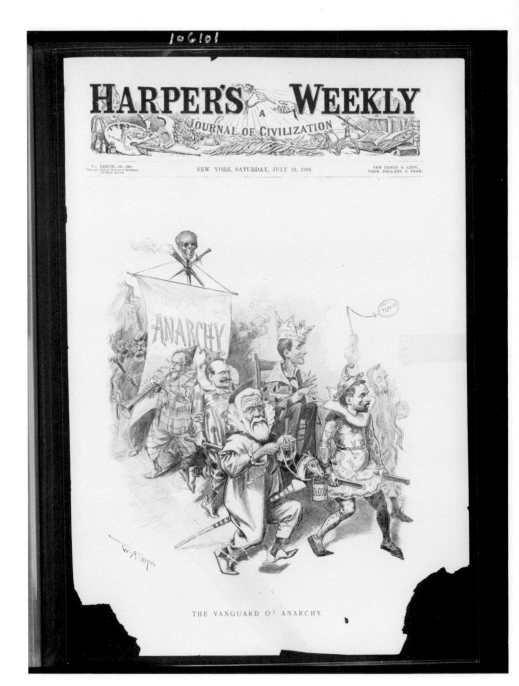

Fig. 27: Edwin Markham claimed that the painting *Man with a Hoe* by Jean-François Millet (painted around 1862) prompted his poem of the same name. However, some have argued that he may have been equally influenced by his life in and around the Sacramento–San Joaquin River Delta, particularly the Suisun marsh area. His sentiments were often taken to be akin to anarchism. Here reproduced is a cover from *Harper's Weekly* that pictures Markham with others considered anarchists (Markham is in the front riding a hobby-horse). The cover was created by W. A. Rodgers and published in 1894. See pages 194–197. (*Library of Congress*)

Right: Fig. 28: This photo of Jack London was published by L.C. Page and Company Boston in 1903. *Tales of the Fish Patrol* was published in 1905. See pages 185–194. (*Library of Congress*)

Below: Fig. 29: This photo pictures Ernesto Galarza, attending a Conference of Industrial Organizations (CIO) conference in 1942 as a relatively young man. In 1936, he had begun working for the Organization of American States in Washington, D.C. He was completing his doctorate at Columbia and later would work for the National Farm Labor Union which preceded the United Farm Workers Union led by Cesar Chavez. See pages 197–200. (*Permission granted by Occidental College Special Collections and College Archives, People Series: Ernesto Galarza*)

Fig. 30: Boxing has long been a featured sport in Stockton, California. What Leonard Gardner saw was the ways employment as a migrant laborer facilitated young men's pursuit of the sport. Earlier at Stanford University, Eaweard Muybridge took a series of films of boxing and boxers, illustrating the animal-like movements of these athletes. This photo was taken in 1881. See pages 200–205. (*Library of Congress*)

Fig. 31: When the Korth family farmed near Rio Vista, nature was a threat as floods were common. Today the restriction of water by dams holds back most floods and nature's wind power supplements the income of farmers. This photo is of a wind farm near Rio Vista in 2012. See pages 206–214. (*Carol Highsmith, Lovelace Collection, Library of Congress*)

Fig 32: Locke is listed in the National Register of Historic Places; photo is form 1984. See pages 214–219. (*Jet Lowe, Library of Congress*)

Fig. 33: The Sacramento–San Joaquin River Delta is part of the western flyway and therefore has an abundance of bird life for much of the year. While most hunting of birds has focused in modern times on "game birds," some cuisines have traditionally served songbird dishes. However, what makes the story that follows clearly Italian is the focus on polenta. The photo from Italy after 1918 shows young boys eating bowls and bowls of polenta for lunch. See pages 219–224. (*Library of Congress*)

Fig. 36: Bruce Robinson, in *Legends of the Strait*, discusses the social relationships engendered by prohibition. While speakeasies and road houses were popular in Sacramento–San Joaquin River Delta towns, prohibition also helped the river steamers keep their popularity. Benicia had grown since it was identified only as a steamboat landing, interim state capital, or a navel arsenal. The photo depicts a thriving community. Its hotels and bars were ready to receive guests attempting to escape prohibition. The photo was taken between 1908 and 1916. See pages 236–238. (*Frank Strumm, Library of Congress*)

Opposite above: Fig. 34: While many Filipino agricultural workers have lived in Stockton and enjoyed an urban lifestyle, others were housed in camps near the fields. This photo was taken by Dorothea Lange, the Depression Era photographer on Ryer Island, April 5, 1940. The caption of this series of photos reads "Company camp for crew of Filipino asparagus field workers. Free wood, no lights, no privy. In world's largest asparagus district on delta of Sacramento River." See pages 224–225. (*National Archive*)

Opposite below: Fig. 35: This picture by Dorothea Lange tells a story of the involvement of children in the Sacramento–San Joaquin River Delta different from William Sheldon's. Here the children are pressed into work carrying water for the family. This photo was taken in 1936 near the American River, which boarders Sacramento. See pages 226–235. (*Library of Congress*)

Fig. 37: Foster's Bighorn Bar and Restaurant in Rio Vista, California, displays one of the most extensive collections of animal "trophy heads" in America; photo is from 2012. See pages 238–243. (*Carol Highsmith, Lovelace Collection, Library of Congress*)

Above: Fig. 40: The Bracero Project set in motion a new day for agricultural labor by introducing a new stream of migrant labor from Mexico. While the immediate result of this infusion was the replacement of workers for those who were sent to WWII or relocation camps, a longer-term effect was the unionization of agricultural labor. The two groups who increasing came to dominate the region's labor force, people from Mexico and the Philippines, joined forces under the leadership of Cesar Chavez, Dolores Huerta, and Larry Itliong to create the United Farm Workers. Significantly, the monument to the success of this movement has been placed in Sacramento, a city that is both California's capitol and a Sacramento–San Joaquin River Delta city. This photo depicts the plaque that has been erected in the old city square now named for Cesar Chavez and was taken in 2012. See pages 260–264. (*Carol Highsmith, Lovelace collection, Library of Congress*)

Opposite above: Fig. 38: Within a month of the christening of the *Delta King*, its passengers were treated to live jazz bands, gambling, fine dining, and prohibition-era booze. The *Delta King* is now a restaurant permanently moored in Sacramento. It was, however, one of the great tourist attractions when it was sailing up and down the river; photo is from 2012. See pages 243–254. (*Carol Highsmith, Lovelace Collection, Library of Congress*)

Opposite below: Fig. 39: Executive Order 9066 was infamous. It began the relocation of residents of Japanese descent, including American citizens. Many families, like Mr. Michael Honda's, were sent out of California to relocations camps far from anything or anyone they knew. Pictured here is the Amanche camp in Colorado where the Honda's were sent. The picture carries the following description of the camp: "12 six-room apartment barrack buildings, a recreation hall, laundry and bathhouse, and the mess hall, constructed by Army Engineers. The Center is made up of 30 such blocks, complemented by hospital buildings, administrative office buildings, living quarters, general warehouse structures and Military Police quarters." It was taken in 1942. See pages 255–260. (*War Relocation Authority, Library of Congress*)

Fig. 41: While the story told by Joseph Small describes the complex relationship between white and black sailors at Port Chicago, only a few miles to the West in Richmond on San Francisco bay, the first naval vessel to be named for an African American (Booker T. Washington) was being completed. The picture was taken in 1942 to record this event, celebrating the cooperation between white and black workers. See pages 264–280. (*Alfred Palmer, Office of War Information, Library of Congress*)

Fig. 42: This photo depicts Bryon Hot Springs resort when it was used as an interrogation center for Japanese prisoners of war during WWII. The photo is from the private collection of Carol Jensen and is used with her permission. See pages 280–298.

Fig. 43: As Hal Schell—famous as a travel writer—documented, many enjoy cruising the Sacramento–San Joaquin River Delta. One popular beginning or termination is the "tower bridge" on the Sacramento River and in the heart of Sacramento. This photo was taken of the bridge and the river in 1985. See pages 299–301. (*Don Tateishi, Library of Congress*)

Fig. 44: Erle Stanley Gardner, the mystery writer and inventor of Perry Mason, documented his Sacramento–San Joaquin River Delta vacations in three books from 1964 to 1969. There he talks of his side trips to Locke as well as of the many marinas and boat houses he passed on his Sacramento–San Joaquin River Delta rambles. This is a picture of the Locke boathouse (once a packing house), taken in 1984. See pages 302–312. (*Jet Lowe, Library of Congress*)

Fig. 45: Levies and bridges have domesticated the Sacramento–San Joaquin River Delta, but are under continuous attack by the forces of nature as George Steward's work underscores. Here is a photo of the damage to a bridge on the Sacramento River taken after a flood in November 1940. See pages 313–319. (*Russell Lee, Library of Congress*)

Fig. 46: Poems about the Sacramento River emphasize nature, but hint at the tension between urban life and the rhythms of the natural world. This picture foregrounds this tension with its contrast between the modern city of Sacramento and the gentle roll of a small boat seemingly arguing for a slower lifestyle. It was taken in 2012. See pages 320–341. (*Carol Highsmith, Lovelace Collection, Library of Congress*)

Fig. 47: The Sacramento–San Joaquin River Delta has provided fisherman and hunters game and relaxation for countless years. This photo is a reminder that the native peoples who lived in the Delta for over 10,000 years began this tradition that continues today. Such human activities bring their participants close to nature and stimulate the impulse to preserve its bounty for the long run. The photo was taken by Edward Curtis, the famous chronicler of Native Americans, and captures a Hupa native fishing for salmon, likely in the Sacramento River. It was taken in 1923. See pages 342–348. (*Library of Congress*)

Fig. 48: The Sacramento–San Joaquin River Delta has many symbols of human attempts to tame nature. This picture captures two of them, the boat and the bridge. The Sacramento–San Joaquin River Delta by some estimates has over 750 miles of waterways, which humans navigate on roads and boats. Captured here in 1992, is the Bacon Island bridge and the so-called Middle River (a former channel of the San Joaquin River). See pages 349–355. (*Steve Pereira, Library of Congress*)

Fig. 49: Jane Wolff argues that the Sacramento–San Joaquin River Delta may someday be allowed to revert to a state where nature rules. However, the evidence of human intrusion will not quickly pass away. This photo emphasizes the natural growth of regional trees and bushes, but also the endurance of a rail bridge spanning a river. It was taken in 1995 on the Stanislaus River which flows into the San Joaquin. The bridge is an Atchison, Topeka & Santa Fe installation. See pages 356–363. (*Ed Anderson, Library of Congress*)

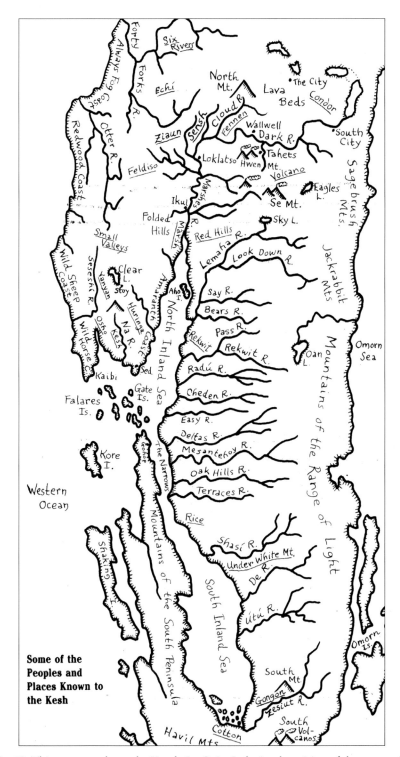

Fig. 50: This map was drawn by Ursula Le Guin. It depicts her vision of the geography of northern California in the future. It appears on page 169 of Ursula Le Guin, *Always Coming Home*, Author's Expanded Edition, edited by Brian Attebery (New York: Library of America, 2019). See pages 363–384.

SACRAMENTO-SAN JOAQUIN

DELTA

NATIONAL HERITAGE AREA

Fig. 51: The Sacramento–San Joaquin Delta National Heritage Area is the first such district in California. The Delta Protection Commission website explains National Heritage Areas, and the Sacramento–San Joaquin Delta National Heritage Area as follows:

"National Heritage Areas (NHAs) are designated by Congress as places where natural, cultural, historic, and recreation resources combine to form a cohesive, nationally important landscape. NHAs are a grass-roots, community-driven approach to heritage conservation and economic development. Designated local coordinating entities collaborate with communities to determine how to make heritage relevant to local interests and needs."

"The new NHA boundaries extend from Sacramento to Stockton to Vallejo. The Sacramento-San Joaquin Delta NHA will promote the Delta's communities, resources, and history. The Delta Protection Commission serves as the local coordinating entity." For more information see pages 5–6 and delta.ca.gov/wp-content/uploads/2020/05/NHA-Factsheet-2020-508.pdf

"And we'll be taken out of her if you don't," Charley replied.

Ole shot an anxious glance at his masts, another at the boat load of armed Greeks, and consented.

The five men were in the bow of the boat—a bad place when a craft is towing. I was watching the behavior of their boat as the great fisherman's staysail, far, far larger than the topsail and used only in light breezes, was broken out.

As the *Mary Rebecca* lurched forward with a tremendous jerk, the nose of the boat ducked down into the water, and the men tumbled over one another in a wild rush into the stern to save the boat from being dragged sheer under water.

"That settles them!" Charley remarked, though he was anxiously studying the behavior of the *Mary Rebecca*, which was being driven under far more canvas than she was rightly able to carry.

"Next stop is Antioch!" announced the cheerful sailor, after the manner of a railway conductor.

"And next comes Merryweather!"

"Come here, quick," Charley said to me.

I crawled across the deck and stood upright beside him in the shelter of the sheet steel.

"Feel in my inside pocket," he commanded, "and get my notebook. That's right. Tear out a blank page and write what I tell you."

And this is what I wrote:

Telephone to Merryweather, to the sheriff, the constable, or the judge. Tell them we are coming and to turn out the town. Arm everybody. Have them down on the wharf to meet us or we are gone gooses.

"Now make it good and fast to that marlinspike, and stand by to toss it ashore."

I did as he directed. By then we were close to Antioch. The wind was shouting through our rigging, the *Mary Rebecca* was half over on her side and rushing ahead like an ocean greyhound. The seafaring folk of Antioch had seen us breaking out topsail and staysail, a most reckless performance in such weather, and had hurried to the wharf-ends in little groups to find out what was the matter.

Straight down the water front we boomed, Charley edging in till a man could almost leap ashore. When he gave the signal I tossed the marlinspike. It struck the planking of the wharf a resounding smash, bounced along fifteen or twenty feet, and was pounced upon by the amazed onlookers.

It all happened in a flash, for the next minute Antioch was behind and we were heeling it up the San Joaquin toward Merryweather, six miles away.

The river straightened out here into its general easterly course, and we squared away before the wind, wing-and-wing once more, the foresail bellying out to starboard.

Ole Ericsen seemed sunk into a state of stolid despair. Charley and the two sailors were looking hopeful, as they had good reason to be. Merryweather was a coal mining town, and, it being Sunday, it was reasonable to expect the men to be in town. Further, the coal-miners had never lost any love for the Greek fishermen, and were pretty certain to render us hearty assistance.

We strained our eyes for a glimpse of the town, and the first sight we caught of it gave us immense relief. The wharves were black with men. As we came closer, we could see them still arriving, stringing down the main street, guns in their hands and on the run. Charley glanced astern at the fishermen with a look of ownership in his eye which till then had been missing.

The Greeks were plainly overawed by the display of armed strength and were putting their own rifles away.

We took in topsail and staysail, dropped the main peak, and as we got abreast of the principal wharf jibed the mainsail. The *Mary Rebecca* shot around into the wind, the captive fishermen describing a great arc behind her, and forged ahead till she lost way, when lines were flung ashore and she was made fast. This was accomplished under a hurricane of cheers from the delighted miners.

Ole Ericsen heaved a great sigh. "Ay never tank Ay see my wife never again," he confessed.

"Why, we were never in any danger," said Charley.

Ole looked at him incredulously.

"Sure, I mean it," Charley went on. "All we had to do, any time, was to let go our end—as I am going to do now, so that those Greeks can untangle their nets."

He went below with a monkey-wrench, unscrewed the nut, and let the hook drop off. When the Greeks had hauled their nets into their boats and made everything ship-shape, a posse of citizens took them off our hands and led them away to jail. "Ay tank Ay ban a great big fool," said Ole Ericsen.

But he changed his mind when the admiring townspeople crowded aboard to shake hands with him, and a couple of enterprising newspaper men took photographs of the *Mary Rebecca* and her captain.

Edwin Markham, "Man with a Hoe" and "The Joy of the Hills"

[Editor's note: Edwin Markham was born in Oregon, but grew up and attended college south of Santa Rosa. He knew the Suisun Marsh area well; he taught in Eldorado County and was a school administrator in Oakland. He published his most famous poem, "Man with a Hoe," in the *San Francisco Examiner* in 1899 and later moved to New York. He claimed the poem was inspired by Jean-François Millet's painting, *L'homme à la houe*. However, it is probable his experience in an around the Sacramento–San Joaquin River Delta region helped form his "socialist" perspective on the dehumanization of workers by the terms of their labor. See Fig. 27.

A second poem presented here, "Joy of the Hills," expresses his appreciation of the natural endowment of the Sacramento–San Joaquin River Delta region, a stark contrast to his view of the social system agricultural work could perpetuate. Both poems were collected in *The Man with the Hoe and Other Poems* (New York: Doubleday and McClure, 1906).]

The Man With A Hoe

Bowed by the weight of centuries he leans
Upon his hoe and gazes on the ground,
The emptiness of ages in his face,
And on his back the burden of the world.
Who made him dead to rapture and despair,
A thing that grieves not and that never hopes.
Stolid and stunned, a brother to the ox?
Who loosened and let down this brutal jaw?
Whose was the hand that slanted back this brow?
Whose breath blew out the light within this brain?
Is this the Thing the Lord God made and gave
To have dominion over sea and land;
To trace the stars and search the heavens for power;
To feel the passion of Eternity?
Is this the Dream He dreamed who shaped the suns
And marked their ways upon the ancient deep?
Down all the stretch of Hell to its last gulf
There is no shape more terrible than this—
More tongued with censure of the world's blind greed—
More filled with signs and portents for the soul—
More fraught with menace to the universe.
What gulfs between him and the seraphim!
Slave of the wheel of labor, what to him
Are Plato and the swing of Pleiades?
What the long reaches of the peaks of song,
The rift of dawn, the reddening of the rose?
Through this dread shape the suffering ages look;
Time's tragedy is in the aching stoop;
Through this dread shape humanity betrayed,
Plundered, profaned, and disinherited,

Cries protest to the Powers that made the world.
A protest that is also a prophecy.
O masters, lords and rulers in all lands,
Is this the handiwork you give to God,
This monstrous thing distorted and soul-quenched?
How will you ever straighten up this shape;
Touch it again with immortality;
Give back the upward looking and the light;
Rebuild in it the music and the dream,
Make right the immemorial infamies,
Perfidious wrongs, immedicable woes?
O masters, lords and rulers in all lands
How will the Future reckon with this Man?
How answer his brute question in that hour
When whirlwinds of rebellion shake all shores?
How will it be with kingdoms and with kings—
With those who shaped him to the thing he is—
When this dumb Terror shall rise to judge the world.
After the silence of the centuries?

The Joy of the Hills

I ride on the mountain tops, I ride;
I have found my life and am satisfied.
Onward I ride in the blowing oats,
Checking the field-lark's rippling notes—
   Lightly I sweep
   From steep to steep:
Over my head through the branches high
Come glimpses of a rushing sky;
The tall oats brush my horse's flanks;
Wild poppies crowd on the sunny banks;
A bee booms out of the scented grass;
A jay laughs with me as I pass.

I ride on the hills, I forgive, I forget
   Life's hoard of regret—
   All the terror and pain
   Of the chafing chain.
   Grind on, O cities, grind:
   I leave you a blur behind.

I am lifted elate—the skies expand:
Here the world's heaped gold is a pile of sand.
Let them weary and work in their narrow walls:
I ride with the voices of waterfalls!

I swing on as one in a dream—I swing
Down the airy hollows, I shout, I sing!
The world is gone like an empty word:
My body's a bough in the wind, my heart a bird!

Ernesto Galarza from *Barrio Boy*

[Editor's note: Ernesto Galarza was born in Mexico in 1905, but his family migrated to Sacramento where he spent his formative years. He later reflected on his coming of age and his early exposure to farm labor in his autobiographical *Barrio Boy*, published in 1971. After high school, he matriculated at Occidental College, completed a master's degree at Stanford, and later finished a doctorate at Columbia. He long worked in labor relations, first for the Organization of American States and later the National Farm Labor Union. The excerpt below is from Ernesto Galarza, *Barrio Boy* (Notre Dame: University of Notre Dame Press, 2011), pp. 293–96. (*By permission*). See Fig. 29.]

Barrio Boy

... It was during the summer vacation that school did not interfere with making a living, the time of the year when I went with other barrio people to the ranches to look for work. Still too young to shape up with the day-haul gangs, I loitered on skid row, picking up conversation and reading the chalk signs about work that was being offered. For a few days of picking fruit or pulling hops I bicycled to Folsom, Lodi, Woodland, Freeport, Walnut Grove, Marysville, Slough House, Florin, and places that had no name. Looking for work, I pedaled through a countryside blocked off, mile after mile, into orchards, vineyards, and vegetable farms. Along the ditch banks, where the grass, the morning glory, and the wild oats made a soft mattress I unrolled my bindle and slept.

In the labor camps, I shared the summertime of the lives of the barrio people. They gathered from barrios of faraway places like Imperial Valley, Los Angeles, Phoenix, and San Antonio. Each family traveling on its own, they came in trucks piled with household goods or packed in their secondhand *fotingos* and *chevees*. The trucks and cars were ancient models, fresh out of a used car lot, with license tags of many states. It was into these jalopies that much of the care and a good part of the family's earnings went. In camp, they were constantly being fixed, so close to scrap that when we needed a part for repairs, we first went to the nearest junkyard.

It was a world different in so many ways from the lower part of Sacramento and the residences surrounded by trim lawns and cool canopies of elms to which I had delivered packages for Wahl's. Our main street was usually an irrigation ditch, the water supply for cooking, drinking, laundering, and bathing. In the better camps, there was a faucet or a hydrant, from which water was carried in buckets, pails and washtubs. If the camp belonged to a contractor, and it was used from year to year, there were permanent buildings—a shack for his office, the privies, weatherworn and sagging, and a few cabins made of secondhand lumber, patched and unpainted.

If the farmer provided housing himself, it was in tents pitched on the bare baked earth or on the rough ground of newly plowed land on the edge of a field. Those who arrived late for the work season camped under trees or raised lean-tos along a creek, roofing their trucks with canvas to make bedrooms. Such camps were always well away from the house of the ranchero, screened from the main road by an orchard or a grove of eucalyptus. I helped to pitch and take down such camps, on some spot that seemed lonely when we arrived, desolate when we left.

If they could help it, the workers with families avoided the more permanent camps, where the seasonal hired hands from skid row were more likely to be found. I lived a few days in such a camp and found out why families avoided them. On Saturday nights when the crews had a week's wages in their pockets, strangers appeared, men and women, carrying suitcases with Liquor and other contraband. The police were called by the contractor only when the carousing threatened to break into fighting. Otherwise, the weekly bouts were a part of the regular business of the camp.

Like all the others, I often went to work without knowing how much I was going to be paid. I was never hired by a rancher, but by a contractor or a straw boss who picked up crews in town and handled the payroll. The important questions that were in my mind—the wages per lug box or per hour, whether the beds would have mattresses and blankets, the price of meals, how often we would be paid—were never discussed, much less answered, beforehand. Once we were in camp, owing the employer for the ride to the job, having no means to get back to town except by walking and no money for the next meal, arguments over working conditions were settled in favor of the boss. I learned firsthand the chiseling techniques of the contractors and their pushers—how they knocked off two or three lugs of grapes from the daily record for each member of the crew, or the way they had turning the face of the scales away from you when you weighed your work in.

There was never any doubt about the contractor and his power over us. He could fire a man and his family on the spot and make them wait days for their wages. A man could be forced to quit by assigning him regularly to the thinnest pickings in the field. The worst thing one could do was to ask for fresh water on the job, regardless of the heat of the day; instead of iced water, given freely, the crews were expected to buy sodas at twice the price in town, sold by the contractor himself. He usually had a pistol—to protect the payroll, so it was said. Through the ranchers for whom he worked, we were certain that he had connections with the *Autorindes (The Authorities)*, for they never showed up in camp to settle wage disputes or listen to our complaints or to go for a doctor when one was needed. Lord of a rag-tag labor camp of Mexicans, the contractor, a Mexican himself, knew that few men would let their anger blow, even when he stung them with curses like, *"Orale, San Afabeeches huevones."*

As a single worker, I usually ate with some household, paying for my board. I did more work than a child but less than a man, neither the head nor the tail of a family. Unless the camp was a large one I became acquainted with most of the families. Those who could not write asked me to chalk their payroll numbers on the boxes they picked. I counted matches for a man who transferred them from the right pocket of his pants to the left as he tallied the lugs he filled throughout the day. It was his only check on the record the contractor kept of his work. As we worked the rows or the tree blocks during the day, or talked in the evenings where the men gathered in small groups to smoke and rest, I heard about barrios I had never seen but that must have been much like ours in Sacramento.

The only way to complain or protest was to leave, but now and then a camp would stand instead of run, and for a few hours or a few days, work would slow down or stop. I saw it happen in pear orchard in Yolo when pay rates were cut without notice to the crew. The contractor said the market for pears had dropped and the rancher could not afford to pay more. The fruit stayed on the trees, while we, a committee drafted by the camp, argued with the contractor first and then with the rancher. The talks gave them time to round up other pickers. A carload of police in plain clothes drove into the camp. We were lined up for our pay, taking whatever the contractor said was on his books. That afternoon we were ordered off the ranch.

In a camp near Folsom, during hop picking, it was not wages but death that pulled the people together. Several children in the camp were sick with diarrhea; one had been taken to the hospital in town and the word came back that he had died. It was the women who guessed that the cause of the epidemic was the water. For cooking and drinking and washing it came from a ditch that went by the ranch stables upstream.

I was appointed by a camp committee to go to Sacramento to find some *Autoridad* (Authority) who would send an inspector. Pedaling my bicycle, mulling over where to go and what to say, I remembered some clippings from the Sacramento Bee that Mr. Everett had discussed in class, and I decided the man to look for was Mr. Simon Lubin, who was in some way a state *Autoridad.*

He received me in his office at Weinstock and Lubin's. He sat, square-shouldered and natty, behind a desk with a glass top. He was half-bald, with a strong nose and a dimple in the center of his chin. To his right was a box with small levers into which Mr. Lubin talked and out of which came voices. He heard me out, asked me questions and made notes on pad. He promised that an inspector would come to the camp. I thanked him and thought the business of my visit was over; but Mr. Lubin did not break the handshake until he had said to tell the people in the camp to organize. Only by organizing, he told me, will they ever have decent places to live.

I reported the interview with Mr. Lubin to the camp. The part about the inspector they understood and it was voted not to go back to work until he came. The part about organizing was received in silence and I knew they understood it as little as I did. Remembering Duran in that camp meeting, I made my first organizing speech.

The inspector came and a water tank pulled by mules was parked by the irrigation ditch. At the same time the contractor began to fire some of the pickers. I was one of them …

Leonard Gardner, from *Fat City*

[Editor's note: Leonard Gardner's *Fat City*, first published in 1969, is set in Stockton and is often classified as a sports story focused on boxing. However, the novel captures the lived reality of migrant labor in the Sacramento–San Joaquin River Delta. His description begins with the recruitment of workers each day and continues with the toll taken by the work itself. This excerpt is from Chapter 9 of *Fat City* (New York: New York Review of Books, 2015), pp. 57–65. (*By permission*). See Fig. 30.]

Chapter 9

Hundreds of men were on the lamplit street, lined for blocks with labor buses, when Billy Tully arrived, still drunk. He had been up most of the night, as he had nearly every other night since the loss of his cook's job; and he had been fired because of absences following nights out drinking. It had been agony getting up after three hours' sleep. After the night clerk's pounding, Tully had remained motionless, shaken, hearing the knocking at other doors, the same hoarse embittered summons down the hall. It had been so demoralizing that he had taken his bottle out with him under the morning stars. In the other pocket of his gray zipper jacket were two sandwiches in butcher paper. He had eaten no breakfast.

The wine calmed his shivering as he passed the dilapidated buses, the hats and sombreros and caps of the men inside silhouetted in the windows. The drivers stood by the doors addressing the crowds.

"Lettuce thinners! Two more men and we're leaving."

"Onion toppers, over here, let's go."

"Cherries! First picking."

"They ripe?"

"Sure they're ripe."

"How much you paying?"

"A man can make fifteen, twenty dollars day he wants to work."

"Shit, who you kidding?"

"Pea pickers!"

The sky was still black. Only a few lights were on in the windows of the hotels, dim bulbs illuminating tattered shades and curtains, red fire-escape globes. Under the streetlights the figures in ragged overalls, army fatigues, khakis and suit coats all had somber uniformity. They pushed to board certain buses that quickly filled and rolled away, grinding and backfiring, and in these crowds Billy Tully jostled and elbowed, asking where the buses were going and sometimes getting no answer. He crossed the street, which was crossed continuously by the men and the few women and by trotting preoccupied dogs, and stopped at a half-filled sky-blue bus with dented fenders and a fat young man in jeans the door.

"Onions. Ever topped before?"

"Sure."

"When was that?"

"Last year."

"Get on."

Tully climbed into the dark shell, his shoes contacting bottles and papers, and waited amid the slumped forms while the driver recruited outside. "If these onions were any good," Tully said, "looks like he could get him a busload."

"They better than that damn short-handle hoe."

"Maybe I ought to go pick cherries."

"You make more topping onions, if we can get this man moving."

The stars paled, the sky turned a deep clear blue. Trucks and buses lurched away. The crowd outside thinned and separated into groups.

"Let's get going, fat boy," Tully yelled.

"Driver, come on. I got in this bus to top onions and want to top onions. I'm an onion-topping fool."

The bus rattled past dark houses, gas stations, the neon-lit motels, and the high vague smokestack of the American Can Company, past the drive-in movie, its great screen white and iridescent in the approaching dawn, a creek beneath ponderous oaks, past the cars and trailers and pickup truck caravans of the gypsy camp on its bank and out between the wide fields. Near a red and white checkered Purina Chows billboard, it turned off the highway. Down a dirt road it bumped to a barn, and the crew had left the bus and taken bottomless buckets from a pickup truck when the grower appeared and told them they were in the wrong man's onion field. The buckets clattered back into the truck bed, the crew returned to the bus, and the driver, one sideburn hacked unevenly and a bloodstained scrap of toilet paper pasted to his cheek, drove back to the highway swearing defensively while the crew cursed him among themselves. The sky bleached to an almost colorless lavender, except for an orange glow above the distant mountains. As the blazing curve of the sun appeared, lighting the faces of the men jolting in the bus—Negro paired with Negro, white with white, Mexican with Mexican and Filipino beside Filipino—Billy Tully took the last sweet swallow of Thunderbird, and his bottle in its slim bag rolled banging under the seats.

They arrived at a field where the day's harvesting had already begun, and embracing an armload of sacks, Tully ran with the others for the nearest rows, stumbling over the plowed ground, knocking his bucket with a knee in the bright onion-scented morning. At the row next to the one claimed knelt a tall Negro, his face covered with thin scars, his knife flashing among the profusion of plowed-up onions. With fierce gasps, Tully removed his jacket and jerked a sack around his bottomless bucket. He squatted, picked up an onion, severed the top and tossed the onion as he was picking up another. When the bucket was full he lifted it, the onions rolling through into the sack, leaving the bucket once again empty.

In the distance stood the driver, hands inside the mammoth waist of his jeans, yelling: "Trim those bottoms!"

There a continuous thumping in the buckets. The stooped forms inched in an uneven line, like a wave, across the field, their progress measured by the squat, upright sacks they left behind. In the air there was a faint drone of tractors, hardly audible above the hum that had been in Tully's ears since his first army bouts a decade past.

He scrabbled on under the arc of the sun, cutting off and tossing, onion tops flying, the knife fastened to his hand by draining blisters. Knees sore, he squatted, stood, crouched, sat, and knelt again and, belching a stinging taste of bile, dragged himself through the morning. By noon he had sweated himself sober. Covered with grime, he waddled into the bus with his sandwiches and an onion.

"You got you a nice onion for lunch," a Negro woman remarked through a mouthful of bread, and roused to competition, an old, grizzled, white man, with the red inner lining exposed on his sagging lower lids, brought from under his jacket on the seat his own large onion.

"Ain't that a beauty?" All the masticating faces were included in his stained and rotting smile. "Know what I'm going to with it? I'm going to take that baby home and put it in vinegar." He covered it again with his jacket.

Out in the sun the scarred Negro at the row beside Tully's worked on in field now almost entirely deserted. Through the afternoon heat the toppers crawled on, the rows of filled sacks extending farther and farther behind. The old grizzled man, half lying near Tully, his face an incredible red, was still filling buckets though he appeared near death. But Tully was standing. Revived by his lunch and several cupfuls of warm water from the milk can, he was scooping up onions from the straddled row, wrenching off tops, ignoring the bottom fibrils where sometimes clods hung as big as the onions themselves, until a sack was full. Then he thoroughly trimmed several onions and placed them on top. Occasionally there was a gust of wind and he was engulfed by sudden rustlings and flickering shadows as a high spiral of onion skins fluttered about him like a swarm of butterflies. Skins left behind among the discarded tops swirled up with delicate clatters and the high, wheeling column moved away across the field, eventually slowing, widening, dissipating, the skins hovering weightlessly before settling back to the plowed earth. Overhead great flocks of rising and falling blackbirds streamed past in a melodious din.

In the middle of the afternoon, the checkers shouted that the day's work was over.

Back in the bus, glib and animated among the workers he had surpassed, the Negro who had topped next to Tully shouted: "It easy to get sixty sacks."

"So's going to heaven."

"If they onions out there I get mo my sixty sacks. I'm an onion-topping fool. Now I mean onions. don't mean none of them little pea-dingers. Driver, let's get paid. I don't want to look at, hear about, or smell no more onions till tomorrow morning, and if I ain't there then hold the bus because I'm sixty-sack man and just won't quit."

"Wherever you go there's always a nigger hollering his head off," muttered the old man beside Tully.

"Just give me a row of good-size onions and call me happy."

"You can have them," said Tully.

"You want to know how to get you sixty sacks?"

"How's that?"

"Don't fool around."

"You telling me I wasn't working as hard as any man that field?"

"I don't know what you was doing out there, but them onions wasn't putting up no fight against me. Driver, what you waiting on? I didn't come out here to look at no scenery."

They were driven to a labor camp enclosed by high Cyclone fence topped with barbed and as the crew rose to join the pay line outside, the driver blocked the way. "Now I want each and every of those onion knives. I want you to file out one by one, and I want every one of those knives."

"You going look like a pincushion," said the sixty-sack Negro.

The crew handed over the short, wooden-handled knives, and the driver frowned under the exertions of authority. "One by one, one by one," he repeated, though the aisle was too narrow for departing otherwise.

Tully stepped down into the dust and felt the sun again on his burned neck. Standing in the pay line behind the old man, he looked down the rows of white-washed barracks. A pair of stooped men in loose trousers, and shirts darkened down the backs with sweat, passed between buildings. In the brief swing of screen door Tully saw rows of iron bunks. A Mexican with both eyes blackened crossed the yard carrying a towel, Tully moved ahead in the line. The paid were leaving the window of the shack and returning to the bus, some lining up again at a water faucet.

"Is that all you picked?" the paymaster demanded of the old man. "What's the matter with you, Pop? If do you can't do better than that tomorrow I'm going to climb all over you."

"Well, it takes a while to get the hang of it," came the grieving reply.

Two dimes were laid on the counter under the open window. "Here's your money." The old man waited. "Huh?"

"That's it."

The creased neck sagged further forward. Slowly the blackened fingers, the crustaceous nails, picked up the dimes. The slack body showed just the slightest inclination toward departing, though the split shoes, the sockless feet, did not move, and at that barely discernible impulse toward surrender, three one-dollar bills were dealt out. With a look of baffled resignation the man slouched away, giving to place to Billy Tully, who stepped up to the grinning paymaster with his tally card.

As the bus passed out through the gate, Tully saw, nailed on a whitewashed wall, a yellow poster.

BOXING
ESCOBAR
VASQUEZ

The posters were up along Center Street when the bus unloaded in Stockton. There was one in the window of La Milpa, where Tully laid his five-dollar bill on the bar and drank two beers, eyeing the corpulent waitress under the turning fans, before taking the long walk to the lavatory. He washed his face, blew his dirt-filled nose in paper towel, and combed his wet hair.

On El Dorado Street, the posters were in windows of bars and barber shops and lobbies full of open-mouth dozers. Tully went to his room in the Roosevelt Hotel. Tired and stiff but clean after a bath in a tub of cool gray water, he returned to the street dressed in a red sport shirt and vivid blue slacks the color of burning gas. Against the shaded wall of Square Deal Liquors, he joined a rank of leaners drinking from cans and pint bottles discreetly covered by paper bags. Across the street in Washington Square rested scores of men, prone, supine, sitting, some wearing coats in the June heat, their wasted bodies motionless on the grass. The sun slanted lower and lower through the trees, illuminating a pair of inert legs, a scabbed face, an outflung arm, while the shade of evening moved behind it, reclaiming the bodies until the farthest the park had fallen into shadow. Billy Tully crossed the sidewalk to the wire trash bin full of empty containers and dropped in his bottle ...

Community Life

[Editor's note: This section highlights two aspects of community life in the Sacramento–San Joaquin River Delta. First, the Sacramento–San Joaquin River Delta threw people from different ethnic traditions together and they learned to share their lives, particularly in times of hardship. Josephine Korth, in her memoir, *Wind Chimes in My Apple Tree,* recounts her family's experience with Japanese neighbors during a flood. Second, Wong Yow, Deborah Gears, and Herb Jamero tell stories about members of an ethnic community bonding in a new land. Finally, William Shelton, returning to the theme of constructing community across ethnic lines, describes the experience of a young boy growing up in the Sacramento–San Joaquin River Delta and participating in a host of different ethnic traditions.]

Josephine Korth, from *Wind Chimes in My Apple Tree*

[Editor's note: Josephine Korth self-published *Wind Chimes in my Apple Tree* in 1978 and is available on the Korth Marina website *korthspirateslair.com/korth-s-book.html*. Here is pp. 65–75. (*By permission*). See Fig. 31.]

Toward the middle of the month most of the smaller islands were under water. Finally it was only Grand Island and our islands, Andrus-Brannan, that were still above water. The tides were running higher each day and we were due for a crest. Already many of our neighbors had left their homes on the mail launch which was still running from Antioch. But my father was stubborn. "Let them go," he said. They passed us by on their way to the launch landing at the district superintendent's store and looked at us with pity no doubt, wondering why a man with such a large family should expose them to so much danger. The day before the highest tide was supposed to crest my father decided to go into Isleton to see how the people there were getting along. He found that most of them had moved to higher ground and had taken their belongings with them. He was shocked when he went to the top of the Isleton levee and saw how high the river was, much higher than on our side of the island, since the Sacramento River is much higher than the San Joaquin River. He lost no time getting home and told my mother that he thought we better get out as things looked bad. There was no way of getting out. In all probability, the mail launch had gone that day and there was only the ferry across the Sacramento River, and even that probably was not running as the floodwaters were running so swiftly the river would be dangerous. To go there we had only a wagon and our two horses to take us.

My mother decided it was too late and we better wait for the mail launch the following day or the steamer that stopped at Wullf's Landing each evening. She immediately started to pack our belongings into two wicker valises and what could not fit in them was stuffed into gunny sacks.

I had always wished I could wear pants like a boy and few months before, my father had bought three pairs of boy's overalls made out of grayish homespun material for us three oldest girls. I was delighted to find that my sister Clara's pair was far too small for her as she had just made her fourteenth birthday and was beginning to fill out. We had immediately taken them to the sewing machine and sewed up the flap in the front. They were very precious to me.

While my mother was filling the gunny sacks I brought my two pairs of overalls and tried to include them in the valises but she said, no, there was no room for them. Then when she started to fill some of the gunny sacks with the soiled clothes I hurriedly stuffed my pants into one of them while her back was turned.

In the meantime, my father and the Japanese workers were building a lean-to on top of the levee right on the road They also built a makeshift manger and moved practically all the hay from the haystack to the top of the levee. If anyone wanted to pass they couldn't except by walking. One thing was very much against us. That part of the levee had been rebuilt during the summer but the rain had softened it because it was not yet quite dry. To help this situation my father covered the area where the horses were going to stand with a good layer of hay.

We had been told by the district pump manager that if the island levee broke that night he would continuously blow a whistle for half hour to try to alert everyone. My father gave last-minute instructions to the Japanese and we all went to bed. I don't think my father went to sleep. There had been some discussion about the time the midnight steamer would pass along the river on the Sacramento side, that it might be a crucial time as it would coincide with the crest of the tide. I think my father had planned to wait until he was sure the steamer had passed before he would relax his vigil and go to sleep. There wasn't a telephone anywhere near where we could get in touch with Isleton to be told that the steamer had passed and that the danger had been lifted for another day.

What were we youngsters doing and thinking all this time? We had never seen a flood. It had not yet been a frightening thing it was to become. We were all rummaging the possibility that we might be going back to Rio Vista to live again and go to the convent school which we wanted to do very badly. I was only eleven years old and not one bit frightened.

It was shortly after midnight that the whistle we feared and anticipated began to blow endlessly. My father jumped out of bed like he had been struck by lightning. There was no wind or rain at the moment. He quickly dressed and started for the little shack that housed the Japanese to awaken them. Outside he noticed Kodama was already coming toward the house with a lantern in his hand. They began moving the horses to their makeshift stall and planting sturdy stakes to tie a couple of cows and calves we had. The hogs were turned loose.

On the road going to Isleton about mile and a half away from us lived a family of three brothers and the wife of one by the name of Raggianti. Mrs. Raggianti was not well and on the days we went to school we left a quart of milk for her. There was a box where we left the milk and in return she would leave some walnuts or sweets for us.

It was not long that night before Mr. and Mrs. Raggianti appeared at our door after we had all been alerted that the island was flooding. They had come in a cart and horse and Mr. Raggianti said he had to go back to help his brothers move their horses out to the levee at Wullf's Landing.

Mrs. Raggianti sat in a chair in our kitchen the rest of the night. She was coughing constantly and chewing cough drops.

We were all up and dressed. There was hot coffee on the wood stove and the Japanese partook of it along with the rest of us. We were now fourteen persons in the group. (Better than the original thirteen.)

Shortly after we were up and dressed my father called us outside so we could hear the roar of the water as it poured into Brannan Island through the break. It sounded like a waterfall in the distance. At that time, we did not know that the break was a half-mile wide. At about six in the morning the water began pouring into Jackson Slough between the two islands. Since it was dammed at our end it wasn't long before the slough had filled and was pouring into Andrus Island right at our door. We watched it in fascination as it started creeping up the asparagus rows so fast as if it were in a great hurry, its depth as it moved along being about six inches.

All day we watched the waters rise higher and higher until there was no more land visible. All the animals were stationed on top of the levee except the chickens. They began to climb the willows as the water rose until the ones on the lower trees were finally engulfed in the water while the others on higher trees kept climbing higher and higher. As the water rose up into the wood pile until it was almost submerged, the rats that were within it began to swim to safety. Some of them swam toward the house and we began a battle to keep them out of the house by using sticks and brooms to scare them.

In the late afternoon, the water reached the gangway that went from the upper story of the house to the levee and we had to abandon the house and take our places on lug boxes under the lean-to and try to keep warm with blankets around us. As it became dark I could see that my father was worried. He kept placing a stick into the ground at the water's edge, hoping each time that the flood had reached its crest and was falling or stationary. Earlier the six men in our group had lifted our rowboat, which was the old sailboat about eighteen feet long, across the levee and into the water in the island. In Seven Mile Slough the water was still rushing so that it was unsafe to try to negotiate it. There was no wind at the time so that inside the island the water was calm.

Fortunately, the space on the levee where we were stationed was higher than the surrounding levee and as darkness descended and the water kept rising we began to envision ourselves on a midget island with the waters flowing on both sides of us over the levee. My mother gave us some cold *linguesa* and bread to eat and cold milk. The Japanese ate their cold rice and hard-boiled eggs. No one talked much. We just sat there huddled together, now and then a pig grunting as it rummaged between the boxes for food. At one time my mother remembered that some heirlooms belonging to a cousin of mine, Uncle Domingo's son John, who was only a child, and which were being kept by my parents for him since both his parents were dead, were still in the house and in a trunk. The water was about a foot or more over the gangway by this time and the levee end was unfastened and floating. My father had to step on it to push it down and then walked through the water and into the house to retrieve the trinkets. Fortunately, he had on some high rubber boots.

As darkness enveloped us so did the wind rise, slowly at first but gaining strength by the hour. It was from the Southeast and soon brought with it a heavy downpour. That was all we needed at that stage for our spirits to sink lower. My sister, Clara, began to sob loudly. That too was all we needed to set most of us crying. Even my mother was wiping her eyes.

My father kept placing the stick at the edge of the water still hoping for a miracle. When things looked bad he wrapped his red bandana handkerchief around the lantern and hung it near the roof of the lean-to but the wind kept putting the light out and he gave that up. As I looked back afterwards I wondered who could have been out there to have been able to give us any kind of help amidst that devastation. There wasn't a soul out in that lonely night that could have helped us. I think he only did it to keep up our courage.

So there we sat. My sisters and I huddled around my mother. Mrs. Raggianti wondered out loud whether her husband and his brothers had gotten out safely and reached Wullf's Landing with the horses, while all the time she kept coughing and chewing cough drops. The Japanese huddled together talking quietly in their language so that we were unable to know what they were thinking. The pigs were as restless as the waters all around us, diving between the boxes looking for something to eat. The horses were also restless, stomping the hay into the mud and sinking into it, keeping my father busy putting more hay under their feet. The cows lay in the mud very unconcerned, chewing their cuds.

And what was my father thinking about? A thousand things no doubt, going over in his mind how we could have gotten out the day before with the Cecchinis, our closest neighbors, who lived on the other side of Jackson Slough. He probably was remembering how they looked at him with pity when he said he was going to stay right there and ride out the flood. His theory was that we would spend the night on the levee and the next day the water would be low enough for us to go back into the house. In his mind, he must have been seeing what we had seen that afternoon which made our hair stand on end. First it was all the sheds, outhouses, barrels, logs, timbers, broken houses drifting by, carried along by the current within the island. After the wind had come up it seemed that our house was bobbing a little as if anxious to join the rest of the floating debris. He probably was glad he and the Japanese had tied the house to the trees around us and was at the same time wondering if the trees would hold. He probably was remembering our other neighbor's horses that had come down the levee through all the mud to eat our hay and how he had tried to drive them back because our horses became so restless, and how the desperate horses took to the water and began to swim across the island and we had watched them until they were a mere speck and wondered if any would reach the other side, a distance of about three miles.

My father stood there at the opening of the lean-to hour after hour staring into space when he wasn't moving the stake higher or checking the horses. He wasn't dreaming. He knew that the pressure of the water would eventually break or go over the levee if the water did not recede soon. But all the time he was scanning across Twitchell Island to where the San Joaquin flowed and wondering if the nightly freight steamer would come up from San Francisco to Stockton that night, since it had to buck a fast-flowing current.

We were all praying, of course. Suddenly he saw the lights of the steamer. It was miles away and we weren't sure it was going to come into the Mokelumne River and go up to the Golden State Cannery as it always did, then back again to Wullf's Landing, before going on its way to Stockton. Everyone now was on their feet watching. As soon as my father was sure it was on the Mokelumne we were hustled into our rowboat, all but the Japanese as the rowboat could not hold us all. When we were ready to untie the boat, the Japanese refused to let us go unless they went too. My father had to explain to them patiently that we would be swamped in the choppy water that was an immense lake now, if we all got into the rowboat, and he raised his hand and swore that after he got his family on board the steamer he would come back to them with the rowboat. So, fearfully, they let us go.

The rain had stopped but the wind was still blowing from the Southeast. It rocked the boat but since we were moving close to the levee it wasn't too bad. We passed our nearest neighbor's house. It was deserted. The workmen he had left there to take care of the horses had left. They had loosened the horses and left them to fend for themselves and probably left on the noon launch. Further on we passed the Everly place. We could hear the water lapping inside at the walls. Even though it was evidently empty there was a dog barking somewhere inside it. We passed the pump house and the district superintendent's house and the water was lapping inside at the walls everywhere. There was no one anywhere and every place was in darkness.

We finally arrived at the landing where we expected to board the steamer. We could not see the wharf. It was under water. On the area, however, where the wharf was submerged there was quite a number of persons sitting or standing on boxes, barrels, or whatever they could find as a place to stand on to keep their feet out of the water. They were all talking very loudly and sounded mostly like Chinese. Mrs. Raggianti was peering through the darkness to see if she could find her husband. My father had rowed the boat right on top of the wharf and we were in the midst of all the refugees. A man came up to our boat walking through the water in his gum boots and started to talk to Mrs. Raggianti. She started to cry loudly. My father had also gotten out of the boat and was walking through the water in his hip-length gum boots. He was talking to the people and soon found out through them that one of the Raggianti brothers had brought the horses out and had them staked on the levee and had left a horse and cart hitched ready for his two other brothers when they finished removing a few belongings from the house. It had not been Mrs. Raggianti's husband who had brought the horses.

Everyone now waited for the steamer to arrive from the Golden State Cannery where it had gone and was now returning. We saw it come into view as it rounded a berm and it looked beautiful with its lights all ablaze. It was called "*Constance*." The crew seemed to know exactly what to do as it tied up and shone its searchlight down upon us. They were all shod in gum boots and oil slickers and made their way through the water to where we still sat in our rowboat. Then we were all carried into the steamer by the deck hands. They even carried my mother and Mrs. Raggianti.

My father went to the Captain and told him about the Japanese and begged him to go into Seven Mile Slough to rescue them. Mrs. Raggianti was crying and trying to tell them about her husband and brother-in-law. The Captain said he was afraid to take the steamer into Seven Mile Slough as the current was too swift and there might be breaks in the levee and since it would be pouring into the slough from the island, it could wash the steamer against the opposite berm and ground it. After a lot of discussion and a lot of tears by Mrs. Raggianti and her other brother-in-law it was decided to go up the slough and rescue the Japanese and also try to find the other two Raggianti brothers. My father left immediately to take the boat back to where the Japanese waited and prepare a place where the steamer could dock and anchor its gangplank.

We were all very comfortable and warm once more, in staterooms provided for us. After loading all the refugees at the wharf, and including horses, other livestock and household goods, we were on our way up the slough, going very slowly. We went out on deck and watched the searchlight play along the levee until we saw my father and the Japanese waiting for us. A deckhand threw a rope to my father but there were too many tules between, and my father failed to get it as it was not long enough. They tried several times and failed every time. Then my father took things into his hands and waded into the water until he was wet up to his neck and succeeded in getting the end of the rope rested on top which of the tules. Then he pulled the gangway until the end rested on firm ground.

There was a discussion as to what to do about the Raggianti brothers as Mrs. Raggianti was pleading for someone to go try to find them. It was very dark but had become quite calm. One of the officers of the ship volunteered to go if the other Raggianti brother went with him. They took off into the darkness dressed in oil slickers, gum boots and with a kerosene lantern. The officer rowed and we waited in the steamer for them to come back.

While we were waiting the rest of the crew and the Japanese began to move the horses and cattle into the boat and also the hay. My father said they could have the chickens if they could catch them. They caught quite a few and tied their legs together. Our two valises and all the gunny sacks filled with soiled and clean clothes were put on board, the valises went into the staterooms and the gunny sacks went somewhere in the lower deck. We also took the blankets and other wraps that we had used to keep ourselves warm.

Meanwhile, according to what the Raggianti brothers said later, they had been too preoccupied drinking wine and did not notice that the water had risen where their house was and that the horse and cart were beyond their reach. They then made their way to the barn and after the water got higher and higher they finally got up on the roof. One of them had been in the war when he was in Italy and he still had the horn he used in the service. He said he had blown his horn all day but that no one heard him. Luckily, he was still blowing his horn so that the rescuers knew where to find him and his brother in the darkness.

When they all walked into the steamer we were in bed but were awakened by the sobbing as the husband hugged his wife and they were all crying. We were peeking through the door and could see how wet they were. We also noted that they were wearing socks on their heads for caps.

For three days, we roamed through the rivers and tules among the Delta islands picking up people and livestock and hay to feed the animals. On one of the days we went back to the Golden State Cannery and my father recognized some of the horses there as the ones belonging to our neighbor which had swum across the island and had reached the other side. There were one or two missing, that had not made it. My father took charge of them and later took them up to the ranch of my uncle above Concord together with our horses, where they stayed for months until the island was dry again.

Back on board the steamer on the morning after we were picked up my mother gave us our best dresses to wear that she had made that winter. We must have been a sight the night before because the officers noticed us and told Clara that she didn't look like she did the previous night and that she looked very nice.

As we wandered through the Delta islands and the steamer kept getting fuller and fuller the officers had to put regulations on the people. At each landing, we all would go to that side of the ship to see the people come in and it finally became dangerous with too many people on one side so they stationed an officer on each end and also a rope to keep the people from crossing to the other side. We children were and were allowed to creep exempt from these regulations under the rope at will, so it was a merry-go-round for us girls.

After the three days and nights of wandering through the Delta we arrived at Antioch. People must have known that the steamer was arriving loaded with flood refugees for the dock was crowded with people waiting for us. There were also news reporters with their cameras taking pictures of the people on the boat. We were all standing at the rail at my father's orders and he held my sister Louise up on top of the rail so we could all be seen to be photographed for the newspapers.

We disembarked together with the Japanese, the horses, cows, valises, blankets and clothes. The Raggiantis and most of the refugees went on to San Francisco. We got rooms at a hotel but the management refused to take in the Japanese, much to my father's disgust. The restaurant where we ate for the next three days also refused to let the Japanese eat there. My father had to buy food for them to eat where they were housed by other Japanese people.

The first thing my father did on arriving at Antioch was to telephone to our friends at Rio Vista that we were all safe. He was told that several persons had tried to go looking for us but had to go back because of the raging waters.

In Antioch, we came across the M family who were also fleeing from the flood. Their only home was under water and they had no place to go so that when it was safe to cross the San Joaquin and the Sacramento Rivers my father hired a launch big enough to take us and the M family to Rio Vista where we had our vacant house on Front Street above the saloon. Here the two families bunched up for the next few days until the M family left.

A few days after arriving in Rio Vista and when my father thought it was safe, he hired a fisherman and his boat to take him back to the island so that he could retrieve the beds, stove and some of the furniture we would be needing and that probably had escaped being destroyed by the water.

To his dismay he found that someone had already ransacked the place and taken every bit of food we had left there. The levee had broken on both sides of the spot where we had made our shelter and the pigs and chickens were also gone. The sailboat was still tied where he had left it so they pulled through one of the breaks near our house into the slough, filled it up with all it could hold including the mast and sail, and towed it behind the launch.

There were things that had to be left behind until he returned to get them, like the marble-topped dressers and parlor tables. In a few days he hired the launch again to get the rest of the furniture. When he arrived at the site where the house had been anchored to the trees, there was nothing there but floating boards and rubble. A terrific wind storm had bobbed the house until it was torn apart.

Nonetheless, my father picked up all the boards he could find and stacked them on top of the levee to help build another house. When we retrieved our luggage and parcels as we got out of the steamer *Constance* at Antioch, the gunny sacks that held our soiled clothes had not been unloaded and went on to San Francisco. We never saw them again and I wondered so often where they could have gone. It made me feel very sad when thought of them for in one of those gunny sacks were my dear and precious pants.

Wong Yow, from *Bitter Melon*

[Editor's note: Wong Yow's story is included in J. Gillenkick and J. Motlow's *Bitter Melon* (San Francisco: Nine Mile Press, 2015), pp. 44–53, along with other stories about the residents of Locke. The life of Locke in the early twentieth century is also pictured in Shana Yang Ryan's fictional account *Locke 1928* (Berkeley: El Leon Literary Arts, 2007), republished as *Water Ghosts* (New York: Penguin, 2010). (*By permission*). See Fig. 32.]

I came to the golden mountain in 1921, when was twenty-one years old. My father had been here for about fifteen years before. He'd worked in Mexico first, doing fieldwork, then found out that wages were higher in the U.S. and came over here.

My grandfather didn't want my father to come; he felt the work here was too hard, that he'd be better off in China. That happened with my great-great-grandfather too. He told my great-grandfather not to come over. You see, even my great-great-grandfather had been to Golden Mountain before. So there's this series of events, where my ancestors warned their sons not to come over here.

But it was my father who bought my papers for me to come over. It was my father who told me work would be available here. Actually, no one needed to tell you. It was general knowledge that work here was better, and you got better pay, and more work. Nobody needed to tell you that.

I came here by myself, on a ship. I didn't a have a thing with me except the clothes on my back. You weren't allowed to bring many valuables in or any valuables at all. I had my own clothes and few pieces of luggage, and very little money with me ... The trip took about a month or so, Hong Kong to San Francisco. I can still remember how crowded the ship was. We slept in bunkbeds in one large room, everyone kind of sleeping together. There were very few women on board. Those that were they kept separated from the men. They ate at different times, in different rooms. They slept in different rooms. We hardly ever got to see the women on board.

I was held on Angel Island for about two months, waiting for my witness to appear, being examined by doctors [and] answering dozens of questions. When my papers were approved, I went over to San Francisco for a couple of days, then came straight up here. My father was living in the Delta at the time. I had just finished learning to be a carpenter in China, so I was ready to do that. Instead, I went straight to work in the orchards, picking pears and trimming trees. Tommy King's father was working in the same place when I started, over near Walnut Grove. There was plenty of work to do if you were interested in doing farm work. We were making about twenty-five cents an hour then, and there was plenty of work if you wanted to do it.

I never did get to use my carpentry skills. It just wasn't done. Chinese people who came over to work usually went to work as cheap labor in the fields or orchards. They weren't expected-I guess allowed -to do anything else. Carpentry work was done mostly by Caucasians or some other culture. Besides, I didn't know how to speak English. That was my major setback right there. There were places that taught you English-there were schools open in Walnut Grove, for instance, that taught English-but because of my age, and because I really needed to just go ahead and work I decided not to go school. Actually, there wasn't any time to. Once you get here, you have to earn money to survive, and that's what I did. School didn't seem that important at the time.

I lived in Walnut Grove with my father for two or three years, then the fire burned down Chinatown there and I came to live in Locke. My father returned to China around then, in 1924. Many of the Chinese people who come to the United States don't like to stay for long.

Once they earn enough money, or believe they've earned enough money, they like to go back to China. Within year or two of going back he remarried in China; my old mother, my real mother, had died already, so he went back to China to remarry. I stayed here and continued to work. Of course, I hoped to make a lot of money eventually. But the fact was, when Hoover was president we were making a dollar a day and work was scarce, so we had a pretty tough time. But as I say, I didn't really expect a lot. As long as there was a job and could get some money coming in, that's what was important at the time. I rented a room up in the boarding houses, the rooms on top, above Main Street there. Locke was a Chinese town; there were very few places suitable for us to live in like that. There were no Caucasians in town, the houses were all the property of local Chinese businessmen here. The restaurant called Al's right now, that used to be a Chinese restaurant. Then as years went by, it went through different hands and eventually Al got hold of it and turned it into an American restaurant. The rent in the boarding houses was about five dollars a month, as I recall. There was a main kitchen, a common kitchen, but we each had our own bedroom so at night we wouldn't have to sleep together in one big room. There wasn't much to it, maybe half the size of this room here. There was a bed, one light. I had very few pictures on the walls or anything else. It was small, just enough for you to sleep in and maybe read the newspaper in, that was about it. We did have a window, but no sink for washing. I hardly ever stayed there for any length of time, though. Most of the time we were out in the fields or the orchards, working. Most of us just rented a place [in town] where we could store our stuff when we left for work. We'd stay there when there wasn't any work to be done. But when you were working, you lived in the camps. You ate and slept right there in the camp most of the year. But every weekend the ranchers would provide a car and driver and send us back to Locke and let us stay for the day, usually on Sunday. We'd stay there the whole day, sometimes till nightfall when the contractor would come and take us back to camp. We could shop, walk around town, go to our rooms. Some of the men gambled. If you had some friends around you'd go and visit them. There were some families back on Key Street, but we rarely had anything to do with them. The children didn't want to play with a bunch of older men! It was a resting day for us on Sundays. Once in a while we would get together and go fishing: that was the main recreation at the time. There were times when we would go up to San Francisco, but this was very rare. There just wasn't time for pleasure trips.

A typical day in town might be to do some shopping, get my hair cut, maybe go to the movies. We would just sit on the benches on Main Street and visit, watching the people go by, or read the newspapers, it really didn't matter. It was just nice to have the day like that, the opportunity of going to town. For dinner, I'd go to this boarding-type cafe: you had to be invited, but you also had to pay for the dinner. Or our employer would take us back to the ranch and we would have our dinner there.

I can't remember exactly how many people were living here. You mentioned 1,500 and that sounds about right. It was over a thousand people. Before, everywhere you looked there were people running in and out, and children everywhere. But those thousand people weren't actually residents of the town. A lot of them were from San Francisco. They'd come in on weekends, and even on weekdays, and go to the gambling houses or just hang around town. Gosh, I can remember all the businesses that were going on-the gambling houses and everything. Of course, you know about the gambling houses, and the gamblers who came into town. It was really exciting! They never caused any problems here at all. The gambling houses were all up on Main Street, and it was up to you whether you wanted to hang around those people or not. If you didn't like gambling, you just stayed away, like I did. I never gambled. I never even worked in the gambling houses. There was always traffic going back and forth, and of course we would have go up there once in a while to get our rides to work; but there weren't any problems at all. They didn't bother you, and you didn't bother them.

Life was busier in the camps of course, because we were working. When you weren't doing orchard work or picking asparagus, you were up picking grapes in Lodi. We got up at six and started working, and we worked every day for a ten-hour shift. For a day's work, you'd get a dollar fifty They divided us up into different jobs. Some of us might be picking pears, some of us irrigating or doing other things. You just went to the job you were assigned to—every boss was different for each camp. But we were never mixed together, like Chinese and Mexican, or Chinese and Filipino. That never happened. We were always separated from each other. There might be other cultures at the camp, like Mexicans, but when it came down to working, we would divide into Chinese groups, Mexican groups. We ate together though, in groups of eight. Our meals were included with our salaries, and prepared for us by cooks in the camp. The food varied with each camp-sometimes it was good, sometimes it was bad, there was no constant thing. At least we didn't have to cook for ourselves.

There was one big house for all the workers, and not everybody had their own room. There was one big room, and everybody had a board bed, a bed made out of boards; there weren't any cushions or anything like that—and the beds would be lined up side by side so everyone would sleep together in the room. I remember going to pick grapes in Lodi, they didn't even have a house for you to sleep in, or a bed. They kept us in stables where the animals were kept. We slept on the hay, or wherever we could find that was comfortable. Another example was after the pear season, we would go pick honeysuckle flowers [used to make herbal tea] in Sacramento. And when we went there we would have find a place on the ground, that's where your bed was.

We got along all right with the Caucasians. don't think there's any problems now. Now if you're talking about back then, maybe thirty, forty years ago, then there were some problems. They even had to separate the races, segregation, you know. But the Chinese workers didn't really associate with the American workers in the Delta, so there was no direct conflict in most cases. There was very little communication between the groups when you're out there working in the fields, you weren't together, so what's the use of causing trouble? We were never put together with the Americans anyway, so this created some distance between us—It was mostly Chinese, some Mexican people. The Americans never really worked in the fields.

In 1935 I went to China, to Zhongshan, to get married. I remember when got there they were celebrating [Chinese] New Year's. It was my family who actually knew the girl, knew my wife, and introduced me to her. So the courtship was started by them, but there still had to be some kind of consent between the two of us. It was still up to us whether we wanted to get married or not. Well, we got married that year, but my wife didn't come back with me right afterwards. She stayed in China. She didn't actually come to the United States until 1969, with my two children, a son and a daughter. They couldn't come until then mainly because it was so hard to get the immigration procedures through. They didn't allow you to bring your wife and children for a long time; my son was already twelve years old by the time he came here. After they all got settled down (I bought this house then, about eleven years ago), they came to work with me, doing farm work.

But you know, I really enjoyed living here. There was always work to do, so was pretty much satisfied. Picking fruit, pruning, irrigation work in the fields there was plenty of work, and Chinese people I could talk to. I'll say the town has changed since then; now there's nobody around. I wish there were more people living in the town. But now there's nothing. There used to be buses and trains and ships going in and out of the area, people getting on and off. It was so busy back then, I do kind of wish it was like that again.

But I'd still rather live here in the United States than there, go back to China. I still have property there. I have a house in Zhongshan, but most of the land has been taken. Besides, the climate's better here in Locke. The air is good and clean. You get a cooling period in the day, but over there [Pearl River Region], it's hot all-day long. Even at night it's hot. Winter times it does get cold here; we didn't have this kind of weather in China. But we got used to it. We'd work for a while and if it got cold then we would go where someone had built a bonfire, and there would be a huge pot of tea; we'd drink some tea and warm our hands and then go back to work. Besides, here you could earn more money. In China, you wouldn't be able to raise enough money for your family.

Now I've got my own roots here–I've got my garden, and my friends here. I don't think I'd ever go back and live. I have family back there too. My younger brother is still back in China, with his family and his children. But my own children are here. My son, Kai, in fact, graduated from Chico [State College] last month. I was very proud of him because of that. He graduated from the School of Communications. Did you know that both men and women are in that same field? My daughter-in-law, Kai's wife, is also in communications, and they're both working in the same printing shop in Sacramento! My daughter is living in Vancouver, Canada, right now. She didn't like school that much; she never chose to go college. She got married and now she's raising her kids, taking care of the family. She went through high school, and that's as far as she got.

I'd like my children to stay here (in the United States). I wouldn't want them to go back to China, but I just leave it up to them. That the way I've always thought-whatever they were happy with, I was happy with too. The best thing to do is to just let your children pursue whatever they enjoy. If you tell them to do something, and force them to do something, they're not going to do it. I saved money to support them through school if they chose to do that, but they didn't have to. Now they can do whatever they want, and if they want to back (to China), then that's their choice.

No, I wouldn't want to live with them. If I was living with them, I wouldn't have the freedom I do now. I just do as I please, go as I please. It's very convenient this way. I'm not lonely here at all. I usually get up in the morning and make some breakfast for myself. And then I'll go out to the garden at this time of year very early in the morning, while it's still cool. I work in the garden for a couple of hours before lunch, then I come in and fix myself lunch. Then, I'll usually stay in during the early part of the afternoon, just to relax, maybe watch some TV or read a newspaper. Then I'll go back into the garden around three-thirty, four o'clock, when it's cooled down a little bit. I'll go out to the garden for a little bit before coming back in to make dinner. Then after dinner I'll relax again and watch a little bit of TV before I go to bed! I can just come in and out as I choose, whenever I choose.

Deborah Gears, "Polenta Birds"

[Editor's note: "Polenta Birds" by Deborah J. Gears is included in Dewey Chambers, editor, *Tales of the Delta Folk* (Stockton: University of the Pacific, 1962), pp. 29–35. This tale describes the way food played a critical role in perpetuating Italian ethnic traditions in a Sacramento–San Joaquin River Delta family. (*By permission*). See Fig. 33.]

"Celia, Celia."

Celia was aroused, momentarily, by the sizzling sound and delicious smells of breakfast. She snuggled down deep in her warm blankets and sniffed the air hungrily.

"Celia! Get up right now!" Her mother's voice demanded.

Eight-year-old Celia rolled over and rubbed her sleepy brown eyes. With her thick dark hair all tousled, she peered out of the covers. It was a cold, foggy morning. She hated to leave her warm, fluffy bed. Her hard-working mother had managed to save enough wild goose down for mattresses. No straw mattresses for the Bava family. She snuggled deep into the feather bed.

Suddenly, Celia bolted upright. Today was no ordinary day! After months of pleading, she was going to help catch the birds for polenta, her favorite dish. It was a job usually left to her two older brothers. But today she was going to prove that she was as good as any boy, her brothers included.

She ran to the window, putting on her dress covering her warm underwear as she went. She peered out at the thick fog. She pulled up her thick stockings and slipped into well-worn shoes. She knew her brother Tony was already out milking the cows. She had better hurry or she wouldn't have her chores done in time for breakfast or for the bird hunt!

"Good-morning, mama," sang out Celia. "I'm going with Tony today for birds, birds for polenta."

"You're not going anywhere if you don't hurry up and finish getting the table ready for your papa's breakfast," her mother said. Celia smiled at her mother's combined language of Italian and English.

Celia quickly set the table. She danced around the room sniffing the frying bacon, and trying to help crack the eggs and pour the milk.

"Celia, get out of my way. Go call your father and brothers to the table," scolded her mother.

The girl pranced out of the room. The familiar damp, bone-chilling fog hit her body as she closed the front door behind her. Unlike the hot, dry summer, the winter time always brought plenty of rain, fog and wind to the Delta. As the water rose with the rains, all her father and the other farmers talked and worried about was the possibility of the levees breaking, flooding their farms and homes.

"Papa, Angelo, Tony. Time to eat," shouted Celia into the thick fog. Shortly thereafter the forms of her father and her older brothers emerged from the thick whiteness. All the Bava men resembled each other. Dark wavy hair, dark completed skin with a short stocky build, testified to their Italian heritage. Celia's father and oldest brother had dark brown eyes. But Tony and Celia both had their mother's green eyes.

"Big day for you today, eh Celia," said her father as he rumpled her hair.

"Today you're going to try to do boy's work. You're no boy. You won't be able to do it." Angelo said. "You belong in the house with mama."

"I'm as good as any boy, you'll see," retorted Celia.

They all filed into the kitchen and sat down. To Celia, the others seemed to be dawdling over their breakfast. She was in a hurry to finish her chores and go.

Finally, breakfast was over and the dishes done. It seemed those two tasks took hours!

"Go feed the chickens and slop the pigs and then you can go," Mrs. Bava told the girl.

Humming parts of Italian songs, Celia snatched her old brown coat and hurried outside. She grabbed the pail to feed the chickens. In her eagerness, her hand knocked the pail over and all the grain spilled.

"Oh," Celia cried, "I'll never get to go." She bent down and scooped up all the seed before she could feed it to the chickens. Finally, the chickens were fed and the pigs were slopped without further mishap. The chickens laying the eggs and the pigs providing the bulk of their meat, Celia knew they were important, but she hated the smell. Especially the smell which came from the pigs' pen. She finished gathering the eggs and hurried inside.

Slamming the door behind her, she ran smack into her mother and two eggs crashed to the floor.

"Oh Celia, when will you learn to be more careful," reproached her mother. Celia was always in a hurry and often clumsy.

"Go on out now, you'll be no help today." Mrs. Bava knew the broken eggs were an accident. She did wish, however, that her daughter would be more careful.

"Tony, Tony, can we go now. Are you ready?" Following the sound of an ax she found her brother replenishing her mother's supply of wood.

"Just a minute," replied Tony. Though only twelve, he worked long, hard days as did all Delta children. His father was one of the few Italian farmers who stayed on the Island all year round. Most returned to Stockton for the winter months. Therefore, the Bava family worked hard even during the winter.

"I'm ready Celia," called Tony as he carefully put away his ax. "I don't know why you are so excited. Catching birds is not all that much fun and it'll be hard for a girl like you."

Celia squared her shoulders. She was determined not to tell her brother even if she did have troubles. She knew a boy who complained was a sissy. Celia was determined not to be a sissy!

"It has to be better than dishes, sweeping, and making beds," Celia snapped.

"Let's go then." Tony tucked the net and burlap bag they would need under his arm. They walked along the levee, down a path, across a footbridge to the far bank.

"How far do we have to go, Tony?" asked Celia struggling for breath.

"There's a good place down the levee, a little ways," Tony laughed.

Although the day was cold, Tony was barefoot as usual. Soon his feet were stained black from the peat-filled dirt. The Delta always had a peaceful feeling. On a clear day, one could look out over wide stretches of land filled with green, growing things. The children always looked at Mt. Diablo as a guide and a friend. But the fog closed everything in on a day like this one. As usual the white mist gave Celia an eerie feeling.

Coming to a stop, Tony unfolded the net. The net was hand made of twine, and was shoulder high for Celia. It was made with a fine mesh, which allowed no bird to escape. These nets had come to the Delta as part of the Italian ways the farmers brought with them.

"Celia, you hold on to this end. You'll walk on this side of the levee, I'll walk along the other." Tony enjoyed being boss. Usually he was the one following orders from his older brother or father.

"Now hold the net up and let the rest fall straight to the ground," he commanded.

Celia held her end up as she was told. It was difficult! She liked being outside, however. She could hear the chirping and the twittering of the small birds. but she noticed that she did not see as many flying around as usual.

"Tony, where are all the birds; they're not flying around," questioned Celia.

"They can't see any better than we can in the Tule fog, stupid. They stay on the ground which is why we can catch them with this net," responded Tony.

With the burlap bag swung over his shoulder, Tony began to walk slowly forward with Celia following his lead.

Celia could feel the cold damp ground under her feet and the wet thick grass around her ankles. If she had been out here with her mother she would be filling her basket with the mustard leaves that were scattered throughout the grass for tonight's dinner. But not now. This was not women's work. Celia smiled broadly.

A squeaking sound interrupted her thoughts.

"Tony, we got one," yelled Celia.

"Shut-up, do you want to scare off all the others? And pay more attention. I had to drop the net over this one all by myself. If there had been more than one bird, we would have lost them," scolded her brother as he shoved the bird into the burlap bag.

"I'm sorry," said Celia and she promised to do better.

"Come on, we have to get a lot more," Tony snapped, thinking of his mother's polenta. The meat from the birds would be added to a thick gravy which in turn would be served over a corn meal mush. Tony could smell the garlic, herbs and tomatoes simmering now. To think of the cheese melting on the polenta was more than he could stand.

Tony and Celia continued walking slowly along the levee. They caught more birds. Celia learned how to trap the bird in the net once it was caught.

Celia's arms began to tire from the unfamiliar work. The fog began to lift a bit. She glanced across the murky waterway and could see a couple of other boys with bats trying to knock down geese. Geese flew low on foggy days. This trick of knocking down geese was an old trick that the Italian farmers often used. "Why waste bullets when you could knock them out of the air," was a joke that went all through Mandeville Island. Her brother waved and wished the boys luck.

Suddenly, Celia tripped over a rock and fell. As she fell the net dropped and two large starlings got away!

Celia sat up slowly. She bit her lip to keep from crying.

"I'm sorry, Tony, I'll try harder." Her aching shoulders told her that catching polenta birds wasn't near as much fun as she thought it would be.

"You're all covered with mud, what are you going to tell mama? Come on let's finish getting these birds." Tony bent over to pick up his sister. He brushed her off as best he could. But the dark peat dirt did not come off very easily. The front of Celia's small body was covered with the dark powder.

They worked awhile longer collecting sparrows, starlings and even an occasional dove that wandered into their net.

Tony, remembering how hard it was to keep up with his older brother, decided that they could take a break before turning back.

"Let's rest here, Celia," he called.

Celia gratefully put the net down and went over to the edge of the levee and sat down on a willow tree that had bent over by the wind. The winter storms were always bad.

"Time to start back," said Tony as he picked up his end of the net. "Tony, how many more birds do we need?" asked Celia.

"Not many," responded Tony. "We'll get a few more and then we'll just forget the net and walk the rest of the way."

Celia picked up her end and promised herself to pay closer attention and not let any more birds escape. The wind was beginning to stir the leaves and make the water ripple. She could feel it right down to the skin. The fog was beginning to get thicker.

"We'd better hurry. We don't want to get caught too far out in this fog," warned Tony.

Swish went the net over a big black starling. It was quickly popped into the bag followed by two sparrows and another starling.

"That should do it, Celia. Help me fold up the net," said Tony. "You can carry the net and I'll carry the birds."

"OK," sang a joyful Celia.

The two children quickly covered the distance home. The house looked warm and cozy on its stilts, and a fire was burning in the wood stove. The two dragged themselves inside.

"Celia, what happened to you? Oh, never mind. Go wash your hands. I've kept some lunch hot for you," mother smiled.

Celia quickly washed her hands and came to the table in the kitchen. They enjoyed the hot minestrone and warm bread covered with rich olive oil. They crowded up next to the hot stove to savor the lunch.

"Come on, Celia, you helped catch them now you have to help get 'em ready too."

Celia was not looking forward to this part at all. She hated cutting off the birds' heads. It was very messy! And the pretty little birds looked so pathetic with no feathers. "The longer you take the longer we have to be out here," said Tony, prodding his squeamish sister. The job of plucking the feathers and cleaning the birds did not take long. It was a job both children had done many times.

They carried the birds inside. The small house already smelled of the polenta. The combined smell of garlic, onion, spices and tomatoes simmering on the stove, tantalized their nostrils.

At dinner that night, Celia sat up tall, proud to have helped put meat on the family table.

"Well, Tony, how did our girl do out there today?" asked Mr. Bava.

Tony looked at his sister and gave her the praise she deserved.

"She was as good as any boy, Papa." Celia's face beamed with pleasure.

When Mrs. Bava brought the large platter of polenta steaming from the oven and placed it on the table, the whole family applauded. It looked beautiful! The rich smell of spices, garlic, tomatoes, mushrooms and cheese covering the birds caught that morning was a special treat. Their Italian heritage filled the kitchen with wonderful smells, and all mouths watered.

Celia didn't join the applause when the polenta was placed on the table. She secretly took a bow.

Herb Jamero, "Pig Party Garcia Campo"

[Editor's note: Herb Jamero, "Pig Party Garcia Campo "is included in Charles Mariano, *Heart and Soul: Farm Workers, Migrant Camps, Other Stories* (self-published, 2018), pp. 88–91. This story demonstrates the way traditions from a country of origin help to bond immigrants together in a new land and in that way, have contributed to the continuing diversity of the Sacramento–San Joaquin River Delta. (*By permission*). See Fig. 34.]

... for decades from the 1940s to the 1970s, my parents operated the Jamero Labor Campo for Filipino migrant farm workers that housed up to 100 men during the peak harvest season. The labor camp no longer exists except through memory and various artifacts which were preserved by my younger brother, George, who continued to live on the property after my parents passed away. It was here that I was able to finalize a simmering dream of developing a family museum dedicated to the memory of my parents and the many *"Manongs"* of that bygone era. Fortunately, the dining area and pool hall which housed billiard and card tables were still in existence. With extensive repairs, it was transposed into the Jamero Family Museum.

In the process of collecting artifacts and transferring furniture, discovery of items was unearthed. Thus. The Picture! While cleaning out the drawers of Mama's buffet table a picture which was somehow wedged toward the rear of the drawer fell out. To my delight, I discovered a familiar scene and some very familiar faces in the picture. Standing on the extreme left clutching a work hat, is Eugenio Amparo. He also was the younger brother of my Godfather, Isidro. Eugenio was perhaps better known as a skilled saxophonist performing in venues up and down the valley during the big band era of the 1930's through 1950's. He married Eusebia Pomicpic, the daughter of a pioneer Filipino family in the Livingston area. Fourth from the left wielding a knife is Anastacio Abucejo, better known to us a Manong Tayo. At the Sunday *Sabongs* (chicken fights), he was the acknowledged master. His expertise covered the range from tying the killing blades onto the rooster's leg to doctoring wounds of the rooster. He was much sought after due to his unique skills. Manong Tayo was also one of the core group of workers who came to our campo every year until forced to retire due to age. Although the faces of others in the picture were familiar, their names could not be recalled.

The identity of the *campo* as "Garcia Campo" is easily explainable. The various camps were usually identified by the given name of the farm labor contractor or the owner of the property. A further possibility here is the fact that most of the men pictured were from the town of Garcia-Hernandez, Boho*l*, *Philippines*—the same home town of my parents, Ceferino and Apolonia Jamero. Typically, men who came from the same or adjoining provinces who spoke the same dialect comprised the camp. At the Jamero Camp, there were *Visayans* from Bohol. Cebu, Leyte and Siquijor. So it was at the asparagus camps in the Delta including Ryer Island, the locale of the picture. *Visayans* with *Visayans, Llocanos* with *Llocano*s. The butchering of pigs and chickens was typical of the campo as the purchasing of meats from a grocery store was much more expensive. The butchering was usually on a weekend of a day off from work since 4–6 men were needed. There were usually several men skilled at butchering with others assisting from blood-letting to shaving its bristly hair to cleaning its innards to quartering into sections. The roasting or *lechon* of the entire pig was reserved for festive occasions.

William Frederic Sheldon, from *Bailing Dust*

[Editor's note: William Federic Shelton's *Bailing Dust* (Walnut Grove, CA: Campus House Press, 1984) is a narrative following a young boy who lives in Terminous, on the San Joaquin River near Lodi. These excepts include Chapter 3 and 6. The experience of the young boy here demonstrates the multicultural world Sacramento–San Joaquin River Delta residents needed to navigate and the way in which it expanded their horizons. (*By permission*). See Fig. 35.]

Chapter 3

The Japanese students went to Japanese School on Bouldin Island after their full school day at the public school and learned the Japanese customs and language from a hired teacher from Japan.

Billie was always interested and impressed by the intensity of their school. The Japanese children were required to read and write Japanese and to participate in Kendo, the Japanese sword fighting.

They did this in full Kendo costume, and the screams of combat "*amag*," "*ada*," "*seke*," and "*pata*" were fascinating to Billie. These words were shouted at the top of their lungs as they struck at each other's extremities with their split bamboo swords.

These swords were round, made up of about six separate pieces of bamboo held together with rawhide. The swords had a hand guard of stiff leather, and the handle was the bamboo sections covered with a two-handed leather end. This was held in front of the combatant in a striking position, straight ahead, and in position to poke the throat or strike the top of the head.

The Kendo costume consisted of bare feet, a black, flowing skirt, and a shiny black lacquered breast plate which reached beneath the arms to protect the rib cage from side cuts. There was a face mask of strong deflecting steel surrounded by heavy felt around the sides of the head and continuing around the top of the shoulders and across the throat. The remainder of the costume included strong gloves that reached up to the elbow with the hand section consisting of a thumb and a hooked part for the rest of the fingers to hold the sword. The sword had a rawhide strip from the tip to the sword guard to tell which was the back.

The blows, when delivered, were struck with sincerity, and to prove it the name of the blow was screamed out when struck. Kendo was fast, and if you hesitated your opponent could counter and hurt.

The Japanese boys would tell Billie that some experts with the sword could make the staves stand apart when striking the exposed arm above the long gloves and pinch the small amount of exposed flesh.

The general effect of this training and the unique costumes was not lost on Billie. Quite often he would find a willow stick to his liking, peel off the bark and attack the nettles in the Japanese Kendo spirit of giving no quarter and expecting no mercy from a superior skill. This Billie would practice on the stinging nettles and consider the consequences of being stung by red hot leaves as a just punishment for not being skillful.

Billie would occasionally be invited to the Japanese picnic which occurred once a year. One year he was invited to the picnic on Bouldin Island across Potato Slough west of Terminous.

This picnic was an all-out affair. There were races for the small children, the older children, the young men and the older men, who were mostly drunk on sake. There were basket filling games where different teams filled a large basket suspended on a pole with colored homemade balls, each team having its own color. There were all kinds of races: sack, three-legged and relay. The teams were made up sometimes on the spur of the moment, and the fast runners were often put in with the very slow.

All this was done with lots of prizes. There were all kinds of trophies: knickknacks, candy bars, oranges, flags. Everybody got prizes.

There was much circulating among family picnic groups.

There were different varieties of Japanese food: pressed fish, white and serrated; all kinds of sushi, each lady had her own special sushi recipe; there was small shrimp and tasteless yellow pudding. Billie loved all this food and would eat all he could get.

The celebration went on all day, and as the sun was beginning to descend, the high point of the day arrived, the Kendo demonstration. This consisted of the entire Kendo class donning full armor and tying a wooden shingle about three inches square on the top of their face-head helmet. Each opposing team wore a red or white colored string around the waist to designate which team was which.

They gathered at the opposing sides of the large squared grassy enclosure. After some rather formal kneeling and bowing, they assumed the classic attack stance, and amid the screams of defiance, began to hit one another, trying to break the shingle tied to the top of their opponent's helmet.

Shortly thereafter, some of the shingles were broken and these fighters retired from combat to sit in disciplined rows facing the remaining combatants. This went on until only one team member was left without a broken board. Then all the remaining opposing members would attack him and break his board. There were several winning team members left standing at the end of a group bout.

Billie liked this battle much more than the individual bouts which followed. The excitement and noise of combat, the flowing costumes, the flying flags, the green grass turning golden in the setting sun, and the intensity of feeling made this the high point of the day.

There were individual bouts among Billie's classmates, but as they were masked by the helmet, he could not tell who was winning the single contests.

All this was prelude to the senior men who participated after students retired to their family groups and changed their clothes back to U.S.A. These were some of the farmers that Billie knew, the fathers of his classmates and the Japanese teacher, who did not participate in the beginning activities but was more prominent as the combative part of the picnic progressed. They donned Kendo armor and demonstrated the more advanced techniques of formal combat. This was as structured and formal as the proceeding contests. The blows were struck harder and the screams of value more sincere.

After this experience in the martial arts, the picnic broke up everyone attempted to go home.

By absolute dark the picnic was over, and the memories of who won and got a prize would be talked about until next year.

Billie had another highlight in his relations with the Japanese. This was New Year's Day. On New Year's Day the whole Japanese community had open house for their friends. At this time the best Japanese foods were the displayed and eaten by the visitors.

Billie would be able to visit up to three feasts. The food was cold but of the special delicate flavor of the sea and garden. Billie's favorite food was sushi. This is a roll of sweet rice surrounded by a leaf of dark blue seaweed with spicy turnips and radishes in the center of this roll. There were pressed fish cakes, white with red tops and sides. There was a formal token lobster with long antenna watching over the spread of food from a raised throne. He presided over the food offering and, as he was not eaten on that day, served as the general theme of goodwill and fellowship.

There were sometimes exotic foods. Whale blubber fried white with an awful grey sauce poured over it. This was a once food. The other foods were not particularly attractive to Billie's taste, and after a small bite of some they were left alone.

This feast went on all day, and to get to some of the outside-of-Terminous ranch houses, Billie rode with his Japanese friends in their cars.

All the Japanese exchanged gifts on Christmas and New Year's Day. Billie did not get any gifts from them on these days and did not expect to get any.

The one gift Billie got from a Japanese man was unexpected and most welcome. Billie was living in Lodi and was out on the street roller skating when a Japanese farmer from Terminous drove by, saw Billie and said, "Would you like to have a BB gun?"

Billie could not believe that anyone could give him a gun, his fondest hope. Billie said, "Yes." He got into the farmer's car and they went down town to the local hardware store. Billie picked out a shiny nickel-plated Daisy BB gun. It cost $1.50.

Billie never forgot this kindness and kept the gun many years till it wore out.

The greatest use that Billie had of this BB gun was roller skating the streets of Lodi and shooting sparrows out of the fronds of the palm trees. These small birds he sometimes took home to feed to his cat, but mostly he just threw them away into the gutter.

The kill was the important thing, and to see your BB pass close to the bird and not hit it required greater concentration for the next shot. Billie was an avid killer. There was nothing that he would not kill if he thought he was justified in shooting it.

There were mud hens in the drainage canals and in the rivers and sloughs around Terminous. These he soon discovered he could kill with a well-placed BB hit.

To get the bird out of the water after killing it from the bank required a large amount of effort. Sometimes long sticks, sometimes a boat rowed a long way, but Billie seldom lost what he shot.

Billie would clean his rare mud hen by cutting it across the stomach with a knife, grasping the flesh on both sides of the cut and pulling in both directions at once. The mud hen was so structured under the loose skin that it was very easy to pull the skin off over the head and over the tail. Billie would then cut off the head and wings, the small amount of skin hanging on the tail, and the two feet, and then have a chunk of red meat to work with. He would then break the mud hen in half and take out the very large gizzard, make a cut around the side of it to where the knife just touched the inner lining of the gizzard and peel the outer gizzard muscle away from the inner lining.

Billie had to clean all the things he killed, whether it was rabbits or catfish or ducks. This was his job, to clean them before his grandmother would cook them.

Billie's grandmother was an indifferent game cook, and Billie never got too much out of the birds he shot. But in Billie's way of looking at it, the pleasure of killing something was the main point of hunting.

Billie was a frequent visitor to his Japanese friends' houses, sometimes walking dusty ways to get there. The arrival at a Japanese house was usually the same. Billie would wait outside until his friends would come outside. They would then talk or the Japanese boy would invite Billie in to his room to look at something he was doing.

This again was the same. As you went into the house, there was a very strong smell of pickles. The next thing was the boy's mother coming out of the general living quarters to greet Billie. Sometimes he was invited into the center of the house but not always.

All the Japanese houses had a small Buddhist shrine in one corner of the main room. Some were closed and some were open. Some had photographs of dim, grey people placed on them.

There was a feature of a Japanese house that Billie wondered about. There was a large stack of magazines and newspapers in one corner of the room. It reached to the ceiling, and Billie wondered what its purpose was. If you would attempt to take out one newspaper or magazine, the whole works would fall down. Billie never did figure out that question to his satisfaction.

Some Japanese houses were very conventionally furnished inside and would compare with any city house, but some of them were as bare as Billie's house. There was no way to tell which kind of house you were going to be presented with from the outside.

All the Japanese farmers were dedicated to hard work. They had great courage in tackling hard problems on their farms, and because of this they prospered out of context to their neighbors. Most of the Japanese farmers in Terminous raised vegetable crops to sell to a large produce company.

There was a group of Japanese farmers who ran Bouldin Island across Potato Slough from Terminous. This group farmed about five thousand acres in one chunk, and it was supervised and managed by one Japanese man. A true shogun, his word was law. And although the island was owned by a large produce company, the ideas of this one man more than prevailed.

Chapter 6

After school was out, Billie walked to the great warehouse to, hopefully, catch a ride home.

In the summer, there was light to see his way past the hurrying trucks, but in the winter, there was early darkness, and the light was provided by truck headlamps and shifting locomotive lights.

The warehouse that Billie was headed toward was at the end of the long shed farthest from school. This allowed Billie to stop at the Western Pacific Railroad office at the front of the warehouse to see what was going on. At this place, there was a telegraph for the dispatcher of the freight cars. Most of the cars were refrigerated and were all designated to be delivered to the east coast from Terminous.

The young dispatcher that ran the warehouse for Western Pacific was friendly to Billie and allowed him to observe the various complications which were required to allow a train to arrive and depart.

When a freight car was requested by a produce company to be spotted in a certain track in front of their warehouse, it went onto an order form. This form gave the particulars of the use of this freight car, whether it was to be iced in Terminous, and what was to be put into it.

The destination and subsequenting *en route* were the final information that came back to the front office after the car was loaded.

The billing for the freight car did not go to the farmer directly but was handled by the home office of the produce company. Billie's father, working for an independent produce company, a local firm, had to handle the billing from the railroad company, and Billie got to see the procedures at first hand.

Quite often the car was sent to the eastern market, Chicago or New York, and the billing came back "red ink." The car had sold at the produce market for less than the freight charges and brokerage charges. There was no recourse to this. Once the car was sent it could not return. The luck of the sale was final.

There were several big seasons for this warehouse with periods of absolute calm in between. The celery was processed for Thanksgiving and Christmas, aimed at all the markets across the United States. The potatoes and onions tried to be sold to avoid the Texas produce which could wipe out California because of reduced freight charges. The green asparagus market was a long drawn out affair lasting for about two months.

The celery was by far the most exciting of the warehouse activities.

Billie, after picking up as much information as he wanted at the railroad office and saying "Hello" to the night watchman who was in that front office also, would start to walk through the various sheds towards the end of the warehouse.

He would pass four or five celery washing machines, each tended by a hundred men. The bright inside lights, the crashing water sprayed on the celery to wash off the peat mud, and the thrashing rumble of the water striking the surface of Potato Slough under the building were normal sounds as he passed the various open doors of the warehouse. Billie would not linger at these other companies' machines as he wanted to get to the farthest warehouse where his father worked.

He would crawl under and over plates of rollers going into the freight cars and dodge hand trucks hurrying across steel plates leading into refrigerated cars. He passed around heavy ice machines ingesting three-hundred pound blocks of ice and transporting them whole to the tops of the freight cars where they were broken by hand and shoved down two holes on each end of the cars into ice bunkers for the initial icing of the celery. The celery was usually iced again in Roseville and, again, halfway across the United States.

The cars traveled by fast freight after they left Terminous and were quite often on the east coast in three days.

This movement of freight cars out of Terminous during the depression was a great help to keep Western Pacific financially alive during the depression. The service that the railroad lavished on this operation attested to the importance of this business. There were sometimes three or four freight engines with full crews smashing and shuffling refrigerated cars all night.

The warehouse, depending on the eastern market sales, would run as much tonnage as they could through the washers, and after the sheds closed down for the night, the refrigerated cars had to be lined up again opposite the warehouse doors. The freight engines would work all night with much huffing and whistling.

Billie would pass through this excitement and finally arrive at the last warehouse. By this time it was dark, and Billie checked in at the office to see if he could get a ride home to Sycamore Slough. He was usually told to wait outside until the warehouse shut its machines down.

Billie liked this part of going outside and watching the celery packing. The first part of the celery operation was the celery coming into the warehouse from the nearby fields. It sometimes came in by river scow, a large, flat boat, with celery piled high in field crates.

These crates weighed about seventy pounds and were the first boxes that the celery was put into. They held about a hundred head of celery each and had a movable slat hooked on the open side of the box. These boxes were put two high on hand trucks and brought into the warehouse and set on the floor beside the celery washer.

Most of the time the celery came out of the fields on ranch trucks which were unloaded and loaded with great rapidity.

The hand trucks just flew, and sometimes Billie was allowed to handle one of them. Billie wasn't heavy enough to pull back on the handles of the hand truck and balance the load, but he could push one into place and let the handles fly up with a satisfying snap.

After the celery was stacked under cover, it went in the field crates over to the washer. This was a great machine with a galvanized steel belt about five feet wide and sixty feet long. The field crates were placed on the dry end of the belt with around six men on each side taking the celery out of the crates and spreading it out one deep on both sides of the belt.

The belt never stopped. The celery plants moved along into a long chamber which vigorously squirted water on them in an attempt to wash off the peat dirt. This water was river water and had been treated with chlorine gas when it was pumped out of the river near the front office.

Terminous had a tall water tower at the railroad office end where the pumps were. This tower received the chlorine treated water and delivered it with great pressure to the washers in the sheds.

Billie had a friend who serviced the chlorine injector. He could scarcely speak. The chlorine which he worked in had burned out his voice. Billie would sometimes go into the small room under the warehouse floor and watch this man put the chlorine into the water. The smell was so strong that Billie didn't see how he could stand it, and Billie avoided this operation.

The well-washed and soaked celery then moved to the main part of the belt which had more than twenty men on each side. These men picked up a head of celery, trimmed the leaves off the individual heads, and threw the unwanted leaves and stalks back on the center of the belt.

The trimmed heads were then sorted to see which were the biggest. These were again placed on the belt and traveled toward the end where they were taken off the belt and stacked in front of the packers.

There were two depths of men working on the wet end of the belt, one the trimmers and one the packers. The packers put trimmed and washed celery into pristine-clean wooden boxes previously prepared by professional box makers. The pungent odor of the celery and the sharp clean odor of the fresh pine boxes gave a pleasant feel to this part of the operation.

The celery leaves came off the belt and dropped into the river below along with a great cascade of crashing water. The amount of celery leaves and stalks was so thick on Potato Slough that the mud hens could walk from one side to the other side without touching water.

One day a city man drove his boat through this thick mat and plugged up the intake of his outboard motor and damaged it. He complained to the Coast Guard about it, and an officer showed up at the front office of the Western Pacific Railroad in Terminous and told them that they would have to clean up the slough.

The Western Pacific then built a flume of galvanized iron under the entire warehouse to carry the trimmings to a central spot between the warehouses. The celery was elevated into large overhead rooms with a trip door on the outside of the room.

The farmers from Lodi who owned cows would come to Terminous, back under these several chutes, and, when the latched door was tripped, get an instant load of heavy celery stalks. Tales are told of whole beds being torn off these trucks from the weight, and the springs under the trucks being shattered from the overhead blow.

Once the celery was packed in the filled crate, the side was nailed shut by a strong frame pressing down on the open side of the box and holding several boards on top of the celery.

These boxes were then shoved along a roller belt into the inside of the refrigerated cars which were being loaded by other box makers. The wooden crates were at each layer nailed with strips of shook which reached across the freight car from wall to wall. Shook is the name for all box making wood and freight car lumber.

The celery was loaded from the back of the refrigerated car to the front with both ends meeting in the center where the doors were. Then heavy two by fours were placed between the stacked celery boxes, and this strong framework was wedged into place with sledge hammers.

The violent movement of the freight train in the three-thousand-mile journey ahead would sometimes tear the boxes loose inside the cars.

This framing was done to all boxed vegetables, and it required some skill to build this bulkhead correctly.

Billie would go into the cars and watch his friends frame the cars. It was very cold in the cars as icing was taking place in each end and salt was being poured on top of the ice to make it melt faster. The way the men treated the cars, sinking the sharp edges of the box makers' hammers into the beautiful wooden walls and the many nails that went into these walls with a general indifference to damage was in evidence, but no one seemed to care. Just get the car out! The workers on these cars were always white men. Billie never saw another race attempt to put these together.

After viewing the loading of the freight cars, Billie would complete his circuit by going into the small office that sat on the far outside corner of the warehouse where his father was working, trying to keep the ranch books straight.

The farm employed a hundred and fifty men to harvest the celery in the open fields and an additional one hundred in the sheds. Also, there were about thirty fulltime employees who lived in various camp houses, scattered around Terminous Tract.

These men were Filipinos, Hindus, Chinese and poor whites from the Midwest. They worked together in the same fields. The work was not exciting but purely physical. In the various seasons of planting and harvest, the work in the peat ground was frantic. The time factor of putting the plants in the ground and the timing of the harvests were vital. No effort was spared to accomplish the survival of the company.

The Filipinos coming from the tropic jungles, the Hindus escaping from the oppression of British India, and the hopeless lot of the poor white were not a consideration of the employer. Get the job done. Get it done on time and get ready for the next planting. This was the only god that counted.

The chance of these men coming together and working alongside of each other under the same circumstances will never come again. The common factor was survival. The great depression was rampant.

The freight trains that Billie would see on his way to Lodi that traveled from Sacramento to Stockton were covered with men going both directions. There was no work anywhere.

Billie went to Sacramento once with his father, and they went into the waterfront district to locate an errant Hindu. The streets were full of wandering men. The open windows of the old buildings framed the ragged men leaning out and shouting down at the passersby.

This was the depression, and it frightened whoever saw it. Those that had a job knew how fortunate they were, and when they did get a job, they held on to it.

The conditions in the Lower Delta for ranch work were extreme, but you did have a job. The peat dust, which never stopped, had alkali salts in it that burn and fester the eyes and skin. The water cannot be trusted and is not drunk. The heat in the summer can be over one hundred degrees. The fog and cold in the winter go on for months.

All this and more was the fate of the ranch workers in the Delta. These extreme conditions drew the men together as nothing else could. The tolerance for the produce companies was enhanced by giving the men a job. The extremes of nature were certainly showered on their employers with impartial generosity.

No one escaped. The people that actually owned the land, the Portuguese, the Italians, the British and the Germans, all shared the same fate as the Japanese, Filipinos, Hindus and poor whites. The bonds of understanding and tolerance were the rule. There was no particular "I am" and "You aren't."

Billie was very sensitive and could pick up on this quickly.

Prohibition

[Editor's note: After the Volstead Act in 1917, the Delta became a weekend destination for those seeking alcohol and gambling. There were hotels and roadhouses galore. One of the most prominent watering holes and hotels, and one that still survives, is the Ryde Hotel. The excerpt from *A Fairer Paradise* sets the scene for the period. An historical account by Phillip Pezzaglia tells the story of prohibition in Rio Vista while Bruce Robinson's novel describes the illegal world that supported this leisure activity.]

Randel Marcus Guitierrez, from *A Fairer Paradise*

[Editor's note: Randall Marcus Gutierrez, *A Fairer Paradise: California River Delta Stories* (Grey Iguana Publishing, 1997), pp. 13–16. This selection paints the ideal world that those who sought the Sacramento–San Joaquin River Delta as an escape hoped to find. (*By permission*). See Fig. 36.]

The steamboat *Delta King* quietly rounds the bend in the river. In the distance Mount Diablo pierces the sky, a lone monument towering above the western edge of the valley. As the steamboat churns up river through the heart of the Sacramento Delta, towns slowly appear and disappear along the tree lined river's edge. Majestic willow trees and river oaks extend from the shallows; branches and leaves spread wildly across the river's glassy shell, casting cool, dark-shadows along the banks. In the pools and along the shaded brim, children swim, fish, laugh and scream, interrupting the peaceful, rhythmic flow of the river current.

Tips of white Victorian farmhouses shaded by great oaks, rise above River Road, concealing flat lands greeting the bottom of the levees on both sides of the river. Lands with fields of asparagus, pears and grain, lay colorfully painted on a checkerboard canvas. Women and children fill the porches and lawns of the farmhouses; the women keep a watchful eye while cleaning, sweeping and dusting their homes. The farm owners surveyed the workers picking and boxing in wooden crates, with colored labels, the fruit and vegetables born in the rich, peat soil of the Delta. The workers' skin, leathered and brown, reveal lines and bends, like the bark of the pear trees in the lands they farm.

Along the river's edge, wooden, weathered buildings stand over the river as small ripples lap gently against their algae covered stilts; their stilts vanishing beneath the surface. Chinese men sit on crates on decks smoking cigarettes from knotted fingers, while Chinese women scrub clothing with soapy, river water in large, tin tubs. Chinese children run and jump into the cool, green water, over and over again like a recurring carnival ride where tickets are endlessly given. Wooden buildings surrounded by alleys, walkways and stairs, lead from River Road to the streets below where shops, bars and diners serve their patrons. The alleys; clouded with the scent of garlic and chili oils, sneak through the windows and cracks of buildings along the narrow streets. When the sun sets, yelling and laughter in musical tone float from Bing Lee's gambling den, where lotteries and Fan Tan are played on green, wooden tables obscured in a gray-haze of tobacco smoke.

Next to Bing Lee's, Al the Wop's bursts with laughter where Joe the bartender reigns king behind the bar stocked with bottles and drums of bootleg liquor. On Saturday nights, crackling gravel under hot rubber tires, of Fords, Buicks and Packards, announce the arrival of men from the cities of Sacramento, Stockton and San Francisco, from Modesto, Merced and Fresno, from Pittsburg, Martinez and Benicia; the Italian, Greek and Portuguese fishing towns lining the river, west to San Francisco Bay. In polished black leather shoes, crisp white shirts, freshly shaven and smothered with splashes of Barbasol and Pinaud; they arrive in anticipation of a visit to Miss Janey's place, after drinking, smoking and telling lies on the stools and wooden bar of Al the Wop's.

Across the river and past the gray-steel drawbridge, the Ryde Hotel bordered by tall, tropical palms, towers majestically and with dignity, above River Road. The hotel gracefully introduces itself in the evenings, announcing its name with a sparkling red, green and blue neon sign; visible a great distance along the winding, levee road. The Ryde Hotel; an oasis, sparkles in the midst of the Delta like a diamond in the setting of a coveted brooch, surrounded by inferior gems. On Saturday evenings, varnished yachts nestle along the wooden pier fronting the hotel; dark automobiles line the levee road with sparkling chrome. Brass trumpets, trombones, clarinets and drums fill the air with the sound of thumping melodies. Men in black tuxedos and women in colorful, flapper dresses; dance wildly to the pulsating beat. Throughout the night, men and women wander through the floors of the Ryde hotel, through doors and rooms of friends, old and new. They sit on chairs and beds; some with crystal glasses filled with wine; some with Champagne and pastel-colored drinks; some with engraved lockets filled with cocaine; some with pipes of opium. As the evening ferments, laughter and inhibitions are slowly swept away by the warm river breeze through open windows, evidenced only by the gentle dance of white-lace curtains.

The *Delta King* slows and nestles along the splintered dock at Walnut Grove. From the passenger decks come those searching for the playful decadence of the Ryde Hotel; others search for various jobs among the settlements lining River Road. The steamboat will carry to and from, "Big River," or "Tai Han," as known by the Chinese laborers upon whose backs the levees were built; the river people, whose dreams have grown beyond and within the boundaries of the Delta.

And their stories ebb and flow, with the timeless tides and free flowing currents of Big River.

Philip Pezzaglia, from *True Tales of the Sacramento Delta*

[Editor's note: Philip Pezzaglia, *True Tales of the Sacramento Delta* (Charleston, SC: The History Press, 2015), pp. 128–36. The Sacramento–San Joaquin River Delta attracted larger-than-life characters who were searching for a place to live idiosyncratic lives. Foster is an excellent example and one whose story continues to bring visitors to Rio Vista. (*By permission*). See Fig. 37.]

Anyone who has grown up in Rio Vista or the Delta knows where the bar/restaurant known as Foster's Bighorn is. The bar and its collection of taxidermy animals are legendary. People from across the United States and the world, for that matter, have walked through the doors of Foster's and gazed in amazement upon the collection of preserved animal heads. Where else can you enjoy a drink or a meal while sitting next to or underneath the head of an elephant, zebra, giraffe, rhinoceros, hippopotamus or dozens of other types of animals? And where else can one stand atop the bar and kiss the moose head after a few cocktails or as a right-of-passage while celebrating their twenty-first birthday?

For the patron who cannot comprehend what it was like to be out on safari hunting such animals, the walls are adorned with photographs of Foster's expeditions taken during 1930s, '40s and '50s. The photos depict Foster, his taxidermist and members of his safari party in a setting reminiscent of an old 1930's Tarzan movie.

But who was William B. "Bill" Foster, and where did the animals in his collection come from? Those who knew him could probably tell hours of stories about the man. In a way, some of the stories have become local urban legends. But one thing is for certain: Bill Foster created a unique local watering hole that became a destination point for travelers the world over who wish to see a one-of-a-kind collection. The story of William Foster begins when he was a young man, still known by his given name, William Frates.

William Frates was born in Hayward, California, in 1893. It is unknown what his parents' names were or how many siblings he had. Newspaper clippings indicate that he had at least one brother, Charles, and a sister, Lulu. At an early age, Bill was hired as an apprentice under Henry Snow in a foundry in Newark, California. This was fine work, but young Bill was not fully satisfied.

For those not familiar with the name Henry Snow, he is recognized as a collector, naturalist, film producer, African big game hunter, museum advocate and one of the founders of the Oakland Zoo, originally located at Nineteenth and Harrison Streets in downtown Oakland. Snow was a strong supporter of the idea of creating a museum with an extensive anthropology and natural science collection. Accompanied by Leslie Simpson, the two big game hunters were dispatched by the City of Oakland on a two-year expedition to Africa. During this trip, the two men collected 169 mammals, 15,000 birds, 5,000 bird eggs and 40,000 insect specimens, all of which would be displayed at the museum in Oakland.

Having apprenticed for Snow, young Bill Frates had the unique opportunity to listen to the exotic tales from Snow himself, which made Frates yearn to travel and try his hand at big game hunting.

In 1919, twenty-six-year-old Frates's dream came true when he secured a position as cabin boy on a ship destined for Africa. The trip sparked a passion in Bill that lasted a lifetime. However, it would take nine years before he saved enough money to visit the Dark Continent once again.

Shortly after Bill returned to the United States from his first trip to Africa, Prohibition in the United States, also known as the "Noble Experiment," began. From 1920 to 1933, the sale, manufacture and transportation of alcohol for consumption in the United States was banned nationally as mandated in the Eighteenth Amendment to the United States Constitution. With Prohibition in affect, Bill saw a financial opportunity and quickly became involved in bootlegging in the Bay Area. Legend has it that he made the finest bootleg whiskey in the East Bay. With bootlegging becoming widespread, organized crime soon got involved and often took control of the distribution of alcohol.

The East Bay's answer to combating the ever growing bootlegging profession was by appointing Earl Warren to the position of district attorney of Alameda County in 1925. This was the first of three four-year terms of office that Warren was elected to. Warren quickly became known as a tough-on-crime district attorney, as he cracked down on bootlegging.

Realizing that his career in bootlegging might be cut short by district attorney Warren, William left the East Bay, changed his surname from Frates to Foster and headed up into the Sacramento Delta.

The exact year that William Foster, as he was then known, arrived in Rio Vista is still unconfirmed. The first mention of William Foster in the local newspaper appeared on May 27, 1927, although it is possible that he might have been a resident town as early as 1925. Another unanswered question concerning Foster's personal life is whether he married Ethel before or after arriving in Rio Vista. No matter, the important thing was that she was always there, at Bill's side.

Shortly after arriving in Rio Vista, Bill Foster purchased a small piece of property located on South Second Street between the homes of C. W. Ownes and J. E. Souza and across the street from the Bailey House. He erected a small, modest home where he could reside peacefully and without fear of the law under his new identity.

Foster walked the streets of Rio Vista looking for a small building in the business district to purchase. Eventually, he found a small shack of a building in the alley behind the old Netherlands Theater building. The building was perfect for what he wished to do. He opened his doors and invited the local male population into his establishment, which was rustically decorated with sawdust on the floors and hosting such entertainments as dancing girls, backroom gambling and Foster's famous bootleg whiskey. It was a "bootlegging joint" frequented by many of the men of Rio Vista and the surrounding area.

Prohibition began when the Eighteenth Amendment to the United States Constitution was ratified in 1920. It was later repealed with the ratification of the Twenty-First Amendment in 1933. However, during those thirteen years, it was illegal to manufacture, transport and sell alcoholic beverages with the exception of use for medical treatment or religious services yet it was never illegal to consume it.

The Delta was far from "dry." There was quite a bit of manufacturing and consumption going on in establishments like Foster's and several others, including the Ryde Hotel, which catered to the individual who wanted to enjoy the "speakeasy" nightlife. Foster's place was as good as any other bootleg joint of the time, and the local authorities turned a blind eye to it. The town was so small, it had a population of 1,309, and everyone knew where Foster's place was and what was going on behind its closed doors.

Oftentimes, fathers would bring their small children with them when they stopped at Foster's place, and the children would play on the sawdust floors, drawing out roads, pictures and whatnot while they waited for their fathers, who were sampling Foster's latest batch of whiskey.

By 1928, Bill Foster had saved enough money from selling whiskey to take his first of eight trips to Africa. It was during this trip that he met and befriended author Ernest Hemingway. From 1928 to 1953, Foster made not only the aforementioned trips to Africa but also ten trips to Canada and Alaska. In all, his travels took him to Africa, India, Mexico, Alaska, Canada, Greenland and points all across the United States. The photographs that currently adorn the walls of Foster's Bighorn showcase Foster on his hunting trips to the Dark Continent and to the north.

In order to preserve the animals in the best way possible, Foster hired John Jonas to accompany him on the majority of his hunting trips to Africa. This way, John could begin to preserve the animals right after the kill took place. Jonas, considered one of the world's premier African taxidermists, was one of five brothers who immigrated to the United States from Hungary and together opened taxidermy studios in Seattle, Denver and New York. On his trips to Alaska, Canada and Montana, Foster was accompanied by North American taxidermist Al Hilbert, who, just like Jonas, would begin to preserve the animals right after the kill took place.

On many of the hunting excursions, Foster also brought along a cameraman who would not only take stills, many of which presently hang on the walls of the bar, but also film motion pictures of the hunt. Foster would later play those films to awe struck viewers at events held in Rio Vista. Rumor has it that the movies still exist but are in the hands of a private collector.

When Prohibition was lifted in 1933, Bill Foster wanted to go legitimate and open a café on Main Street. He heard a rumor that Frank Asta was going to close down his cigar shop and that the landlord, John I. Fiscus, was looking for a new tenant., But that was just the rumor that Foster had heard, and he would need to talk to the parties involved to see if there was any truth to it.

The rumor did have some truth to it, and in December 1933, Frank Asta, proprietor of the Club Cigar Store, closed his business. Because the lease technically would not be up until October 1934, several rumors regarding the reasons of the closure circulated about town. One rumor had owner Fiscus putting a property lien on the business, and the fixtures owned by Asta were held for payment. The precise facts concerning the negotiations between Asta and Fiscus never surfaced. Nonetheless, the outcome was the same: a vacant building. And Bill Foster wanted that building.

Foster entered into a long-term lease with Fiscus on the Main Street building located between Front and Second Streets. The building had to undergo extensive remodeling to change its usage, and Fiscus agreed to pay for the majority of the repairs. The building was divided into two businesses: Asa Brooks would operate a restaurant on the east side while Foster's portion would be an L shape on the. right, or the west side of the building.

The building ended up needing more work than was initially thought. Beams in the floor had deteriorated, and a new foundation was put in place. A new "party wall" was required and placed between the building and the adjoining Chase building to the east. The interior was finished in the popular Art Deco style of the era, complete with cove-shaped ceilings and a color scheme reflective of the times.

The façade of the building was designed by a "specialist" in exterior architecture design. It was an impressive façade, designed in a modernistic manner, with embellishments of black slate and anti-rust mona metal. Iron scrolls were placed in the three windows above the two entrances. There were four columns, two evenly spaced in the middle and two on either end. The exterior of the building was green against a mauve-and-tan background.

When completed, a modern restaurant was in place for Brooks's establishment while Foster's business included a liquor store, taproom and clubroom. The grand opening, held on Saturday, February 10, 1934, for the club was well attended. Foster's landlord presented him with a large horseshoe flower arrangement of carnations with the inscription "Good Luck Bill." A large portion of the merchants and citizens were on hand to tour the new establishment and wish Foster the best of luck.

In 1949, the City of Rio Vista constructed a municipal swimming pool with money that the town received from natural gas royalties. On hand to cut the ribbon during the official dedication held on September 25, 1949, was Foster's old nemesis, Earl Warren, who was, at that time, California's governor. Foster, most conveniently, was called away that weekend for a pressing business matter. You could draw your own conclusions, but it seemed that Foster did want to take the chance of Warren recognizing him from his days as a bootlegger now that he had spent the last two decades a legitimate businessman.

In February 1952, Bill Foster decided that after eighteen years and numerous hunting excursions, he needed to slow things down and spend more time at home rather than traveling the world.

Foster decided to combine the things he loved most, his extensive collection of taxidermy animal heads and his bar. He decided to display three hundred animals, 95 percent of which were shot by Foster himself, in his bar. Foster could then bartend, show off his collection and entertain his patrons with stories of his safaris.

It took two and a half months to remodel, and Foster had no idea how the public would react. Little did Foster know that what he was creating would become a one-of-a-kind showplace that would still be drawing individuals from all over the world more than sixty years later.

The animals were arranged with the elephant head as a focal point. The head measures thirteen feet from base to the tip of the truck. The tusks weigh 110 pounds each and are five feet in length. It is considered the largest mammal trophy in any collection in existence, and It cost $4,000 to mount the elephant, $800 for the giraffe, $450 for the hippopotamus and $350 for the rhinoceros.

From 1952 to 1963, William "Bill" Foster spent his days working behind the bar and greeting customers at his bar/restaurant.

In November 1963, Foster passed away and the town of Rio Vista mourned the lost of one of its most well-liked and respected citizens.

What would happen to Foster's was the question on the minds of local citizens. Would the widow Foster put the town's most famous bar up for sale? Foster's widow, Ethel, did decide to sell; however, she did make it known that her wishes were for the collection to remain in Rio Vista and for the interior to stay much the same as it looked when her late husband had operated the establishment.

In 1964, Ethel Foster sold the business to a local businessman. Unfortunately, financial difficulties arose, and Ethel found herself, once again, the owner. Because of some back taxes due, there were worries that the collection might get sold and leave town. Legend has it that at that time, Walt Disney, Howard Hughes and Bill Harrah were all interested in purchasing the collection and approached the widow Foster. However, she was not interested in seeing the collection leave Rio Vista, and she turned them down.

Fortunately, a local couple stepped up and purchased the establishment from Mrs. Foster in 1969, and Foster's legacy remained intact, locally. Since Foster's passing in 1963, the business has changed hands a few times, but each time, the keys were passed to another local owner. Bill Foster's legacy has been kept alive.

Bruce Robinson, from *Legends of the Strait*

[Editor's note: Bruce Robinson, *Legends of the Strait: A Novel about Benicia, California during the Prohibition Era* (Bloomington, IN: Authors House, 2011), pp 325–338. While fiction, this account dramatizes the dangers which accompanied those who attempted to profit from prohibition as so many in the Sacramento–San Joaquin River Delta region did. (*By permission*). See Fig. 38.]

Chapter 23: "You Took Advantage of Me"

By February of 1928, Tucker's new enterprise was thriving. Word had traveled fast among the hundreds of speakeasies and roadhouses along Lincoln Highway—all the way from Napa to Oakland. With the opening of the new Carquinez Bridge the year before, many new establishments had sprung up along the back roads winding eastward into the hills of Contra Costa County and westward in the shorelines of the Napa River and San Pablo Bay.

Tucker's two tanker trucks made the long round trip between Jamestown and Oakland twice each week, usually on Mondays and Thursdays. Apart from two alternate Lincoln Highway routes, one to the north and east through Sacramento and the other directly east through Stockton, most of the roads east of Sacramento and Stockton were unpaved and unmapped. Often little more than hay-wagon trails, those few roads marked by signs had names like Gopher Gulch and Blackbird Hollow. It was only by exploring these routes months ahead of time that Tucker had managed to plot the best routes.

Armed with pistols, Billy and Patrick drove one tanker at night, using the southern route. Adam and Eddie Zhao followed them in separate car. Adam carried an Army-issue Colt automatic; Eddie, a double-barreled shotgun. Also armed with pistols, Jack and Francis drove the second tanker during daytime hours. They used the northern route through Sacramento to Placer and then headed southeast toward Jamestown. Larry followed them accompanied by a new member of Tucker's gang, Ted Sena. Both men wore shoulder-holstered pistols. Sena also carried a Tommy gun.

Jack had known Sena from the days when he worked as a shoeshine boy in Huey's barbershop. "You can trust this man," he had assured Adam. "He's been in the business long time, and he knows how to keep a secret."

Still, Adam was skeptical. "We's in a war here, boy," he cautioned. "We needs somebody can use a machine gun an' ain't scared t' die."

"Sena's your man," Jack said. "I've done some checking. He was machine gunner for the French air corps during the Great War. Earned the Croix de Guerre. Just like you, Adam, he's a tough old geezer, and he isn't scared of anybody."

"Le' me talk to him," Adam said. When he did, Adam hired Sena immediately. That was late in June of 1927.

When, a month later, Sam demonstrated his well-developed aeronautical skills, Adam quickly saw the value of air reconnaissance and hired him. "Now you gotta get yourself a plane," he told Sam.

"That's easy," Sam said. "I'll talk to Sharon and Todd."

"How you know you can trust 'em?" Adam asked.

Sam smiled. "Because they're in the bootlegging business too. Not like you, exactly. They provide air courier service for a bunch of distilleries all the way from Fresno to Chico. They'll rent us a plane and a hangar, if the price is right."

"Whatever it takes," Adam nodded. "You set it up, boy."

The Rivers were eager to cooperate. They agreed not only to provide hangar and use of their airstrip but also to lease to Adam an Army surplus, de Havilland DH-4 biplane. This two man aircraft was equipped with two .30-caliber Marlin machine guns in the nose and two .30-caliber Lewis machine guns in the rear. Its 421-horsepower engine delivered both the range and speed Adam would need to provide protection for his vehicles as they traversed the deserted back roads between Jamestown and Davis. The Rivers also offered room and board in the bunkhouse on their ranch so Adam's flight crew would have ready access to the de Havilland.

Since air reconnaissance would be effective only during daylight hours and Ted Sena was the only member of the gang familiar with aircraft machine guns, Adam switched him from daytime follow-car duty to gunner on the de Havilland.

"So, who's taking Sena's place in the follow car?" Larry asked.

"How about Sean?" Patrick suggested.

Tucker frowned. He still did not trust the older Irishman, but he knew he needed a white man.

"Why don't you let Jack ride with Larry?" Francis said. "Sean can go with me in the truck. Don't worry. I'll keep him on the straight and narrow."

Adam studied Francis' face for several seconds. Though only nineteen, Francis had the hard eyes of man twice his age. Better still, Adam knew Francis was a committed teetotaler. "You's gonna have t' watch 'im like a hawk, boy," Adam warned.

"Don't worry. I know all his dumb harp tricks. I'll fix it so he moves in with me. That way I can watch him day and night. He gets out o' line, I'll kick his Irish ass all the way back to Cork!"

Larry and Patrick both laughed. Jack said, "I'll vouch for that. I'll keep a close eye on him too." Reluctantly, Adam nodded. "He don't get no gun. He jus' a extra set o eyes, you hear."

"Agreed," Francis said.

[Editor's note: change of scene in author's text]

At first, Gail did not recognize the tall young man standing in her doorway. His face was in shadow cast by the bright mid-morning sunlight behind him. His voice, deep and resonant, was even less familiar. "Jack?" she asked hesitantly, feeling rather than perceiving his identity. "Is that really you?"

"Hello, Mother," Jack said softly. He was shocked and saddened by the changes in her. Though her figure was still slender and graceful, crow's feet were visible at the corners of her eyes. Her long brown hair, tied up in a tight bun at the back of her head, revealed strands of gray at the temples.

"Yes, Mother," he replied. "I know it's been a long time, but I'd like to talk to you about something. Can I come in?"

"Oh Jack, of course!" Gail exclaimed, throwing herself at him and clasping his face in her hands. "It's good to see you! My God! How you've grown!" Her eyes filled with tears as she said, "Come in, dear. I'll fix you a nice breakfast."

"Thanks, but I've already eaten," Jack said as he followed her inside. He had forgotten how small her apartment was and suddenly felt remorse at not having visited her sooner. *How lonely and sad you must be*, he thought.

"Sit down, Jack," his mother urged. "I'll make a pot of tea." Quickly filling an iron pot with water and setting it on the stove to boil, Gail sat down in her armchair, its mohair fabric worn smooth as silk. "Are you still working for the bridge company?"

"No, Mother. They let everybody go as soon as the bridge was finished. I'm back working for Adam now."

She turned to face him, a worried look on her face. "Really! So what are you doing? Has he opened another garage or something?"

"No. He still works as a mechanic for an outfit over in Vallejo. But he's started another business on the side." Suddenly Jack stopped himself, realizing that any information he shared with his mother about Tucker's trucking enterprise she would probably share with Soames.

Gail was not to be put off. "What kind of business?"

"Trucking," Jack replied, hoping she would ask for no additional details. "I'm one of his drivers."

"Well! You certainly are a Jack of all trades, aren't you?"

They both laughed at her pun. Apparently satisfied with Jack's explanation, she moved on to another topic. "Have you seen anything of Del or Sam lately? I understand Sam earned his pilot's license and is working for the Forestry Service."

"Yes. I heard that too." Jack spoke hesitantly, worried that his mother's questioning was again leading him into dangerous territory. "I haven't seen Del for long time. I did a get a couple of letters from her while I was in jail. But she's moving in different circles. You know-high society and all that."

"There's no reason you can't still be friends," his mother observed, but there was a note of fatalism in her tone. Smiling sadly at her son, she said, "We all go our separate ways as we grow older, don't we, dear?"

Jack seized his mother's hand. "Mother, I want you to move out of here! Get yourself a nicer place, a house maybe. I'm earning good money now so I can help you."

Gently releasing herself from his grasp, she stood up and moved toward the stove. "Why would want to move? I've been living here for almost twelve years now. It's close to my job, and I'm really quite comfortable. A single woman doesn't need much, you know."

"But this place is so small. You need more space, Mother—at least a place with hot and cold running water! And look at this," Jack said, pulling at some loose strands of stitching on the cushioned arm of her sofa. "You need new furniture. And you should have an electric iron and a washing machine. They have wonderful new kitchen appliances these days. I can buy them for you."

"Jack!" she said firmly. "I don't need it. Save your money. You may meet a nice girl someday and want to get married. That would make me much happier than any new furniture or appliances." She reached over the stove, opened a cabinet door, and extracted a round metal box. Removing its lid, she placed it on her kitchen table. "Have some sugar cookies. I baked them yesterday. It's a recipe from your Grandmother Tillie."

Tillie Westlake was Jack's paternal grandmother. She had died just before his father was killed in the Great War. Though the old woman had lived with them while Jack was very young, he remembered very little about her. Since Tillie's death, Gail had rarely mentioned her, except occasionally to praise her baking skills. Jack knew his mother was using the cookies now as a distraction.

He stood up and walked toward her. Taking both of her hands into his own, he implored, "Mother, you have to listen to me! I want you to free yourself of Soames. He's a very bad man a thief and a murderer! You've got to break up with him before it's too late."

"No, Jack!" Gail retorted, pulling away. "You listen to me! My relationship with Soames has nothing to do with you! It's none of your business! Do you understand?"

"No, Mother. I don't I understand. I guess I never will."

The pot of water was boiling now, so Gail filled her porcelain teapot and a dropped in a tea caddy. "We'll have to let it steep for a few minutes," she said. Again, she motioned toward the cookie tin. "Go on, Jack. Have one. It will sweeten your disposition."

Defeated, Jack took one of the cookies and sat down again to nibble on it.

"Have you heard that Charles Lindbergh is coming to California?" Gail asked. "I'll bet Sam is very excited."

"Is he coming to the Bay Area?" Jack asked, aware now that all he could do was try to make small talk.

"I don't know. I think the paper said San Diego. But one never knows these days. They say soon there will be passenger air service all the way from Los Angeles to New York. I find that hard to believe." Gail tested the strength of her tea and filled a cup for each of them. "Do you still take cream and sugar, Jack?"

"A spoonful of sugar will be fine, thanks."

As she served the two cups and saucers and motioned him to sit down at the table, Jack felt like a little boy again. But the feeling dissipated quickly when Gail said, "So tell me more about this new a job of yours. You said you are truck driver. What kind of trucks and where do you drive them?"

"It's a delivery service," he answered, desperately searching for a way to remain ambiguous. "We cover a lot of different areas, all around the Bay."

Gail looked at him suspiciously over the edge of her teacup. "And what kinds of things do you deliver?"

"I really can't say." Jack decided it was the only right answer to offer. He was not going to lie to his mother, even now when he was so thoroughly disappointed in her.

Gail eyed him warily. "Is it something illegal? Jack, you're not involved with bootlegging again, are you?"

Jack pushed back his chair and stood up. Carrying his cup and saucer over to the kitchen counter and setting it down. Then, without turning to face her, he sighed. "I guess it's just as you say, Mother. What I do has nothing to do with you. It's none of your business! I'm leaving now!"

Gail remained seated and silent as Jack stepped outside and closed the door. Only then did she begin to weep.

[Editor's note: change of scene in author's text]

Florin Geddis leaned on her kitchen sink and stared out at the row upon row of deteriorating wooden merchant ships anchored in Southampton Bay. Etched against the gray late October sky, the old ships were like gloomy ghosts silently reminding her she was now completely alone.

Three months before, Sam had moved out to share lodging with Ted Sena at the Rivers' ranch in western Calaveras County. Although Sam told his mother in January that he had accepted a job with the Forestry Service, he did not explain when that job would start. When he was away during the spring and early summer, she assumed he was working but did not know where or for whom. She had ceased to care. *C'est comme son père!* she thought bitterly.

Now this latest blow! Two days ago, Merriweather had taken her Tee-Tee away and sent him to a private boarding school in Grass Valley, more than a hundred miles away. The foolish doctor had made some feeble excuse about Tully's needing a "good" Quaker education. "*Quelles bêtises!*" she declared aloud.

But there was no one to hear her, no one who felt any compassion for her lonely plight. Since Florin had been released from the sanitarium four years before, even her friend Gail had avoided her. Nor, despite all her protestations to the contrary, did that Quaker woman Natalie Brighton show any sympathy. Natalie's initial solicitousness had been purely political! *Quest-ce-que je faire? [sic.]* Florin asked herself.

She knew the answer, the only answer. Entering her bedroom, Florin found the small bottle of laudanum she had hidden in a drawer beneath her undergarments. She brought it back into the kitchen and emptied its contents into a wine glass. Then, filling the glass with a Merlot she had recently purchased, she carried it into her living room and sat down in her favorite wingback chair.

She considered putting a record on her Victrola, but then dismissed this thought. She knew the laudanum would quickly take effect. In a matter of minutes, she would be completely free of her loneliness.

[Editor's note: change of scene in author's text]

Sean regained consciousness and opened his eyes. He was sitting alone in complete darkness, his wrists and ankles bound tightly to a straight-back chair. The only sounds he heard were those of wood intermittently bumping against wood; the only sensation, that of bitter cold seeping into the very marrow of his bones.

Sean's first impulse was to call out, "Hey! Anybody here?" His instincts told him to keep silent, though. Wherever he was and whoever had put him there had done so with malice. He tried to control the terrifying thoughts that were racing around in his head.

After a few minutes, his eyes became accustomed to the dark and he was able to make out the dim outline of large rectangular opening at one end of the building he was in. Through this opening, he could see two lights shining in the distance, several hundred yards away. Gradually, he became aware that separating him from these lights was a wide expanse of open water. The much closer sounds of wood clunking against wood told him he was in some kind of a boathouse.

His fingers were numb with cold. He thought of rocking his chair, hoping the weight of his body might cause it to break and loosen the ropes around his wrists and ankles. He quickly abandoned this idea, realizing he might be close to the edge of a dock and could tumble himself into the water. Sean closed his eyes again, the vaguely remembered words of an old Gaelic prayer drifting through his head. At length, he again slipped into unconsciousness.

"Ding-dong! Ding-dong!" mocked a reedy male voice.

Jolted into wakefulness, Sean saw a rat-like face, only inches away from his own. "Did you have pleasant rest, Mister Hanrahan?"

Sean blinked, almost blinded by the bright light from a kerosene lantern the stranger was holding. The light revealed two other men standing on either side of his interrogator. They looked vaguely familiar to Sean, but he couldn't remember where he might have seen them before. "What's goin' on?" Sean demanded angrily. "Why you got me tied up like this?"

The rat-faced man stepped back, at the same time bringing the lighted lantern so close to Sean's left cheek that he could feel its heat. "We have a few questions to ask you, sir."

That reedy voice again, caressing but menacing! Sean stiffened with terror. "W' what d' y' want?" he stuttered. "I d' don't know from nothin'!"

"Aw, come on, old chum," one of the other men said with mock solicitousness. "Don't give us that line. After all what you told me and Seth the other night at the Casa de Vallejo? You know plenty!"

Desperately Sean tried to remember, but his brain was still foggy from whatever it was he had been drinking earlier. "Like what?" he asked fearfully.

"Like what routes your nigger boss uses for his deliveries," hissed the man with the reedy voice.

"Who the hell are you?" Sean demanded, trying to recover some of his own Irish bravado.

"Allow me to introduce myself. My name, sir, is Emmett Spears," the rat-faced man said, brushing the side of Sean's cheek with the white-hot globe of his lantern. When Sean yelped in pain, Spears added, "That's just a little taste of what's in store for you, muttonhead!"

Terrified, Sean felt the warmth of his own urine—a response Spears was quick to detect.

"I see you're beginning to catch on." The other men chuckled derisively.

"Come on!" Spears snarled. "We don't have all night. Spill it!"

"I only went with Tucker's boys once," Sean whimpered. "It was the night route they took from Livermore through Stockton and then straight across to Jamestown."

"What nights of the week?"

"Just Tuesdays, I think."

"Where do they keep their trucks?" Spears barked.

"Back of Schuster's Garage in Vallejo, where Tucker works."

Spears nodded to Stark. "Very good, Mister Hanrahan. But we also need to know the day route the nigger uses and which days of the week?"

Desperate, Sean tried to remember what Tucker had said months before. "Up Lincoln Highway through Sacramento and then to Placerville. From there, I think they take some road south toward Jamestown. I don' know for sure!"

"I know that road," Stark said. "It's the old Forty-Niners' route. Goes through Columbia."

"Which days?" Spears repeated, moving the hot lantern close to Sean's face again.

"Jesus!" Sean yelped in pain. "I don' know!"

"Not good enough, my friend," Spears snarled. Turning to Stark, he said, "We're done with this fool. Get him into the boat."

"What d' y' mean?" Sean cried out. "I tol' y' everythin' I know!"

"Take look at your dogs, old buddy," Stark chuckled. "You got some new shoes."

Glancing down, Sean suddenly realized both of his feet and the legs of his chair were stuck in a box of hardened concrete. When Stark and Seth grabbed the corners of this box and lowered Sean into the stern of a run-about, Sean cried out, "What are y' gonnah do?"

"We're goin' fishin'," Stark explained, as he started the boat's engine. "And you're gonnah be the bait."

Speechless with terror, Sean began to scream. Instantly, Stark gunned the big inboard on his Chris. Craft, completely drowning out Sean's screams as they sped out across the open water into San Pablo Bay.

[Editor's note: change of scene in author's text]

Since it was Mischief Night, Adam was not surprised both of tank trucks had been splattered wet with his yellow paint. Parked in the open behind Schuster's Garage, they were easy targets for pranksters. "Wipe that stuff off before it dries," he told Patrick Finn and Eddie Zhau, handing them several rags he had retrieved from the back of his car. "An' hurry it up 'cause we's runnin' late."

While Billy warmed up the engine of the truck they were going to use that night, Patrick and Eddie quickly carried out Adam's orders. Ten minutes later they were on Lincoln Highway, heading south toward Livermore.

Using the southern route, it was more than a three-hour drive from Vallejo to Jamestown. Once they were past Stockton, though, the roads across the Central Valley were level and straight. At that time of night, their truck and follow car were the only vehicles in transit, so they made good time. As they entered the foothills of the Sierras, their progress was slowed by long hill climbs and sharp curves.

"What's that?" Patrick exclaimed as they came over a rise and the truck's headlights revealed an obstruction in the road ahead.

Billy shifted into low gear and the truck's engine whined in protest. "Looks like tree fell across the road."

Seconds later, they saw figures moving behind the obstruction. Then, simultaneously, eight sets of automobile headlights flashed on—four on each side of the road.

"Jesus! It's an ambush!" Patrick shouted, quickly unholstering his pistol.

"Hang on!" Billy ordered, shifting into high gear and flooring his gas pedal. Their heavy rig quickly picked up speed on the downward slope. But as they roared through the gauntlet of bright headlights, dozens of men opened fire on them with pistols, rifles and Tommy Guns.

Without doors or windows, the truck cab gave Billy and Patrick no protection. Torn to pieces in hailstorm of bullets, Billy lost control of the truck, which careened off the road into a ditch. The empty tank trailer rolled over on its side, toppling the cab and hurling Patrick out onto the rock-strewn embankment where he was knocked unconscious.

Following in their car more than a hundred yards behind, Adam and Eddie had not seen the roadblock until they crested the hill. The tank truck had already run off the road. Adam slammed on the brakes, stalling his engine. Eddie reached for his shotgun in the back seat. Instantly, several in the ambush party turned their fire on Adam and Eddie.

With bullets pinging off the hood and grill of his vehicle, Adam restarted his engine and backed up the car to turn it around. Eddie tried to fend off the attack by firing both barrels of his shotgun. But the rear wheels of Adam's car spun in the loose gravel at the side of the road for several seconds before he could gain traction. That's when two bullets smashed the front windshield and slammed into Eddie's right shoulder.

By now, the tank truck had caught fire. Just as two of the ambush party's vehicles began to move onto the road in pursuit of Adam, the truck's gas tank exploded. This gave Adam the time he needed to get a head start on his pursuers.

Thanks to Francis, the V8 engine of Adam's 1924 Buick sedan had been modified to provide maximum speed. Because of this and his superior knowledge of Calaveras County's back roads, Adam easily eluded and outran his pursuers. Eddie Zhao was bleeding profusely, though. Adam knew his partner would be unconscious, perhaps even dead, before they reached the Rivers' ranch.

"What the hell happened?" Todd Rivers asked as he helped Adam lift Eddie's limp body out of the car. Awakened by the sound of voices, Sam and Ted ran toward them from the bunkhouse, both shouting the same question.

"We was ambushed. Somebody leaked our route," Adam replied angrily.

Sharon held the front door open as they carried Eddie inside and gently laid him on the Rivers' living room sofa. His clothes were covered with blood and he seemed to have stopped breathing. Sharon leaned over Eddie and pressed her fingertips against his throat. "I'm afraid he's gone," she said.

Adam shook his head slowly. "They got Billy and Patrick too."

"We've got to go back and rescue them!" Sam declared. "We can take the plane."

"You'll have a tough time doing that in the dark, Sam," Sharon gently reminded her former pupil. "Biplanes don't have headlights." Adam collapsed in a chair, his face twisted with anger and grief. "Ain't no use. The truck blew up. They's gotta be dead."

"I still say we should try!" Sam insisted.

Todd glanced at the clock on the mantel piece. "It'll be light in a couple of hours. I'll take our truck. Adam, you can come with me, and Sam and Ted will cover us from the air."

Adam closed his eyes and slumped forward. "He's been hurt!" Sharon shouted, moving swiftly to catch Adam before he collapsed on the floor. Yanking open the front of his jacket, she exposed a bleeding gash just below his collarbone. "Looks like a glass cut. Todd, go get my kit!"

[Editor's note: change of scene in author's text]

All Saints' was an important and solemn feast day in the Lanham household, as it was for many parishioners of Saint Dominic's Church in Benicia. Indeed, sometimes it seemed to Del that Catholics generally were obsessed with death. Despite the early hour, Saint Dominic's was filled to capacity-mostly gray-haired men and women, kneeling with their heads bowed in studied grief.

Every year since her mother's death, Del and her father had attended 6:30 Mass on All Saints Day to pray for Clarabel Lanham's immortal soul. Though she was only five years old when her mother died after a long bout with influenza, Del felt a special kinship with her now as Father Cardoni led the congregation in their recitation of the Canticle for the Dead.

"Salvation, glory, and power to our God," the priest began.

"Alleluia," all responded in unison.

"His judgments are honest and true."

"Alleluia."

"Sing praise to our God, all you his servants."

"Alleluia."

And so it went, on and on. The continuous pattern of utterance and response was supposed to ease the troubled spirit and soothe the grieving heart. But for some like Del, it was only numbing to a still sleepy brain.

Images of her dead mother came back to Del in fleeting fragments as she tried to concentrate on the meaning of the priest's incantations: "The wedding feast of the Lamb has begun and his bride is prepared to welcome him." What is the connection between these words and the living, breathing being that was your mother? asked a voice somewhere deep inside of her. Who was your mother? Why should she matter to you?

Dell trembled in fear of these questions. Surely it was blasphemous to entertain them. How often had the nuns warned her that Satan is forever at work trying to poison our conscious thoughts, especially when we pray. "Always say the words aloud," Sister Rosemary had repeatedly urged during Catechism class. "The very act of uttering holy words will protect you from the Evil One."

But Dell's thoughts continued to meander. They were not thoughts, really, but the recalled images of women she had known: those of her mother, pretty, slender and frail; of Ruby, most of the time jovial and always sturdy and steady; of Craig's mother, Betsy, petite and perky as a Scotch Terrier; of Jack's mother, full of sorrow and stoic determination; of Sam's mother!

It was this last image that loomed large and frightening, Florin's dark and beautiful but empty eyes during the murder trial coupled with the recent newspaper report of her attempted suicide. Del shifted her gaze toward the bank of lighted candles to the left of her pew. Each burning candle represented some parishioner's prayer for a dead or a living soul. Del became aware that she was really praying now not for the soul of her own mother but for that of a mad woman!

"Hail Mary, full of Grace, pray for us sinners now and at the hour of our death," Del murmured. The words on her lips were not the same as those others spoke at that moment, neither the words of the priest, "Bring all who have died into the company of heaven with Mary, Joseph and all your saints" nor the response of the people, 'and give us also a place in the unending fellowship of your kingdom."

Everyone stood up, Del included, and together recited the *pater noster* in Latin. Del felt a sudden flood of warmth overwhelming her-a feeling of love and forgiveness that could not be expressed in the words of any language.

10

World War II

[Editor's note: The Sacramento–San Joaquin River Delta was changed dramatically by World War II. First, it was home to a large number of Japanese families who were subsequently resettled in relocation camps. A number of them wrote haiku poems describing their experience. See Violet Kazue de Cristoforo, *May Sky: There is Always Tomorrow* (Los Angeles: Sun and Moon Press, 1997). Included here is a reflection by a Japanese American congressman, Mike Honda, about the "less than human" experience suffered by his family from Walnut Grove.

Secondly, as a result of the draft and the relocation of the Japanese, there was a shortage of agricultural workers in the Sacramento–San Joaquin River Delta as in the rest of California. The governmental response was the Bracero Project, which encouraged migrant labor from Mexico. Daniel Bacon has long been a chronicler of migrant labor in the United States and offers an oral history of a family who participated in the Bracero Project in and around the Sacramento–San Joaquin River Delta.

Finally, the Sacramento–San Joaquin River Delta was the location of large military facilities, selected because of its safe distance from San Francisco, which was considered a target and because of its strategic location on the water. One of the most significant events to occur at these installations was the Port Chicago munitions explosion and subsequent mutiny. Joseph Smart sets the stage for these events with his description of the day in the life of a black seaman at Port Chicago just before the accident. Another installation of note was the interrogation facility at Byron Hot Springs. Here Japanese prisoners of war were questioned about issues of strategic significance. An interview with one of the interrogators, Louis Lipkow, is includes to provide a sketch of the working of that facility.]

Mike Honda, "When My Japanese American Family Was Treated as Less Than Human"

[Editor's note: "When my Japanese American Family was treated as less than human," by Michael Honda, December 21, 2015, was posted as a blog for Reuters and later on medium.com. Clearly the scars left by the relocation experience impacted families and communities long after the war was over. Michael Honda did not return to Walnut Grove but served as congressman, representing a portion of San Jose from 2001 to 2017. Mr. Honda has provided edits of the original blog. (*By permission*). See Fig. 39.]

In the aftermath of the Paris and San Bernardino, California, terrorist attacks, the dangerous and destructive discourse about Muslims and Muslim Americans has reached a tipping point. Some Republican presidential candidates are calling for a ban of Muslims entering the country, and a Democratic mayor in Virginia is demanding the internment of Syrian refugees.

I can't help but fear that history could be on the verge of repeating itself.

I am a third-generation American of Japanese ancestry, born in Walnut Grove, California. Yet my family and I were classified as enemy aliens simply because we looked like the enemy. In the days before we were taken from our communities, the life we knew was ripped from us.

In the aftermath of the attack on Pearl Harbor, on Dec. 7, 1941, the United States blamed us for the Japanese attack. Because of what the 1988 Civil Liberties Act labeled "war hysteria, racism and a failure of political leadership," President Franklin D. Roosevelt signed Executive Order 9066, which confined the Japanese American community in internment camps—and forever changing our lives and our community.

On Feb. 19, 1942, the U.S. government announced that all "aliens and non-aliens of Japanese ancestry" would be relocated. Our government didn't even have the decency to call us citizens or noncitizens. So the military carried out Executive Order 9066 and confined us to "American-style concentration camps."

All Japanese Americans were allowed to take only what we could carry. As our community prepared for the evacuation, opportunistic neighbors came to our house to bargain for what we had to leave behind. They would make their best offer for our family heirlooms, or even our household goods for mere pennies on the dollar.

Other residents in our neighborhood barged into our house while we were having dinner. Without a second thought, they took our belongings. In the eyes of these people—and of our nation—we were nothing. We didn't matter.

The land and prized treasures of my family and of all Japanese Americans were sold, stolen, and, in rare cases, preserved by caring neighbors. Families burned or buried ancestral documents for fear the papers would be misunderstood. It was a fire sale of everything we held dear.

My grandfather, for example, had a fledgling gas-station business in a rural area near the levee of the Sacramento River. The first time the U.S. authorities came, they took his radio and personal fire arms. They returned the following week and took his flashlights and remaining electronic gadgets. For fear they would return yet again to take more, my grandfather took the wheels off his brand-new pickup truck and pushed it into the Sacramento River. "If I can't have it," he said angrily, "they can't have it."

My grandfather wasn't a citizen, then (because of the anti-Asian exclusionary immigration laws), but in his heart, he was an adopted loyal American. That is why he had so much hurt, anger and resentment at being distrusted and challenged. Because of his "resistance," he was separated from our family, and sent to a different internment camp for those considered "high risk," Tule Lake, California. At the end of the war, he went back to Kumamoto, Kyushu, Japan.

Our government had told us our relocation was for our safety and protection. But when we saw soldiers with M1s or other rifles coming to our house to take us away, there was no doubt in our minds that they would shoot us if we made the tiniest false move. My family was relocated from the Sacramento valley to the fairgrounds in Merced, California. On arrival, we were all forced to clean out horse stalls to make them our new home. Many elderly and babies ultimately died because of dysentery from these unsanitary conditions.

After a few months, we were then transferred to the Amache internment camp in Colorado. Soldiers with rifles loaded us onto trains. The shades were pulled down so we couldn't see where we were going.

Once settled inside Amache, we organized ourselves. We built stores, post offices, schools and even held Boy Scout meetings—anything to regain some semblance of life and normalcy. My father used to tell me, "If we were sent to internment camps for our own protection, then why was there barbed wire and machine-gun posts pointing their machine guns inward, and not outward?"

To pass the time, we even played the good old American sport baseball. But when a ball went out beyond the barbed wires, the guards menacingly yelled at the person retrieving it: "Don't go out there, or you will be shot." One elderly man was shot because he didn't hear the guard in time.

Our constitutional rights were trampled; our loyalty and citizenship ignored. Yet many still wanted to volunteer for the military. At first, we were denied enlistment as enemy aliens. Then later, the government came back and imposed the draft on the young men. Many served in the 100th Battalion and the 442nd Combat Infantry group, which became the most highly decorated combat regiment of the military.

The military also came looking for people who knew the Japanese language. My father volunteered to serve in the Military Intelligence Service, where he taught the language to the naval intelligence officers. It was a cruel irony that my father willingly served the same government that locked his family and community behind barbed wire without due process.

At the end of the war, many Japanese Americans returned to their homes, only to find their land and houses occupied, their possessions stolen. For the lucky few, however, some neighbors had faithfully preserved property and belongings, knowing that our incarceration was wrong. They carefully safeguarded our belongings—and were our true friends. This friendship mattered.

The postwar world greeted us with suspicion. Like many young Japanese American boys growing up at that time, I was bullied and teased. Many grew up feeling ashamed of our Japanese ancestry.

The trauma of this dark chapter of U.S. history long haunted the Japanese American community, especially our seniors. Their pain and experiences were unspeakable, and buried deep within their souls.

In 1988, Congress passed, and President Ronald Reagan signed, the Civil Liberties Act, a formal apology to U.S. citizens of Japanese ancestry who were unjustly interned. Our government made a mistake, but it apologized and healed many wounds as a result.

Then in 2011, 70 years after the Pearl Harbor attack—the event that changed our lives forever—President Barack Obama signed the bill that awarded the Congressional Gold Medal to the Japanese American veterans of World War II. I was particularly moved because I, along with my mother, accepted the award on behalf of my late father.

The United States can do better, and by apologizing for its injustice to our community, it finally did.

This holiday season, many around the world are fleeing their homelands and running from terror. Millions of Syrians are living in refugee camps with only the items they were able to carry with them. Here in America, many Muslim Americans, Sikh Americans and others are living in fear of harassment and violence simply because they happen to resemble and practice the same faith as those who committed the atrocities in New York City, Paris and San Bernardino.

We cannot move forward if we continue to repeat the same mistakes. We cannot let racism and bigotry overrun Americans' conscience and good faith. The tragedy of Japanese American internment cannot, must not, be repeated.

Ultimately, I don't want the internment to be a Japanese American lesson. This should be an American lesson for all those under the protection of the U.S. Constitution.

In November, 2011, Congress honored Japanese American World War II veterans with the Congressional Gold Medal, the nation's highest award for distinguished achievements. My father, Giichi "Byron" Honda, is one of these honorees. In a brutal irony, he served in the Military Intelligence Service, even as his family lived behind barbed wire in a Colorado internment camp.

The deeds of the 6,000 MIS volunteers were long shrouded in secrecy. These bilingual Japanese Americans served their country as translators, interrogators and Japanese-language instructors. Not only did they help win the war in the Pacific, their understanding of the Japanese built a pathway to peace after the war. Because MIS work was classified until 1972, their heroism was often hidden from public view.

My father was born in Walnut Grove, Calif., and was a Boy Scout growing up. He graduated high school and was a member of the California Scholarship Federation. He then worked as a truck driver to pay for community college, pursuing his dream of becoming a doctor.

But his dream was dashed on Feb. 19, 1942, when President Franklin D. Roosevelt signed Executive Order 9066, declaring the West Coast a military zone and forcing more than 120,000 Japanese Americans, my family included, to evacuate. My family was hauled to Merced Assembly Center and incarcerated behind barbed wire at the Amache internment camp in southeast Colorado. I was less than a year old.

Men of Japanese ancestry were originally prohibited from enlisting in the armed forces. Despite their patriotism and willingness to fight for freedom and democracy, countless Japanese American men were classified "4C"— enemy aliens.

But when the military needed servicemen who could read and write Japanese, 6,000 men quickly joined the MIS. In 1943, my Dad left Amache to teach Japanese under contract to the Navy Intelligence Service at the University of Colorado at Boulder. He was later transferred to Northwestern University. He was able to bring his family, including me, to join him in Chicago.

Life in Amache had taught me that being Japanese in America was bad. In the years after my internment, Dad was quick to teach me that Japanese Americans had been treated unjustly and our constitutional rights as Americans had been violated. My father's lessons guided my work in Congress even as we approach the 70th Anniversary of Executive Order 9066.

The Congressional Gold Medal recognizes the strength that Japanese American servicemen demonstrated in volunteering to risk their lives for their country – even as their families were imprisoned back home. As President Harry S. Truman told these veterans at the end of the war, "You fought not only the enemy, but you fought prejudice, and you won."

The military volunteers' service and the MIS protected America in the darkest of hours. Their legacy as Japanese Americans is a lodestar for every future generation—inspiring us to work tirelessly to forge a more perfect union.

The thousands of Japanese American war heroes from MIS, the 100th Infantry Battalion and the 442nd Regimental Combat Team, are now etched in U.S. history. Their devotion to country is an indelible reminder that we must never let "war hysteria, racial prejudice and a failure of political leadership" derail the continuing mission of America—to live as one nation, indivisible, with liberty and justice for all.

However, we should realize that EO 9066 can still be legally applied to other "enemy aliens," because of the existence of the Alien Enemy Act of 1798. Representative Ilhan Omir from Wisconsin and Senator Mazie Hirono from Hawaii are currently sponsoring a bill to repeal the final remnants of the Alien and Sedition Acts of 1798.

Rigoberto Garcia Perez interviewed by David Bacon

[Editor's note: Rigoberto Garcia Perez (interviewed by David Bacon) in "The Story of a Bracero," *dbacon.igc.org/Imgrants/24BraceroStory.htm* (*By permission of the interviewer*). See Fig. 40.]

[Author's comment: Are braceros going to make a reappearance in California fields? The old program for bringing contract workers from Mexico, which started during World War II, was finally ended as a result of a massive outcry in 1964. One of the main organizers against it was the young Cesar Chavez, who brought unemployed farmworkers in Oxnard, displaced by contract workers brought from Mexico by growers, into the streets to demand jobs. Chavez said that it would have never been possible to go on to organize the United Farm Workers if the bracero program had not been cancelled.

Yet in the discussions back and forth between President George Bush and Mexican President Vicente Fox, it is becoming clear that a contract labor program may be all they can agree on. Before his last trip to Monterrey, Bush told reporters that he opposed any kind of amnesty for the eight million undocumented workers in the U.S., but favored programs "to link willing employers with willing employees." That language is administration shorthand for advocating a program in which employers might once again bring contract laborers from Mexico on a large scale.

The U.S. already has smaller-scale guest worker programs, but growers generally do not use them because they require pay scales higher than they presently pay to their mostly undocumented workforce. New grower proposals would abolish those restrictions.

So what was it like to be a bracero in the old days? Rigoberto Garcia was one of many thousands who came every year, and remembers the experience with a mixture of anger and resignation. Some of his memories document the brutal exploitation and callous treatment suffered by the contract laborers themselves. But other memories puncture some of the stereotypes about the program. Braceros not only went on strike (and suffered deportation as a result), but their experiences laid the groundwork for later strikes by the U.F.W., when those same workers came back after the program was abolished. Also, Garcia remembers the solidarity of a Japanese grower, interned during World War II, who finally helped him win his legal status.

As the country begins to debate whether or not to move towards a new bracero program, it is important to look at what happened in the old one, and who better to tell that story than a bracero himself?

On a recent night in the desert of the Palo Verde Valley, as the scent of the surrounding citrus groves made its way into the old trailer where he now lives with his wife, Rigoberto Garcia Perez told his story to David Bacon. In the accompanying photo, he sits with her at the table in their tiny kitchen, with his old bracero work contracts spread out before them.]

I was born in Lalgodona, Michoacan, January 26, 1934. My father owned some land, but he had to keep selling it off, and in the end, he lost all of it. He became a bracero when the war started with Germany.

They always made good money, the braceros. He rebuilt his house and tried to recover his land, but he couldn't. But he was a fighter, so he started a small store and went into business. And he never went to the U.S. again.

When I began to think about crossing the wire, my father was against it. It was as if I had told my parents I was going to work down in the mine. His idea was that when you work for someone else, you never get free of it. For him, working on the land we were working for ourselves, not someone else. When you work for someone else, the profit from your work stays with them. That was his advice, and it was true. Because here you work just to survive, and you don't own anything. You just survive and survive, but someone else owns your labor.

I was an *alambrista* the first time I went to the U.S. We got to Mexicali, and got on a train. There were two trains that went from San Diego to Phoenix, and traveled a ways on the Mexican side. At the border, you'd have to get off, because the immigration was there. So you'd get off outside town, and cross the border on foot. It wasn't a big problem, like it is today, where they're keeping such a watch. The border was almost free then.

I worked in Stockton, in the cherries, where the *migra* caught me twice. After that, I didn't want to go back. I decided to work in Calipatria, where if they caught me, I was closer to the border, and it wasn't as hard to get back. Because we were so near Mexicali, when we'd hear on the radio that some famous artist would perform there, we'd all go. We didn't need papers. We'd go to Mexicali and have a good time. And that night, we'd cross back over. It was easy. Now it costs a lot of money for everyone to cross. Poor people suffer a lot.

I went back home and got married, and I stayed home a year. Then I decided to cross again, but as a bracero. Instead of hopping freights and all that, we could go a different way. I went to the contracting station in Sonora, in Empalme. It was very easy to get work. There were people there who would sign you up, for $300 a month at that time. They'd get a thousand or two thousand people a day.

I went as a bracero, four times, but I didn't like it. We got on the train in Empalme, and went all the way to Mexicali, where we got on busses to the border. From there, they took us to El Centro. Thousands of men came every day. Once we got there, they'd send us in groups of two hundred, as naked as we came into the world, into a big room, about sixty feet square. Then men would come in in masks, with tanks on their backs, and they'd fumigate us from top to bottom. Supposedly we were flea-ridden, germ-ridden. No matter, they just did it.

Then quickly, they took a pint of blood from every man. Anyone who was sick wouldn't pass. Then they'd send us into a huge bunk house, where the contractors would come from the growers' associations in counties like San Joaquin, Yolo, Sacramento, Fresno and so on. The heads of the associations would line us up. When they saw someone they didn't like, they'd say, "You, no." Others, they'd say, "You, stay." Usually, they didn't want people who were old—just young people. Strong ones, right? And I was young, so I never had problems getting chosen. We were hired in El Centro and given our contracts, usually for 45 days.

It was an agreement from one government to the other. The contract had to have the signature of the mayor of your town, guaranteeing your reputation. You also had to have experience picking in Mexico. It was a kind of blackmail. My wife's father had to work in the Yaqui River Valley to complete his period of time before he could go to Empalme and sign up. When your contract was over, they'd put you on a bus back to El Centro. And there they'd give you the passage back to Empalme.

I went to Santa Maria, where we picked strawberries. From there they renewed our contracts and sent us to Suisun, and we picked pears there. When we were through, the rancher said, "now we're going to Davis." And from there they sent us back to Mexico.

I think at that time our wage was 80¢ an hour. In the tomatoes, it was piece work, 20¢ a box. That was pretty good if you could pick a hundred boxes. But the work was a killer, really hard. They'd give you two rows, which could give you 50 boxes, and you could do that in half a day.

In Tracy I was with a crew from Juajuapa de Leon, in Oaxaca, and one of those boys died. Something he ate at dinner in the camp wasn't any good. The kid got food poisoning, but what could we do? We were all worried because he'd died, and what happened to him could happen to any of us. They said they'd left soap on the plates, or something had happened with the dinner, because lots of others got diarrhea. I got diarrhea too. But this boy died.

We slept in big bunkhouses. It was like being in the army. Each person had their own bed, one on top of the other, with a mattress, blanket and so on. They'd tell us to keep the place clean, to make our beds when we got up. We woke up when they sounded a horn or turned on the lights. We'd make our beds and go to the bathroom, eat breakfast, and they'd give us our lunch—some tacos or a couple of sandwiches, an apple and a soda.

When we got back to camp, we'd wash up before we went to eat. In the tomatoes, you really get dirty, like a dog, so you'd want to go in there clean, with your clothes changed.

We could leave the camp if we wanted to go into town. In Stockton, there was a Spaniard who had a drugstore and a radio station. He would send busses out to the camps to give people a ride. He was making a business out of selling us shirts, clothes, and medicine.

The foremen really abused people. A lot was always expected of you, and they always demanded even more. We were obligated to really move it. There were places where braceros went out on strike, or stopped work. One of my brothers went on strike in Phoenix because they were picking cotton and the crop was bad. They always said you could never make money doing it. A lot of work for nothing. They threatened to send them back to Mexico. They put them on a bus to El Centro, and from there they sent them to Fullerton, to work in the oranges.

My brother was one of the leaders. He got it into his blood, and later worked with Cesar Chavez for many years. I was too. There was always exploitation then. They would say that a bucket would by paid at such and such a price, and you'd fill it up, and then they'd pay less. When the farm workers' movement came along, we already knew about organizing and strikes from people who'd participated in those movements. My father had been on strike in Mexico too. He'd tell me that when the boss doesn't understand you have to hit him where it hurts, in his pocketbook. If you don't, he won't see you. I think it's that way everywhere in the world.

Those who can exploit, do it. That's what Cesar said when he died in San Luis, "*Hay que educar a que pisa, y hay que educar a les deje pisar. Hay que educar a los dos.*" You have to educate both, the exploiter and the exploited. If you don't educate both sides, you can't have a future.

I was a bracero from 56 to 59. I was in Watsonville six months before I got married. That was when my wife and I were just lovers. We'd write each other, and I'd ask her to wait for me, until I returned. So we got married. She didn't like my leaving, but she stuck with me. I told her, "I'll just go this once, and

I'll be back in time to do the planting." I went off to work, but always with the idea I'd come back and we'd use the money to do more on our farm. We had four hectares of onions, but the price fell, and the crop just stayed in the ground. So I said, "Well, I better go to the United States."

The next year, when I came back, we had a good crop of camote. We put our backs into it, and irrigated, and we had no competition. We were the lords of the market. But afterwards, I thought again, "Well, I better go to the United States." A human being is never satisfied. We all have one thing, and want another.

The last time I came as a bracero, I was in San Diego. There I worked for a Japanese grower named Suzuki, a good man. During the war, they had put him into one of the camps. He talked a lot about it. He told us, "I know what your life is like, because we lived that way too, in concentration camps. They watched over us with rifles." So he got papers for all of us. He fixed us up, and told us to come work with him. That was the last contract I worked.

When I fixed my immigration status. I decided I wouldn't go back, because my father had died, and I decided to bring my wife here instead. I was tired of being alone. That was the hardest thing, the loneliness. You have the security of three meals, a place to stay, your job. But you get depressed anyway. I missed my land and my wife. And since I met her, I can't go with another woman. My parents and grandparents gave me that tradition. One wife for one strong family.

But it was important to send my kids to school. That's what I was trying to do as a bracero. I wanted a real future, and we knew that we were just casual workers. I would never be able to stay. I had to look for another future.

It was the beginning of the life I'm leading now. Thanks to those experiences, we survived, and here I am. I have two countries, just me, one person. I can cross the border, and live in my own land, and I can live happily in this country too. I came as an *alambrista,* and then back came as a bracero. Eventually I got my papers and lived like any other person. But I always remembered how I got here. Illegal, a bracero.

I still have a house on the land my father gave me. And I haven't let it go, because that's where all my children were born. Anytime we want to go to Mexico, we have a place there. I tell my son your grandfather was a visionary. Don't sell it, he said, because we don't know what will happen. Maybe one day we'll go back.

Joseph Small, "A Day at Port Chicago"

[Editor's note: Joseph Small, "A Day at Port Chicago" in Richard Allen, *Port Chicago Mutiny* (Berkeley: Heyday, 2006), pp. 1–20. The author mixes the military and civilian conventions for telling time; his usage has been kept here to indicate the confusion of recruits between the two worlds. (*By permission*). See Fig. 41.]

This story could start on any day of week and almost any moment of the day during the years 1943 to 1946. Let's take the 14th day of one of the months in 1944. The day started a usual. The fall-in call came at 6:45 A.M. I never liked powdered eggs so I didn't answer chow call at 5:00 A.M. I also didn't like the white officers—and they were all white—and though l was part of them they didn't like the all-black enlisted-man crew.

The barracks petty officer burst into the overcrowded crew quarters yelling, "Fall out! Fall out, you sons of Satan!" The men who didn't respond quick enough were rolled out of their bunks, mattress and all.

We could hear the clank of metal striking metal outside the barracks window. That would be T.J. He had gotten up at 4:30, stood beside his bunk and used it to relieve his bladder, hung his sneakers around his neck, and gone outside in his skivvies to pitch horseshoes. He had done this every morning for the past two months. We all wondered if he would be successful in getting the Section Eight discharge he was after.

In the spring, rains had turned the streets of the entire base into sea of mud, with the exception of the sidewalls around the base officers' quarters. Lieutenant Ernest Delucchi was one of those base officers, in fact, he was the commander of Division Four in Barrack 11, my division.

He was a short man in his middle thirties who was making a desperate attempt to change the color of his bars from silver to gold. To get his gold bars he had to prove he could get maximum work out of a crew of black sailors under impossible conditions, and he was doing just that. Everybody was rushing around talking about last night's liberty, making beds, and listening for the lieutenant's barking voice over the intercom. The petty officer was going from bunk to bunk bouncing a dime on the blankets. If the dime didn't bounce high enough for him to catch it, he ripped the bunk apart and we had to tighten the blanket before we met roll call.

The rains had stopped, the sky was clear of clouds, and it looked like we were in for a nice day. T.J. was dragging around getting his bedclothes together to hang on the fence to dry. He had a date with the medical officer as he had every morning for three weeks. They were running tests on him to find out why he wet his bed every night. His sneakers were still tied together by the laces and hung around his neck. Every time he bent over he had to hold on to them with one hand and then readjust them to keep them from falling off. He mumbled something under his breath about "this stinking bed."

Hoppy, a real black black man, who wore a size 30 suit, stood five feet four inches tall, and weighed 118 pounds soaking wet, crossed the center aisle of the Barn, as we all called the barracks, and said something to T.J. T.J.

exploded, hitting Hoppy in the chest with both fists, sending him stumbling backward down the aisle. Hoppy ended up tangled up in two bunks with T.J. screaming at him, "You are just mad because I am getting out and not you!" We all made a break toward the commotion to break up what we thought would be a fight, but there was no need.

Time had run out. It was 6:45. The intercom blasted the louie's voice from the quarterdeck. "Now hear this, now hear this. Division Four, Barracks B, fall out, fall out!" From that moment we had two minutes to line up in the street, mud or no mud.

I reached after my overshoes to put them on, at the same time my mind was pondering the probable events of the day. There was no reason to believe they would be any different from all the days that had gone before. The shavetail louies always underfoot, the inspectors always yelling to show their authority, the bombs bouncing off the hull of the ship as they rolled down the ramp from the boxcar door across the dock, stopped short of falling into the bay by the ship onto which they would eventually be loaded. And most of all the race. We were always in competition to see which division could load the most ammunition in one eight-hour shift.

A new ship was in and I found myself hoping she had electric winches. We had just sent one to sea with eighteen thousand tons on her. She was drawing about thirty-five feet of water and she was barely gunwale high. One foot waves flooded her weep holes and put her decks awash. More than one old Liberty had broken in half during a heavy storm under such a load. Her welded seams were rusted, her bulkheads strained out of alignment, her steam lines leaked, and her steam winches looked like they may have been taken off of the steamship that Fulton built. Their valves were leaking and loose, and my hands still bore the blisters of fighting those long iron handles trying to find neutral, which was always in a different place.

The division was lined up in the street, all except me and the POs. I never marched in ranks. It was my job to call cadence for the marching men. The PO stood on the curb waiting for me to call the division to attention. He became impatient and yelled something. I didn't hear what he said I but I knew what he meant. I yelled at the top of my voice, "Division, attention!" and waited for the men to pass the word along through a series of yells, elbow jabs, and shoulder shoves. It took a couple of minutes for them to settle down, stop talking, and give me their attention. Then I spoke in a more subdued tone, "Space off to the right." After the "Ready front" the PO called the roster. Every man present answered "Here" after his name was called. Two men that were late returning from liberty somehow had their names answered too.

We saw the cattle car pull up at the end of the street and our DCO came out of the BOQ. I gave the command "Right face, forward march," and began to call cadence. I moved the four lines of men at the rate of sixty-two steps per minute, which was pretty rough in that mud, but that was regulation and the louie was waiting.

The cattle car was our transportation to the docks. It was a forty-foot trailer with a row of small windows along each side about five feet off the floor. It had four rows of benches in it, and fully loaded and packed, it carried about eighty men. It didn't do any good to get the front of the line to get a seat, because even if you sat for the mile and quarter ride there was usually someone sitting on your lap, standing on your feet, or standing over you with hands stretched out leaning against the wall. The whole rig was battleship-gray, drawn by a tractor too small for the load.

The doors were closed, locked from the outside by the lieutenant's chauffeur, who jumped back in the lieutenant's jeep and hit his horn twice. The tractor driver started to pull off in first gear. The motor strained, coughed, and died. He started the engine again, this time shifting to low low. He popped the clutch, the truck jumped, picking the front wheels clear off the ground. It piled all against the rear doors of the cattle car. Hoppy swore at the driver in his deep bass voice. By the time we got straightened out the truck had pulled up in the parking lot, the doors had opened, and the louie was peering into the trailer. "Are you boys okay?" he inquired. I ignored his question, because I knew he was not concerned with our welfare.

I took my usual position to the left and about one third of the way back from the front of the columns of men. A lot of the men were grumbling and cursing. A few were limping. Kong, a short, stocky, gorilla looking man from Detroit, broke out of ranks and started toward the driver, who had gotten out of the cab and started around front of the truck. Kong was stopped by the PO and told to get back in ranks. He obeyed after shaking his fists at the driver and promising to see him on the beach.

The DCO of the Third Division was briefing his men on the day's work ahead. They had gotten off a cattle car a few minutes ahead of me and were ready to move out. He made a motion with his finger that brought his PO to stand at attention in front of him. Lowering his voice and looking over his shoulder to see where Lieutenant Delucchi was, said, "Tom, this hull needs two hundred fifty ton to sail. Tell the boys if we get it by fifteen-thirty, they can hit the beach at eighteen hundred." The PO turned on his heels without answering and walked toward the four columns of men who were talking softly. I didn't hear the command, but I saw the men lean forward in anticipation of the command to march, and every left foot started at the same time. Lieutenant Delucchi came around the head of Division Four and met the CO of the Third Division right in front of me. They patted each other on the right shoulder, and Lieutenant Brickland said, "Ernie, you want to kick that another fifty?" My boss said, "Sure." They shook hands very quickly. Lieutenant Brickland moved off up the dock behind his men. Lieutenant Delucchi turned to me and said, "Okay, move them out."

I gave the usual commands and the division moved out. The cadence call came from my lips automatically, but my mind was on the little girl had met on the beach last night. I don't know whether I picked her or was picked up by her. Now that I think of it, she really hung one on me.

I didn't like this little town when I first heard about it. It had a soldiers' camp in it, and any sailor would automatically be considered an intruder. Nevertheless, I decided go. When I got off the bus at this dark corner I didn't know where I was. There was street sign and streetlight. Everybody went around the front of the bus and turned left, so I just followed the crowd. I was told that in this town sailors stuck together, and everyone that got off the bus had on Navy blues.

I finally reached a little storefront building and peered inside. It had shelves along each wall, and five or six wooden benches in the center of the floor. There was a curtain wall about twenty feet back from the front door. The wall had a door in it with a half-round hole and a shelf at the bottom of the hole. There were five men in the place, all soldiers. A sign over the little window read, "Last Navy Bus Leaves One Thirty A.M." The sounds of talking and laughter were fading away, so I started to trot to catch up. I made mental notes of landmarks in case I had to find my way back alone.

We passed a movie house. The lights lit up the whole street. The marquee stretched all the way to the curb, held up by two enormous chains. The name the place was the Star. I tried to see what was playing, but my eyes were drawn to the cashier, who sat in a brightly lighted booth in the center of the entrance. She was a beautiful blonde about eighteen or twenty years old. She had a broad smile on her face, but she wasn't smiling at anyone in particular. I think that with the crowd going by, she expected a customer to come by the window.

The sailors were no longer walking in a bunch. The crowd had thinned out and was crossing a street at an angle. In the corner where the leaders were turning right was large brownstone building. The steeple jutting into the black night sky told me it was a church. There was a light over the door but I didn't see the sign until I started to turn the corner. It was encased in a brick wall about six feet by six feet at an angle to the building. It could be seen from both directions on the street.

According to the sign on the corner, we were walking on Third Street and had just crossed Beach Way. Halfway down the block I could hear water splashing against something, the smell of fish was very strong. I was used to the smell of salt water, but somehow this smell was different. Then I saw another street sign. This one read, Beach Way and Fourth. I looked back at the sign at the church: someone had turned it around. I thought myself, kids are the same all over the world.

As we crossed Fourth Street it seemed we had entered a new world, at a different time. The buildings were one-story frame structures, shabbily built, needed paint, and of all things, seemed to be built on poles. The water came right up to the edge of the street, the houses jutted out into the bay. Though the fronts of the houses rested on the edge of the street, the backs of them were as much as eight feet above the water, supported by poles sticking up out of the sand. All of the buildings I could see were either a saloon, pool hall, chicken shack, or café.

I was thirsty and needed a beer bad. I went into the first saloon I came to. It didn't look bad on the inside. The place was filled with military men, all black except one. At a table at the rear of the room sat two men that were not with the crowd. One black MP and an SP, the only white man in the place.

There was plenty of noise, a jukebox was blasting in the corner, above the laughter and conversation. There seemed to be two women for every man. The most popular thing in any saloon was missing from the bar, beer bottles. The bar, the floor, the tables, and a GI can in the corner was loaded with paper cups. I didn't have to ask why. A broken beer bottle was a perfect weapon in a barroom brawl, and I am sure here were plenty here.

I ordered a beer. The bartender set a bottle on the bar but promptly poured it into a paper cup and shoved it to me; the bottle went out of sight behind the bar.

I had passed up the fried eggplant they had for supper at the base, so by this time I was feeling the sting of hunger. A ham sandwich would hit the spot with the beer, but when asked the bartender for one he said very sarcastically, "We have an agreement with the café across the street. They don't sell beer and we don't serve food." I thanked him, gulped my beer, and headed for the ham sandwich.

I gave the batwing doors of the saloon a vicious push, but they only opened halfway out. I heard a little scream and as I stepped through the opening she was standing there rubbing her right hip. I apologized for the accident. She smiled, and I continued across the street. I looked back over my shoulder wondering, what she was doing there, and who she was waiting for. She waved her hand and I imagined I saw a smile. I waved back, stepped through the café door, which was open.

I stopped just inside the door to look for the menu, but saw none. The sign over the door read "Tender Rib Café." I started toward a long glass counter that had, among other things, a pan stacked high with corn bread. Inside case were eight or ten glass baking dishes of meat. Though they were all the same color, and all cooked in deep brown gravy, I recognized two of them: the chicken and the pork chops. I looked for the tender ribs, but saw none. There was no ham in sight either; least if there was, I could not recognize it. I ordered the dish that I thought was chicken, the gravy was a little lighter brown, rice, black-eyed peas, candied yams, and corn bread. I moved across the room, selected a seat, and sat down. There was half a newspaper on the table. I picked it up, it was two days' old. I threw it on a chair against the wall. Just then the waitress called, "Hey, sailor, pick up your plate."

As I leaned forward to get up, she came in the door. I knew she was the girl from across the street by the shorty coat and the pleated skirt she had on. I had never really seen her face. I said to myself, "Damn, she's beautiful!" I picked up my plate from the top of the glass counter and returned to my seat. I began to eat, and suddenly realized I had nothing drink. Just as I looked up the waitress "Coffee, sailor?" I nodded my head and swallowed the mouthful of food I had been chewing. The waitress brought the coffee, cream, and sugar and the bill. The meat didn't taste like any chicken had ever eaten, so I looked on the bill to see what it was. The bill said, "Dinner $1.90." She had signed her name at the top, Pat.

I was spreading butter on a piece of corn bread when I heard a light giggle. Turning slightly left and looking up, the girl from across the street had been joined by another girl. I saw something else, everything., That is, had it not been for the green panties under the pleated skirt I would have seen everything. My jaws stopped moving and I looked up into her face. She was looking directly at me, with a half-smile. I tried to let her know what was happening by the movement of my eyes, but she didn't seem to catch the hint. She whispered something to her girlfriend and looked back to me and the smile broadened.

I couldn't eat any more so I stood up, took two dollars and the bill, and laid them on the glass case. I turned and walked straight toward their seats. Her knees were in a normal position and she had a sick look on her face. The other girl was gone.

I said, "Pardon me, miss, I wanted to tell you …"

She looked up at me and said, "I don't feel good, will you take me home?" I said sure and reached for her hand. She stood up and said "My name is Lou." She turned to go to the door.

I put a quarter on the table and picked up her handbag. I waved to the waitress, said, "Good night, Pat," and turned to leave.

Just as I got to the door Pat said, "Good luck, sailor," and waved at me. That put on my guard and I vowed to be careful.

We had backtracked on Beach Way across Fourth, Third, Second. First, I wondered what street could be left. We turned right on Front Street, which was well lighted. We hadn't said much to each other, but I did find out that the name Lou was short for Lucinder. That happened when I called her Louise, and she corrected me. I had searched her bag, there was no weapon in it. I had felt her pockets for a knife or maybe brass knucks. There were two other possible places. One I had ruled out; she wouldn't have hidden there and showed it to me. The other was her hair. I stopped her in her tracks, took her head my hands, kissed her. She didn't resist and there was no weapon.

Just about that time we halted in front of a two-story frame house. I saw a thin line of light at the edge of one of the front windows but the porch was dark. As we walked up the steps, I could make out the lines of a porch swing in the shadows. She moved toward the swing, and looking back at me she said, "This is where I live. My mother is waiting for me." I believed her and ruled out the thought of men waiting in the shadows. If I was going to be robbed it would come as a surprise, because from now on my mind was going on to other conquests.

The footfall of the column leaders on the wooden dock boards brought me back to the present. I called out, "Division halt!" and then, "Fall out!" We were at work and I was tired already.

I heard the clang of metal against metal and looked up. There she was, riding high in the bay. A brand new Liberty. I knew she must be electric all the way. I bet she hadn't been out of Kaiser Ship Yards long enough to roster her full complement of merchantmen. The graveyard shift was just getting off. I asked the PO, "How much did you get?" He spoke out of the corner of his mouth.

"A hundred ninety, and is he mad."

I stepped around five one-ton bombs in a huge wire net and headed for the gangplank. I was almost eager to get to those beautiful electric winches, running them was a breeze. I walked up between the two control panels. Each had a handle about six inches long about belt high, and comfortable to the grip. I stood on a rubber mat right at the edge of the hold. I could see all the way to the bottom of the ship. She had three decks, and the bottom of the hold was about fifty feet down.

Hoppy was signalman for today. He stood at the edge of the hold talking with Kong. The hook was in the bottom well of the hold so there was nothing for him to do until we started the first lift from the dock. The net still had two other bombs on it, and the crew was slowly making their way down the series of ladders that were welded to the steel hull of the ship. Kong yelled my name and started toward me on shaky on legs, looking more like a tamed gorilla than a human. He said, "Man, I got loaded last night."

"That I can see and so did Lieutenant Delucchi," I said.

"Oh, damn Tubby!" Kong said. "He got pretty tanked up himself last night. He staggered in the same time I did this morning. I want to tell you about this broad I met last night. But then it wasn't a broad after all. I met her in the J Bar on Seventh Street. I spent over twenty bucks on her. Man, was she fine! Anyhow we got this room about two-fifteen this morning. Man, was I ready for Freddie!"

"I noticed she didn't turn on the lights when we went in, but I didn't care, there was enough light from the Navy Yard across the street for me to see what was in the room. I could see the bed and I headed straight for it. The light went off under the bathroom door, it opened, and something flew across the room and landed half on, half off the chair. The shadow that passed between me and the window was wrong. There were a few things missing. The long hair, the full bust, and the wide hips. Man, did I flip!"

"Instead of coming around the bed, it got lost in the shadows against the wall. I heard the key rattle in the door, the tumblers fell over, and the key came sliding toward me across the floor. It went under the bed."

I asked him, "Why didn't you get out of there?"

He said, "Man, I had taken off my pants, shoes, and hat, and didn't know where they were! I rolled out of bed and went to the bathroom. There were the hips, the bust, and the long hair all piled up in the bathtub. There was a funny-looking object lying on the sink. I picked it up to examine it. It was a straight-edge razor blade that slid back in a metal handle. When you compressed the button, it slid forward exposing the blade and locked in place. I pulled the bathroom door open and headed across the room to the switch by the door. I flipped the switch, the light came on. I heard a scuffle and whirled around. The punk was headed for the bathroom, but he was late on the move, I had his knife."

Hoppy cut in in an excited voice. "Man, what did you do?"

Kong continued, "Without looking around, I made a dive for my pants that were on the floor at the foot of the bed. By the time I had them on he was headed toward me naked, at a dead run. He reminded me of a goat on a charge. He was running in a crouch with his head down."

Waves began running up the cable from the hold. That told me the net was ready. I looked over the hold, pulled back on the inboard control three clicks, and told Kong he better get to work. I took up four clicks the outboard line and waited for the net to come into view above the edge of the hold. Hoppy moved over to his position at the rail to await the descent of the net. All movement and safety of equipment, material, and personnel depended his signals from the time the net dropped below rail until the time it came back into my field of vision. He was standing facing me and looking over the rail at the men loading the nets. By holding his hand in front of him and clinching his left fist, he stopped the net six inches above the dock. The men pushed the net to the side about ten inches off center. By holding his hand out in front of him, pointing his left index finger downward, and moving it in a circular motion, Hoppy gave me the signal to lower the outboard line. I pushed the outboard winch control two clicks forward and dropped the net on the dock.

A clinch of his left fist told me the hook was low enough for the men to unhook the empty net and hook up the loaded one. The hook swung back to center, across center, and stopped, hanging at an angle. A loud handclap from Hoppy brought my eyes back to his hands. Rubbing his palms together slowly meant slow movement: the left index finger pointed upward meant up on the outboard line. I pulled the outboard winch control back one click, never taking my eyes off his hands. Moving his finger, a little faster meant more power. I added one more click to the winch. I could hear the net dragging down the dock until it came back to center directly below the outboard boom. The clinching of his fist stopped all motion. I pushed the control back to neutral. Hoppy brought the tips of his fingers together on each hand and then brought his two hands together in a backward and forward motion, first touching his fingers together and then parting them, followed by touching them together again. This meant fast movement. The left index finger pointed upward and moving fast, and the right index finger pointed upward and moving slowly, gave me my orders. I pulled four clicks on the loaded line and two clicks on the slack line. I had watch both Hoppy and the line, him to catch any signal for an emergency stop, and the line to see the load when it cleared the rails.

As the loaded net rose above the rails, I added two more clicks to the slack line and backed off two on the loaded line. As the inboard line became taut and started to draw the net in over the rail of the ship, l let it pull until the net got high enough to clear the edge of the hold. As the net crossed between us we had to inspect the net and the load that was in it. If a bomb fell out or the net came loose and dumped the load into the hold, it would mean disaster. There is absolutely no place to run or hide in the hold of a Liberty ship being loaded with ammunition.

The load and net seemed fine, but as the side of the hold came into my field of vision. I saw something. Hoppy saw him the same time I did. He yelled, "Hot!" at the top of his voice. I had to act almost without thinking. l stopped the inboard reversed the outboard winch full speed. That took the net and load almost straight up. The load was about twelve inches above the deck before I got a chance to stop it and look down. A 90-Day Wonder [new officer] was kneeling at the edge of the hold. I let off the inboard line, the net began to shift back toward the rail of the ship. When it was far enough away from the edge of the hold, I let off the outboard winch and landed the net load of bombs on the deck of the ship.

Lieutenant Delucchi came running. I expected him, because under the strain of five tons of bombs and both winches running under load, the springs started to sing, and he heard it. This holdup meant a loss of tonnage to him and he was hot as a pepper mill. The shavetail lieutenant had a bloody mouth that he received when the net hit him and he bumped it on the side of the hold. He was lucky. If the net had been two inches lower he would have gotten knocked into the hold. The lines and springs were inspected and found to be unbroken. The shavetail was led away and returned to work. Lieutenant Delucchi came over, patted me on the shoulder, and said, "Make it up, Randy. We need three hundred tons."

The twenty-fifth load was headed up when the ship's bells tolled 1200 hours. I dropped the load back on the dock and went to chow. We were five lifts, or twenty-five tons, behind. I knew I had to make up before 1530 hours or face the maddest Italian in the Navy.

The chow wagon had arrived, manned by two cooks and three KPs. The men were lined up in single file, all jabbering about one thing or another. I fell in behind Hoppy, goosed him with my knee, and looked around to see if one of the marine guards had seen me. Hoppy yelled and grabbed the sailor in front of him in a bear hug. He immediately began to say "I'm sorry" over and over and to point back over his shoulder at me. The sailor laughed and said forget it. We picked up our trays from the ammo box at the side of the truck and gripped them firmly in both hands. Experience had taught us that the KPs always seem to enjoy serving chow, because that's when they get even with the Navy by trying to knock the bottom out of the trays with their serving spoons.

The fare was liver and onions, or bacon. I got bacon. Though I was raised on a farm and grew up eating onions, I quit when a girl refused to kiss me one night because I had onions on my breath. It turned out I didn't need kisses to fire up her boilers anyhow. It was a good thing the Navy used stainless-steel trays, as the KP tried to poke his fork through the bottom of it. After that, it was it safe to turn one side of the tray loose with one hand.

I picked up two pieces of hand-sliced bread and a cup of coffee, and looked around for place to sit. Hoppy and Kong were saving me a place on a rope dock bumper the edge of the water. I set my mug down on what used to be an 8-by-8-inch dock edge guard. Now it was about 8 by 4 half round. Kong spotted the driver who had given us the rough time coming to work, now sunning himself in the parking area and started to get up. I put my hand on his shoulder and said, "The beach is better." Kong said, "Yeah," and stuffed a piece liver in his mouth.

One of the KPs was headed toward us with a handful of liver and an apple pie. He said, "You guys missed your pie. They were getting some more when you went by." We each got two slices of pie and a piece of liver and the KP turned to go back to the chow wagon. He stopped short and turned around and said, "You guys from 4B?" We all answered yes at the same time. Then he asked, did we hear about T.J.? None of us answered, we all stood up. He continued, "We heard they gave him some sort of shock treatment in sick bay, and he went blind. They took him to the hospital across the bay." Hoppy said that ends the pissy smell in the barn. I said maybe he will get a medical instead of S[ection] 8. Kong said he ought to get a BCD for stinking up the barracks.

We picked up trays and headed for the GI can at the rear the truck. The marine on guard looked over each tray carefully, to make sure there was no food being thrown away. You took all you wanted, and you ate all you took. The truck was all closed up and loaded except for the GI can, the trays, and eating tools. The cooks were already screaming, "Let's roll 'em!" They had been on duty since 4:00 A.M. and their day finished after serving second chow. The cooks who came on at 1200 served third chow at 1700 hours. The night shift served first chow at 0530.

Lieutenant Delucchi was getting out of his jeep. He had driven himself to the BOQ for lunch. I had discussed with him many times the possibility of an explosion on the dock, but he always laughed it off. I told Hoppy and Kong to go aboard and waited to talk to him. He walked up alongside of me, looked at his watch, and asked, "How are things going?"

"Rough, I think we are pushing too hard." I said.

He looked at his watch again and asked, "Do think you can lift thirty by fifteen-thirty?"

"Sure, if the place doesn't blow up, and someday it will."

"If it does," he said, "neither you nor will be around to know about it," and broke out with one of his belly laughs.

That made me mad, so I quickened my step and mounted the gangway at a dead run.

Hoppy wasn't at his post so I couldn't go right to work. I thought about Lou. I could have had her right there on the swing, at least I thought so. But maybe that was my ego talking. She somehow didn't act like that sort of girl. I had walked many hookers to their bed or bunk, and by this time they had told me how much and showed me a health card.

The inside door opened and a small-built woman in a beautiful floor-length pink housecoat asked, "Is that you, Lucinder?"

The girl moved across the swing and answered, "Yes, Momma." Just as the light flicked on and the screen door opened, I stood up. The lady said, almost whisper, "Oh, you have a friend with you. Come in, both of you."

I looked at my watch. It was 11:30. I said, "No. thank you. I think I will be heading back."

Lou took me by the arm and gave it a little tug. Her mother said, "Not on your life! This is Lucinder's first night home and she has met a friend already. Come in, young man, come in."

Lou had slid her arm around my waist as if to keep from running away. She squeezed gently, and when I looked down at her she smiled, touched two fingers to her lips, then touched them to mine. I placed my arm her shoulder and my fingers touched her breast. I squeezed the nipple, expecting a lightning swing from her right hand. Instead, she let out a little squeal and laid her head on my shoulder. I had to change thoughts immediately. Those tight sailor pants would have given me away when we entered the living room. It was very brightly lit, and there was the distinct odor of new paint.

I saw Hoppy coming up the gangway taking three steps at a time. The winches whirred into action, and we were off and running. My first lift off the dock I noticed the winch pulled a little too hard. I paid close attention to the drums to see if the lines were fouled or bedded. When the load started to cross the deck, I could see why the springs were tight and the winches dragged. There was an extra bomb in the net. We were lifting six tons instead of the regular five. The POs were really trying to get that extra twenty-five tons.

The ship the other side of the dock was almost loaded. She was getting ready to sail. I could hear the crew battening down hatches. She would probably sail with the tide tomorrow morning. I found myself hoping she made it across. The Atlantic was thick with Germans and the Pacific was overcrowded with Japs. If God smiled on her and the Japs and Germans missed her, there were still storms and the high seas. We had just gotten the report that half a Liberty had been towed in. She broke in half in twenty-two-foot seas, and the stern half went down. They didn't tell us how many men were lost but we all knew the crew's quarters were in the fantail. If those boxcars weren't there, I could see if the rats were leaving the ship. That was a sure sign there would be trouble on the trip.

I dropped a load in the hold, and instead of setting it down, the PO stopped it about six inches short of the deck. The crew swung the net to one side and I lowered it gently to the deck. Instead of waiting for the crew to unload the net, I was waved out of the hold. I soon found out why. Lieutenant Delucchi had added another net. There was no more resting between lifts. There was always a net loaded and ready to go aboard, and always one empty and ready to be lifted out of the hold. The DC was going to win his fifty or burn up the winches and kill the crew.

The bombs hitting the ship and the dock edge guard became louder and more frequent. The cursing and swearing were more constant. A few fights erupted, but the crew chief was there to quiet things down. I had no time to gab with Hoppy or anyone else now. I paid close attention to my winches, for I expected the brakes to start heating at any time. After all, I was lifting six tons at a clip and, what was worse, stopping six tons in almost freefall. I could usually smell the brake bands before they started smoking. But if the wind was blowing the wrong way, I might not see or smell the hot bands until it was too late. That would be when I had to make an emergency stop because of someone in the drift path, or someone standing under a descending load that I couldn't see until after the load started to descend.

I noticed civilians coming down the dock. Each carried a flight bag, a small suitcase, or duffel bag. They had to be the crew of the ship in the next berth. They all swaggered in their walk as if the screws that held their knees together were loose. Learning to keep your balance while walking on a moving floor causes sea legs after a few years, and when you walk on land you swagger at the shoulders and often appear to be slightly drunk. When I noticed the smoke billowing from the ship's funnels I knew she was getting up steam. She would convert the steam to energy that would carry her on a journey not yet known, to encounter she knew not what. But go she must, for men were waiting on what she was carrying to kill other men who were waiting on other ships to do the same.

The appearance of the jitney to switch boxcars meant a ten-minute break. I was glad, it would give my winches a few minutes to cool down. Kong came up the gangway with a canteen in his hand. He grabbed Hoppy by the shoulder and continued to where I was sitting between the two winches. Hoppy sat on the edge of the hold. Kong jumped up on the winch brake drum but immediately jumped down, it was hot. I asked him what was in the canteen. Kong opened his mouth to say something, but Hoppy grabbed it and opened it. At the same time he said, "What happened to that punk last night?"

Kong rubbed his buttocks and said in an excited voice, "What happened to the punk?" Man, what about me? That was the strongest man I ever tangled with. I ducked that first charge and he ran into the wall. While he was getting himself together and untangled from the clothes tree he ran into, I dragged the bed away from the wall to find the key. I found it but before I could get it in my pocket he was all over me. We wrestled for a while and he got a bear hug on me. Man, I couldn't move! He was squeezing the breath right out of me. I tried to butt him in the face with the back of my head. I tried to break his ribs with my elbow. He kept calling me a son of bitch and squeezing harder. I finally got a handful of his privates and then did some squeezing. He bit me on the shoulder and then started to weaken. He released his hold enough for me to break free. He called me a motherfucker several times and started slipping to the floor. I gave his balls a squeeze as hard as I could and let go. He slumped to the floor, out cold.

"I thought I had plenty of time so I got dressed and started for the door. Then I thought about his money, he must have had some somewhere. I found his handbag but there was absolutely nothing in it. Man, I mean it was empty! There wasn't even a pin in it."

"I know that guy had some aching nuts this morning," Hoppy said.

"His nuts! My ribs feel like they need cementing back together."

"Did you find any money?" I asked him. "They always keep a bundle somewhere."

"Let me tell you, you won't believe this. I found the money, three hundred dollars. It was in the pocket of a pair of dungaree shorts in the bottom of a grocery bag he used as a clothes hamper in the bathroom."

Hoppy jumped up. He said, "Man, you been holding out on us! When we hit the beach tonight the juice will be on you!"

"I ain't got the money," Kong said.

"What happened?" I asked.

"If I had squeezed a gorilla's nuts that hard he would have stayed out for week. But when I opened the door he was getting up off the floor."

I tried to get past him to the door. I made it but the damn door was locked. I had to take the money out of my pocket to get the key. By that time, he was on his feet and headed for me. I got the key in the door and unlocked it, but I didn't have time to open it. He came at me with his head down just like before. All of a sudden, he fell flat on the floor and came at me sliding on his stomach. He grabbed my legs and upset me. I fell back against the door and knocked the light out. I jumped up and opened the door. I could see him getting up, so I turned on the fan. He followed me out into the hall buck naked.

I asked again, "What happened to the money?"

"I dropped it when hit me. It was three one-hundred-dollar bills. Anyway, I lost him when I crawled through hole in the Navy Yard fence across the street."

Two short toots from the jitney whistle, asking for a clear track off the dock let us know it take was time to go back to work. It would take the dock crew about five minutes to open the doors and set the skids, so I decided to get a drink of water.

Darn the girl! Every time she finds my mind unattended she moves in. I remember hurrying across the room to a deep stuffed chair and sitting down. Lou's mother skirted around canvas-covered furniture in the dining room and into the kitchen. The pivot door swung back and forth four or five times and then there was silence. The light expected to come on never did. The offer to have coffee I expected never came. Lou had put on some records and turned out some lights. As she crossed the room and sat on the arm of the chair beside me, Mahalia Jackson was singing "He's Got the Whole World in His Hands."

"Where is your mother?" I asked.

"Don't worry about her. She likes and trusts you or she be sitting right there. She's gone to bed."

I thought that was my cue. I pulled her down on my lap, but she swung around and stood up. I stood up with her. I pulled her to me and kissed her hard and long, When I let her go she drew a deep breath and said, "Honey, don't rush me. I don't even know if you are married or not."

She backed away, straightening her skirt. I noticed the rapid rise and fall of her breasts and surmised that that kiss had really started the fire. I couldn't let it die now. I pulled her up to me and asked her, "Why the display in the café?"

She looked up at me and said, "I'm sorry. That was a mistake. I didn't mean to tempt you. I am ashamed of how it looked to you." She stopped short and looked straight at me. She asked, "What is your name?"

This stopped me cold, so I covered up the moment for thought by squeezing her nipple. She never blinked an eye. I pulled her up to me and kissed her. Then I told her, "I have several names. I have one when I wear civvies and another when I am a sailor, so tonight my name is Randolph."

The bombs started crashing against the ship. I went back to my winches. Delucchi got his tonnage and his fifty dollars and it was quitting time. The cattle car was back; the night crew was unloading and we were forming ranks to march off the dock. I was in my place at the side the column about to yell "Forward, march" when the louie tapped me on the shoulder. He had the tally sheet in his hand. He put his arm around my shoulder and with big smile said, "Thanks, Randy. You did a fine job. We got five ton over." I said, "And fifty dollars." He turned a pale green, gave a grunt like pig, walked off toward the cattle wagon.

As the cattle car wound its way through the ammo bunkers over the bumpy road, its motor screaming and Hoppy cursing the driver, my mind pondered the possibility of the whole place blowing up. True, the bombs had no detonators in them, and as far as the Navy was concerned, it couldn't happen, but those bombs were full of gunpowder and the way they were handled anything could happen. I found myself hoping that if and when it did, I would be miles be away from there.

Someone mentioned T.J.'s name and I cocked my head to listen. All I could hear was that he got a bad conduct discharge. I started forcing my way to the door. My mind was in a whirl and I had to get the straight of this. After all, if the man was blind, how could they give him BCD? When the door opened I was the first one to hit the sod. I didn't wait to march the men off. I headed for the supply room. That punk that ran it would have the complete story on everything. I mounted the steps two at a time and threw my weight against the door.

It squeaked and swung open. There was no one behind the counter. I yelled as loud as I could, "Tony, where are you?" Tony answered from the back room, "Be right there."

I picked up a couple pair of socks and stuffed them in my pocket, hoping they were the right size, and had just got my fatigue jacket down when Tony came out, brushing his straight black hair with his hand. I asked him, "Man, what happened to T.J.?" Tony started cracking up. That made me feel better. His laughter seemed to take the importance out of what I had heard. I knew then that it must have been a lie.

"T.J. is in the brig. He went to the hospital for examination after someone told the doctor that he saw T.J. wetting in his bed after he had gotten out of it. The shock treatment was a fake. They thought it would scare him into giving up his schemes to get out. When he pretended to go blind."

"Pretended?" I said.

"Sure, there never was anything wrong with him. When he claimed he couldn't see he really shook up them doctors. He even threatened to sue the whole damn bunch. They thought maybe he had taken some kind of drugs and sent an MP to search his locker."

Just then the back door opened and closed again but no one came in. It almost chow time so I said to Tony, "They found dope?"

"No. They found a book about a woman who was in a car accident and sued because of an injured back. She won the case because they couldn't prove her back wasn't injured."

I started laughing and pounding on the counter. I said, "So he tried it with his eyes?"

"Yes, but you haven't heard the best yet," Tony said. "They thought he was faking, so they got one of the female nurses to take off everything except her bra and panties and walk through the room he was in."

"And the fool got hard-on." said.

"They couldn't tell. He had his sneakers on his lap, but they took movies of him. Once the nurse got in front of him, his eyes his followed her all the way across the room and out the other door. He's still trying to fake it. "

[Author's note: Here the story breaks off and poor T.J.'s fate remains unrecorded. Joe Small, "Randy" in this account, never completed the story, though he lived through to the finish.]

Louis Al Nipkow, "Interview about Byron Hot Springs during WWII"

[Editor's note: The Byron Hot Springs resort was commandeered by the Armed Forces during World War II to house prisoners of war, primarily from the Asian Theater, during interrogation. This is a transcript prepared by the Fort Hunt Oral History Project. The person interviewed is Louis Al Nipkow, who was stationed at Camp Tracy. The interviewers include Brandon Bies, Vincent Santucci, and Steven Kleinman. The interview was conducted on February 17, 2008. The transcript has been slightly edited where there is the potential for a confusion over who, in fact, the speaker is. (*Permission by the National Park Service*). See Fig. 42.]

INT: Can you say in your own words what happened at Byron Hot Springs?

LN: You mean as to what my personal job was or—

INT: What was Byron Hot Springs set up to do?

LN: Well, it was set up to interrogate prisoners that returned for further information, to the mainland here. And we were required to get the information from them that was requested.

INT: Were these only Japanese prisoners?

LN: Only Japanese prisoners, right.

INT: When the time that you were at Camp Tracy, you don't recall there being any German prisoners?

LN: No, there were none.

INT: Okay. Was it only interrogation or did you use any other techniques to obtain information?

LN: Only interrogation.

INT: Did you do any monitoring?

LN: Yes.

INT: You listened?

LN: Yes.

INT: Okay. We'll probably want to talk in detail about that.

LN: Okay.

INT: And was there any looking at captured documents?

LN: No, there were no documents to my knowledge that we saw, and the monitoring was done basically by the Nisei listening into the conversations.

INT: So you never—do you recall going into the [interrogations].

LN: No, I never did it.

INT: So, looks like we have about two minutes. When you drove, I assume you drove, to Byron Hot Springs.

LN: Right.

INT: When you came to the gate for the first time what did you see? Was there a gate?

LN: There was a closed gate. At the time it was a wonderful place for the camp because you couldn't see anything from the road. It was a lightly traveled area anyway and there was a hill that hid the whole camp itself. And there was just a gate there that you

LN: Right. Now, I personally didn't do any monitoring but I'm not sure that some of the others didn't.

INT: Do you remember ever being briefed in what the purpose of the monitoring was, or did you know what the purpose of the monitoring was?

LN: Well, we were briefed as to what we wanted to find out and then we took it from there.

INT: Was the focus of the monitoring on the monitoring of the actual interrogations or the monitoring of the individual rooms where the prisoners stayed in between interrogations?

LN: Well, it was general information that we thought we get from that particular prisoner.

INT: Did you focus on the monitoring that took place when conversations among two prisoners when they were alone in their rooms? Or, were their rooms bugged?

LN: All the rooms were bugged, yes.

INT: And how do you know that?

LN: Well, I was told they were bugged. I didn't know that personally but I was told they were bugged.

INT: Did you ever see any of the bugs or microphones or anything?

LN: No. No.

INT: Any idea where they may have been hidden?

LN: No, I don't.

INT: Was there a room where the monitors were located in Byron Hot Springs?

LN: No, I was told that all of the rooms were bugged, but not where the bugs were, but each room apparently was bugged.

INT: And for those people that were listening, the Nisei that were monitoring, would they be in a specific location to listen, a quiet room or—

LN: Well, I believe there was a room where they went to listen, one central room.

INT: Was there a specific interrogation room that you used?

LN: No, we went to certain rooms that—well, they may have been. We were directed to a certain room on certain days. I don't think it was the same room though.

INT: In a typical interrogation, would have been an Anglo officer, a Nisei, and a prisoner?

LN: Correct.

INT: Were the prisoners in a room by themselves or did they share a room.

LN: I believe there were two to a room.

INT: Did you get to see transcripts of the monitoring?

LN: No.

INT: You never saw them?

LN: No.

INT: Do you remember if the Nisei who were doing the monitoring would ever report back to you about something that maybe they heard in a room conversation?

LN: No. See, I think that—I don't know about the rest of the places or the rest of them but I think the Nisei that we had there were pretty truthful, dedicated people. I think they reported everything and asked everything that they were required to do.

INT: Do you know, was there an officer that was assigned to supervise the activity of monitoring and the Nisei?

LN: Well, I think that Colonel or Major Swift was in charge of that.

INT: I think we know the answer but I'll ask it. When you arrived at Byron Hot Springs there were already prisoners there, there were already staff there?

LN: Right.

INT: Do you have any recollections in terms of the numbers of about, first let's talk about the American staff who was there. Can you recall ballpark how many people were there?

LN: No, I really—I would be guessing. I wouldn't know how many there were, but—you mean excluding the Nisei?

INT: You could certainly—if you can remember a distinction that would be great. Just anything whatsoever you might remember about numbers of people there.

LN: Well, all I remember is when we used to sit down for a meal I guess most of us sat down together and I guess there were 30 or 40. Now that's not including the Nisei, but I would say the everyday number of people were probably, when we sat down to eat, were probably or so, and that's just a guess.

INT: Did you associate whatsoever with the guards who were there?

LN: No.

INT: Did they essentially serve as the whole support staff? You mentioned earlier the Nisei were doing all the cooking.

LN: Yes

INT: So do you remember if there were—what the non-intelligence personnel, the people who were not interrogators or Nisei, what they were doing? Was that just guarding and that was about it?

LN: They were guarding really.

INT: Along that same line, did you ever go down—whatever the downtown Byron looked like at the time, did you ever go off base for meals or—

LN: Yes, occasionally we did.

INT: Did you encounter locals?

LN: Yes.

INT: Did they ask you what you did?

LN: No. You know, at that time Byron and the area there was just virgin territory. I mean, I think there was one roadside restaurant and, of course, at that time if they saw a Japanese or a Nisei, they freaked out, you know. So the Nisei didn't go anywhere but we did go out to dinner once in a while locally, but there was very little going on there.

INT: Did they inquire as to what you were doing?

LN: No.

INT: Did they seem to have any problem [with the facility]?

LN: They probably knew. I'm sure they knew but there were no questions asked.

INT: How were the Japanese prisoners brought there?

LN: Trucked in.

INT: Like for instance at Fort Hunt when they were brought down from Pinegrove Furnace they had buses and the windows were tinted out so they couldn't see out and people couldn't see in.

LN: It was the same.

LN: So they'd see a bus go by so—

INT: Yeah. Did you have actual MPs at Byron or were they just guards?

LN: I think they were just guards.

INT: Were they armed?

LN: No, not that I know of. Not that I remember. I mean, they were—I don't remember them looking like they were armed.

INT: Was there anybody stationed at the entrance?

LN: Oh, yes. Yes, yeah.

INT: And, let's see, did they ever use dogs?

LN: No.

INT: Horses?

LN: No.

INT: With the MPs, who moved the prisoners around? Was it—if you were going to interrogate someone, did you go and get the prisoner or did the MP go and—

LN: No. Somebody brought them down to the room. I don't remember whether it was an MP or not, but they were brought to the room and then taken back.

INT: And likewise, when they were going to and from Camp Tracy to or from Angel Island, would any interrogators or Nisei or anyone accompany them or would it just be the MPs?

LN: It would just be them.

INT: Okay. Did you—obviously, the MPs knew what was going on? They obviously could tell, but did they ever sit in on any of the questioning or interrogations?

LN: No.

INT: Do you get the sense of the MPs were from the local area?

LN: I'm sure they weren't. Well, besides which, like I say, that was just absolutely virgin territory there. There was no place to—nobody to hire there so they were definitely from the outside.

INT: Do you remember how were the prisoners contained? What would have kept a prisoner from trying to escape? Was it simply the fact that they were Japanese   and would have stood out like a sore thumb?

LN: No, they were locked in. There was no way they could get out. I mean their rooms were locked.

INT: Were the windows closed off or did they have—could they see out of their room?

LN: I don't remember that, but I do know that they were locked in. I don't know about the windows.

INT: Do you know about how long the average stay was for a Japanese prisoner at the facility?

LN: Well, it wasn't terribly long. Of course, it depended a little bit on what they might have to say or what we thought they might have to say; but I would say probably not more than a week or days.

INT: Okay. That's very similar to Fort Hunt. I'm really fascinated to find out

what percentage or how would you characterize the prisoners in terms
of their resistance to interrogation?

LN: I would say that the ones that we had were very easy people to deal
with. I mean, I don't remember any of them being belligerent or hard to
talk to, not that we got what we were supposed to get from them, but I
mean they were pleasant people.

INT: Did any of them ever resist answering questions, specific questions?

LN: Oh, yeah.

INT: How would they resist?

LN: Well, they would say they didn't know. I mean, they didn't resist to the
point where they were belligerent about it, but they'd say they didn't
know or they couldn't tell you they didn't know mainly but there was
very little tough questioning. Mostly as I recall it seemed like they
answered what they could.

INT: How would you then characterize the strategies that were used to ask
questions? Since you didn't have interrogation training, how did you
know about how to approach these people?

LN: Right. I think that's where we lacked what we should have had. We
didn't have that training, but we were told what we were trying to find
out. That's the best we could do was ask them what we were told to
find out. But we really lacked training on that phase of what we did.

INT: Did you have instances where you felt you were being lied to?

LN: Well, of course, you don't know when they say they don't know, it's—

INT: Right.

LN: You being trained in it you probably have a way of going about it, but
if you're not trained and they say they don't know, unless you torture
them I don't know how you find out.

INT: Were there ever instances of what anybody might describe as coercion?

LN: No.

INT: How about any tricks? Any tricks that you would use to try to entrap them?

LN: Well, you see, that's another phase where we weren't trained in that, so
really the best we could do—it's surprising, a lot of that was just like
you're trying to find out about now. We were—we really didn't know
either, you know. We were told what to ask and try to get it, but I mean
we weren't really trained in the fine art of finding out what you wanted.

INT: Would there be cases that you could reward them with cigarettes or a
shot of whiskey or something that if they

LN: Their main pleasure was getting their food and being well treated
which I think was a hell of a note when you think about what they
went through before they got here. I mean, they were well treated at the
end of the line.

INT: It's a pretty comfortable setting, right?

LN: Oh, yeah.

INT: We might get to that later but the layout of the rooms that the prisoners were in, how they were furnished to what kind of bedding, that sort of thing.

LN: Well, I didn't see the rooms but I'm sure they were double bunk because there were two to a room as far as I remember, and so I don't remember anything more than they both had beds but I don't know much more about it than that.

INT: Do you remember if there were—did they have bathrooms in their rooms or was there a latrine somewhere?

LN: Well, see, that I don't remember.

INT: Did you have a bathroom in your room?

LN: Yes.

INT: Okay. Did you ever go to the third floor?

LN: No, wait a minute. We didn't have a bathroom in the room. I think we had a sink but we had to go out down the hall to the bathroom.

INT: Did you ever go to the third floor?

LN: No. No.

INT: What prohibited you from going up besides being told not to perhaps?

LN: Well, I don't know that there was anything stopped us but we certainly never went to the prisoners' rooms, that's for sure.

INT: During your time in Japan, you spent a long period, did you feel like you understood the culture pretty well, the highly ritualistic nature of Japanese?

LN: Well, you see back in those days we lived up in what they called the Bluff which was Tokyo Bay. It was up high off the Bay there and we really—there were all foreigners that lived up there. And we really didn't associate much with the Japanese. I mean, we went shopping or something, yes, but the country club was Americans, French, Britishers and those were the people we associated more than we did with the Japanese.

INT: Okay. Did you understand the tradition of bushido? Okay. Would it be possible for you to run us through a typical interrogation? Anything else that you might remember about how an interrogation would go.

LN: No, Swift would tell us what they wanted to know and find out what you can find out and we were always briefed on what to ask which we relayed to the Nisei which was parlayed to the prisoner. But, that's about it. We were just—it was pretty lax, you know? There wasn't anything that was cut and dried about it. I think today it would be different but it was, I guess by today's standard it was almost a parlor game.

INT: Did you feel you were effective in getting information?

LN: Well, I think we tried to get what we could. We couldn't get everything, but we certainly tried and I think some of it was effective, yes.

INT: Do you know what happened to the information when you concluded?

LN: No. No. No. Swift is dead, isn't he?

INT: We haven't found him. Unfortunately, the way we're going about doing this, people with more common names are very difficult to find. You have a more distinctive name. That's how we found you.

LN: Because Major Swift could answer all those questions they asked me precisely. He was in charge of all that.

INT: Do you remember if he was older than you?

LN: Oh, yeah. I knew him as an old man out there and I'm sure he's probably not around anymore, but I'd say at the time he was probably—well, I thought he was an old man. He was probably fifties then, so I imagine he's gone. But there's the man that could have answered all these questions precisely.

INT: Do you remember writing up a report after you were done with a prisoner, did you type something up or a briefing statement?

LN: No, no. I think like Swift ended up with the Nisei to find out fluently. I mean he was very fluent both ways and I'm sure he, if there were further questions, he asked them.

INT: So you think Swift himself asked questions of the prisoners, or he asked them of you?

LN: No, he didn't talk to the prisoners. I'm sure he talked to the Nisei.

INT: Okay.

LN: He was in charge of the Nisei and it's just a shame that he's not available.

INT: Were you told that your interrogations, your actual interrogation sessions also monitored?

LN: Well, we didn't know it at the time—

INT: What, they didn't tell you that?

LN: —but obviously I got a list of the prisoner's name and how long, what room, and how long it lasted, but we were not told that they were monitored but I assume they were.

INT: Are you describing, was this a transcript of the interrogation? Or was it just—

LN: No, it was a transcript. That's where I got the Fontaine name.

INT: We do have some information with the Fontaine on it, but it's a listing, if you will. It's just a running list of—it's the name of the prisoner, the name of the interrogator, the alias, room number.

LN: Right.

INT: Okay. So not necessarily a monitoring sheet?

LN: No.

INT: So they described him with the alias of Fontaine? Yeah, he had Fontaine and what was the other one we were discussing?

LN: Nelson.

INT: Nelson, yeah.

LN: But the Fontaine one absolutely baffles me.

INT: Were you a Nelson Eddy fan back then by chance? Nelson Eddy?

LN: No.

INT: Is that what we were speaking of? You may have to flip it over a page or two into the part of that one got cut off. But, you'll see your name is underlined a couple of places there.

LN: Yeah. Well, the one I got had—this one was filled out with the room number.

INT: If you flip another page or two, I believe it gets to some that are like that.

LN: Yeah. Do you want me to get it? I've got—

INT: No, that's okay and you can keep that copy. We don't want to overload you with paperwork but you can keep that as well. But do you remember ever filling something like that out?

LN: No. It's a funny thing, this is not regarding Tracy but when I say Fontaine and I were very close and I still call her every birthday, and I guess she's or something now, but I called the other night just—you know, I was waiting for dinner and I thought I'm going to call somebody and talk to somebody, and I called Joan, and so I called her and she was very fond of all of us in the family and it was a strange thing because what made me think of it was I saw my Fontaine there. Where it came from I have no idea because I didn't even know I was referred to as Nelson, but I called her and she—it was very funny because she always says, "Oh, you dear boy" when I call her, but she said, and this came right after I called her, she said, "You know, it's very funny that you should call because I had a dream last night." She came to say goodbye to us, my family, and my grandmother the day she left Japan and she said, "I had a dream last night about your grandmother." And isn't that funny that I should open that the day before and see Fontaine and call her and she had a dream about it?

LN: It was weird.

INT: That was really interesting.

INT: And so, again, with the interrogations, would you be working with the same prisoner over the course of a number of days?

LN: I think it changed every time. I don't think we—I don't remember interrogating the same prisoner twice.

INT: So, do you think other staff at Tracy interrogated the same prisoner as you did?

LN: They may have rotated. I don't know. But I don't remember. It may have been but I don't remember duplicating interrogation.

INT: Did you ever see transcripts or write-ups of somebody else's effort to interrogate somebody before you went in and interrogated that same prisoner?

LN: No. As I recall, the prisoners were not there very long. I mean, they were questioned and then sent back, but if they called to say they had something more to say, then we brought them back and interrogated. That way there might have been a duplicate question session. I don't know. I don't remember.

INT: About how long do you remember a typical interrogation going for?

LN: I think it was like a half hour, maybe   minutes, something like that. It wasn't that long.

INT: So, we're not talking about all night or five or six hours?

LN: No, no. It was an hour—I think an hour tops.

INT: How many interrogations might you conduct in a single day?

LN: Oh, not more than a couple. I don't remember, see, how many people interrogated along with me. I don't remember that, but there were quite a few of us. And I don't remember doing more than maybe two, three at the most a day.

INT: Did you have additional duties besides your interrogation responsibilities?

LN: No, that was basically it. It was really a very pleasant place to be during the service. We had lots of free time and people were very pleasant, but I don't imagine that's the way it would be today. I think we're going way back when things were a lot easier. I think today it would be a lot tougher.

INT: Were you ever allowed to take a prisoner outside of the building—

LN: No. They were strictly down from their rooms, questioned, and taken back up to their room. They didn't go out. They were brought there and when they left they went back to where they were from. But there was no associating with them at all other than questioning.

INT: Were they fed up there on the same floor?

LN: They were fed in their room.

INT: In their room. Okay. They didn't get any opportunity to get out and walk around and exercise for minutes or—

LN: No. But like I said, I don't think they were there more than a week or days, but not that I know of. I don't think they were allowed out. I never saw any of them let out or heard that they were let out, but come to think of it, I don't know if they weren't because they couldn't be shut up. Well, maybe for a week. As I say, I don't think they were there for more than a week or days at the outside. But they were not allowed out as far as I know.

INT: Do you know of directly or heard any rumors of any attempts to escape?

LN: No, no, none that I know of.

INT: Sounds like if they did, they'd try to get back in for the food.

LN: Well, that's right. See, I came from a pretty quiet family and our life was pretty quiet, and as I look back now, life in the military, when I got there to Camp Tracy, was really very pleasant and I'm sure these prisoners went through holy hell before they got there and they thought this was a pretty nice place. So I don't think there was any desire on their part to escape, there anyway.

INT: Probably about a minute. Are there any particular prisoners, any specific prisoners that you remember back—

LN: No.

INT: Okay. Along those lines, do you recall if these were any particular types of prisoners, which had strategic information or certain jobs in the military that may be of importance?

LN: No, that we didn't do, and as I say, I didn't know—I'm really not helpful on that at all, but see, I don't know, there were prisoners taken from all different parts. It wasn't just one part, and then they were questioned and I think eventually they returned to Hawaii and were segregated there; and the ones that they thought had further information were sent back here. So, where they came from, whether it was Japanese Navy or Japanese Air Force or what, they were mixed up I'm sure. But I'm sure they were mostly army.

INT: But you don't remember that you had a Japanese prisoner from Iwo Jima or from the Aleutians?

LN: No. No. I obviously knew where they were but I don't remember any specific places that they came from.

INT: What about branches of the service?

LN: They were mostly army.

INT: Would you ever work with a naval prisoner?

LN: Yeah, there were some navy. I'm sure navy. I don't think any air force, but mostly army and I think there were some navy.

INT: You interrogated both enlisted men and officers?

LN: Yes

INT: And any particular ranks that you can recall?

LN: Well, I don't recall anything above like the majors or colonels, but mostly if they were, I'd say captains. I don't remember any—

INT: No generals or anything like that?

INT: At Byron did you interrogate anybody who was non-military?

LN: No.

INT: So at Ft. Hunt you did work with the Diplomatic Corps?

INT: Okay. Do you remember in terms of the questioning and the information you were trying to get, was it more of a strategic value in terms of information about the Japanese military or was any of it related to technology, like weapons development or anything like that?

LN: No, it was mostly weapons. I mean if there are any.

INT: Okay.

LN: And the military part of it.

INT: Do you know if there were interrogators at Tracy who specialized in certain areas?

LN: No, my feeling is, and maybe you probably know more about that than I do, I think the bulk of the investigations were done—interrogations were done in Hawaii, weren't they? Brought to Hawaii and then they were sent back here, but I don't recall. It may have been, but I don't recall anything like a colonel or higher; I mean maybe captains, but I think probably anything like generals or anything major was taken care of in Hawaii.

INT: There weren't very many flag officers.

LN: I guess not.

INT: But the mission, from what I read in the archives, the mission of this umbrella program under the Military Intelligence Service at Camp Tracy and Fort Hunt was conducted with what they called special interrogation. What that meant was that carefully selected prisoners who had very specific information which is why he's asking the questions about—Fort Hunt had a lot of technical assignments

LN: Yeah, it was all military—the questions were military, not armaments or science or anything like that in what was coming up in their secret archives or weapons, nothing like that.

INT: Did you ask anything about life back in Japan; for example, trying to gain understanding of the effects that the Allied bombing campaign was having. Did you ever ask about their wives, their children or how often they could write, anything like that?

LN: Well, it was pretty pleasant, yes, probably some questions like that, just to not be too abrupt or trying to warm them up a little bit, a few questions like that and then that ended the questioning proper.

INT: So, was that typical to try to warm them up, per se?

LN: Well, it was on my part because I'd lived out there and, you know, if you live in a country and you get more or less accustomed to the people and what they think or feel, and so I'm sure the ones of us that were questioning that had lived out there probably approached in the same manner.

INT: Did you ever tell prisoners that you had lived in Japan?

LN: No.

INT: Okay. Did the prisoners you interrogated sustain wounds while they were in combat requiring medical care, and was there medical care at Tracy?

LN: There was no medical care—well, there may have been medical care but if there were any medical problems they were taken care of before they came to Tracy. So that was not a real problem at Tracy because they were all taken care of before they got to Tracy which made it simpler.

INT: Yeah, the reason I asked my question, you mentioned going out to the armament plant and somebody saying, "Aren't you registered? Don't you need to check with the immigration?" And that's an American but the Japanese didn't see anything. That's funny.

LN: No, no. Well, I guess to a certain extent they were under real stress when they got to Tracy and I think they thought more about themselves than the person questioning them. I think they were pretty uptight and afraid. But they certainly enjoyed it there so they loosened up some I think, which was helpful if you wanted to get something from them rather than to be brutally mean and have them shut up completely.

INT: Did you hear any of the prisoners ever make any—or did the Nisei translators ever share with you something they heard from the prisoners where the prisoners were asking about the status of these apparent Japanese in American uniforms. Did they challenge them where their allegiance were, or were they surprised that they had so many Japanese Americans? Any comments at all from the prisoners?

LN: Well, I think the prisoners were very surprised that there were Japanese, to them they were Japanese, not Nisei; and I think they were very surprised to have a Japanese question them and they didn't realize that they were really Americans. And I think it's a hand to the Nisei; you know, I think it was totally unfair that they were all rounded up and sent to camps. And when you think about it, the 2nd Regiment that was—I mean, they were all from the camps that volunteered. So the prisoners themselves had no knowledge that they were going to be questioned by what they thought was Japanese who was essentially American. So I think they probably were surprised but they probably were happy that to them it was a Japanese talking to them, their language and everything.

INT: Do you recall an occasion where you interrogated a Japanese prisoner who spoke English?

LN: No, never one. Maybe if they did they didn't let on that they did, but none of them ever spoke to me in English. Not a word.

INT: Was there ever a security investigation or security concerns about any of the Nisei translators?

LN: Well, I'm sure there was. Now, Swift would, if he were around he would be able to answer that because I'm sure there was, but I was not part of it or aware of it.

INT: Do you remember if the Nisei lived in the main building with you or if they lived outside—

LN: No, I think they lived outside. No, they lived outside for sure. There were a lot of buildings there like the map that I got which are undoubtedly no longer there, but there were a lot of barracks there and they had their own barracks I'm sure.

INT: Do you remember there being more Nisei than interrogators or about the same number or just a handful of Nisei?

LN: No, they were all interrogators that were there.

INT: I'm sorry. In terms of the numbers of people, was there one Nisei for every Anglo interrogator, or were there more Nisei—

LN: No, I think there were less Nisei.

INT: Okay.

LN: Yeah. I think less Nisei.

INT: Were any of them commissioned officers?

LN: No. None of the Nisei were in the military that were questioning.

INT: Really?

LN: Now, I don't make a flat statement about that but as I recall they were civilians.

INT: Did they wear a uniform?

LN: No, I think they were dressed as civilians as I recall.

INT: Do you know if they attended any sort of training prior to this?

LN: Oh, I'm sure they did. Not at Tracy. I think wherever they came from.

INT: You don't know where—

LN: No. Possibly whatever the name of the camp was that was in Tracy. It was a big one, not necessarily for Japanese prisoners but I think that was bigger than I think when they originally landed, that was on the bay here, Angel Island, but a lot of them went back to Tracy I think when they were returned.

INT: During an interrogation, would you wear your rank?

LN: Probably.

INT: Would you ever change your rank?

LN: No.

INT: Okay. So, even if you were interrogating a Japanese officer of a higher rank?

LN: As I recall, we were in our same uniform all the time, and as I recall, I would say or percent were not a very high rank in the Japanese military.

INT: Ever any concerns about prisoners taking their own lives?

LN: No. I do think that they saw new life out there. I don't think they were—I think they were delighted there was a place where they were treated fairly nicely. There was never any question that I knew about anybody wanting to take their life.

INT: Any conversations regarding family at home?

LN: No.

INT: Any discussions about their inability to return home because of becoming a prisoner of war?

LN: Well, I'm sure they had that worry but there was no way to talk about it.

INT: In terms of, and you may not know this, but in terms of the capacity of that third floor, was it always full? Did you ever come upon a situation to where you had more Japanese prisoners than could fit?

LN: No.

INT: Never used another facility?

LN: No.

INT: You were limited to what amount of prisoners would fit on the third floor?

LN: I don't know how many; probably if there were rooms, probably no more than at a time. And I say that with I don't think they were there longer than a week or days.

INT: But you're pretty confident they didn't use another building to house—

LN: No, I don't think they did. I'm sure they didn't. Is that building still standing?

INT: Yes, that building is still standing and most of the rooms you can still make out the rooms. In addition to—the first and second floors have one large open area in them. Really, it's on the first floor but it expands through two stories.

LN: Right. Right.

INT: And then there are additional rooms on the rest of the first floor, on the rest of the second floor and then the entire third floor is nothing but rooms. In addition, there's a basement under a cellar underneath it.

LN: That's where we worked most of the time. Downstairs, that's right. And the main entrance there was basically where we all ate.

INT: Okay. That large with the double.

LN: Right. And all the activity was in the basement, I mean as far as— the interrogation was separate but as far as we were concerned. The basement was the main area.

INT: Did you have—were there offices down there?

LN: Well, we had a desk. There was no specific area. It was—I don't know if you went down in the basement—

INT: We did.

LN: —I don't know what it's like now but it was a wide-open area where we all worked down there.

INT: What did you do down there? What type of work?

LN: Well, basically it was getting preparation for an interrogation. We didn't do any monitoring as far as listening in, and you know, that's a good question. I mean, we were down there and boy, I don't recall a lot of the stuff that we did other than getting ready to interrogate and what we were trying to find out. You know, it wasn't that long a period that we were there really that I was there, for instance. It was a pretty short period so what happened before me and after me, I don't even know when it closed.

INT: Again, not wanting to bias your memory but in that basement area do you remember a room that was closed off, that might have served as a monitoring room where the guys actually sat with headphones?

LN: Yeah, I think so. Well, I think it was—if you go into the main building, down in the basement it would be in the back of the basement. I think there was a room back there that was for monitoring.

INT: Do you remember there's a marble staircase kind of, looked like fairly opulent. I don't know if I—

LN: Yeah. Yeah.

INT: Anything else in the basement that you remember? Was there any recreational areas?

LN: No recreational area, no. There was a—the only recreational area really was there was a tennis court that was used. I was a big tennis player in my younger years and we had the chance to play quite a bit of tennis there. But other than that I don't think—there was no—other than the—see, the hot springs were not used. They were closed by the time I got there and that captain I'm thinking of, that was a very nice captain from Dallas. His name was Howard Keys—

INT: —yeah, came in as a first lieutenant and left as a captain.

LN: That's it.

INT: Left about on the same—very similar to when you left actually.

LN: And he one day went down to that hot springs which I say was a devastated area except for this broken down wooden building, but the marble baths were still there which they used in the s I guess, and he went down the stairs I remember, to the hot springs and about two feet down from the top of the hot springs there was a wooden platform. And I tell you, if you put your hand six inches down into the water you couldn't even see it there the water was so murky; and I remember him putting his feet down in there and it was warm water. Now, what it is now I don't know if it's still there or not. I guess it is, but not the building I'm sure.

INT: Oh, down in that basement area were there any subject area specialists that were supporting your interrogations? People who could answer questions or fill you in with what was known about Japanese order of battle at the time?

LN: Well, I would say the only one that I recall was Major Swift. He was really sort of the key to this whole thing there. I don't remember the name of the—was it a colonel who was in charge of the operation there?

INT: There was but he looks like he may have left prior to you being there. The first colonel was a Daniel Kent who actually later came back. He looks like he was probably replaced, let's see, by Zenas Bliss.

LN: No, but as I recall, he had nothing much more than basic running of the camp and the other guy, the one we were talking about—

INT: We were talking about Swift. The one in intelligence.

LN: —he was actually the fellow that ran the intelligence.

INT: Any civilians involved in the interrogation?

LN: No, other than the Nisei.

INT: Okay. Did you ever receive any high-level visits, general officers or other colonels coming to inspect or visit or just look around.

LN: Not that I'm aware of. Now, see, like I say, I wasn't there that long. It's possible a month or two months before I was there, there might have been somebody, but not when I was there that I'm aware of. I'm sure there probably was contact. There might have been somebody there but not to my knowledge.

INT: Do you remember the switchboard on the main floor?

LN: No.

INT: Do you know if there was anybody that communicated with the Pentagon?

LN: Not personally, no, I don't know who was in touch. I'm sure they were. Although, you know it surprises me that there are so many questions that you people don't know. I'm sure there was a lack of communication; must have been because there's so much that they really ought to have knowledge of, but anyway, like I've forgotten. So much time has passed, it's a shame that this didn't happen a year or two earlier where like that Swift could have answered these questions so easily.

INT: See, part of the problem is General Strong, Major General Strong who was the senior intelligence officer at the Army at the time, after the war was over he was so concerned that this information, the way we went about interrogations and some other programs was so sensitive that they couldn't risk it ever getting out to the enemy—If you could kind of repeat again a little bit of what we were saying before we were recording, which we were showing you some pictures of the basement and the acoustic tiles—could you just mention again what your conclusions were from that?

LN: Well, as far as whether they might have been listening in on conversations, I do remember that there was a room in the back of the basement that was closed off, and I would guess that that is where they were monitoring the conversations upstairs; and I think on top of it if you have those wires coming out of there, that makes sense that that's what that was and where it was.

INT: And then finally, and this comes care of Major Corbin, this is a document that is believe it or not meant to represent a floor plan, we believe, of the third floor. You see, there's individual rooms listed one, two, three, four and all the way on down with two prisoners in each room.

LN: Interestingly, a lot of them appear to have been civilians on this particular date but then there's also a lot with military ranks on them. There's a slot listed for the Captain of the Guard as well as for the stairs where you would have walked up, so this almost was treated as kind of a rough floor plan, if you will. Some of the rooms appear to be empty, but it would appear by this numbering system 1 through that there were rooms—

INT: So now that we've grilled you a great deal on Tracy I think we will shift a little bit to talking about you happen to remember about P.O. Box 1142. Could you first tell us, you mentioned earlier that you had never heard of P.O. Box 651 in Washington.

LN: Right.

INT: How did your transfer come about? Was it kind of all of a sudden?

LN: Well, all of a sudden I was called into the office of, Colonel Bliss. And he said that seven of us were being transferred immediately to, I don't think he mentioned but to the Washington area, and I think we had to depart in a day or two. And that's where I got the information and then that's what happened.

INT: Do you remember about when this was? We're relatively certain because we have the dates on the list, but I just wanted to see if you off the top of your head remembered about when it might be.

LN: Well, when you told me that it was something like March, was it?

INT: All right.

LN: It could have been June or July.

INT: Okay, and then I believe that list has it shown as late July.

LN: All right. That makes sense.

INT: Okay. And you said there a group of you, a group of seven.

LN: Seven of us.

INT: Do you remember if any of the Nisei or any other enlisted men were being transferred?

LN: There were no Nisei and they only one I remember by name was this captain—well, the name doesn't come to me, but he was a captain in the Army and he was one of the ones that was transferred.

INT: Was he transferred with you?

LN: Yeah, with me. And—

INT: And he was of Japanese language. Did he speak Japanese as well? Was he an interrogator?

LN: Well, he was an interrogator but I don't remember him living in Japan or anything. And the others, I don't remember their names.

INT: Okay. We can probably surmise who they were from that list because they all—I believe you all departed on the same day. The list actually lists the day you departed on July

LN: Well, there would have been seven of us and we were all together.

INT: Okay. And were you at the impression at this point that Camp Tracy was being shut down?

LN: No.

INT: No? Okay. So you were just being transferred but everybody else was going to be staying there.

LN: Right. And I have no idea when it was closed down.

INT: Do you remember where you flew into in Washington? Did you fly right into Washington, D.C.?

LN: Yes, we flew into Washington, D.C. I think we had to transfer at Chicago. I think we had to change planes, but we flew into Washington, D.C. and were greeted there at the airport, but that's really about all I remember of the trip.

INT: And were you briefed at all prior, or just when you got there you kind of figured out what this location was for?

LN: No, we were told—as far as I remember, I was told by Colonel Bliss that the Japanese Diplomatic Corps [from Germany] was there and that we were going to be interrogating them, but we were told nothing about—the only thing I do remember about Camp Tracy is that that was the rear echelon interrogation center for the top German prisoners before it was only for the Japanese

LN: That had sort of an association with Hunt, but that was the rear echelon interrogation headquarters of the German prisoners before the Japanese got there.

INT: So you remember knowing that Tracy had at one time German prisoners? But when you were at Tracy—

LN: There were none.

INT: —it was just Japanese. Okay. Meanwhile, when you arrived at P.O. Box 1142 did you, again, we had this discussion a little bit. Camp Tracy you said you called it just Byron Hot Springs?

11

Leisure Time

[Editor's note: The invention of the outboard motor and the mass production of pleasure craft open the Sacramento–San Joaquin River Delta to weekend cruising and leisurely vacations. While these outings begin before World War II, they increased dramatically after the war. Water skiing and enjoying drinks at a host of marinas become a way of life in the Sacramento–San Joaquin River Delta. Hal Schell wrote popular guides to the region during these years. Earle Stanley Gardner, the famous detective writer, was one of the many who enjoyed wandering the ways and byways in a houseboat.]

Hal Schell, "Introduction," from *Cruising California's Delta*

[Editor's note: Hal Schell, "Introduction," *Cruising the California Delta* (Stockton: Hal Schell, 1995), pp. 6–7. (*By permission*). See Fig. 43.]

It is not easy to get a handle on the elusive Delta. All too often when its praises are sung, its geographical attributes are ticked off one after another, laundry list style as if it were these mere physical things that make it such a wondrous place. In reality, it is the people who make the Delta. Consider:

> It is a warm summer afternoon on Lost Isle and Delta-dweller Jerry Patterson decides to take a snooze down by the beach. So as not to sully his sweaty body by lying on the ground, he plunks himself down atop a handy hunk of Styrofoam. The tide comes in and when Jerry awakens he and the Styrofoam are merrily floating up the San Joaquin River toward Stockton.
>
> John Parent is leading a flotilla of four new yachts, at speed, past Antioch and Pittsburg heading to Alameda to display them in a boat show. John is

in charge because he knows the way. He falls prey to the nefarious shoal known as Middle Ground. In quick succession, he is followed by two of his compatriots. The fourth boat is spared this fate when its skipper figures out why those three boats made such abrupt stops.

A love struck Delta crop duster is wooing the cute daughter of a marina owner and in his early morning versions of Dawn Patrol swoops in low over the marina to parachute love notes to her.

Tow-truck operator Gary Dilday is summoned by the Highway Patrol to retrieve an automobile that ran off Highway 4 and submerged beneath the waters of Trapper Slough. After pulling two "wrong" autos from the slough, Dilday finally retrieves the "right" vehicle.

Jim Van Dyke, a one-time commodore of the Stockton Sailing Club, is heading to San Francisco in his vintage Bird Boat. The water is rough, each wave sending the bow of the sturdy boat crashing into the water. It emerges from one such dive with a giant sturgeon thrashing around on deck as the Bird Boat crew looks on in wide-eyed wonder. It then crashes into the next wave, this time emerging with a deck uncluttered by denizens of the deep.

Jus Ducky skipper Ed Krampert rescues a dog that has been floating around the Delta for 36 hours in its life vest and ultimately gets the treasured pooch returned to its grateful owners aboard the Lady Di.

Dexter Coffman lands his hot-air balloon on a nearly inaccessible alfalfa field on Terminous Tract and its retrieval van gets mired down in a drainage ditch while trying to fetch the balloon and crew. Highway Patrol and sheriff's officers converge and argue over who is going to haul these trespassers off to the pokey. To the rescue comes landowner John Morais, who sends the gendarmes on their way, pulls the vehicle out of the peat bog with his farm tractor, and then helps the balloon crew consume the traditional bottle(s) of champagne.

The owner of a large old wood-hull motorsailer down in the Bay has a few days to spare and could do with an activity that might net him a bit more than pocket change. He catches the next tide up to the Delta to prospect for lost anchors at two anchorages that are rumored to have a bountiful crop of this item, Mandeville Tip and Three River Reach.

You can see that there is nothing so fancy or fanciful about this Delta. Yet these are the sort of happenings that lend a personality to the place, the kind of happenings that make you chuckle and want to be a part of this crazy, wonderful scene.

I do not mean to downplay the importance of the geography of the Delta, but only wish to put it in its proper perspective to make it secondary to the people who prowl this unique area. The Delta is touted as having 1,000 miles of navigable waterways, a nice handy round number that might be a slight exaggeration. But to be sure, there are more waterways here than you will ever find time to explore. Within this vast Delta are nearly 150 marinas and waterside resorts. At one time or another, I have visited all of them.

For the denizens of the Delta, its borders are only vaguely defined, almost by preference. A Delta with such vague boundaries seems better suited to the free-spirited folks who call this home. Sure, in more recent times politicos have drawn up boundaries for their Delta, but the boating community takes little note of them. If pressed for practical boundaries, I would draw a line from Pittsburg to the west, to Courtland to the north, to Stockton to the east, then on to Tracy and back to Pittsburg.

This boxes in what I normally think of as the Delta, but you may apply your own boundaries. It makes not a whit of difference. This book covers a larger territory, in what are logical extensions of the Delta cruising waters. To the north it extends to Sacramento then 22 miles beyond, on up to where the Sacramento River is joined by the Feather River. To the south it meanders through the Suisun Marshes to Suisun City, then goes with the flow downstream to the quaint river town of Benicia.

The Sacramento River and the San Joaquin River are the lifelines of the Delta, its major thoroughfares, its grand boulevards. Its other rivers and streams, however, play important roles. In spite of its profusion of waterways, the Delta is surprisingly compact and easy to get around in. It is close enough to major population centers to make commuting to it practical. The majority of boats berthed in the Delta belong to people who live in the greater Bay Area, up in Sacramento, or down in the growing San Joaquin Valley communities. They need only make commutes of up to two hours to enjoy their off hours aboard their boats in the Delta. And wherever the boat's home port may be, it takes but a few minutes to leave civilization behind, to ease out into the tules and come under the spell of the Delta.

This book makes an effort to capture this elusive Delta scene and spice it with a dash of history about who and what was here before us. And then there's the "asphalt sloughs," those often narrow and twisty ribbons of macadam that slice and meander through Delta Country. To feel this area in your bones, you must sometimes take to its roads, perhaps crossing waterways via lumbering ferries and over drawbridges that groan open to let boats pass through. Occasionally this book will point out things of interest shoreside, and places you may need wheels to get to.

This Delta is honest to the core, a place with purpose. It is not gussied-up to please the tourist. It has no "must-see" sights. It does not suit everyone. But if it sounds like your kind of place, the river rats and anglers and farmers and tule island dwellers who have long been Delta-smitten, will cheerfully move over and make room for you. I invite you to join us.

Erle Stanley Gardner, "A typical cruise," from *Gypsy Days on the Delta*

[Editor note: Erle Stanley Gardner, *Gypsy Days on the Delta* (New York: William Morrow, 1967), Chapter 4. (*By permission*). See Fig. 44.]

A Typical Cruise

My adventures in the Delta country during the summer of 1964 had been largely confined to the North Fork of the Mokelumne River and to the country to the east. I wanted to get a look at some of the country to the west.

Jean Bethell, Richard DeShazer, Sam Hicks, and I decided to take a trip in the River Queen house cruiser, starting from Richard's Yacht Center at the Bethel Island Bridge, skirting Frank's Tract, passing Korth's Pirates Lair, going to the B & W Resort; then turning into Georgiana Slough, and from there into the Sacramento River just below Walnut Grove, and following the Sacramento River to Sacramento, and on up to Knights Landing.

For some years I had been a member of the Knights Landing Outboard Motor Club, and we had explored the river between Knights Landing and Colusa, a rather considerable distance when one takes into consideration the force of the current of the Sacramento River, which is something to be reckoned with.

However, I knew that the army engineers had been ordering trees removed from the slopes of the levees, and I wanted to see to what extent this had been carried out above Sacramento and what effect it had had on the levees themselves.

As I remembered it, some of these trees along the levee banks were eighty to a hundred feet in height. They were magnificent shade trees which made boating and tying up for a few hours an unmitigated pleasure.

In the places where the trees have been removed and rock faces put on the river side of the levees, the river becomes relatively uninteresting. One has to get his pleasure from the boating rather than from the scenery.

People with whom I have talked seem to feel that the levees are more permanent where the trees have been removed and rock faces placed on the sides. However, this is an ambitious undertaking and it is not going to be finished overnight or in the course of a year or two. I have also noticed that there are plenty of places where the trees have been removed from the levee and, before the levee has been faced with rock, the river has exerted an alarming toll of erosion.

I personally have the feeling that about the time the trees have all been removed, practical considerations will show that it would have been better to have left them where they were.

However, the Delta is fertile country. Trees seem to sprout everywhere. Vegetation even grows from the tops of old pilings which have been placed in the channel. I intend to be philosophical and rejoice at what we have left while we have it, the remaining shade trees and the leisure and freedom to enjoy them. There are places where the trees continue to remain in place, and there is always the charm of boating on the water.

It is difficult to analyze this charm.

I remember many, many years ago when I felt the same way about an automobile. It was a pleasure to get behind the wheel of a good car and drive leisurely along the highway, noticing the scenery and experiencing the exhilarating sense of motion.

These automobiles and the roads on which they were operated would get you there and get you back; but the pleasure of driving and watching the scenery was such that, on a free afternoon, one could go for a drive just for the sheer pleasure of driving.

Then the public demand for speed and ever more speed made for faster cars, wider roads, and shorter driving time when the road was clear.

The net result is that nowadays, on a free afternoon, one can travel much farther in a much faster car but at a much slower pace than one wants to go, hampered by the numbers of other cars and whipped by occupational impatience. Saturday and Sunday afternoon driving is no longer any pleasure at all.

Boating now gives me the same pleasure I got from driving years ago. I like to glide over the water, the breeze in my face; I like the freedom from restraint, the sense of motion.

I get this same feeling boating on the river, no matter what type of boat I am using. All I want is a good boat.

There is this feeling of independence, of being a part of nature; and, of course, the feeling of motion has always appealed to man. There is, moreover, a sense of freedom from the cares and worries which tend to surround the individual when he is part of a human ant colony struggling in endless turmoil in what, at times, seems to be a hopeless treadmill.

There is also the marvelous feeling which is inherent in the anticipation experienced in getting ready for a boating trip. Sam and I started storing ice, clothing, and provisions, preparatory to this Knights Landing trip. Jean went to the market and planned the menus. Dick DeShazer struggled manfully with a whole series of last minute problems so that he could get away at the earliest possible moment.

As I have said earlier, the *River Queen* is a floating deluxe apartment. It has a steel, watertight hull with hatches which open up to disclose huge storage spaces-and we took full advantage of all this storage space.

The cruiser has an electric refrigerator with a freezing compartment, but since we had lots of plastic containers which would keep ice for a long time and loads of room, we loaded aboard extra supplies of ice for chilling watermelons, a varied assortment of cold drinks, and keeping fresh vegetables.

The day was hot, but the steel body of the River Queen resting on cool water made the interior so comfortable that we didn't even bother to turn on the air-conditioning unit.

The boat was in one of Bud Remsburg's covered berths, the light was dim, the shade was cool and Sam doing the heavy work while I carried cameras, films, and lighter stuff.

Sam is a good-natured giant tall and strong, with long legs, big wrists and hands, and an unlimited capacity for responsibility and achievement.

As I get older, it is a pleasure to let these younger men take over.

Dick DeShazer is a real yachtsman. When he came aboard he carried his extra clothes, shaving kit, and the things he needed in a briefcase.

Yachtsmen and aviators are certainly accustomed to traveling light.

Personally, I travel heavy.

When I would take pack trips on hunting expeditions into the wild mountainous country, I always told the outfitter, "You've got packhorses; I've got money. Put an extra packhorse in the string."

I will admit that at times I carried a weird assortment of articles.

For instance, noticed that the "dudes," who had previously ridden the horses I was destined to ride later, would let the bridle reins drag when they stopped and got off. The heavy-footed trail horses would step on a rein and break it off, whereupon the wrangler would "splice" the rein.

As the next dude in line. I would have bridle reins that were spliced in one or two places.

This can be exceedingly annoying. The average dude horse wants loose reins. He is in a string of horses on a narrow mountain trail. He knows where he is going. He knows the other horses. He knows the trail. He knows the wrangler. He knows exactly where they are going to camp that night, and he has a pretty good idea of how long it is going to take to get to that camp. If he is a good, conscientious horse, he is going to keep his place in the string.

He doesn't want the dude to ride him, he wants to carry the dude.

Therefore, at regular intervals, the horse will bite down on bit, give his powerful neck a surge, and jerk the reins through the fingers of the surprised dude.

If the bridle reins are spliced, when the splice comes ripping through the fingers of the dude's hand, it can give him an uncomfortable sensation.

Therefore, I always made it a point to carry my own bridle reins.

I remember on one trip in the primitive area of Idaho when a famous Bill Sullivan and his brother-in-law, Ted Williams, were piloting us, a wrangler from a nearby outfit came riding to our camp one night to pass the time with Ted Williams, whom he knew quite well.

The wrangler took a look at our outfit and particularly at the duffel bags. He wanted to know how in hell any dude could fill up all those duffel bags with material which by any stretch of the imagination could be considered necessary or useful on a trip of that kind.

I held my peace because there was nothing else for me to do.

It happened, however, that this wrangler had tied his horse a tree by the bridle reins. He sat visiting with us until quite late and then, in the darkness as he approached the horse, his cowboy boot caught in a root and the wrangler stumbled. He instinctively threw out his hands to catch himself, his horse snorted, jerked back, and broke both bridle reins about six inches from the bit.

That wrangler had a picturesque vocabulary. The thought of trying to splice bridle reins and riding over trails in the darkness made him use purple language and lots of it.

Spliced reins might be all right for a dude, but you never see a wrangler riding with spliced reins.

So I got up, walked over to one of my duffel bags, reached in, took out a new pair of bridle reins, quietly walked over to where the wrangler was standing, and handed him the brand new pair of expensive bridle reins.

"Just take these, " I said.

He looked at me with wide-eyed amazement. "Where in hell did you get these reins?" he asked.

"Out of my duffel bag," I told him casually. "You see. I'm a veteran camper, and every once in a while some damn fool wrangler will tie up a horse by the bridle reins, then 'spook' the horse and break the reins. I always go prepared to help out at such a time."

"You'll find these reins are very strong and hard to break."

I turned and walked away.

The guy was so grateful for the reins he was willing to take a little ribbing, yet he wasn't entirely certain he was being ribbed.

My talk had the effect of paralyzing his vocal cords.

Ted Williams came out to help him. They put on the new bridle reins and the wrangler rode away.

The next year when I was in that country, Bill Sullivan tipped me off. "Don't let that wrangler know you're here," he said, "or he'll take a shot at you."

"How come?" asked.

"The damn fool went into a bar in Challis and told the story," Bill Sullivan said. "Prior to that time, he had always been considered an honest man, but the story of a dude taking a pair of bridle reins out of a duffel bag for a wrangler who had tied up his horse by the bridle reins and then spooked him was too much for the people in the bar to take."

"They promptly branded the guy the biggest and most imaginative liar in the Middle Fork. Just keep away from him."

I kept away from him.

But I still maintain the habit of traveling heavy. However, the *River Queen* is built to take it and, after all, a couple of extra duffle bags only means one more trip up and down the ramp—for Sam.

Sam had the motors warmed up by the time Dick had everything settled, and we were off.

The *River Queen*, powered with twin Ford Interceptors with an inboard-outboard drive and cruiser bow is capable of maintaining a very satisfactory cruising speed, yet the interior is such that one moves about at will from main cabin to dining room, galley, bedroom, and "head" without constantly ducking and twisting.

It is made to sleep six comfortably, but it has ample space to carry sleeping bags, and decks which enable camping out, so that in clear weather quite a crowd of people can be accommodated.

The four of us on the *River Queen* were surrounded with lots of room.

Courteous yachtsmen go no faster than five miles an hour when cruising past docks which line the shores of the slough. In this way, the wake is not sufficiently violent to rock the boats at the mooring; and, in leaving our mooring, we had about fifteen minutes of five-mile-an-hour progress in Dutch Slough before we got in the clear.

Then we turned into Sand Mound Slough and began to open up the engines.

We were in no screaming hurry. We kept the engines from two-thousand to twenty-five hundred revolutions, although we could have gone up above thirty-five hundred to four thousand had we so desired.

However, we were as cozy as though we had been visiting in an apartment. Sitting there in the living-room cabin of the *River Queen*, we relaxed in comfortable chairs or on a padded davenport and stretched our legs, knowing that we weren't going to have any interruptions. No problems, no stress, no strain.

It is a wonderful feeling!

We glided along Sand Mound Slough to the border of Franks Tract.

Franks Tract needs a little explaining. It was at one time a huge ranch, but, like all the Delta country ranches, the agricultural ground was below the water level. The levees kept out the water.

Then, one night, something happened. The levee broke, the water came pouring in and, as a result, what was once one of the most prosperous ranches in the community is now the enormous lake some five miles across.

The owners of the land, claiming that the government had taken over the responsibility of maintaining the levees, insisted that the government "get its water out of here." The government couldn't find any way of getting the water out of there. There was too much of it.

So now a part of the property has been taken for a state park and there is a huge shallow lake of water, which is something of a landmark in the Delta region. Rumor has it that there is an orchard with the tree limbs just a few feet, and in places only a few inches, below the surface. Fishermen may get their lines snapped on a submerged tractor or a piece of expensive farm machinery.

Personally, I have never been anxious to find out, and most of the conservative boaters feel the same way. They skirt around the outside of Frank's Tract, back of the line of the old levee until they come to the Old River; then to the San Joaquin River, cross the Stockton deep water channel, pass Korth's Pirates Lair; and then go up the Mokelumne River past a whole series of interesting marinas and resorts.

Someday I hope to have the time to explore some of these resorts and clubs. Later on, we will take a look at Perry's, a short distance above the Pirates Lair. We were familiar with the Beacon Resort when Meuhlbauers had it, but haven't been there recently; and I have yet to explore some of the other interesting marinas and restaurants which dot the west bank of the river. (The resorts are on the west bank because it is possible to reach them via a good road.)

So, we went on to the B & W Resort, a beautiful place which I hope to explore on another trip-but today it was simply a junction point where we turned to the west, left the Mokelumne River, and entered Georgiana Slough. We followed the leisurely windings of Georgiana Slough up to the drawbridge, then into the Sacramento River and up to Walnut Grove and, just above Walnut Grove, the city of Locke, which is really worth a chapter in itself.

At Locke, there is one of the old warehouses, hundreds of feet long, built out at the level of the levee with piles supporting the building out over the river.

In the old days, boat after boat landed at this warehouse to take on passengers and produce.

The warehouse was designed so that wagons could drive from the road along the levee right into the warehouse and unload. Then, when riverboats came, a chute could be rigged down to the loading deck and the produce slid down by gravity.

This was a conventional, easy method of loading these boats. Passengers could step out from the buildings at levee level, which put them on the upper passenger decks of the boats. The produce could be slid down by chute to the freight decks, where stevedores would be engaged in stowing it away.

The whole loading operation gave employment to a large number of men, and the river was a very busy maritime thoroughfare.

Whenever I see one of these loading arrangements, I think of a story told me by my old friend, Captain Madden, who always chuckled over the story of "Hog" Riley.

It seems that Captain Riley had a little boat which was operating up the coast, picking up supplies here and there and running them in to San Francisco.

The boat, as Madden described it, was one with a little peanut-power motor which had a regular run carrying hides, produce, etc., in to San Francisco. Captain Riley—who was later to become known as "Hog" Riley—was a man of rather generous beam, and he was engaged in shipping hogs to San Francisco from a point down the coast.

The hogs were being loaded with a chute. That is, the fore feet and hind feet were tied together; the hog was lifted onto the chute and turned loose. The force of gravity would carry the hog sliding down the smoothly polished chute into the hold; and the man in the hold would call out, "A hog, one-a hog, two-a hog, three-a hog, four" and then at the fifth, he would call out, "A hog, tally."

In that way, the shipment could be checked against the bill of lading.

It happened that after the fourth hog had gone down the chute, Captain Riley, heaving and tugging at a huge hog, somehow managed to get the hind legs of the animal untied, or the animal kicked his legs out of the knot.

The hog didn't want to go down that chute and didn't intend to go down. Captain Riley found himself caught off balance and suddenly realized he was catapulting down the chute.

The man in the hold, seeing a huge black body cascading down the chute, duly made a tally, raised his voice and reported to those above, "A hog, tally."

From that day on, Riley was known throughout the trade as "Hog" Riley.

Captain Madden also tells another story of "Hog" Riley. It seems Riley was casting off from one of the smaller ports at night. He was loaded with every bit of cargo he dared put on his little ship, and had huge bales of hides piled along the afterdeck obstructing the view of the helmsman to the rear. But Riley had lookouts out front and, since he was a veteran who sailed by compass course and made many of his runs at night, he didn't care about visibility. It was late at night when he finally gave the signal to cast off and started the motor, easing out into Stygian darkness.

The men stood watches; the Captain stood by the helmsman, giving him directions on times and compass. And then, about the time Captain Riley thought he should be picking up his familiar landmarks off San Francisco, a deep fog came in.

The Captain sounded the foghorn and, almost immediately, had an echo hurled back at him.

The use of an echo is, of course, one of the standard means of navigating in a fog. The whistle is blown, the time is taken for the echo to return to the ship; the time is multiplied by the speed of sound, divided by two-and that is the distance the ship is offshore.

The promptitude with which the echo came blasting back at Captain Riley caused him the greatest consternation. He was within a few hundred feet of shore, somewhere at a place where he had no business having land anywhere around him.

Again, the whistle sounded, and again the echo came blasting back.

Riley tried changing course and easing offshore, but he couldn't get offshore. The shore seemed to follow him. Wherever he went, he seemed to keep just a certain distance from the shoreline.

It wasn't until the first streaks of daylight blew away the few streamers of fog that Captain Riley realized someone had neglected to turn loose the stern line, and the boat had been pulling against the mooring of the wharf all night, changing courses, but never getting anywhere.

The story may be apocryphal; but Captain Madden vouched for its truth and used to tell it from time to time with the greatest glee.

It would, of course, take a certain combination of events to bring about such a happening, but Captain Madden was a veracious individual who insisted it was true. He was a hard bitten salt who had had a variety of experiences throughout the world and could hold an audience fascinated telling stories of the Seven Seas.

To return to our trip, our house cruiser went on past the warehouse at Locke, the mysterious town that still has so much of the Oriental atmosphere. One almost feels he is in a provincial Chinese village when he starts wandering around the narrow side streets, down below the level of the levees.

There is a wonderful Chinese market here operated by my friends, the Kings, with a meat department under the guidance of George Marr. And there are several other markets in the place where one can obtain all sorts of Chinese delicacies.

There are, of course, logical reasons why the Chinese settled in Locke.

Many years ago, California was literally swarming with Chinese. The Chinese coolie did the heavy work in the hot sun for wages so small that one wondered he could live at all.

But the frugal Chinese lived, saved money, sent it back to China; and many of them returned to China relatively wealthy men. Chinese merchants opened stores, became shrewd buyers, selling their wares at a low margin of profit, and soon infiltrated the economy of the country.

When I was a young lad living at Oroville, the Chinese situation was as hot an issue as is the bracero program today.

Newspapers of the period talked of "the yellow peril."

The Chinese were a minority group suffering indignities which one can hardly realize.

Many kids considered it smart to throw rocks at a "Chinaman" whenever they saw him. There is, I believe, a decision in one of the old justice's courts that killing a "Chinaman" was no crime because murder consisted of killing a human being and a Chinese was not a human being.

Be that as it may, the Chinese had no rights, no status. They worked for a pittance; they did work that the American laborer wouldn't consider; they saved their money; they became prosperous; and, eventually, they won the respect of the citizens everywhere.

Today, the Chinese, what few of them can be found in the country, are consummate merchandisers. They are shrewd buyers who recognize quality and operate on a small margin of profit.

The market operated by the Kings at Locke is a shining example.

George Marr has some of the choicest meat one can find anywhere, regardless of the size of the city or the market. The merchandise in the market is high quality and is well displayed, the prices are reasonable; and there are all sorts of Chinese delicacies-canned fresh lychee nuts, dried bean noodles, Chinese oyster sauce, and pickled scallions which the Chinese call "*sohn kayeu tau*"—but which are now being produced in quantity by the Japanese.

There is also the Chinese bean cake cheese, made out of bean curds which presumably are fermented in some way and then preserved. The squares of this Chinese cheese have an absolutely indescribable flavor, as pungent as horseradish, as rich as Camembert, as strong as Limburger.

I will admit that some of these Chinese delicacies require little period of acquaintanceship before the palate develops a full-flavored friendship, but I love the Chinese food.

Years ago, I lived in China with a Chinese family. There wasn't knife, fork, or silver spoon in the house, as far as tableware is concerned. We ate with chopsticks and porcelain china spoons. Naturally, I became quite adept with chopsticks, and think back with nostalgic memories of the times when the family sat around the table—each with his individual bowl of rice, but all of the other dishes in the center of the table. Each individual reached in with his chopsticks, picked out what he wanted, put it on his bowl of rice, ate a layer of rice, then returned to the central dishes for more of the food.

Those were in the days of long ago, as far as the Orient is concerned. At that time, the Chinese had the greatest respect for the Americans as a race.

I think back on those days and contrast them with what is happening today.

Now, the average Mainland Chinese hates our guts. This has been brought about because we didn't like the communist leadership of the Chinese and so, in order to punish the Chinese for going communist, we harassed them economically and politically in every way we could.

The inevitable result, of course, was that we managed to alienate the Chinese people and thereby made the communist rulers that much more secure in their jobs.

I sometimes wonder what would have happened if we had simply tried to keep the friendship and respect of the Chinese individual.

Perhaps the communist leaders would have been able to have turned the citizens against us anyway, but it would have been more of job than if we ourselves hadn't helped do it.

I suppose I am unspeakably naive in international affairs, but I like people. I like to travel in foreign lands. I like to study foreign customs and try to appreciate types of thought which are not based on American patterns.

More and more in my travels, I have found a creeping atmosphere of hostility and a spirit of "Yankee, go home!"

I suppose this decreasing prestige has been the inevitable result of necessary foreign policies, but sometimes I wonder.

I particularly wonder about Mainland China, where my former friends have now quit writing to me, but where thirty-odd years ago the American was universally respected.

But all this is a long way from the Delta country.

Anyhow, on this trip to Knights Landing we decided to pass up Walnut Grove and Locke, and kept moving smoothly on up the Sacramento River.

It was getting along in the afternoon when we passed Walnut Grove, but we didn't have to bother about the hour.

That is part of the charm of house-boating.

We had our beds along; we had our electric plant and electric lights; we had radio, television, and air conditioning if we wanted it; and we had an abundance of food.

We were as much at home as the Canadian goose which had decided to spend the summer in the Delta country, and which went swimming majestically by.

So we kept on up the river until it began to get dark. Then we pulled in to the bank, tied up to a couple of trees, broke out the portable barbecue outfit, used the electric generator to fire up some charcoal, spread thick steaks on the broiler, brought out ice cold beer, sourdough French bread which we toasted and buttered, had a crisp salad, and sat there in our little private domicile as completely isolated as though we had been on the ocean a thousand miles from shore, yet along the roads on the riverbank, there was a fairly steady stream of automobile traffic.

Those steaks were juicy, thick, and tender. They came from another market where we have always been able to get positively superb meat.

I think this is so largely true of the Delta country because markets cater to boatmen who want barbecues and, therefore demand the best.

I know that the markets at Bethel Island have some of the best meat I have ever been able to buy; and like so many boatmen, we make it a point to obtain the very best money can buy.

Sitting around the table on our house cruiser, dining leisurely and in an unhurried atmosphere, with tender juicy steaks two and a half inches thick and barbecued to perfection the cares of the world certainly seemed far away.

The hot water tank of the *River Queen* gave us an abundant supply of scalding hot water. The dishes presented almost no problem and, shortly after dinner, we turned out the lights and sat there in the warm darkness listening to the purling waters of the river, watching the occasional lights of passing automobiles on the riverbank.

Soon the tempo of conversation slowed; we became drowsy and went to bed.

I know that I had a night of deep, untroubled sleeping; waking once or twice long enough to roll over, listening to the gurgling of waters as they swept past the steel hull. Tied to overhanging tree limbs some eight or ten feet offshore, we were completely isolated, thoroughly relaxed.

Nature: Challenging and Appreciated, Engineered and Restored

[Editor's note: In the modern era, from the 1960s forward, reflections on the Sacramento–San Joaquin River Delta have focused on the struggle to tame the environment and to restore it. Much of the reflection has been about water and habitat. The Sacramento–San Joaquin River Delta is key to the redistribution of California's water from north to south and from agriculture to urban uses. Further the significance of the Sacramento–San Joaquin River Delta for species of birds and fish—not to mention its rich agricultural promise—have raised the temperature of the debates. Much of the early twentieth century focused on strategies for regulating floods and the devastation they could bring.]

George Steward, from *Storm*

[Editor's note: George Steward, *Storm* (Lincoln: University of Nebraska Press, 1983), pp. 275–81, 336–40. (*By permission*). See Fig. 45.]

Tenth Day, Section 7

Once the water had begun to spill over the weirs, the gauge readings rose more slowly; but still they rose. People going out after breakfast to stand on Colusa Bridge saw the brown swirling water just a hair above twenty-one. At noon they looked, and said, "Twenty-one-point six." By three o'clock the water was just below twenty-two. But the levees stood up high and firm on either side; the river would have to rise seven feet more, and touch twenty-nine to reach the danger-point, and even beyond that the levees, with luck, might stand a foot or two.

For every inch that the water rose at the gauge, another inch spilled over the weir. By mid-afternoon a depth of two feet was pouring over the quarter mile length of Colusa Weir; that flow itself already equaled a large river. But from the other weirs also great streams poured out. Over Fremont the flow was twenty inches deep and nearly two miles wide. Peering out through rain-sluiced windows, the people in cars crossing the long viaduct on U.S. 40 looked out to see the Yolo By-Pass, a mighty river, three miles wide, of swiftly flowing flood water.

Sacramento gauge, close to the point where the American flowed into the main stream, stood in early afternoon at twenty-one point five. It was rising slowly, but as at Colusa, the city would not be endangered until the water rose seven and half feet more, and touched twenty-nine. Before that happened, the weir gates could be opened.

In the General's outer office three assistants had been kept busy all day. Each had a telephone, and all three lines were busy most of the time.

One of the assistants flipped the switch for the General's private telephone.

"Yes?" said the General from the inner office.

"Folsom reports seven point eight, up nine-tenths in an hour. I thought you'd like to know it right away."

"Yes, thanks. We're in for some trouble with the American, I think."

"And, General, Orville wants you, Mr. L. D. Jackson. He wants you personally."

"Put him on," said the General with resignation. He had never heard of L. D. Jackson, but felt that he had been talking to him under different names and in different towns all day.

"Yes, General," said the long distance operator. "And when you're through talking to Oroville, would you mind not hanging up? I've three more long-distance calls waiting for you."

The General talked with Mr. Jackson, giving him information and reassurance. Then he talked to Red Bluff, Redding, and some ranch house out of Marysville. It was the same story with slight variations; each man had his worries which in his own mind loomed larger than the possible flooding of all the rest of the valley.

Fortunately, at this stage the General could usually quiet people's fears very quickly. The water was flowing over the weirs and flooding through the bypasses on a much greater scale but with the same simplicity that water spills from one basin of a fountain into the next. Everywhere the gauges stood several feet below the critical point. With the rain still continuing, there was no telling what height the flood crest would finally reach, but as yet the tremendous capacity of the by-passes was not even severely taxed.

So far, the damage reported had been only incidental and fortuitous. Two boys venturing out in a rowboat had lost their heads apparently, and overturned in the swirling channel; one of them had been drowned. A sudden outbreak of Stony Creek had swept away two hundred sheep. Seepage, caused probably by gophers working in the levee, was being fought near Meridian; local authorities reported the situation controlled. An incipient break in the Feather River levee had been discovered by a patrol before it had time to develop. The near-by ranchers had mobilized hastily. One of them donated some bales of hay, and these clogged the flow until a sand-bag defense could be built up.

"Hold up any more calls for me," said the General into his telephone. "Unless there's an emergency; I've got to do some figuring and get out a forecast."

The American was the immediate problem. Reports from the mountains indicated very heavy rain was falling everywhere in that basin. Even worse, it was a warm rain and was washing off the snow cover up to the five-thousand foot level. Every creek and gully flowing into each of the three forks must be a-boiling. And of all the rivers the American was the most flashy because of its steeper gradient and shorter length, its waters crested quickly, and came out with a rush. With Folsom gauge rising so rapidly, the lower country would soon feel the effects; by latest report Sacramento gauge had risen to twenty-one point eight.

The General dictated: "The Feather, Yuba, and upper Sacramento Rivers are rising slowly, but gauge readings are not excessive; flood levels are not to be expected within the next twenty-four hours. The amount of water flowing through the bypasses will increase moderately. The American River is rising rapidly, and will reach twenty-five feet at Sacramento about midnight. This will necessitate closing the main highway between Sacramento and North Sacramento, and rerouting the traffic via Jib-boom Street."

The General settled back in his chair and looked at his desk-clock. That statement would go out immediately, and in about twenty minutes he could expect the Committee.

The Committee consisted of three businessmen, a type of humanity for which the General as a military man had no liking. Two of them were tall and thin, but the chairman and the most aggressive was short and fat.

"General," he stated emphatically, "this has got to stop. When that road is closed, business in North Sacramento falls off fifty to a hundred thousand dollars each day. Sacramento clearinghouse receipts fall off five hundred thousand dollars, each day!"

The man's overemphasis made the General think of a dog's barking; he disliked it intensely. Also, as a former officer he disliked being shouted at by a civilian. But he kept his temper.

"Look here," the man barked on, "if you open those gates at the twenty-five foot gauge reading, that road won't flood. We represent the State Businessmen's Association, and we pay a lot of taxes. We're about ready to turn on the heat!"

In the long years since he had ceased being a junior officer the General had got out of the habit of keeping himself tightly reined in, but he still held on.

"Gentlemen," he said, "what happens to the Delta's farmers when those gates are opened?"

"They get flooded of course, but they take that chance. And there's not half, not a quarter, the loss of crops that there is loss of business here."

The General reflected a moment, wanting to argue. Damage to land and crops was real to him, but as a military man he could never quite figure out the meaning of loss of business. Someone didn't spend money today because he didn't like to go out in the wet, but he must do something with the money some time. But that was not the point.

He put his last thought into words. "Gentlemen, that's not the point. There is the matter of an agreement. Possibly conditions have changed, and flooding the highway is more costly than flooding the farmers. That's still not the point; I hold the gates until I consider that the safety of the city is endangered."

The three men of the Committee looked at one another, and then got up. Last to go was the fat chairman. He turned around in the doorway.

"All right, General, " he barked. "And say, you don't by any chance own stock in the Delta Asparagus Company?"

The General was on his feet. He did not bark, but he roared: "Get out of my office!"

The General strode back and forth the length of the room. By God, by God, but civilians were a poor lot of mammals, by God! Didn't they ever learn that you had to work together, even sacrifice yourself, for the whole? That very moment the General limped as he walked, and he had that limp from the day he took his regiment against a too strong German position. Everybody knew it was a hopeless attack. But it pegged some German reserves, and kept them off the neck of another American outfit somewhere. The men who died, and there were a lot of them, at least knew that they helped the whole army. In war, you fought a common enemy. But these buyers and sellers, faugh! They strangled each other. They squabbled even when the storm allied itself with the river, when hour by hour the readings of the gauges were higher and the rising water lapped searchingly along the levees. Suddenly the General felt a great disgust with man as a species. It might be a good thing if the situation pictured in his favorite passage should happen again and on a larger scale, if the whole valley (or the whole world perhaps) should become only a far stretching welter of brown waters with a few heads bobbing about here and there for a little while.

Still, he would like to have an ark to save some of the better ones, a few good soldiers, and some of the men who were out there patrolling the levees right now in the rain, fighting the river and the storm, not figuring how to get a dollar and thirty-six cents out of some other fellow.

Twelfth Day, Section 4

The General had jumped from bed at four thirty Friday morning when the cloudburst suddenly beat against his windows. During the night when Friday passed into Saturday, he did not consider the question of bed.

As he looked from his office windows in the still hours of the morning, he felt a curious sense of unreality. The full moon was brilliant; street lights shone upon dry asphalt; branches of trees and shrubbery swayed in a steady breeze. It was no night to imagine floods and disaster. Apparently, the inhabitants of the valley felt a similar sense of safety. Few long distance calls came in from panicky ranchers and businessmen demanding the news and asking advice.

The storm was over. But for the General the crisis had not yet passed. Far and wide, he could feel those billions of cubic feet of water, penned in behind the levees, pouring toward the Bay. The water level in the rivers stood far above the valley floor, high as the roof eaves of the cottages in the river towns, high as the second-story windows in Sacramento. Along hundreds of miles of levee top, in the bright moonlight, his patrols walked their beats, back and forth. The men needed no slickers tonight; each carried a shovel on his shoulder. On one side, each man looked far down the slope of the levee, and saw the streetlights of some little town still burning or perhaps only the wide stretches of the valley where the scattered houses showed no lights. On his other side, the patrol looked out almost on his own level, and saw the brown backwater among the leafless willows of the stream, on the margin beyond the willows flowed the swift water of the channel.

At one o'clock word was telephoned from Kennett, far north under the peak of Shasta, that the upper Sacramento had crested at twenty-four point six, and was falling. This crest was high enough to be dangerous, but it would not arrive in the lower river for several days and could be disregarded for the moment.

The critical stream was still the American. Although the rain in the foothills had ceased twelve hours previse, the crest had not yet had time to descend to the plain. Every fifteen minutes the General had a telephone call from his deputy at Sacramento gauge where the American poured into the main river. Hour by hour the water rose, twenty-seven point seven, twenty-eight, twenty-eight point one.

By now so much water was flooding from the American that it almost monopolized the main channel below its mouth. The water from the upper river had topped the wickets of Sacramento Weir, and was flowing across in streams two feet deep. At either end of the long weir a man stood on guard; the moonlight glinted upon the star of a deputy sheriff and showed the bulge of the pistol at his hip. There were many people who might like to have those wickets opened, and the General was taking no chances.

Between two and three, the gauge held steady. Perhaps, thought the General, the crest had arrived; perhaps he had held the American. But then the gauge crept up—twenty-eight point three, twenty-eight point five. Beyond twenty-nine it must not go. The trouble, the General suddenly realized, was with the Sacramento itself. Under present conditions the four miles between the weir and the mouth of the American should be practically still water. But now the outlet through the weir was not sufficient, and the water still pressed down against the outflow of the American and rose against the levees around the sleeping city. The telephone rang, and the deputy reported twenty-eight point seven. On top of that was another call, police headquarters, a patrol car just reporting, three inches of seepage water covering a street. Again, the telephone, northwest wind freshening, waves slopping at the top of the American levee, we're holding it with a row of sand-bags; not dangerous, yet.

The General shrugged his shoulders. Like a good soldier he had held his lines until he could retreat with honor. He gave his orders.

Men hurried along Sacramento Weir. They knocked out the pins holding the wickets in place. An eight-foot wall of water swept through.

Then occurred what might seem a miracle. Along four miles of its course the great swirling river grew still, and then reversed its flow. Water which had passed the weir on its way to the sea, now turned and flowed back up stream. The suck of the suddenly opened wickets seemed to annul the power of gravity. Even the American felt the pull; part of its waters continued down the main channel, but part took the up channel, and flowing through the weir entered the bypass. The level at Sacramento gauge fell half a foot in ten minutes.

The General started home to bed. As he drove his car along the dry streets under the bright moon, he again felt that sense of the unreality of disaster on such a night. Yet the opening of the weir was sending down water which would flood thousands of acres in the delta. Already he had sent out the warning.

He had lost both his fights. First, he flooded the highway, and in the end, he had to open the wickets. Flooding the asparagus country was a nasty business, but at least it saved the city, like sacrificing a platoon to save a battalion. And somebody had to take the responsibility. The next few days might raise some excitement. But barring accident, the levees and bypasses would carry the run-off; the rivers would crest successively, and the storm was over.

Yet other storms would come; again, the brown water would rise against the levees. In the end, the levees would go down, a hundred years, a thousand years; but in the end, they would go, and the men who built them.

Perhaps. It was only that he had lost a night's sleep; he felt old. He sensed a great weariness, of storms that came and went, of water that fell as rain and rushed through the rivers, only to return again as rain. He knew there was a quotation, not Bret Harte this time, something more ancient. What was it all about, this ceaseless, ineffective activity of storms, and of men? Then he found the quotation somewhere back in his mind: "All the rivers run into the sea; yet the sea is not full; unto the place from whence the rivers come, thither they also return again." The cold northwest wind eddied about the General's neck, and he shivered.

The River

[Editor's Note: Following the fictional account by George Steward of a devastating flood (above), in the next three chapters, three groups of writers/poets celebrate the Sacramento and San Joaquin Rivers, the "fauna" of the Sacramento-San Joaquin River Delta, and finally the interaction between human actors and the environs.]

Laura Ulewiecz, "Notes Toward the River Itself"

[Editor's note: Laura Ulewiecz was a Polish poet who joined the so called "Beat" movement in San Francisco. However, she later moved to Locke and became a social worker. Her poems during this latter period were limited in number, but show the power of the Sacramento River to stimulate reflection. Laura Ulewiecz, "Notes Toward the River Itself," in Berg, P. (ed.), *Reinhabiting A Separate Country* (San Francisco: Plant Drum Foundation, 1978), pp 101–109. (*By permission*). See Fig. 46.]

1.
Where the water rises,
again I go, older
and older now; to touch
little where it rises from
fresh, the quiet, the pool,
tender of our powers;
touch where, inside
the dark, young layers of onion

squeak in older layers.
Always the aging outside
is what shows, arranged
in shawls around the new—
tough protection from
these terrible winds-
as in the cabbage.

2.
Where does this water rise?
Why, in the earth.
Same entrails, new hairdo,
I go. Or to the river.
Not for renewal,
but continuance. She, too,
lamenting her protection,
ay, her wrinkles, goes
in her bikini, showing
her yoga body off
to young men. Oh, men,
young, she clasps them to her.

3.
Light. More light. The weight
of its heat pressing layers
of your flesh down, till hope
is a small dried bird. That's
why the time in the middle
is called an age. It's heat,
light. As if the earth
in the chicken yard flew up
and buzzed in your face. As if
the only breeze came
from the wings of mosquitoes.
Heat, following drought.
So it is that the half-formed
figs thud on the Macadam.
Yet here are these round, hot
Chinese pears flecked
like the bark they are growing on/
from. They still hang.
And you're amazed.

Did you think we are spun
between fire and dark
on spits, gutted like game?
We swing through the flame of the sun
sustained by the dark through our navels.
We turn the dark in our minds
Like an unripe pear
for a long time before
we let go into it.

4.
I place myself in the water
to cool me. My whole life cools
here in the slough. They sing:

"Sorrow is all I owe you
song of my sorrow," Voice
of the unseen bird. I have
this in me.

            "Shade is my joy,
hot sun, water to dip into.
Mosquitoes that sip your blood,
I feed on. Fruit that I eat,
you plant. We are the good neighbors."
The song of the seen bird sits
on my shoulder. We do not touch.

Those two bird songs are not
contradictory.

5.
Somehow I have not spoken,
really, of the river-
so big, so obvious
to our lives. Surely
it wraps itself around
all of our words and moistens
them. It's hard to remember
the important things. Summers,
it's why we're cool at night

with breezes in the cottonwoods;
and what the boaters come for;
and why we're not a desert;
and how, if you drive off
the road you drown. And it's hard
to say the important things.
Late in Spring, if tradewinds
from Hawaii come
melting the mountain snow
fast, you do not say,
the river is rising', but, 'the levee
may not hold.'

                    To speak
of the river itself is to talk
about mud, how it's churned
in that water. I refuse to go down
to the dark home of the carp,
to the crayfish crawling through sunken
automobiles. Yet, sometimes,
I think I've caught it out,
this river, stealing in Tule
fog across the land
back to its vastness. It's not
the river I've found, but a dream
of our past. Or dark of the moon
when old men lean hour
after hour against
the bridge, I hear them cast
their lines into that dark
something they trust is there
enough to wait. But it isn't
the darkness they fish; it's the light
from the bridge. Just as it's not
the river I get a sense of,
but of old men. Or when
the full moon crowns it, or when
the sun sets on its
iridescent esses,
it is not the river I see
at all; but the changes on it.

Back by the slough along
Twin Cities Road, a Redwinged
Blackbird lights upon
A head of grass so deftly.

6.
"Houses beyond decay"
to live in-a thing to think
about. Walls of the past
to build new walls within.
Twelve whites, eighty Chinese,
Six Philippinos—
Population count.
So that's our village. Expanding
in circles around it-
artifice of the delta:
plains between levees, tomatoes,
mechanized pear trees. Then
the sloughs, sedate or sluggish,
how you choose it. Remnants
of original marshes. Birds.
Oh, so many kinds of
so many whirring wings
and, everywhere, mosquitoes.

"You should go there full
confusion and anguish," he said;
and the other replied, "I did.
That's when it's good." To like
yourself again in the river
air, the tides of the transient
ocean pulling your blood.
His friend, the medium,
said, "I feel no ghosts here,
but much low energy
pulling, pulling down."
No Chinese went for a year
where the house burned down
in respect of the ghosts.

"What do you think of first?"
He said, "Community

and panorama." I was thinking
of gardens and river air.
"You will get more involved each day
in the life of the whites," they said.
Twelve whites, eighty Chinese,
six Philippinos.
So then this architecture,
built in that year, inside
this panorama, it comes
in the end down to the people.

Today, I take a vow
of silence against the smallness
of this town, silence
against the angry slowness
of my mind. There is nothing
to be angry about, but I am
angry.

7.

Tell me:

How somberly I squat the levee
Catching autumn between my legs,
My thighs heavy, my back hunched over
The last zinnias, the spent cucumber vines.

Tell how I walk down into the field
Lower than rivers, gather these pumpkins
Against me, my lovers. That is the end.
There will be no more summer.

Say shake the burnt-out stalks
of sunflowers, shake till seeds fly out
Of their heads, that I pick the seeds with a laugh
Out of my hair. spit them around my face.

Say the river is quiet as sleeping frogs,
These tiny frogs, tucked in the clefts
Of leaves, they can sing like birds. I turn
The earth upside down in my sureness of rain.

But you stand above on the slope detached
In your past, without need, like bones. I do not
Say love you, at last, I do not love.
am here, barefooted, stepping on pears.

Tell me:

Slide me into my future
With the palms of your voice.

8.
Those who belong nowhere
yearn to keep goats. They hoe
in the garden once and are
depleted. They move on.
The air of the delta is streaked
with their comings and goings, chalked
with tenuous jet streamers
from Mexico to Boulder.
Any wind can whisk them
away as if it all
did not matter. As if
it did not matter, their quest
from land to city, between
cities; as if between
earth-insect and nest, between
tree and tree did not matter—
the movements of the oriole.
As if the climbing harvest
Of pear trees, the growth of this year's
safflower; as if transient
life investment, it did not
matter, and there were
no such thing as renewal.

9.
Look!

It is on all sides of
us. It is circling
us. Out there where they
packed it—pushes always

to come back. Can't
you hear it easing under
us to shovels down?
Keep it channelled, buy land,
buy tractors, buy
pear trees even as it rises
hard with rain to say
whose land this really is.

Julia Connor, The Delta Poem

[Editor's note: Julia Connor has been an active poet in the Sacramento region over many years. Here she related experience of the Sacramento–San Joaquin River Delta to classical and Biblical texts. The poet implies that the experience of the Sacramento–San Joaquin River Delta is not dissimilar to experiences rooted deep in the Western Cultural Tradition. The orthography of the poem including the words split by a hyphen are the poet's. Julia Connor, "The Delta Poem" (Sacramento: Vernacular Editions, 1987). (*By permission*).]

And when she could not longer hide him, she took
for him an ark of bulrushes, and daubed it with
slime and with pitch, and put the child therein;
and laid it in the flags by the river's brink.
Exodus
2:3

O to be summoned here
before even the hope of Spring
can attend her grand uncertainties

wherein each argument of Form,
of Green

must resurrect
must fuse to flame

must,

so that even to what
does not yield

we have called the bee
and given a name.

The Sacramento takes its rise on the
southern slopes of the Klamath mountains and provides the central channel
into which all streams flow.

Here, flood waters built a land that
sloped away from the river, forming
great enclosed tule basins that held
water most of the year.

Where I am most ardent
small birds perch

three now are jewel
to the hemlock stalk

behind which
the river bends
are they lost chorus
or emissaries

of some future
loveliness?

At dawn in the early spring, mist rises
off the river to reveal some sleeping
thing, some figure of the water's cast
that's curved, moth-like, and feminine.
Too young to be described as color,
it is mauve; tulip-shadow.

Is there more to beauty
than your storm of early white
that drops upon
the almond orchard floor

O Zagreus,
O torn flower

strewn down
by the sun.

Early writings depict a valley with
vast herds of antelope, elk, and
black-tailed deer.

The last elk were killed in the
Suisun marshes.

Deer tracks can still be seen leading to
the stout, erect, diffusely branched California Rose, whose dense thickets form
wild rows of pink along levee banks from
May to November, and whose bright
orange winter hips light the barren bush,
draped in blackberry and grape; the
sanctuary of birds.

Have we forgotten
all signs are braziers

all betray light
or how

as bird
the slightest peck

will ignite
the Red Bud of Spring;

have we forgotten
betrayal's color?

The word *delta* refers to the triangular
shape of the forth Greek letter and means
the fan-shaped alluvial plain formed at
the mouth of a river where, upon meeting
quiet waters, the stream drops part of
its load of sediment.

What breaks surfaces
breaks words
breaks and

multiplies
the stored nuclei
where larvae swarm

inexorably drawn
to the flame
understanding in a flash
the form of events,

vera iconica;
Veronica's veil.

In ancient Hebrew each letter is
articulation of the Holy Tongue,
having numerical value, sound,
form, and mantric effect.

There, *delta* becomes *daleth*, whose
number is four and whose symbol,
the door, is both threshold and ob-
stacle of manifestation; as a dam
might impede a flow …

What is true
is portent of
the image cast

worm casing,
shell,
hollow tube of grass
the woman, Veronica,
was a poet.
Was she like Helen
to be seen everywhere

was she known
for her intensity

was she,
ephemeral wretch,

to become
the apotheosis
of woman?

You think the valley's level, but it's not.
The river falls in sequences and gradients,
each becoming factor of velocity. The
great tract it plows is, in actuality, a
structural depression, the result of a sea.

Was she one of the many
would-be-saints

honey-questing
the inviolate

or had she read
so ardently

she dared step forth
to wipe the brow

of Eros:

We know only that a woman appeared
offering a cloth and that when he
returned it, it bore the imprint
of a face.

Were her hands
like those of the men
traveling with him

stained
by the sulphur
of their trade;

was she
reviled
for being both woman
and mage

hence,
forever stricken
from the books?

It is said she was later in Rome and
cured Tiberius with the relic.

... and, that she was the woman Christ
cured; that she went to France and
married Amadour. That the common
speedwell is named after her.

Had they forgotten
that Asclepius

took foul letters
from his patient's brow

or that Moses' face
was veiled

after discourse
with the God;

had they forgotten
the art conceals

or had they never seen
what this woman saw

rapt
in words?

Where even Joseph had discovered things
by gazing into water

was it forbidden for a woman
to fish

was it folly to imagine her slender hands
plying the heavy nets

was it that rare?

Was it rare
that a poet speak

or a woman's rag
veil the face she called

                              "Master ..."

so that the word
crept in like a bee

and the flower
unfurled;

honey stain
on flax.

When he said
"you are just a girl"

is it a wonder
her nerves failed

and she hid the thing
slipping it

into a box,
weeping as he fell

and then swept back
by the angry crowd

she recognized the bird
a heron, or a crane perhaps;
or was it incidental
he wore the Ibis crown

of Thoth?

Where land and water meet in a marsh
Of cattail, sedge, and tule grass, the
White-Faced Ibis appears. Seeming at
first black, it is actually rich purple
with iridescent head; white around the
eyes. Like the crane, the ibis flies
with neck extended announcing its
arrival with a low pitched cry that it
repeats three times.

Already the small thorns cling,
fragments
of some unseen whole;
evergreen, bumblekite,
berry,
word.

The path of the Pacific Flyway origin-
ates in the Arctic, then stretches south
across the Gulf to the mouth of the
Columbia, where it swings to the interior,
Tule Lake, and the Sacramento basin.

Had not Osiris
once the opener of ways

set free the rivers
of Spring

to swamp
the bulrush bird;

> *Ah Helpless One*
> *how fair are you that rise today*

had not the words themselves become
a *kalamos,*

sweet mystery
of the fragrant reed.

What augury returns
to haunt the brambled mass

beneath which spreads
the pale blue spell

eye   *arvensis*
Veronica's flower;

what garment wraps the word,
what prophecy?

what salt
yet clings
to the sinuous lore

via dolorosa,
rapture
of the way?

... forehead, white; sides of crown,
black; neck, pale grey; throat, marked
with white; chin and cheeks, white; upper
parts, slate-blue; shoulders, grey; tail,
slate-blue; inner wing quills, slate-blue;
plumes of breast, grey; abdomen, black
with rufous streaks; under tailfeathers,

white; bill, yellow with dusty ridge; legs
and feet, dusty; soles, yellow; bare space
around eye, greenish-blue; iris, chrome
yellow ...

The Great Blue Heron can be found in
shallow waters, lifting each foot above
the surface and then replacing it, so as
not to cause a ripple.

Was she drawn
(ephemeral wretch)

to his torment,
what had he

Miserere,
born of the waters,

expected
from a girl;

what caprice
had they not already suffered

what veil
not torn?

It is certain they knew
each other's terror

and by secret
exchanged some sign

thru which they wove
the cloth

she held
and he cast the image on;

it is certain
they recognized

the beauty
of what they were doing

for that moment
did forever bond

beauty
to the poet's hand.

An imperative that spins the chrysalis
Spins the caterpillar
in line with the sun

to hold the dark
as if it were a star
come into the hand

> *root of Hemlock*
> *digg' d i' the dark.*

Had she left then
or did she watch the catastrophe

had she heard *the Eloi,*
Eloi, lama sabachthani

had she seen him drink
from the moistened reed,

had she seen the
spear enter?

Was it then her hand
as if aerial

entered the hive
extracting from each cell

some young unwinged
yet honeyed thing

she'd found
inside?

Or paused, did she think
some miracle occurred

some strange,
uncanny thing

that being poet
she equated with words;

had she touched
or only imagined she touched

that wound?

Bees swarm on the walls of the Araña
Cave near Valencia, as a figure ascends
a rope of corded grass to rob honey
from a crevice in the rock.

And in Athens, where from the moon-
hive the stars still swarmed, the bees
were honeyed priestesses, whose
phrenic song was Hermes' gift, Apollo's
nurse, and intoxicant to the Honey Lord.

While of Eros it was said:
> He lay among the rose blooms smiling,
> bound fast by sleep, and above him the
> tawny bees were sprinkling on his
> dainty lips honey dripping from the
> comb.

There is a story of a certain Melissa
of Corinth, who, initiated by the goddess
herself, was plagued to tell her secrets
by women of the neighborhood. Infuri-
ated by her refusal to speak, they tore

her limb from limb. From these, we are
told, the goddess brought forth bees.

These whom the Pleiades, rising Doves,
roust to store the hive, are called *bright
with gleaming scales*, whose web is sealed,
wherein *sweet streams drip* .

Alder's wood bleeds red
when felled
buds in spirals
along stream beds

male flowers
from naked twigs
sans leaf,
sans cover

green from the flower
brown from the twig
red pearls
from the bark

used to paint the heads
of arrows.

What foreign hand unwound
the tiny thing sewn
to its precious hem

what dissembler confused
this seasoned Art
with real estate;

what Fleet-Footed-One was lost
that the cloth might hold?

What breaks surfaces
breaks words
are crises of matter
life rises to include

breaks and rises
like blooms
snapped free
of the stem

to become
butterflies.

Prepare

(O radiant nets!)
Love's hero

to dissolve
and resolve again

O Delphi, Christos,
Amor ...

Your oracular spring!

Joshua McKinney, "Down in the River"

[Editor's note: Joshua McKinney teaches writing in the Sacramento area. He published the poem below in a collection of poems by area writers, *Late Peaches*, edited by Bob Stanley (Sacramento: Sacramento Poetry Center, 2012), p. 136. (*By permission*). Here the poet is on the edge of hearing nature speak; there is a long tradition in American letters of longing to grasp directly nature's secrets.]

Down in the River

bottoms, I went walking at dawn,
through the thought-out grass
to where the last rabbit track failed
among dredge tailings, which loomed
like cairns around me. That brumous
landscape destroyed all compass,

and I stopped, cloaked in the cold fog
listening. Off to my right, a dog
barked, distant, practicing
its old partisan art: something joyful,
something doleful as the oldest
sound. And it seemed to drift

toward me as greeting, nearly
tangible, but breathable, too,
like the cloud I stood hidden in, all
bearing lost in a cold inspiring,
vapor drawn into my body entire, sown
in the furrows of the brain's tilth.

How long I waited I can't say.
Then I heard the cry again, more distant
still in that heartbroken place
where shaken, I took a step forward,
solitary and slow, and started at a sound
made myself, an almost human name.

Fauna

Chiura Obata, "Frosty Dawn Near the Delta"

[Editor's note: Chiura Obata is renown as a painter. In 1937, he published a limited-edition art book that contained the haiku poem below. Chiura Obata, *The Sierra to the Sea* (Berkeley, Archetyne Press, 1937). (*By permission*). Here he captures the experience of birds while fishing the Sacramento–San Joaquin River Delta. See Fig. 47.]

Ducks whirring past ...
A shooting star
Brushes the tip
Of a fisherman's rod.

Everard Jones, "The King of the San Joaquin"

[Editor's note: Joel and Coke Hallowell have edited a book of stories featuring residents of the San Joaquin River region, *Take Me to the River* (Berkeley: Heyday, 2010). They include a poem by Everard Jones on p. 11. (*By permission*). Jones discusses the challenge of pursuing salmon in the San Joaquin. The battle is almost medieval.]

Out of the Pacific and through the Gate, and up
   the river to spawn,
comes a gallant knight with plenty of fight
to cope with the dangers beyond.

He carries no scars, this warrior king.
He's king of fish in the San Joaquin.

His hardships are many, his dangers untold, as he journeys
   against the stream,
yet onward and onward he battles his way, impossible
   that it may seem.
He navigates using no compass or stars.
He's the king of the San Joaquin.

He has many names this warrior bold, from warm
   waters to the cold.
Chinook, Quinat, Silverside, Red, he's known quite
   well unto all.
He's fat when he starts, but later gets lean,
He's king of fish in the San Joaquin.

They've heard that he's coming, the salmon so fine.
they've rigged up their outfits and tested their line.
They've checked their boats and are waiting to greet
The king of the San Joaquin.

I tried a cast I had tried before:
the current carried it away from shore.
was winding it in, as I always do,
when the line snaps tight and the rod bends true.
The king of the San Joaquin.

The battle is on and there's plenty of fight.
I thumb the reel with the greatest delight.
The rod is high and he takes out line.
No need to hurry; he's a-biding his time.
He cuts the water so swift and clean,
He's king of the fish of the San Joaquin.

My thumb is burned, my fingers are sore,
I'm ready to quit, but he's asking for more.
When out of the water with a mighty splash,
a glimpse I get, a silver flash.
and back he goes a with a terrific thrash.
The king of the San Joaquin.

He finally tires as all fish do.
I thought he had quit, I thought he was through.
I reached for the gaff, started to gloat, as I brought
    him alongside the boat.
The king of the San Joaquin.

I was ready to gaff him and end it all there,
when he takes a last jump straight into the air.
It took him a second, a second too soon, to shake
    his head and toss a spoon.
The king of the San Joaquin.

I relaxed in the seat and lowered the rod,
reached for my pipe and for that I thank God.
I draw on the "burner" and smoke fills the air.
I think of that warrior, that salmon so fair,
The king of the San Joaquin.

Pete Otteson, from *The Black Hole: Creating a Balanced, Sustainable Wetland Habitat*

[Editor's note: Peter Otteson authored a privately published description of a habitat restoration, *Creating a Balanced Sustainable Wetland Habitat: The Black Hole* (2020). It recounts the commitment of Dino Cortopassi to the creation of a duck habitat. Cortopassi clearly developed a deep affection for the Sacramento–San Joaquin River Delta and the duck hunting it provided; this story demonstrates the potential cooperation between farmers, hunters, and environmentalists in the region. Below are excerpts pp. 3–7. (*By permission*).]

Becoming A Delta Swamp Rat

Dino's Italian immigrant father, Amerigo Cortopassi, started him working summers at the Vignolo and Cortopassi Farms on Wright Tract, six miles east of Stockton, instilling old country values of work and perseverance early on. In 1947, Amerigo started Dino, age 10, driving grain trucks in the field to unload barley from the harvester to the truck, his first experience in operating farm machinery. "All of the men in my family—three uncles and my father—were farmers," Dino explained. "So that's what I grew up with. They were my heroes and anything having to do with farming I always thought of as really cool."

That was the start of Dino getting his hands into the dirt, in parallel with a developing passion for Delta hunting that soon followed. At age 14 he was driving back and forth from Stockton's eastside to Wright Tract because, when you were a farm kid, you could get an early license. So, in addition to entire summers doing farm work, when fall arrived there was no holding Dino back from hunting before and after high school classes.

As it turned out the teenager was handy with farm machinery and progressed up the Wright Tract Filipino worker hierarchy. Soon, Amerigo had Dino working Christmas vacations planting barley. He started out riding the grain drills keeping seeding discs cleaned of moist peat, with Amerigo driving the tractor, to which later Dino graduated. "For my Dad, the name of the game was work, work, work. But because I loved it, I didn't see it that way." To the youngster, the Delta seemed romantic and exciting. Farming below water level meant that during times of high water, days and nights were spent in flood fights, protecting levee low spots with rows of three-high sandbags for 100-yard stretches

A Seminal Moment

Dino's love of farming grew, and so did his love of hunting and fishing on Wright Tract, where he could watch waves of pintails in 5,000-bird flocks wheeling above in stunning aerial displays. White-fronted geese, "specks" in today's parlance, inundated the island in flocks so large their atavistic calls awed the senses. "If you want to talk about seminal moments, I think routinely seeing so many ducks and geese, in numbers that most people today cannot conceive of-had a lot do with my love affair with the Delta," he said. "Observing nature's might and such huge numbers of waterfowl are visual memories I'll carry to my grave."

Getting Ahead

Years later, shortly after Dino and Joan's marriage, while working as a country buyer for a Stockton-based grain-trading firm, Dino began part-time farming, literally starting from scratch on rented land. By 1961 Cortopassi Farms was renting enough land to support full-time farming, which Dino continued to expand on farmlands northeast of Stockton. A decade later he was chosen as one of four Outstanding Young Farmer awardees by the U.S. Jaycees, a national leadership organization.

As the years went by, Cortopassi Farms grew and began to acquire small parcels of ag lands with mortgage debt. During those growth years, Dino continuously searched for the "why" of things, a habit learned from his mother, Teresa Avansino Cortopassi. The constant search for "why" provided Dino the impetus to see problems as opportunities to get ahead. While not all problems are opportunities, by constantly pushing the envelope, Cortopassi Farms continued to increase its capital base and expand its scope.

In addition to farming, Dino occasionally partnered with Fritz Grupe, his friend from college days at UC Davis. Their first deal was a mini-commercial property in Stockton north of Hammer Lane. "It was our first deal together, but I knew there would be more to come," Grupe recalled.

Later in the 1980's, Grupe was shopping to buy a trout-fishing ranch in Oregon on three miles of headwaters of the Williamson River, in which Dino volunteered to be a partner and bought a half interest with Fritz, sight-unseen. "That's how far back we've done habitat projects together," said Grupe.

Then they joined the Butte Ranch Duck Club together in the Sacramento Valley. Dino was ready to buy into the Wild Goose Club and urged Fritz to join with him. Fritz was leaning toward joining Butte Ranch and suggested he and Dino join at the same time. However, soon it became clear the Butte Ranch wetlands weren't being efficiently utilized and before long, Dino offered to relevel additional wetlands with equipment and manpower he brought up from Stockton. The other Butte Ranch members were reluctant to spend money, and finally, in frustration, they both left the Butte Ranch Club. Fritz joined the Greenhead Club and Dino the Wild Goose Club, both premiere duck clubs in the Butte Sink area east of Colusa.

At the Wild Goose, Dino was soon drawn to gamekeeper Gary Kerhoulas, who managed the club and had set the gold standard of professional, private wetland management. For his unprecedented accomplishments Kerhoulas would later be inducted into the California Waterfowler's Hall of Fame in 2012.

"Gary had deep knowledge developed from hands-on experience," Dino said. "He thought like a mallard duck, understood how to manipulate the proper timing and depths of water, how to provide food and cover for the birds-water grass and native plants, and state-of-the-art tree planting, and so much more." Dino said. "He was the champion of wetland management and the mentor from whom I chose to learn all I could about habitats. Each morning that we hunted together was like a seminar, with Gary teaching me about habitat, blind placement, and what ducks liked."

Recreating a Butte Sink Marsh

Dino's idea for doing something like the Black Hole Habitat was, in a sense, to teleport the look, feel, and behavior of a riparian Butte Sink mallard marsh into the Delta. Nobody, including Dan Nomellini, often called the "King of the

Delta Duck Hunters," could help him. Creating a riparian marsh consisting of trees, tules, and grasses had never been done before in the islands. The Delta had always been open water shooting focused on northern pintail rather than mallards.

Dino recalled his teen years when there were tons of northern pintail that Delta guys called "sprig." There were so many in fact that bag limits were too liberal for a species that decoyed easily.

"In the 1950's, when the Delta loaded up with sprig, I'd get in my pickup before high school, just me and my dog, travel to Wright Tract and jump into temporary barrel blinds held down with sand bags in the middle of flooded barley stubble. On good days I'd shoot a limit of cock sprig, no hens and no mallards, in time to make my second class!"

"All you had to do was stay concealed with plenty of white around the blind," Dino said. We often used folded newspapers for decoys. Like everyone else I blew a sprig whistle, but really didn't have to call at all. There were so many working birds soon they would be spiraling down to feed on waste barley left by the harvester."

Nomellini's most famous club, the Venice Island Duck Club, boasted a favorite hunting spot called "The Mallard Hole" that, simply described, was a deep-water honey hole, surrounded by tall, indigenous trees that attracted mallards without fail. But its creation was one of levee failure, not of natural design.

Dino explained, "The Venice Mallard Hole is one of blowouts that Venice Island experienced in its history. On Delta islands, there are a number of such "holes" created by a levee blowout that scoured out the peat down to sandy clay and created a deep pond surrounded by a ring of cottonwood and willow trees. That's where mallards congregate because riparian habitat is what mallards like. They love trees and screened protected areas."

Dino euphemistically calls mallards "Wild Bill" ducks because Wild Bill Hickok always sat with his back to a wall when playing poker, and that's what mallards like to do, sit with their backs protected by a tree line. "During my many years in the Butte Sink, mallard drakes became the noble duck to hunt, much more so than pintail," Dino said. "Mallard hunters need to be good callers, experts in decoy-placement, prepare well-hidden blinds that blend into the riparian habitat, and be patient at working wary greenheads into range."

Change of Mindset

When Dino began hurning greenies in the Butte Sink, it was like an epiphany. "I mean, you had to fool those greenheads," he said. "And, during my 25 years hunting the sink is when I really got focused onto riparian habitat, which led to the genesis of the Black Hole."

He also learned about the history of mallards in California, including the fact that the Sacramento Valley nests and grows most of its own mallards, more than 50 percent allowing hunters to bag locally grown birds. Scientific studies and banding data proved that reality.

Delta islands don't work the same way, because they only provide wintering habitat on massive sheet water spread atop peat soils. Most of the Delta's wintering ducks, including northern pintail, wigeon, and green-winged teal, nest in the prairies of Canada and mid-Western states, Alaska, and the boreal forests of the Northwest Territories. The Delta historically was a wintering habitat, not a nesting habitat, and, unlike the Sacramento Valley, raised very few mallards or other local-nesting ducks such as wood ducks.

Part of the Black Hole Habitat and its creation stemmed from Dino's yearning "to put something back." Reflecting on the number of ducks he had bagged in a lifetime, he decided to do something about it, something really big.

"When Dino said he wanted to do habitat work in the Delta, I never saw anyone with a passion like him," said Grupe, his old, partner and hunting buddy. "His love of the Delta is without parallel and when he sets his mind on doing something, it will be the best. He's a perfectionist, a visionary, and knows the way he wants something," Grupe continued. "He'll move a ditch a few yards, he's that much of a perfectionist and, I may add, not an easy person to work for. He doesn't tolerate fools. He's got the advantage of having earned the money to accomplish some amazing habitat work and combined with his passion, he does it right. If someone has more knowledge, he'll bring them in to get their ideas. He isn't a know-it-all. He doesn't mind trying a new idea and if it doesn't work out, he'll tweak it until it does work or toss it."

That's why the Black Hole Habitat is unique. By the way, the name "Black Hole" was coined by Grupe, who saw the habitat project as an unending hole in a Delta island into which money was poured, and persuaded Dino to name it that!

The Human/Nature Interface

[Editor's note: William Everson/Brother Antoninus is often associated with the "Beat" poets but his fascination with the environment of the Central Valley and his religious explorations set him apart. In these poems, he describes his sensitivity to the beauty of the Sacramento–San Joaquin River Delta landscape. These poems were published originally by New Directions in 1948 in a collection entitled *The Residual Years*. (*By permission*). See Fig. 48.]

William Everson, "San Joaquin"

This valley after the storms can be beautiful beyond the telling,
Though our city folk scorn it, cursing heat in the summer and
    drabness in winter,
And flee it: Yosemite and the sea.
They seek splendor, who would touch them must stun them;
The nerve that is dying needs thunder to rouse it.

I in the vineyard, in green-time and dead-time, come to it dearly,
And take nature neither freaked nor amazing,
But the secret shining, the soft indeterminate wonder,
I watch it morning and noon, the unutterable sundowns;
And love as the leaf does the bough.

William Everson, "The Dusk"

The light goes: that once powerful sun,
That held all steeples in its grasp,
Smokes on the western sea.
Under the fruit tree summer's vanishing residuum,
The long accumulation of leaf,
Rots in the odor of orchards.
Suddenly the dark descends,
As on the tule ponds at home the wintering blackbirds,
Flock upon flock, the thousand-membered,
In for the night from the outlying ploughlands,
Sweep over the willows,
Whirled like a net on the shadowy reeds,
All wings open.
It is late. And any boy who lingers on to watch them come in
Will go hungry to bed.
But the leaf-sunken years,
And the casual dusk, over the roofs in a clear October,
Will verify the nameless impulse that kept him out
When the roosting birds and the ringing dark
Dropped down together.

Paula Sheil, "Out the Gate"

[Editor's note: Paula Sheil teaches creative writing in Stockton and manages a community writing center. She is also an avid sailor. Here she explores the emotional interface between the Sacramento–San Joaquin River Delta and the San Francisco Bay. The orthography is the poet's. (*By permission*).]

plowing gently through Delta
        from the center to the sea
            rushing with the flood tide
            to the Golden Gate
                in merry anticipation
                for the bucking
                    breakers of the Bay
                        betting on not puking
                            my salami and cheese
                            pouring out of California
                            pulsing 'way in heartbeats

the drone of the engine
the scream of the gulls
beating my way out
of the Valley to the Bay
the sun flies a banner
across a faultless sky
my pirate friends tend
the helm and force our party
through the middle passage
passed the farms and levees
ignoring the vultures
and the solitary seal
nodding at the rip rap
and wondering what beavers eat
when there's no trees
a hemorrhage need
spilling out to the Bay
the gush of ocean is
big like dreams
big like love
big like death
all surrounding cold
out the Gate
to meet the maker.
join the joiner
hammer home the truth of water
the sharp wind of motion
moves through my nostrils
empties past my whistle
I am for blowing
a California melody
playing through the Gate

[Editor's note: Steven Federle teaches creative writing in Solano County. He has written many poems about the Sacramento–San Joaquin River Delta. These two emphasize two Sacramento San Joaquin River Delta bridges of which there are many. The bridges are one of the major human modifications to the Sacramento–San Joaquin River Delta environment. See his collection of poems on *poemhunter.com*. In each case, the bridge facilitates human presence, but also provides a fleeting vision of the threat nature represents. (*By permission*).]

Steven Federle, "Bridge at Montezuma Slough"

We drive to see
where the twisted road will lead.
Salty river, winding slough,
dark water
rising to frothy cap
slapping concrete pier,
moon driven waves race
back to beckoning bay.
Finally we must decide.
Cross the low bridge
or turn back.
But the flood is too close to the deck!
We feel tidal vibrations,
basso profundo,
rattle sub-sonic
in our ears
as together
we face our fear,
and slowly cross,
eyes always ahead
til again we feel sure earth
solid beneath our tread.

Steven Federle, "The Bridge at Rio Vista"

The bridge stands low
over the swollen
Sacramento,
black water,
rushing to
darker seas,
hypo-thermal,
sucking breath
from the fallen,
the overboard,
the suicide.
Its sturdy stanchions,
hold fast,
give refuge

from the maelstrom,
a way across
or a place
to jump

[Editor's note: Kati Short has been honored as the poet laureate of the city of Brentwood. Here reprinted with permission are two poems from a collection she edited, *In Mt. Diablo's Shadow* (San Ramon: Falcon Books, 2011). Both celebrate aspects of the suburban lifestyle available in the Sacramento–San Joaquin River Delta. They envision the Sacramento–San Joaquin River Delta environs as supportive of human life and sensibilities. (*By permission*).]

Carol Smith, "Stone Fruits"

It's summer in the Delta
And tolerating the summer heat with me are the
Delicious stone fruits, and my favorites are the
Apricots, particularly the Blenheims
With their fleeting season making them desirable
As memories of summer love.
Its summer in the Delta
When I can rise in the morning and jump
Into a pair of shorts and leap
Into my paddle boat, and if I have no
Pressing business, such as buying apricots,
Pedal all the way to China.
An improbable notion
Nevertheless, an interesting option at my age
Jumping or leaping into anything
Whether shorts or boat
But not impossible, and I could bring along
A large bag of apricots.
It's summer in the Delta,
And I digress from the point of this poem:
The stone fruits that I love, especially the apricots.
And who's to say I couldn't jump
Into my paddle boat and pedal all the way
To China?
Even at
my age.

Kati Short, "My Brentwood"

He brought me through golden hills,
I came from emerald green ones
He brought me to the edge of the middle of nowhere
I came from a crowded place, there was no solitude anywhere
He brought me to a town with eighteen thousand folks at most
I came from a city of thirteen million souls at least.

His house became my house,
His Brentwood took longer to become my town.
I missed what had been my home,
yet from the beginning was enchanted by downtown:
The fountain, the trees at night,
the smell of the cherry blossoms, the charm of the picture show
The little shops with friendly keepers, the library in the park,
the gazebo, the roses,
the bike lanes and paths where we could ride in safety
all were part of my conversion.

Brentwood folks smile and say hi,
where I came from we bowed
I relearned to smile and it felt good.
Then from the soul of this small town an energetic arts network
emerged and drew me to it.
For years I thought I'd lost my niche,
but my Brentwood showed me
where to carve a new one.
Our town pulled me into it and made itself mine.
Brentwood has become home.

Alyssa Langworthy, "Delta"

[Editor's note: Alyssa Sierra Langworthy is a queer storyteller born and raised in Stockton, California. She is a founding member of the With Our Words Youth Poetry Collective and is an alumna of the Brave New Voices, International Youth Poetry Slam. After earning her BA in Critical Gender Studies and Communications from UC San Diego and spending a decade in Southern California, Alyssa has returned to the Central Valley to continue her work as a teaching artist, performance poet, and healer. Her poem "Delta" expresses the tensions inherent in the urban Sacramento–San Joaquin River Delta. (*By permission*).]

I am a resident of Stockton, California
the southern sister of Sacramento
the baby cousin of the bay area
that was standard reply number one five years ago
When I was eleven
When it was 2005
And George W. Bush was 9 months into the second term of a presidency
He shouldn't have even won in the 1st place
and Katrina wrecked Louisiana's 9th ward
Her levees broken like the wings of a fallen angel
Disaster sounded like a drowning jazz band
Like I said that was the standard reply five years ago
And is still widely acceptable today
Because no one knows the San Joaquin Valley
Bakersfield, Fresno, Merced, Modesto, Manteca,
Stockton
We feed you
20 million tons of your produce is produced within my home soil
Fertile like 17 year old baby daddies without a condom
The delta, the heart of my city is soon to be broken
Like teenage hearts
after broken condoms lead to pregnancies which lead to broken futures
Like broken levees lead to broken economies which lead to broken futures

Fast-forward five years
And you will know us as Katrina's big bitch of a sister
She may have been spinning sorrow and pain through the center of her eye
but she was solo suicide
and we have Columbine and Virginia Tech double-helixed into our spines
Weston Ranch is on the south side; built damn near entirely on levees
And is predominantly populated by african-american people
So every fall we play Russian roulette
Dodging droplets like bullet shots on the east side,
The north side, where crimson Nortenos and cobalt Surenos beat and box
purple rhythms into
    each other's skin
The west side where Bloods and Crips turn streets into blood flooded crypts
Except nobody cares when a population is killing itself
But I know for damn sure you sure will care
If you don't get your strawberries, cherries, almonds, walnuts, broccoli
Or any of the other dozen crops we grow in the San Joaquin Valley
Our levees are slowly crumbling with age

Like the bones of grandmothers
Letting paranoia seep through like raindrops with each storm
They were supposed to fix this
They told us change was gonna come
These past five years we've waited
Hoping that change doesn't look like death.
Doesn't taste like water logged street corner fruit stands

We are praying that change will not sound like submerged suburbs
Hoping that thunder won't boom like god's pistol, spraying precipitation like
bullets
When his skies open up and pour
Because I don't know if FEMA will help either
Our crops aren't predisposed to endure a single day of disaster,
let alone sit underwater for three
I don't wanna live in the next New Orleans
Katrina deserves to be an only child
We don't have to be her bitch of a sister
We are the southern sister of Sacramento; baby cousin to the Bay Area
A fat, violent, miserable city
Home of the foreclosure crisis
And I would rather keep it that way
… I would rather keep it that way …

16

Dreams of the Future

[Editor's note: In what has gone before, authors have reacted to the Sacramento– San Joaquin River Delta as it is more than as it might be. These last two selections explore what the future might hold for the region. Jane Wolff is a professor of landscape architecture. She reviews the history of the Sacramento–San Joaquin River Delta and concludes that one possible future is a return to nature, the recreation of a "wild" space between Northern California's urban and agricultural geometries. Her vision is in keeping with the impulse of the environmental movement to return threaten landscape to the control of natural processes. Ursula Le Guin, the well-known science fiction writer, developed unique view in her final novel, *Always Coming Home*. She envisions a world after a great calamity hits Northern California. After the destruction of San Francisco, there is a return to village life. Here survivors trade and develop interrelationship not unlike those formed by native peoples before Europeans came to California. The short story included here is embedded in a novel that is organized as a collection of anthropological materials; taken together, these materials sketch the culture of a new Sacramento–San Joaquin River Delta society. Le Guin's parents were anthropologists and wrote extensively on the native peoples of the region. In many ways, what Le Guin offers is a return to the values that her parents discovered among those who first inhabited California.]

Jane Wolff, from *Delta Primer, A Field Guide to the California Delta*

[Editor's note: Jane Wolff, *Delta Primer: A Field Guide to the California Delta* (San Francisco, William Stout, 2003), pp. 37–44. (*By permission*). See Fig. 49.]

If you stood in the middle of one of the islands in the Sacramento-San Joaquin Delta, where the Great Central Valley of California drains into San Francisco Bay, you might not know that you were twenty feet below sea level. You might not realize that the rational agricultural geometry around you ended abruptly at the meandering river on the island's edge. You might not understand that the ditches running through the fields were dug for drainage rather than irrigation. You might not think that there was anything strange about the Delta until you saw an ocean going freighter cruise by in the distance, eighty miles from the Golden Gate and fifteen feet above your head. If you climbed to the top of the levee that separates the island from the river, though, you would see land and water together, and then you might wonder how the landscape became such a paradox.

A History of Unexpected Consequences

In 1850 the Delta was still wild. A tidal marsh, it consisted of low-lying islands among the distributary channels of California's two great rivers, the Sacramento and the San Joaquin. It moved, water levels were a landscape in flux: river channels varied, and land flooded and dried out with changes in the seasons and the tides. The history of its dilemmas begins in that year, when Congress passed the Swamp and Overflowed Lands Act and made marshlands available for settlement on the condition that they were reclaimed for agriculture. The act specified small holdings and prohibited the resale of land. Claims were made, but reclamation at the scale of the small farm was difficult. After legal changes in the late 1860s ended the limits on parcel size and consolidation, groups of investors accumulated large tracts of land and undertook the Delta's wholesale reclamation.

The early settlers built low levees around the islands to stop seasonal flooding, and they drained and cultivated the interiors. These interventions had an unforeseen result: the land began to sink. The region's peat soils were extremely fertile, but they were unstable. The peat oxidized when tilling exposed it to air, and it blew away as it dried out. The ground began to subside at a rate of several inches year.

To compensate, farmers made the levees higher and stronger. Starting in the late 19th century, they used the clamshell dredger, developed in the Delta, to move alluvial material from the river channels to the levees. The fortification of the levees had its own unanticipated effect; the rivers began to rise. Because they eliminated flood plain, the levees increased the volume of water in the river channels during the rainy season. The channels began to silt up with the alluvial sediment that had formerly replenished the surface of the islands, and the level of water in the rivers rose even when they weren't flooding. Hydraulic mining in the Sierra Nevada sent huge amounts of soil and rock into the Delta and made the channel bottoms still higher. Flooding became a constant threat rather than a seasonal one.

As the scale of cultivation increased, the infrastructure needed to support it became more extreme. The land fell so low that groundwater had to be pumped up and out of the fields. Levees required constant repairs and additions to compensate for shrinkage, cracking, and damage caused by hydro-static pressure. Engineering was not able to create stasis in the fluctuating systems of the Delta; each intervention had consequences that made new interventions necessary. The landscape became a hybrid of cultural intention and natural process, and the line between nature and artifice grew more and more difficult to draw.

The Multiplication of Complexity

The Delta is a rural landscape, but the transformation of its geography over the last 150 physical geo-years has been closely connected to cities. Urban capital and urban markets drove reclamation and the subsidence it produced. Building levees was expensive, and many reclamation projects were funded by consortia of investors. The large scale land ownership needed to make reclamation feasible meant that the region was never characterized by subsistence agriculture. By the 1870s farming was being carried out at a commercial scale: early vegetables were sold in central California towns; peaches, pears, livestock, hay, and dairy products were sent to San Francisco; and after the completion of the transcontinental rail lines, fruit was exported to markets in the East.

By the late 19th century the economic agenda for the Delta had expanded, and the consequences of human intervention had multiplied. Commercial fisheries introduced striped bass and American shad in the 1870s and 1880s, and these exotic species began to compete with natives. The transport of goods to market also complicated the region's ecology. Invasive species were inadvertently brought to the Delta in the ballast water of ships; since 1933, when the Stockton Deep Water Channel was completed, ocean going boats carrying organisms from other ecosystems have been able to cruise as far as ninety miles inland from the Golden Gate.

After World War II, the Delta became the centerpiece of the infrastructure that supplies water to Southern California. The large scale export of water from the Delta began in 1951, when the Delta-Mendota Canal opened. Funded by the Federal government, its purpose was to provide irrigation water for the Central Valley. An ancillary installation, the Delta Cross Channel, was built to carry water across the Delta and toward giant pumps that fed the canal. In

1973 the State of California opened another canal, the California Aqueduct, to take water from the Delta to Los Angeles and San Diego. It had its own pumping plant; next to the pumps, a new forebay allowed sediment to settle out of the water before it was sent to the south.

The export canals transformed the meaning of the Delta's rivers. They had been local transportation systems for farmers and produce, and they became the center of a giant plumbing network extending for hundreds of miles and serving distant constituencies. Water export changed the rivers' ecology, too. Sending vast amounts of water to the canals instead of the ocean allowed salt water from San Francisco Bay to migrate upstream. The force of the pumping changed the direction and quantity of water flow significantly enough to confuse the native fish that migrate through the region. Instead of swimming toward the ocean they went into the pumps, and their population began to decline dramatically.

Unlike the consequences of earlier interventions, the changes wrought by water export provoked conflict. Water export threatened the farmers in the Delta; salty water in the rivers would produce salty groundwater in the soil, and land could quickly become unfit for cultivation. It also mobilized environmentalists, who were concerned about its devastating effects on native species.

The conflict produced new institutions and new management strategies. Local agencies were chartered in the Delta to negotiate with the Department of Water Resources about water quality. New measures were developed to protect endangered species. Enormous screens were installed to remove fish from the mouth of the pumps. A protocol was developed to identify, count, measure, and record the collected fish; to take them in specially adapted tanker trucks across the Delta to a point just above the mouth of the Sacramento, out of reach of the pumps; and to put them back into the river. Even this well organized, highly choreographed strategy has had unexpected consequences, though. The striped bass that were introduced for fishing follow the schedule and location of the fish drops. They wait for the trucks, and they eat the fish that have just been rescued from the pumps. So far nothing has been done about this development. Measures that could eliminate the exotic predators would also destroy the native species whose welfare is legal mandate.

Disputed Territory

All of the powerful and conflicting forces that are shaping the California landscape today converge in the Delta: suburban development, environmental politics, the changing economics of agriculture, and the endless demand for water.

The range of people who want something from the Delta has grown to include: local farmers; farmers in the Central Valley; ecologists and environmental activists; boaters, fishermen, windsurfers, birdwatchers, hunters, and other recreational users; suburban developers in the cities and towns that ring the Delta; and the inhabitants of Southern California. Their goals for the landscape are different; they understand it in different ways; and they imagine its future differently. The fault lines among the Delta's constituents are complicated, variable, and sometimes counterintuitive. They do not fall according to simple boundaries: urban interests against rural interests, for instance, or water exporters versus water conservers, or local constituencies against distant ones; and they shift from case to case.

One source of dissent is water use. Some groups depend on keeping as much water in the rivers as possible, and others want to maximize exports. Delta farmers need enough fresh water in the rivers to keep the salt water of San Francisco Bay out of the groundwater that runs through and below the land, and environmentalists and ecologists want sufficient flows to support native plant and animal species. On the other side, farmers in the San Joaquin Valley irrigate their crops using water from the Delta, and the expanding cities of Southern California demand more and more water, especially as their right to Colorado River supplies is challenged by states upstream.

Conflicts also arise over land use and management. Farmers in the Delta want to stay in business, but environmentalists propose to turn prime agricultural land into nature preserves, water engineers suggest flooding subsided islands to create reservoirs, and suburban developers are active all the way around the region's perimeter. Delta farmers and ecologists struggle with boaters and jet-skiers, but for different reasons. The wake from the boats and skis erodes the levees that the farmers must maintain, and the fuel additives emitted by two-stroke engines are harmful to flora and fauna. Such alliances shift with respect to different questions, though. For instance, farmers advocate the dredging of river channels to reduce flood hazards, but environmental legislation severely restricts dredging because it increases sediment in the water and harms fish.

In 1994, state and Federal agencies formed a consortium called CALFED to negotiate the Delta's contested future. CALFED's contradictory mandate is to meet the increasing demand for water in Southern California and to maintain and enhance environmental quality in the Delta. Its advisory board crosses the spectrum of groups with interests in the Delta: the Central Delta Water Agency, Ducks Unlimited, the Natural Resources Defense Council, the Paskenta Band of Nomlaki Indians, the United Farm Workers of America, the Pacific Coast Federation of Fishermen's Association, the California Farm Bureau Federation, the City of West Sacramento, the Bay Institute, the Inland Empire Utilities Agency, the Metropolitan Water Agency, and the Kern County Water District of Southern California comprise only partial list.

CALFED has entertained a wide range of proposals. One was to flood subsided islands to make a reservoir and wetland system that would run through the middle of the Delta; another was to build a canal that would carry water around the edge of the Delta rather than through it. It was impossible to reach consensus on the more radical strategies, and the group has decided on a program that simply makes adjustments to the current situation. No one's goals are truly satisfied. Local interests are concerned that limits have not been set for export, but water exporters believe that the system does not guarantee adequate supply. Chances are good that the current plan will change.

There is no end game in the Delta. The cost and difficulty of maintaining the region's infrastructure are only increasing. On the other hand, if the levees fail and the region is inundated, salt water from San Francisco Bay will migrate upstream. Giving up the struggle would mean losing things that society wants from the landscape: fertile agricultural land, the remnants of a unique ecosystem, and, not least, the water supply for nearly two thirds of California. Management is not a question, but how the landscape should be managed, and to what end, are fiercely contested topics. The outcome is likely to be determined through a public process.

New Nature?

In 1860 what people in cities wanted from the Delta was produce. In 1960, it was water. Today it is something less tangible: the illusion of nature. That illusion is being made by an improbable concurrence of interests: CALFED is offering funding for ecosystem restoration as a condition of water export, and so environmental groups have allied themselves with constituencies in the southern part of the state. In a certain way, the alliance is not so strange. Like the increasing demand for water, the desire for nature is a product of urbanization. As cities expand, that longing becomes more urgent: the homogeneous suburban mat becomes more oppressive, and wild places (or even places that look wild) are harder and harder to find. The interest environmentalists have in protecting endangered fish is not exactly the same as the one that Los Angeles has in obtaining water, but like all of the positions advocated by the Delta's constituents, it assumes that people can and should determine an agenda for the landscape.

To make new nature, subsided land is taken out of agricultural production and native wetland plants are grown instead. CALFED is currently studying the purchase of one of the largest of these efforts, which will transform four very low lying agricultural islands in the middle of the Delta. Two of the islands will become wetland areas and two will become reservoirs that can compensate for seasonal differences in the availability of water. Beyond that, new nature may help to make development at the Delta's perimeter possible: developers in nearby cities and suburbs have proposed to pay for wetlands projects in the Delta to fulfill legal requirements for environmental mitigation.

New nature does not imply freedom from human control. It depends completely on the levee system built to overcome wilderness: without the levees, the Delta's subsided islands would flood. Giving up control would make the Delta into a wild inland sea completely unlike the landscape that existed before reclamation.

It is possible to see unmanaged nature in the Delta. It exists at Franks Tract, a former island that was reclaimed for agriculture and cultivated until 1938. That year the levee was breached and the land behind it flooded. Because the cost of repairing the breach and pumping the land dry again was prohibitive, the island remained inundated. Wind created waves strong enough to erode the levee from inside, where it was not reinforced, and it deteriorated into small fragments overgrown with cattails and tules. The island has become an open lake with enough erosive force to threaten the levees that protect neighboring farmland. Its agricultural past is under water, and the marshy ecosystem that preceded it is irrevocably lost.

What Next?

There are 32 million people in California now. If the population continues to grow at its present rate there will be 50 million people in 2025. The more people there are, the more complicated their agendas for the Delta will be. The negotiation of their competing desires is likely to transform the landscape, and what happens will have a powerful effect on the economy and ecology of the whole state.

Most of the 20 million people who depend on the Delta today don't even know that it exists, and conventional planning is not educating them about what's at stake. There are many threats to the Delta's future, but the greatest one is its invisibility.

Ursula Le Guin, "The Trouble with the Cotton People"

[Editor's note: Le Guin, U., "The Trouble with the Cotton People (Written by Grey Bull of the Obsidian of Telina-na, as part of an offering to his beyimas.)" in *Always Coming Home, Expanded Edition* (New York: Library of America, 2019), pp. 164–176. (*By permission*). See Fig. 50.]

When I was a young man there was trouble with the people who send us cotton from the South in trade for our wines. We were putting our good wines on the train every spring and autumn, clear Ganais and dark Berrena, Mes from Ounmalin, and Sweet Betebbes they like down there, all good wines, selected because they travel well, and shipped in the best oak casks. But they had begun sending us short-staple, seedy cotton, full of tares, in short-weight bales. Then one year they sent half in bales and the rest stuff already woven; some of it fair sheeting weight, but some of it sleazy, or worse.

That year was the first I went to Sed, with my teacher in the Cloth Art, Soaring of the Obsidian of Kastoha-na. We went down with the wine and stayed at the inn at Sed, a wonderful place for seafood and general comfort. She and the Wine Art people had an argument with the foreigners, but it got nowhere, because the people who had brought the cotton to Sed said they were just middlemen; they hadn't sent the lousy cotton, they just loaded and unloaded it and sailed the ships that carried it and took the wine back South. The only person there, they said, who was actually from the cotton people, wasn't able to speak any language anybody else spoke. Soaring dragged him over to the Sed Exchange, but he acted as if he'd never heard of TOK; and when she tried to get a message through the Exchange to the place the cotton came from, nobody answered.

The Wine Art people were glad she was there, since they would have taken the sleazy without question and sent all the good wine they had brought in return. She advised them to send two-thirds of the usual shipment, and no Sweet Betebbes at all, and to take the rest back home and wait to hear from the cotton people. She refused to load the sleazy stuff onto the train, so they put it back into the ships. The ship people said as they didn't care, so long as they got their usual share of the wine from us for doing the shipping. Soaring wanted to cut that amount, too, to induce the ship people to pay attention to the quality their cargo; but the other Valley traders said that was unfair, or unwise; so we gave the sailors a half carload, as usual, all Sweet Betebbes.

When we came home there was discussion among the Cloth and Wine Arts and the Finders Lodge and the councils and interested people of several towns, and some of us said: "Nobody from the Valley has been to that place where the cotton comes from for forty or fifty years. Maybe some people from should go there, and talk with those people." The others agreed with that.

So, after waiting awhile to see if the cotton people would send a message on the Exchange when they got their sleazy back and less wine than usual, we set out, four of us: myself, because I wanted to go, and knew something about cotton and fabrics; and three Finders Lodge people, two who had done a lot of trading and had been across the Inland Sea more than once, and one who wanted to keep up the Finders' maps of the places we were going. They were named Patience, Peregrine (Yestik, the peregrine falcon, is a common Finders name) and Gold. We were all men and all young. I was the youngest. I had come inland the year before with a Blue Clay girl, but when I said I was going to the end of the Inland Sea she said I was crazy and irresponsible, and put my books and bedding out on the landing. So I left from my mother's house.

I had been busy learning with the Cloth Art and had not given much thought to joining the Finders Lodge, but the trip to Sed had made me want to travel more, and I knew I had a gift for trading. I saw no reason to be ashamed of it. I have never cared much what people say. So I went as a novice of that Lodge, both a traveler and a trader.

In the books I read and the stories I heard as a kid, the Finders were always travelers, traders, and they were generally on snowy peaks in the Range of Light singing to the bears or getting toes frozen off or rescuing each other from chasms. The Finders I was with appeared not to favor that style of travel. We rode the Amaranth Train sleeping car all the way down the line to Sed, and stayed at the inn there again, eating like ducks in a slug patch, while we asked around about ships and boats.

Nobody was sailing south. We could get a ship going across the East Coast, to Rekwit, sometime in the month; or as soon as we liked, a boat would take us across the Gate to the Falares Islands. From either Rekwit or the Falares we could try to find a coaster going South, or else go on foot down the inner side of the mountains. The Finders decided the chances were better on the west side, and that we should cross the Gate.

I sorry when l saw the boat.

It was about fifteen feet long with a little farting engine and one sail. The tidal currents run in and out the Gate faster than a horse at a gallop, they say, and the winds the same. The boat's people were skinny and white with fishy eyes: Falares Islanders. They talked enough TOK that we could understand one another. They had been in Sed to trade fish for grain and brandy. They sailed those little boats way out west of the Gate, out on the open ocean, fishing. They were always saying, "Ho, ha, go out to big waves, ha, yes?" and slapping my back while I was throwing up over the edge of the boat.

A north wind was coming up, and by the time we were out in the middle of the water of the Gate the waves were getting very steep and hard, like bright little cliffs. The boat climbed up and dropped down and jerked and slapped. Then the low fog that had been lying over the Inland Sea, which I had taken for distant land, blew and faded away in a few moments, and there a hundred miles to the east of us was the Range of Light, the far glitter of the peaks of snow.

Underneath the boat there, Patience told me, the bottom of the sea was all buildings. In the old times outside the world the Gate was farther west and narrower, and all its shores and the countries inland were covered with houses. I have heard the same thing told in the Madrone Lodge since then, and there's the song about the old souls. It is no doubt true, but I had no wish at the time to go down and verify it, though the harder the wind blew the likelier it seemed that we were about to do that. I was too bewildered, however, to be really frightened. With no earth to be seen but those tiny white sawteeth half over the world's curve, and the hard, bright sun and wind and water, it was a good deal like being dead already, I thought.

When the next day we finally got ashore onto one of the Falares Islands, the first thing I felt was lust. I got a big, long hard-on, and couldn't turn my mind from it. The Falares women all looked beautiful, and I had such mindless desires that I was really worried.

I got alone, with some difficulty, and masturbated, but it didn't help. Finally, I told Peregrine about it, and he was decent enough not to laugh. He said it had to do with the sea. We talked about living on the coast, being chaste, and coming inland, when you stop being chaste, and all that may be reversal-language. Sex is always turning things around and upside down. He said he didn't know why being on the sea then coming ashore had that particular effect, but he had noticed it himself. I said I felt as if I'd come back to life with a vengeance. At any rate, a couple of days eating what the Falares people eat cured me. All the women began to look like seaweed, and all I wanted was to go on somewhere else, even on a boat.

They weren't doing any sailing down the inland coast at that time of the year, but were all going out on the ocean for the big fish. But they were generous people, and some of them said they would take us along the inland coast as a place they called Tuburhuny, where one of them had family living. We had to get off the island somehow, so we accepted, although we weren't sure where Tuburhuny was. The Falares people chart the seas, but not the lands, and none of our place names seemed to fit with theirs. But anything on the South Peninsula suited us.

When we sailed south the weather was quiet and the fog low. The fog never lifted. We passed a few rocks and islands, and around midday, passing a long, low one, the Falares people said, "City." We couldn't see much of it in the fog; it looked like bare rock and some yerba buena and beach grass and a couple of tall, slender towers or masts supported by guywires. The Falares people carried on about it: "You touch, you die!" and they acted out electrocution or asphyxiation or getting struck by lightning. I never heard any such thing about the Cities, but I had never seen one before, or since. Whether it was true, or they were having one of their little jokes with us, or they are superstitious, I don't know. They are certainly rather undereducated and out of touch, on those islands in the fog; they never use the Exchange at Sed, as if it too were dangerous. They are timid people, except on water.

Tuburhuny turned out to be called Gohop on our maps, a little town a short way south of the northern tip of the Peninsula on the inland side. It was sheltered from the everlasting fog of the Gate. Avocadoes grew all over town, and they were just coming ripe when we were there. How they there could stay thin, I don't know, but they were thin, and whitish, like the Falares people; but not quite so much out on the edge of things. They were glad to talk to travelers, and helped Gold plan our trip on his maps. They had no boats going out any distance, and said none came by their little port regularly so we set off south on foot.

The Peninsular Range between the ocean and the Inland Sea is so buckled up by earthquakes and subsidences and so deeply scored by faults and rifts that walking the length of it is like crossing a forest by climbing up every tree you come to and then back down. There was usually no way around. Sometimes we could walk along the beaches, but in many places, there wasn't any beach; the mountains dropped sheer into the Sea. So we would plod up and up, clear to the ridge, and from there we saw the ocean on our right and the sea to our left and ahead and behind the land falling away in fold after fold forever. As we went farther south there were more long, narrow sounds and inlets in the faults, and it was hard to know whether we were following the main ridge or had got onto a hogback between two rifts, in which case we would end up on a headland staring at the water, and would have to go back ten or fifteen miles and start over. Nobody knew how old the maps we had were; they were from the Exchange, sometime or other, but they were out of date. Mostly there was nobody to ask directions of but sheep. The human people lived down in the canyons with the water and the trees. They weren't used to strangers, and we were careful not to alarm them.

In that part of the world the young men, late adolescents and older, often form groups and go out and live a hunting life, like our Bay Laurel Lodge, but less responsibly. The bands are allowed to fight each other, and to raid each other and any town except the one they came from, taking tools or food or animals or whatever they want. Those raids lead to killings, of course, sometimes; and some of the men never come back and settle down, but stay out in the hills as forest living people, and some of them are crazy and kill for the sake killing. The townspeople make a lot of fuss about these wild men of theirs, and live in fear of them; and so the four of us, young men and strangers, had to behave with notable propriety and good manners even at a distance, so as not to be mistaken for marauders or murderer.

Once they saw we were harmless they were generous, talkative, giving us anything they thought we wanted. Most of their towns were small, pleasant places with wood-beamed adobe houses stuccoed white, shaded by avocado trees. They all stayed in town all year, because a family would not be safe from the bands of young men in a summerhouse; but they said they used to go to summerhouses, and it's only in the last couple of generations that the young men have gotten irresponsible. They seemed to me foolish to let such an imbalance occur and continue, but perhaps they had some reason for it. The different peoples of those many canyons speak several different languages, but their towns and way of life were pretty much all alike. There were always people in the towns who could use TOK, so we could converse. At one of their Exchanges we sent messages to the Wakwaha Exchange to tell the Finders and our households that all was well with us, so far.

Towards the inner base of the Peninsula the ridges flatten down into a hot, sandy country, not lived in by human people, which runs two full days to the southwest coasts of the Inland Sea. The beaches are broad and low, with sea marshes and dunes and brackish, boggy lakes inland for miles; farther south, steep, desolate mountains run between east and west. The Inland Sea along that coast is very shallow, crowded with sandbars and islands, and on those islands, is where they grow the cotton.

The cotton people call themselves Usudegd. There are a lot of them, some thousands, living on the islands and at places on the coast where rivers come down from the mountains; they have salt water everywhere, but not much fresh. The sea is warm there, and it is warm country, though nothing like so hot, they say, as across those desolate mountains on the shores of the Omorn Sea. There are some severely poisoned areas in their country, but since it's so dry the stuff stays put in the ground, and they know where not to go.

Across the Inland Sea in the northeast the cotton people look up to that tall peak of the Range Light which we call South Mountain and Old Lion Mountain. Usually all one can see is the murk from the volcanoes south of it. It is important in their thoughts, but they never go to it. They say it is sacred, and its paths are not to be walked. But what about the Gongon people, who live all around South Mountain? That sort of idea is typical cotton people. They are not reasonable about some things.

It is my opinion that people who have too much to do with the sea, and use boats great deal, have their minds affected by it.

At any rate, their towns are different from the towns of the Peninsular peoples.

The cotton people dig in and build underground, with only a couple of feet of wall above ground for windows, like a heyimas. The roof is a low dome covered with sod, so from any distance you don't see a town, but a patch of hummocks. In among the roofs are all kinds of shrubs, trees, and vines they have down there; palm, avocado, big orange and lemon and grapefruit trees, carob and date, the same kinds of eucalyptus we have, and some I never saw before, are some of their trees. The vines flower splendidly, the trees make shade above ground and the houses stay cool underground; the arrangement looks odd, but is reasonable. They have no problems draining their houses, as we do our heyimas, because it's so dry there; though when it rains sometimes it rains hard, and they get flooded out, they said.

Their sacred places are some distance outside the towns, and are artificial mountains, hillocks with ritual paths round around them, and beautiful small buildings or enclosures on top. We didn't mess with any of that. Patience said it was best to keep clear out of foreigners' sacred places until invited into them. He said one reason he liked the Amaranth people, with whom he had stayed several times, was that they had no sacred places at all. People tend to get testy about those places.

But the cotton people were already testy. Although they hadn't replied or sent any message on the Exchange, they were angry that we had sent back their woven goods and hadn't sent the usual amount of wine, and right away we were in trouble there. All we had to do was say we had come from the Valle of the Na and the hornets began to buzz.

We had to get into one of their boats, flat things that felt very unsafe, and go out to the most important island. As soon as we got on the water, though it was entirely calm and smooth I got sick again. I have a very delicate sense of balance and the unsteadiness of boats affects my inner ear, the cotton people had no understanding of this at all. The Falares Islanders had made jokes about it, but the cotton people were contemptuous and rude.

We passed many large islands, and the cotton people kept pointing, saying, "Cotton, cotton. See the cotton? Everybody knows we grow the best cotton. People north as Crater Lake know it! Look at that cotton," and so on. The cotton fields were not very impressive at that time of year, but we nodded and smiled and behaved with admiration and propriety, agreeing with everything they said.

After coasting miles along a flat-island, we turned northeast and landed on a small island with a good view of the mountains, all the south end of the Range of Light and the bare, raw Havil Range in the south. The whole island was a town, hundreds of hummock roofs, some of them turfed, others naked sand, trees and bushes in patterns among the hummocks, and flowerbeds, also in patterns, with little paths between and through. They are strong on paths, down there, but you have to know which ones are to be walked on.

We had been travelling all that day and thirty days before it, and it was sunset by the time we landed on this island, but they hardly stopped to give us dinner before they took us straight into the town council meeting. And there they hardly said anything polite or appropriate about our having coming all that way to talk with them before they started saying "Where's the Sweet Betebbes?" and "Why did you send our goods back? Do we not have an agreement, made sixty years ago? Every year since then it has been honored and renewed, until this year! Why have you of the Wally broken your word?" They spoke good TOK, but they always said Wally for Valley, whine for wine.

Patience knew what he was doing when he took his middle name. He listened to them endlessly and remained alert, yet never frowned, nodded, or shook his head. Peregrine, Gold, and I imitated him as well as we could.

After a great many of them had said their say, a little woman stood up, and a little man beside her. They both had twisted bodies and humped backs, and looked both young and old. One of them said, "Let our guests have a word now," and the other said, "Let the Whine People speak." They had authority, those little twins. The others all shut up like clams.

Patience let there be silence for some while before he spoke, and when he spoke his voice was grave and soft, so they had to stay quiet to hear what he said. He was cautious and polite. He said a lot about the fitness of the agreement and its admirable age and convenience, and the unsurpassed quality of Usudegd cotton, known to be the best cotton from Crater Lake to the Omorn Break, from the Ocean Coast to the Range of Heaven, he got fairly eloquent in here, then he quieted down again and spoke a little sadly about how Time blunts the keenest knife and changes the meaning of words and the thoughts in human minds, so that finally the firmest knot must be retied, and the sincerest word spoken once again. And then he sat down.

There was silence. I thought he had awakened reason in them and they would agree at once. I was very young. The same woman who had talked the most before, got up and said, "Why didn't you send forty barrels of Sweet Betebbes whine like always before?"

I saw that the difficult part was only beginning. Patience had to answer that question and also say why we had sent back their woven goods. For a long time, he didn't. He kept talking in metaphors and images, and skirting around the issues; and after a while the little twisty twins began answering him the same way. And then, before anything that meant much had been said, it was so late they called the meeting off for the night, and finally took us to an empty house where could get some sleep. There was no heating, and one tiny electric light. The beds stood up on legs, and were lumpy.

It went on like that for three more days. Even Patience said he hadn't expected them to go on arguing, and that probably the reason they argued so much was that they were ashamed of something. If so, it was our part not to shame them further. So we could not say anything about the poor quality of the raw cotton for the last several years, or even about the sleazy they had tried to foist off on us. We just stayed calm and sad and said that indeed we regretted not shipping the sweet wine which we grew especially for them, but said nothing about why we had not shipped it. And sure enough, little by little it came out that they had had a lot of bad things happen in the last five years: a cotton leaf virus mutation that was hard to control, and three years of drought, and a set of unusually severe earthquakes that had drowned some of their islands and left the water on others too saline even for their hardy cotton. All these things they seemed to consider their own fault, things to be ashamed of. "We have walked in the wrong paths!" they kept saying.

Patience, and Peregrine, who also spoke for us, never said anything about these troubles of theirs, but began talking about troubles we had had in the Valley. They had to exaggerate a good deal, because things had been going particularly well for the winemakers, and the fourth and fifth years before had been great vintages of both Ganais and Fetali; but in any kind of farming there are always troubles enough to talk about. And the more they told or invented about unseasonable frosts, unsuccessful fermentations, the more the cotton people went on about their own troubles, until they had told everything. They seemed relieved, then, and they gave us much nicer house to stay in, well-lighted and warm, with little paths all marked out with white shells and Fumo balls [Author's note: Fumo is a word for concretions, usually whitish or yellowish, of ancient industrial origin, of nearly the same specific gravity as ice. There are fumo belts in certain parts of the oceans and some beaches are almost entirely composed of small particles of fumso.]

And last, they began to renegotiate the contract. It had taken Patience seven days to get them to do that. When got down to it at last, it was very simple. The terms were about the same as they had been, with more room for negotiation each year through the Exchange. Nothing was said about why they hadn't used the Exchange to explain their behavior earlier. They were still touchy and unreasonable if you said the wrong thing. We said that we would accept short-staple until they had the long staple in quantity again, and we would send a double quantity of Sweet Betebbes with the spring shipment; however, underweight bales would be refused, and we did not want woven goods, since we preferred to make our own. There was trouble on this point. The woman with the thirst for Sweet Betebbes got poisonous about it, and went on for hours about the quality and beauty of the fabrics of Usudegd. But by now Patience and the little twisty twins were friends of the heart; and the contract at last was spoken for cotton in the bale only, no fabrics.

After speaking the contract, we stayed on nine days more, for politeness, and because Patience and the twins were drinking together. Gold was busy with his maps notes, Peregrine, a person whom everybody everywhere liked, was always talking with townspeople or going off in boats with them to other islands. The boats were little better than bundles of tule reeds. I generally hung around with some young women who are weavers there. They had some fine mechanical looms, solar-powered, that I made notes on for my teacher, Soaring, and also, they were kind and friendly. Patience warned me that it's better not to have a relation of sex with people in foreign countries until you know a good deal about their customs and expectations concerning commitment, marriage, contraception, and so on. So I just flirted and did some kissing. The cotton women kissed with their mouths wide open, which is surprising if you aren't expecting and disagreeably wet, but very voluptuous; which was trying, under the circumstances.

Peregrine came back from another island one day with a queer expression. He said, "We've been fooled, Patience!"

Patience just waited, as usual.

Peregrine explained: he had met, in a town on one of the northernmost islands, some of the sailors of the ships that had brought the cotton to Sed and taken our wine back, the same people who had explained that they were sailors and knew nothing about the cotton people and didn't speak their language. There they were living in that cotton town and speaking the language like natives, which they were. They were sailors by art or trade, and hadn't wanted to get into trouble with arguing about the goods or the contract, they hadn't told anybody except the people on their own island about their private supply of Sweet Betebbes, either. They laughed like crazy about it when they met him, Peregrine said. They told him that the man they had told us was one of the cotton people was the only one who wasn't; he was a poor halfwit who had wandered in from the desert, and couldn't speak much of a language.

Patience was silent long enough that I believed he was angry, but then he began to laugh, and we all laughed. He said, "Go see if that crew will take us back north by sea!"

But I suggested that we go home by land.

We left a few days later. It took us two months to go along the eastern coast of the Inland Sea to Rekwit, from which we sailed across to Tatselots in a great storm, but all that journey is another story, which I may tell later.

Since we went down there, there hasn't been any more trouble with the cotton people, and they have always sent us good, long-staple cotton. They are not an unreasonable people, except in making little paths everywhere and being ashamed.

Bibliography

Introduction

Briones, L., "The Blues in the Delta Breeze," poemhunter.com/poem/the-blues-in-the-delta-breeze/
Delta Narratives project, scholarlycommons.pacific.edu/cop-facreports/7/
Marx, L., *The Machine in the Garden* (New York: Oxford University Press, 2000)
McWilliams, C., *Factories in the Fields: The Story of Migrant Labor in California* (Berkeley: UC Press, 2000)
Turner, F. J., nationalhumanitiescenter.org/pds/gilded/empire/text1/turner.pdf

Chapter 1

Gifford, E. W., "Miwok Myths," *Publications in Archaeology and Ethnography*, Vol. 12, No. 6 (Berkeley: UC Press, 1917), pp. 332-333.
"How the Dum'nah World was Made," and "The Paht-win World," in F. F. Latta (ed.), *California Indian Folklore* (Exeter, California: Brewer's Historical Press, 1936/1999)
Kroeber, A. L., "The Patwin and Their Neighbor," *Publications in Archaeology and Ethnography*, Vol. 29, No. 4 (Berkeley: UC Press, 1935), pp. 304–305.
Kroeber, T., *The Inland Whale* (Bloomington: Indiana University Press, 1959)
Margolin, M., "The Basketmakers," "The Shamans," and "Sacred Time" in *The Ohlone Way* (Berkeley: Heyday, 1978)
Meadows, S., "Reweaving the World Ohlone" in Margaret Dubin (ed.), *The Dirt is Red Here: Art and Poetry from Native California* (Berkeley: Heyday, 2002)
Merriam, C. H., *The Dawn of the World: Myths and Weird Tales Told by the Mewan Indians of California* (Cleveland, OH: The Arthur K. Clark Company, 1910)
Rummerfield, J., "Keepers of the Land," *Stockton Record*, January 21, 2011
"Sacramento Valley Drainage (Maidu)" and "Dancing Song for a Yokut Wedding" in Robert Pearsall and Ursula Erickson (eds.), *The Californians: Writing of their Past and Present*, Vol. 1 (San Francisco: Hesperian House, 1961)
Stuart, D., "The Native Peoples of San Joaquin County, Parts One and Two," *The San Joaquin Historian*, Winter 2016 and Summer 2017

Stuart, D., "Paradise Lost: An Indigenous History Timeline for the Sacramento-San Joaquin Delta," *Soundings Magazine*, June 25, 2021

West, N., *Eye of the Bear* (Sacramento: Bridge House, 2001)

Chapter 2

Atherton, G., *Rezanov* (New York: The Authors and Newspapers Association, 1906)

Beebe, R. M. and Senkewicz, R. (eds.), *Lands of Promise and Despair: Chronicles of Early California, 1535–1846* (Norman: University of Oklahoma Press, 2015)

Duhaut-Cilly, A., Frige, A., and Harlow, N. (trans.), *A Voyage to California, the Sandwich Islands, & Around the World in the Years 1826–1829* (Berkeley: University of California Press, 1999)

Duran, N. and Chapman, C. (eds.), *The Expedition on the Sacramento and San Joaquin Rivers in 1817* (Berkeley: Academy of Pacific Coast History, University of California, 1911)

Font, P., and Brown, A. K. (trans.), *With Anza to California, 1975–1776: The Journal of Pedro Font* (Norman, Oklahoma: Arthur H. Clark, 2011)

Russell, C. H., *From Serra to Sancho: Music and Pageantry in the California Mission* (New York: Oxford, 2009)

West, N., *River of Red Gold* (Sacramento: Bridge House, 1996)

Chapter 3

Bidwell, J., *Echoes of the Past* (Reprint: New York: The Citadel Press, 1962)

Gudde, E. G. (ed. and trans.), "The Memoirs of Theodor Cordua: The Pioneer of New Mecklenburg in the Sacramento Valley, "*Quarterly of the California Historical Society*, Vol. 12, No. 4 (Berkeley: UC Press, 1933)

March, J., "Letter to Hon. Lewis Cass," *California Historical Society Quarterly*, Vol. 22, No. 4 (Berkeley: University of California Press, 1943)

Shebl, J., *Weber! The American Adventure of Captain Charles M. Weber* (Lodi, CA: San Joaquin Historical Society, 1993)

Sutter, J. A., *Diary,* Library of Congress, loc.gov/item/34013250/ and on the website of the Museum of the City of San Francisco, sfmuseum.net/hist2/sutdiary1.html

Hanel, D., *In the Shadow of Diablo: Mystery of the Great Stone House* (Virginia Beach, VA: Create Space Independent Publishing Platform, 2018)

Winters, I., "John Sutter" in R. L. Barth (ed.), *The Selected Poems of Yvor Winters* (Athens, OH: Swallow Press, 1999)

Chapter 4

Branch, E. M. (ed.), *Clemens of the Call* (Berkeley: University of California, 1969)

Derby, G. H., *Phoenixiana: Or Sketches and Burlesques* (New York: D. Appleton, 1903)

Frost, R., "A Peck of Gold" in *Complete Poems of Robert Frost* (New York: Holt, Rinehart and Winston, 1949)

Harte, B., "The Legend of Monte del Diablo," gutenberg.org/files/2599/2599-h/2599-h.htm#link2H_4_0002

Holliday, J. S., *The World Rushed In: The California Gold Rush Experience* (New York: Simon and Schuster, 1981)

Taylor, B., *Eldorado: Adventurers in the Path of Empire* (New York: G.P. Putnam, 1850)

Chapter 5

Bade, W. F., *The Life and Letters of John Muir* (Boston: Houghton Mifflin, 1924)

Barnes, M. J., *The Opposite Shore* (Self-published, 1961)

Farquhar, F. P. (ed.), *Up and Down California in 1860–1864, the Journal of William H. Brewer* (New Haven: Yale, 1930)

Gillis, M. and Magliari, M., *John Bidwell California* (Spokane, WA: Arthur H. Clark Company: 2004)

Hunt, R., *The Boyhood Days of Mr. California* (self-published, 1965)

MacMullen, J., *Paddlewheel Days in California* (Stanford: Stanford University Press, 1944)

Minnick, S. S., *Samfow: The San Joaquin Chinese Legacy* (Fresno: Panorama West Publishing, 1988)

Nordhoff, C., *Northern California, Oregon, and the Sandwich Island* (1874) archive.org/details/northerncalifor00remygoog/page/n6/mode/2up

Norris, F., *The Octopus* (New York: Doubleday, 1901)

Royce, J., *The Feud at Oakfield Creek* (Boston: Houghton Mifflin, 1887)

Chapter 6

Payne, W., *Benjamin Holt: The Story of the Caterpillar Tractor* (Stockton: University of the Pacific, 1982)

Schmidt, L., "California Packing Corporation Plant #22," *Rio Vista Short Stories* (Bend, OR: Maverick Press, 1991), pp. 35–40.

Schmidt, L., "Inventing a Sugar Beet Harvester," *Schmidt's Short Stories and Poems*, Vol. I (Detroit: Harlo Press, 1986), pp. 99–109.

Thompson, J. and Dutra, E. A, *The Tule Breakers: The Story of the California Dredge* (Stockton: The University of the Pacific, 1983)

Chapter 7

Bernardo, R., "In honor of Labor's Dead" in Pearsall R. and Erickson, U. (eds.), *The Californians: Writing of their Past and Present*, Vol. 1 (San Francisco: Hesperian House, 1961)

Didion, J., *Run River* (New York: Random House, 1991)

Dillon, R., *Delta Country* (San Francisco: Presidio Press, 1982)

Galarza, E., *Barrio Boy* (Notre Dame: University of Notre Dame Press, 2011)

Gardner, L., *Fat City* (New York: New York Review of Books, 2015)

London, J., *Tales of the Fish Patrol* (1905) gutenberg.org/ebooks/28693

Markham, E., "Man with a Hoe" and "The Joy of the Hills" in *The Man with the Hoe and Other Poems* (New York: Doubleday and McClure, 1906)

Chapter 8

Clarksburg

Smith, T. R., *Clarksburg: The Water, the Land, and Its People*, second edition (Clarksburg, California: T.R. Smith, 2017)

Benicia

Benet, L., *When William Rose, Steven Vincent, and I Were Young* (New York: Dodd Mead, 1976)

Bussinger, J. and Phelan, B., *Benicia* (Charleston, SC: Arcadia Publishing, 2004)
Dillon, R., *Great Expectations: The Story of Benicia, California* (Benicia: Benicia Heritage Books, 1980)
Rubay, D., *With a Dram So Proud: The Life of Stephen Vincent Benet* (Benicia, CA: Benicia Literary Arts, 2016)

Antioch
Anderson. C., "Fenced Off, Parts One and Two," *Soundings Magazine* (October 3 and 9, 2019)
Bohakel, C., Hiebert, P., Rumbault, E., and Davis, C. A., *Antioch* (Charleston, SC: Arcadia, 2005)

Courtland
Graham, K. M., *Discovering Courtland* (Walnut Grove, CA: The Sacramento River Delta Historical Society, 1987)

Crockett
Robinson, J. V., *Crockett* (Charleston, SC: Arcadia, 2004)

Isleton
Crawford, B., *Isleton* (Charleston, SC: Arcadia, 2003)

Oakley
Jensen, C., *Oakley Through Time* (Charleston, SC: Fonthill/Arcadia, 2019)

Pittsburg
Aiello, M., *Pittsburg* (Charleston, SC: Arcadia, 2004)

Rio Vista
Drady, A., *Rodney Newton* (New York: P.J. Kenedy, 1929)
Drady, A., *Red Morton, Waterboy* (New York: Appleton, 1932)
Korth, J., *Wind Chimes in My Apple Tree* (self-published, no date)
Pezzaglia, P., *Rio Vista* (Charleston, SC: Arcadia, 2005)
Schmidt, L., *Schmitty's Short Stories and Poems*, Vol. I (Detroit: Harlo, 1986)
Schmidt, L., *Rio Vista Short Stories*, Vol. 1 (Bend, OR: Maverick, 1991)
Schmidt, L., *Schmitty's Short Stories*, Vol. 3 (Bend, OR: Maverick, 1998)

Ryde
Graham, K., *Ryde* (Walnut Grove, CA: The Sacramento River Historical Society, 1987)

Suisun
DeCaro, E. A. and Ewing, L. M., *Suisun City and Valley* (Charleston, SC: Arcadia, 2013)

Walnut Grove
Graham, K., *Discovering Walnut Grove* (Walnut Grove, CA: The Sacramento River Historical Society, 1985)

General Books, Multiple Communities
Blanton-Stroud, S., *Copy Boy* (Berkeley: She Writes Press, 2020)
Chambers, D. (ed.), *Tales of the Delta Folk* (Stockton: University of the Pacific, 1992)

Didion, J., *Where I was From* (New York: Knopf, 2003)

Graham, K., *Discover Paintersville, Vorden, and Ryde* (Walnut Grove, CA: The Sacramento River Historical Society, 1987)

Hanel, D., *In the Shadow of Diablo: Ghosts of Black Diamond* (Virginia Beach, VA: Create Space Independent Publishing Platform, 2018)

Hayes, P. J. (ed.), *The Lower American River: Prehistory to Parkway* (Carmichael, CA: American River Natural History Association, 2005)

Jacobs, M. (ed.), *Lady Constance: The Collected Letters of Constance Miller* (Stockton: The Stockton Record, 1991)

Mariano, C., *Heart and Soul: Farm Workers, Migrant Camps, Other Stories* (Self-published, 2018)

Pezzaglia, P., *Towns of the Sacramento River Delta* (Charleston, SC: Arcadia, 2013)

Shelton, W. F., *Bailing Dust* (Walnut Grove, CA: Campus House Press, 1984)

Russell, K., *Dead Game: A John Marquez Crime Novel* (San Francisco: Chronicle Books, 2005)

Ethnic Communities
AFRICAN AMERICAN
Angelou, M., *Mom & Me & Mom* (New York: Random House, 2013)

Angelou, M., *The Collected Autobiographies of Maya Angelou* (New York: The Modern Library, 2004)

CHINESE
Chan, S., *This Bitter-Sweet Soil: The Chinese in California Agriculture, 1860–1910* (Berkeley: UC Press, 1986)

Graham, K., *Discovering Locke* (Walnut Grove, CA: The Sacramento River Historical Society, 1985)

Kingston, M. H., *The Woman Warrior* (New York: Knopf, 1976)

Leung, E. (ed.), *Remembering 100 Years, 1915–2015* (Locke, CA: The Locke Foundation, 2015)

Leung, P. C. Y., *One Day, One Dollar: Locke, California and the Chinese Farming Experience* (Taipei, Taiwan: Liberal Arts Press, 1994)

Motlow, J. and Gillenkirk, J., *Bitter Melon: Inside America's Last Rural Chinese Town* (San Francisco: Nine Mile Press, 1987)

Ryan, S. Y., *Locke 1928* (Berkeley: El Leon Literary Arts, 2007)

JAPANESE
De Cristoforo, V. K., *May Sky: There is Always Tomorrow: An Anthology of Japanese American Concentration Camp Kaiko Haiku* (Los Angeles: Sun and Moon Press, 1997)

Maeda, W., *Changing Dreams and Treasured Memories: A Story of Japanese Americans in the Sacramento Region* (Sacramento: Japanese American Citizens League, Sacramento, 2000)

Sato, K., *Kiyo's Story: A Japanese-American Family Quest for the American Dream* (New York: Soho Press, 2009)

Shimamoto, C. M., *To the Land of Bright Promise: The Story of a Pioneer Japanese Truck Farming Family California's San Joaquin Valley* (Lodi, CA: The San Joaquin Historical Society, 1990)

Wildie, K., *Sacramento's Historic Japantown: Legacy of a Lost Neighborhood* (Charleston: The History Press, 2013)

MEXICO

Galarza, E., Barrio Boy (Notre Dame, IN: Notre Dame Pres, 2011)

Hernandez, J., *Reaching for the Stars: The Inspiring Story of a Migrant Farmworker Turned Astronaut* (New York: Center Street, 2012)

PHILIPPINES

Bulosan, C., *America Is in the Heart* (New York: Penguin, 2019, first published in 1946)

Mabalon, D. B., *Little Manila is in the Heart* (Durham: Duke University Press, 2013)

Chapter 9

Graham, K., *Discover How the Games were Played: Dai Loy Gambling House in Locke* (Walnut Grove: The Sacramento River Delta Historical Society, 1987)

Gutierrez, R. M., *A Fairer Paradise: California River Delta Stories* (Grey Iguana Publishing, 1997)

Harvie, J., *Discover the Dai Loy Gambling Hall Museum* (Walnut Grove. CA: The Sacramento River Historical Society, 1980)

Pezzaglia, P., *True Tales of the Sacramento Delta* (Charleston, SC: The History Press, 2015)

Robinson, B., *Legends of the Strait: A Novel about Benicia, California during the Prohibition Era* (Bloomington, IN: Authors House, 2011)

Chapter 10

Allen, R., *The Port Chicago Mutiny* (Berkeley: Heyday,1989)

Bacon, D., *Communities without Borders: Images and Voices from the World of Migration* (Ithaca, NY: Cornell University Press, 2006)

Charles River Editors, *The Port Chicago Disaster: The History of America's Deadliest Homeland Incident during World War II* (no date)

Corbin, A., *The History of Camp Tracy* (Fort Belvoir, VA: Ziedon Press, 2009)

Honda, M., "When my Japanese-American Family was Treated as less than Human," December 21, 2015, medium.com/@RepMikeHonda/when-my-japanese-american-family-was-treated-as-less-than-human-768d8f72a87c

Jensen, C. A., *Bryon Hot Springs* (Charleston, SC: Arcadia, 2006)

Sheinkin, S., *The Port Chicago 50: Disaster, Mutiny, and the Fight for Civil Rights* (New York: Roaring Brook Press, 2014)

Chapter 11

Brandeis, G., *Delta Girls* (New York: Ballantine, 2010)

Gardner, E. S., *Drifting Down the Delta* (New York: William Morrow, 1969)

Gardner, E. S., *Gypsy Days on the Delta* (New York: William Morrow, 1967)

Gardner, E. S., *The World of Water: Exploring the Sacramento Delta* (New York: William Morrow, 1965)

Emery, W. and Squire, S., *Edges of Bounty: Adventures in the Edible Valley* (Berkeley: Heyday, 2008)

Schell, H., *Cruising California's Delta (*Stockton: Hal Schell, 1995)

Walter, R. E., *Cruising the California Delta* (San Francisco: Miller Freeman, 1972)

Chapter 12

Arax, M., *The Dreamt Land_*(New York: Knopf, 2019)
Graham, K., *Discovering the Sacramento River Delta* (Walnut Grove, CA: The
    Sacramento River Historical Society, 1982)
Steward, G., *Storm* (Lincoln: University of Nebraska, 1941/1983)

Chapter 13

Connor, J., *The Delta Poem (*Sacramento: Vernacular Editions, 1987)
McKinney, J., "Down in the River" in Bob Stanley, editor *Late Peaches* (Sacramento:
    Sacramento Poetry Center, 2012), p. 136.
Ulewiecz, L., "Notes Toward the River Itself," in Peter Berg editor, *Reinhabiting A
    Separate Country (*San Francisco: Plant Drum Foundation, 1978), pp 101–109.

Chapter 14

Hallowell, J. and C. (eds.), *Take Me to the River* (Berkeley: Heyday, 2010)
Otteson, P., *The Black Hole: Creating a Balanced Sustainable Wetland Habitat*
    (Stockton: Privately Published, 2020)
Obata, C., *The Sierra to the Sea* (Berkeley, Archetyne Press, 1937)

Chapter 14

Everson, W., "San Joaquin" and "Dusk" in *The Residual Years* (New York: New
    Directions, 1948)
Federle, S., "Bridge at Rio Vista" and "Bridge at Montezuma Slough" see
    poemhunter.com
Langsworthy, A., "Stockton" (unpublished)
Sheil, P., "Out of the Gate" (unpublished)
Short, K. (ed.), *In Mt. Diablo's Shadow* (San Ramon: Falcon Books, 2011)

Chapter 15

Le Guin, U., *Always Coming Home, Expanded Edition* (New York: Library of
    America, 2019)
Moffat, A. (ed.), *2020: Visions for the Central Valley* (Berkeley: Heyday, 2010)
Wolff, J., *Delta Primer: A Field Guide to the California Delta* (San Francisco,
    William Stout, 2003)

Additional General Materials on the Delta

Bohn, D. and Minick, R., *Delta West: The Land and the People of the
    Sacramento-San Joaquin Delta* (Berkeley: Scrikshaw, 1969)
Cohen, A. N., *Gateway to the Inland Coast* (Crockett, CA: Carquinez Strait
    Preservation Trust, 1996)
Commission, Delta Protection, *Delta Narratives: Saving the Historical and Cultural
    Heritage of The Sacramento-San Joaquin Delta* (2014), scholarlycommons.pacific.
    edu/cop-facreports/7/
Graham, K., *Discovering the Sacramento River Delta* (Walnut Grove, CA:
    Sacramento River Delta Historical Society, 1982)

Jensen, C. A., *The California Delta* (Charleston, SC: Arcadia, 2007)

Parker, C., *Up-Delta in the Early Days: A Cruise into the Past of the California Delta* (Self-published, 2000)

Trimble, P. C. *Riverboats of Northern California* (Charleston, SC: Arcadia, 2011)

Westhoff, A., *Feasibility Study for a Sacramento-San Joaquin Delta National Heritage Area* (West Sacramento: Delta Protection Commission, 2012)

The Sacramento–San Joaquin Delta National Heritage Area

Congress designated the Sacramento-San Joaquin Delta National Heritage Area (Delta NHA) as California's first National Heritage Area in 2019. NHAs are a grassroot, community-driven approach to heritage conservation and economic development. Designated local coordinating entities collaborate with communities to determine how to make heritage relevant to local interests and needs. NHAs support historic preservation, natural resource conservation, recreation, heritage tourism, and educational projects through public-private partnerships.

The Delta NHA boundary extends from Sacramento to Stockton to Vallejo with the junction of the Sacramento and San Joaquin rivers at its heart. The history of California's Delta and Carquinez Strait is a rich tapestry of indigenous peoples and immigrants from around the world, natural beauty and wildlife, engineering marvels, bustling metropolitan areas, and picturesque rural towns. The native peat soils provide for fertile cropland and its water supports 29 million Californians.

Visitors to the Delta NHA have many experiences to choose from while winding along the scenic roads, cruising the 700-plus miles of waterways, and spending time in the area's many towns and cities. There are opportunities for water recreation, birding, fishing, agritourism, heritage tourism, and so much more.

The Delta NHA, managed by the Delta Protection Commission, is committed to supporting the region's economic development and the preservation of its historical significance. You can obtain more information about management of the Delta NHA at www.delta.ca.gov/nha or by contacting the Delta Protection Commission at (916) 375-4800. For information on Delta tourism and recreation, explore www.visitcadelta.com.